AMERICAN ALLY

AMERICAN ALLY

TONY BLAIR AND THE WAR ON TERROR

CON COUGHLIN

HarperCollins books may be purchased for educational, business, or sales promotional use. For information, please write: Special Markets Department, HarperCollins Publishers, 10 East 53rd Street, New York, NY 10022.

FIRST EDITION

Designed by Joseph Rutt

Printed on acid-free paper

Library of Congress Cataloging-in-Publication Data

Coughlin, Con.
    American ally : Tony Blair and the war on terror / Con Coughlin.— 1st ed.
    p. cm.
    Includes index
    ISBN-10: 0-06-073126-5
    ISBN-13: 978-0-06-073126-7
    1. Blair, Tony, 1953—Relations with Americans.   2. Terrorism—Prevention—Government policy—Great Britain.   3. Great Britain—Foreign relations—United States.   4. United States—Foreign relations—Great Britain.   5. Great Britain—Foreign relations—1997–.   6. United States—Foreign relations—2001–.   I. Title.

DA591.B56C68 2006
941.086'092—dc22   2005049492

06 07 08 09 10 WBC/RRD 10 9 8 7 6 5 4 3 2 1

For my beloved sister,
Dominique (1964–2003)

CONTENTS

ACKNOWLEDGMENTS

ONE OF THE GREAT FRUSTRATIONS of writing a work of contemporary history is that it is not possible to name many of the officials who have provided me with invaluable help, guidance, and insight. The requirements of Britain's Official Secrets Act are particularly onerous in this regard, and I find it hard to believe that any of the information I have gathered in the course of my research could possibly pose a threat to national security. Many of those I have interviewed in Britain and the United States hold positions of great influence and power in their respective governments and have played a central role in the formulation of transatlantic policy in fighting the threat posed to Western security by the forces of Islamic extremism. Because of the obligations and responsibilities placed upon them by their positions, they have asked that I preserve their anonymity in the sourcing of direct quotations. While I am unable to thank them publicly for their contributions, I would nevertheless like to express my deep gratitude to them all for their helpfulness and openness, as I do to those who are in a position to be publicly identified and quoted.

Writing a book of this nature is a daunting challenge, and I am particularly grateful to Lord Powell, Lord Renwick, Lord Guthrie, Lord Butler, and Lord Robertson for laying the foundations by helping me to understand the dynamics of the transatlantic alliance from both the political and military perspectives. In London, Jonathan Powell, Downing Street's chief of staff, was invaluable in guiding me through the labyrinthine complexity of Whitehall. John Williams at the Foreign and Commonwealth Office assisted in setting up interviews with the key diplomatic players. Matthew d'Ancona, my former colleague at the *Sunday Telegraph,* elucidated some of the more obscure areas of British political discourse.

Colleen Graffy, the indefatigable London-based representative for Republicans Abroad, made sure I got to see the key players in Washington, as did Devon Cross of the Pentagon's Defense Policy Board and Dan Fried at the National Security Council. Gary Schmitt of the Project for the New American Century explained the origins and principles of American neoconservatism with admirable clarity, while Danielle Pletka, of the American Enterprise Institute, provided her characteristically frank take on the value of the Blair government's contribution to the war against international terrorism.

Finally, I am indebted to Dan Halpern and Emily Takoudes at Ecco for their professionalism, enthusiasm, and encouragement in guiding this book into print, and to my agents, Melanie Jackson and Gill Coleridge, for making it happen.

PART ONE

One

THE MAKING OF AN ALLY

THE RESULT OF THE 1997 British election had yet to be declared, but in Washington, President Bill Clinton was excited at the prospect of the imminent victory of his young protégé Tony Blair. With the exit polls suggesting a landslide victory for the New Labour leader, Clinton was pacing the Oval Office wondering when he could telephone his congratulations. The State Department urged caution, pointing out that until the result was officially declared, John Major, the Conservative leader, was still technically Britain's prime minister. Blair, meanwhile, sat in the living room of his house in the northern England constituency of Sedgefield, watching the results on the television with his wife, Cherie.

Jonathan Powell, Blair's chief of staff, called Blair to pass on the message that Clinton was trying to reach him but the State Department would not yet let him. Blair was flattered, but even though all the available information pointed to the biggest election victory in Labour's history, he refused to believe it until the result was official. "What do they know?" Blair asked Cherie as they watched the predictions of the television pollsters.[1]

The result was finally announced several hours later, and Blair was declared the winner with the biggest majority in British postwar politics. Clinton was delighted as the extent of Blair's victory was confirmed to the

White House. Clinton had struck up a close relationship with Blair, whom he regarded as a potential political ally, and members of Clinton's successful 1996 campaign team had been brought to Blair's Millbank election headquarters to assist the New Labour Party. Having finally been allowed to phone Blair personally to congratulate him, Clinton issued a glowing tribute to the American press. "I'm looking forward to working with Prime Minister Blair," declared the American president. "He's a very exciting man, a very able man. I like him very much." Clinton's enthusiastic response to Blair's victory was echoed by Sidney Blumenthal, a senior White House aide, who declared: "At last the president has a little brother. Blair is the younger brother Clinton has been yearning for."

This somewhat patronizing attitude toward the new British prime minister was just some of the widespread acclaim that greeted Blair's arrival at 10 Downing Street, the official residence of Britain's prime minister. It is unlikely though that anyone among the crowd that gathered outside 10 Downing Street to cheer Blair's triumph thought they were witnessing the arrival of a man who was to become one of the most important and controversial wartime leaders in British history.

The election campaign that had swept Blair and his New Labour Party to power had been fought predominantly on domestic issues, such as improving the state of Britain's woeful public services. This was reflected in the selection of the pop group D:Ream's song "Things Can Only Get Better" as New Labour's official campaign anthem. The British public, or rather the ever-diminishing percentage of the electorate that actually turned out to vote, wanted better hospitals, schools, and roads. To this end, they had voted Blair into power with an impregnable 179-seat majority in the House of Commons, while the Conservatives had suffered their worst electoral defeat since the Great Reform Act of 1832. After eighteen years of Conservative rule, Britain was ready for a change in direction, and that day appeared to herald the dawn of a new era in British politics.

Tony Blair was four days short of his forty-fourth birthday when he was elected prime minister on May 2, 1997. Born in Edinburgh in 1953, Blair spent most of his childhood in the northern former coal-mining city of Durham. At fourteen, he was sent to the prestigious Fettes College boarding school and from there went to Oxford to study law.

As a young man, Blair gave his contemporaries little indication that he would one day emerge as a leading figure in world politics. To his fellow students, the long-haired Blair, who was usually dressed as a hippie, seemed like a noisy and exuberant public schoolboy rebel who steered clear of the university's intellectual establishment. At school, Blair had played Captain Stanhope, the lead part in R. C. Sheriff's antiwar play *Journey's End*, and at Oxford, he continued to pursue his thespian interests, playing Matt in a college production of Bertolt Brecht's *Threepenny Opera*. Blair also maintained a keen interest in rock music. His favorite bands were the Rolling Stones, Led Zeppelin, and Cream, and in his last year at university, he became the lead singer and bass guitarist of Ugly Rumours. Blair took to the stage in purple pants and a cut-off T-shirt and, according to his fellow band members, did a passable impression of Mick Jagger, "a bit of finger-wagging and punching the air."[2] But despite his exposure to the decadent milieu of rock music, Blair, unlike many of his contemporaries, avoided drugs. In an interview many years later, when there was controversy over whether or not President Clinton had taken drugs at Oxford, Blair was asked if he had ever smoked dope. "No, I haven't," replied Blair. "But if I had, you can be sure I would have inhaled."[3]

Blair showed little active interest in politics at university, although fellow students recall he was an avid supporter of the Labour Party. But while at Oxford, he acquired the deep religious conviction that was to lay the foundations for the moral certainty that would dictate his conduct in later life. In 1972, he befriended Peter Thomson, an Australian Anglican priest, an older student who had a profound influence on Blair's personal development. As a result of many lengthy late-night discussions with Thomson about moral philosophy, Blair became a practicing Christian, and it was as a result of his Christianity that he became actively involved in the Labour Party. As Blair conceded after he had become Labour leader in 1995, "my Christianity and my politics came together at the same time."

After university, Blair followed in the footsteps of his father, Leo, and his elder brother, Bill, and trained as a barrister. His Christian beliefs made him a committed socialist who was particularly concerned about inequality, and he formally joined the Labour Party in 1975, whereas most people of his class and background would generally have joined the Conservatives. As Blair himself later remarked, "With my class background, if all I wanted to do was to exercise power, I could and would—let's be blunt about this—have joined another party."[4]

After standing unsuccessfully for the Labour Party in a by-election, he finally won the northern England seat of Sedgefield in the 1983 general election at age thirty. Blair was rapidly promoted through the Labour ranks, and in 1992 became the opposition spokesman for home affairs, such as the penal system and immigration. He married Cherie Booth, another young barrister, in 1980, and the couple had four children. Euan, the eldest, was born in January 1984, followed by Nicholas in December 1985, Kathryn in March 1988, and Leo in May 2000. In 1994, after the sudden death of the Labour leader John Smith from a heart attack, Blair became Labour's leader.

Blair's youth and vitality, together with the arrival of his wife and young family at Downing Street, inevitably drew comparisons with John F. Kennedy, who had been the same age as Blair when he entered the White House. The last time a British prime minister of such a young age had occupied Downing Street was under Lord Liverpool in 1812, when Britain was in a battle for survival in the Napoleonic wars.

Europe still remained a vexed issue for British politicians in 1997, and one of the main campaign issues had concerned the extent of Britain's involvement with the European Union. Although Blair himself was pro-European and keen to have Britain become a member of the Europe-wide single currency that was due to come into effect in January 1999, he realized that it remained a divisive issue with the British electorate. Apart from Europe, international issues, such as the Atlantic alliance, the civil war in the Balkans, resolution of the long-running dispute with Iraq's Saddam Hussein, and Britain's role in confronting rogue regimes and Islamic terrorists, did not feature. Most postwar British elections had concentrated almost exclusively on domestic issues, and the 1997 election campaign was firmly set in that pattern.

The new British prime minister reflected the nation's more parochial concerns when he gave his victory address on the steps of Downing Street before hosting a celebratory family lunch. Having paid tribute to his predecessor, John Major, Blair set out his immediate objectives for the newly elected government. New Labour, he promised, would provide Britain with a world-class education system; it would modernize the nation's health-care provision; and it would create a competitive economy. His sole reference as to how he would conduct his foreign policy was a rather vapid statement that he would give Britain "strength and confidence in leadership both at home and abroad, particularly in Europe." The only hint of Blair's underlying leadership qualities he had given throughout the entire electoral campaign was at a speech he gave in Manchester just two weeks before polling day. "Century upon century it has been the destiny of Britain to lead other nations," he declared. "We are a leader of nations or nothing."[5] This was the language of a man who would soon be responsible for leading his country to war five times in the next six years.

At this stage in his political development, Blair had not given much thought either to being a wartime leader or to countering the threat posed by rogue states and the rising tide of Islamic terrorism. His primary goal leading to the election had been to get New Labour elected to power after eighteen long years in opposition, and then for the party to stay in power for as long as possible. The only international issue on which he had made any firm pronouncement concerned Europe, where he had changed from supporting the traditional 1980s Labour hostility to the policies articulated by the European Union to becoming an active cheerleader for closer political and economic integration with the European mainland. His experience with international political communities was limited to his many visits to the United States to meet with members of the Clinton administration, but these meetings were more to advance his own domestic electoral prospects than to seek a deeper understanding of world affairs.

Clinton's friendship with Blair developed after he became Labour leader in 1994. Blair did not formally meet Clinton until November 1995, when the American president, en route to Ireland, stopped in London to attend a dinner hosted by the American ambassador, Admiral William Crowe. Links between Blair's Labour Party and Clinton's Democrats were already well established. Philip Gould, Blair's chief pollster, had stayed at Clinton's campaign headquarters in Little Rock, Arkansas, during Clinton's 1992 election campaign and had befriended Stanley Greenberg, one of the candidate's key aides. The previous April, Labour had suffered its fourth successive electoral defeat and Gould wanted to see if there was anything to be learned from Clinton's campaign strategy. Gould returned from Little Rock brimming with enthusiasm for the professionalism of the Clinton campaign and its policies. Gould encouraged Blair to travel to Washington to see for himself the Clinton phenomenon, and in January 1993, he flew to the United States with Gordon Brown, another up-and-coming proponent of reforming the Labour Party to make it electable.

Blair knew little about America. He had visited the United States just once previously, in 1982, when he traveled to Tennessee to represent a client in a legal dispute. Blair and Brown were regarded as too junior to be granted an audience with the incumbent American president, but they were introduced to a number of key Clinton aides who were important to Clinton's successful election. Brown and Blair were struck by the similarities in what Clinton had achieved in broadening the appeal of the Democrats in the United States with what they needed to do to revive their own party in Britain. Under Clinton, the Democrats had sought to move away from their reputation as the party of "tax and spend" and as being soft on core issues such as welfare, crime, and defense. Blair understood that Clinton's appeal to what he called "the forgotten middle class" could be replicated in Britain. Labour needed to reassert its reputation for fiscal probity and social responsibility if it was to stand any chance of gaining power. Apart from policy issues, the other important lesson that Blair learned from Clinton's electoral success was the need for his party to display unity and discipline. This meant being aided by a highly sophisticated operation to deal with the demands of the twenty-four-hour cycle of the international news media.

By the time Blair and Clinton met, Blair had adopted many of Clinton's policies and strategies, to the extent of rebranding his party as New Labour, a direct imitation of Clinton's New Democrats. Blair's open admiration for Clinton was reciprocated, and in April 1996, Blair was invited to Washington, where he received the warmest reception granted to a British opposition leader since Winston Churchill made his famous "iron curtain" speech in 1946. At a dinner held at the British Embassy, Blair charmed the assembled guests with his self-assuredness and charisma. The next day, he was given an hour with Clinton in the Oval Office. The *New York Times* reported that Clinton "welcomed Blair to the White House with the kind of exuberance (and the attendant flood of words) that he seldom lavished on overseas guests."[6] Blair and Clinton spent more than an hour discussing issues that mainly related to Blair's election campaign—such as the problems of financing welfare reform without raising taxes, and the continuing attempts to find a peaceful settlement in Northern Ireland. "They hit it off straight away," said one of Blair's aides who accompanied him on the trip. "They shared a lot of common ground, and there was a lot of mutual admiration. There was also a meeting of minds on the big political issues."[7]

It was not just Clinton whom Blair charmed during the visit. In a whirlwind forty-eight hours of meetings in Washington and New York, he met the UN secretary-general Boutros Boutros-Ghali and chairman of the Federal Reserve Alan Greenspan, spoke in New York at a breakfast meeting hosted by Henry Kissinger, and addressed the New York Chamber of Commerce, where he assured the audience that his pro-European outlook would not get in the way of his respect for the Atlantic alliance. He consolidated his profile with the American media by addressing the National Press Club and by giving interviews to the major American television networks. He also had a private meeting with Hillary Clinton that was organized by Sidney Blumenthal, a key Clinton aide who was already billing Blair as Britain's new prime minister. The first lady and Blair spent thirty minutes discussing politics and public policy in their respective countries. She later wrote: "I instantly felt a connection."[8]

Clinton's open support and encouragement for Blair certainly did the Labour leader's election prospects no harm, and the next time the two men met was after Blair had secured his landslide election victory. But Blair's relationship with Clinton at this stage was very much confined to learning how to turn the American president's proven electoral success to his own advantage. It did not go unnoticed by seasoned Washington observers and Clinton's political opponents that Blair's primary focus was almost exclusively the campaign and election issues rather than the nitty-gritty of policy, particularly foreign policy.

In view of the pivotal role that Blair would later play in leading the war on terror, it was, perhaps, surprising that he appeared to display so little interest in Clinton's approach to foreign policy issues, particularly the threat posed by international terrorism to Western security. Perhaps Blair was being naive, or perhaps he was just playing smart, calculating that it was not in his interests to challenge Clinton in an area where he was in no position, at least for the time being, to exert influence. "The bottom line was that Blair knew nothing about foreign policy," said one of Blair's close advisors. "Frankly, it is not an issue that wins elections. We thought it was something we could sort out once he got elected. That was always the primary objective."9

Relations between Clinton and Blair's immediate predecessor as prime minister, John Major, who had succeeded Margaret Thatcher as British prime minister in November 1990, had never been particularly warm. They got off to a bad start after it was claimed that Major's Conservative Party had been trying to dig up, on behalf of American Republicans, information regarding Clinton's participation in demonstrations against the war in Vietnam while he was a student at Oxford University. The Republicans wanted the information to use against Clinton during the 1992 presidential election campaign. Nevertheless, Clinton and Major managed to sustain a professional working relationship, although Major discovered that the American president was rarely willing to take his advice seriously. As the crisis in Bosnia deepened, Major's appeals to Clinton to become more engaged in the issue generally fell on deaf ears.

Clinton, who had Irish ancestry, took an active interest in the negotiations to end the violence in Northern Ireland between Ulster Unionists and Irish Republicans. The Northern Ireland peace process was one of the few tangible achievements of the Major government, but Major believed that Clinton's involvement was too biased in favor of the Republicans. Major deeply opposed Clinton's decision to grant a visa to visit the United

States to Gerry Adams, the leader of the Republican's Sinn Fein movement and a military commander of the Irish Republican Army. Major insisted that Washington should only grant Adams a visa once he had given an unequivocal promise to renounce violence. Adams was asked by the American consul in Belfast to give such a promise, but his response fell well short of what was expected. Even so, the White House, to Major's fury, granted the visa.[10] "It was a rather brutal demonstration of where the real power lay," said a senior Downing Street official who worked with both John Major and Tony Blair. "For all the effort that Britain invests in maintaining a strong working relationship with Washington, there are occasions when the Americans will do just as they please, irrespective of our views on the subject."[11]

AS THE DATE OF the British general election drew close, Jonathan Powell, Blair's chief of staff, arranged a series of seminars with retired diplomats and foreign policy experts to bring the future prime minister up to speed on the main policy issues he would face. Robin Renwick, the recently retired British ambassador to Washington, was one of those who attended the meetings, which took place at Blair's Islington home on Friday mornings. In all, six "seminars" were arranged for Blair between late 1996 and early 1997, and the meetings covered a broad range of subjects, including Britain's relations with Washington and Russia, the Balkans, and the new European currency that was soon to be introduced to mainland Europe.

Blair's foreign policy "tutors" were impressed both by his inquisitive mind and by the quality of his questions. He was particularly interested in Europe and eager to move away from the period of paralysis that had defined John Major's relations with the European Union, and indicated that he thought Britain should join the Euro so that it could consolidate its position at the top table of Europe's decision-making bodies. He revealed that he was not entirely unaware of Clinton's tendency to prevaricate on important international issues, such as the Balkans. His tutors recall that he was particularly inquisitive as to why Britain's involvement in the Bosnia conflict had not been more effective in the mid-1990s, and why the United States was so critical to bringing peace to the region. If Clinton did not want to involve American troops in Bosnia, why couldn't Britain assume a bigger role? Was it only possible for Britain to act with its European allies, or could it go it alone? It was clear to those who participated in these seminars that Blair's foreign policy outlook was starting to take shape, and he saw that it was not simply a case of Britain allying itself either with Europe or the United States. Britain should work with both, and its unique position as a traditional ally of Washington as well as its burgeoning relationship with Brussels meant that it was perfectly placed to be a bridge between Europe and America.[12]

The cardinal importance of Britain's relationship with America was forcibly driven home during Blair's tutorial sessions. It was pointed out that Britain had developed a close strategic relationship with the United States since the end of the Second World War, even though the relationship had become increasingly one-sided in Washington's favor over the recent decades. Apart from the obvious commercial, cultural, linguistic, and historical ties between the two countries, the three pillars upon which the strategic alliance was founded were military, intelligence, and nuclear cooperation.

Blair showed a strong interest in the dynamics of the Atlantic alliance and was particularly keen to learn about Britain's military capabilities and how they could best be deployed. Robin Renwick, who had helped set up Blair's foreign affairs tutorials, arranged for the Labour leader to meet General Sir Charles Guthrie, the chief of the defense staff, Britain's leading military figure, at Claridge's Hotel in London in early 1997. The British commanders had become restless under John Major's leadership because of his indecision over Bosnia and his failure to address the structural problems of the British armed forces, which were still geared up to fight the Cold War. "Major was all over the place and we were all very demoralized because of Bosnia," recalled one of Guthrie's close aides. "We thought it was crucial to get New Labour on board on defense."[13] Guthrie was pleasantly surprised by the interest Blair showed in defense issues. He understood the need for Britain's armed forces to be restructured into an expeditionary force able to deal with threats posed to Western security throughout the world. One of Blair's first acts as prime minister was to order a strategic review of Britain's defense capabilities.

Margaret Thatcher was another important influence on Blair's early development as a war leader. There were many areas of domestic policy where Thatcherism and Blairism were opposites. Nor did they share much common ground on the question of Europe: Blair was for closer integration, Thatcher was steadfastly against. Defense and the threat posed by international terrorism were, however, two important policy areas where Blair was keen to emulate the leadership and moral certainty that the Iron Lady had demonstrated in tackling these issues. After being forced out of Downing Street by opponents within her own Conservative Party in late 1990, she had become Baroness Thatcher in 1992, and remained a powerful influence on world affairs throughout the 1990s. She had, for example, openly criticized her successor John Major—and, by implication, President Clinton—for the West's ambivalence in tackling the bloodshed in Bosnia. She campaigned for the arms embargo on the region to be lifted to allow the Bosnian Muslims, the primary victims of the ethnic cleansing, to arm themselves. As she argued in her book *Statecraft*, "The West's equivocation damaged our interests too."[14] Blair had reached conclusions similar to Thatcher's about the West's failure of leadership over Bosnia.

Despite their political differences, Thatcher warmed to Blair and praised him for being a "thoroughly determined person," and she acknowledged his achievements in modernizing the Labour Party.[15] Thatcher's praise attracted headlines and, although traditional Labour supporters were aghast that their former adversary was lavishing such praise on their young leader, Blair was privately flattered. He responded by acknowledging her achievements in office, when he was guest of honor at a conference hosted by Rupert Murdoch for his senior executives at the Australian resort of Hayman Island. In an attempt to demonstrate that their outlooks were similar, Blair declared, "Mrs. Thatcher was a radical, not a Tory."[16]

Blair was keen to meet Thatcher before he became prime minister, but Thatcher was hesitant about being publicly associated with Blair while a Conservative prime minister still occupied Downing Street. She was already being accused of treachery by Conservative officials and was advised that it would be unwise to attach herself too closely to the Blair camp. A line of communication was, however, opened between Jonathan Powell, Blair's chief of staff, and Thatcher's private staff. The facilitator of this unlikely arrangement was Charles Powell, Jonathan's elder brother, who had been Mrs. Thatcher's foreign policy advisor in Downing Street. It was agreed that no formal meeting would take place until Blair won the election. Until that time, contact was confined to chance meetings at official functions and ceremonies, where Blair deployed all his charm to flatter the grande dame of British politics. "Blair basically modeled himself on Thatcher so that he would be taken seriously on the world stage," said Charles Powell. "He had learned a lot from Clinton about campaigning and how to win elections, but when it came to leadership he looked to Thatcher, rather than to Clinton."[17]

Blair did not officially meet Thatcher until his 1997 election had been secured. She wrote him a note to congratulate him on his victory, in which she said she would be happy to meet him to talk about any issue, including the administration of his private office, the future of NATO, or any other subject he might find helpful.[18] An invitation for her to visit the new prime minister duly arrived and Thatcher and Blair spent an hour together on May 22. They mostly talked about international issues, ranging from Russia to the future of the British colony of Hong Kong, which was due to be handed over to Chinese control later that summer. Thatcher expressed her well-known hostility to the European single currency. A significant proportion of the conversation concerned Britain's historic relationship with the United States, which she urged Blair to maintain at all costs. "Her message to Blair was very straightforward," said Charles Powell. "Thatcher told Blair that it was the primary duty of a British prime minister to get on with a U.S. president."[19]

WHEN TONY BLAIR ENTERED Downing Street in May 1997, he was well briefed on the many challenges that he would face. But he and his colleagues had little or no experience of government or the wider world.

The size of his victory could not conceal the fact that the new Blair government was the most inexperienced to take office for nearly 150 years. Of Blair's new ministers, only one had sat at the cabinet table before—John Morris, the attorney general—and they had no experience in running a department or giving orders to civil servants.

For all of the briefings Blair received in private, in public he didn't display much interest in world affairs. He had not served on any of the parliamentary committees that dealt with foreign affairs and had not made a speech of any significance on world issues. Before becoming party leader in 1994, he had not involved himself with any of the political pressure groups campaigning on foreign issues, be it the plight of the Kurds under Saddam or the collapse of Yugoslavia. He spoke passable French, and holidayed regularly in France and Italy. Little else was known about Britain's new leader.

It is ironic that Blair, who would risk his political career and reputation on his alliance with the United States, should have spent much of his first days in office laying the ground rules for his future dealings with his new European colleagues. The vexed question of Britain's role in Europe and the nature of its relationship with the bureaucracy of the European Union had brought the Conservative Party to its knees, and led to its devastating defeat in the 1997 election. Most of the newly elected Labour members of Parliament were pro-European, having been seduced by the attractive social welfare, employment, and human rights provisions advocated by Brussels. The majority of the British press, however, remained deeply Euroskeptic, and Blair was mindful that he needed to choose his words carefully if he was not to upset his otherwise supportive media. Labour's election manifesto had skillfully managed to be both pro-European and patriotic, with Blair indicating that he was in favor of playing a more constructive role in Europe. But on the question of Europe's new single currency, Blair had not come to a firm decision, although his gut instinct was that Britain should join when both the political and economic conditions were right. When asked about the subject shortly before the election, Blair had answered that it was "no big deal either way,"[20] although many of Blair's close advisors were enthusiastic advocates of British membership.

Blair calculated that he could use his impressive domestic election victory to become a dominant force in European politics. His first priority was to establish good relations with Helmut Kohl, the German chancellor, and French president Jacques Chirac. Blair figured that with Kohl nearing the end of his remarkable career, and Chirac weakened by the defeat of his government in recent French parliamentary elections, he was in a strong position to be a dominant figure in European politics. His first European summit took place in Noordwijk in Holland on May 23, 1997, when he spoke enthusiastically about the politics of the Third Way, of which he had become a close adherent following his discussions with Bill Clinton in Washington. Chirac, the leader of France's right-wing Gaullist party, was so confused by Blair's remarks that he later asked him if he was sufficiently right-wing to be "an honorary member of New Labour."[21]

Two weeks later, Blair gave a clearer exposition of his likely approach to European issues when he delivered an address to the Congress of European Socialists, held at the Swedish port of Malmö on June 6. Having overseen a radical overhaul of his own party to broaden its appeal and make it electable, Blair believed that he was well equipped to do the same in Europe. Blair complained that, in his view, the institutions established by the European Union were "impossibly remote" from the people. "Am I satisfied with Europe?" he asked his audience. "Frankly, no." The union, he declared, must "modernize or die." Blair's comments caused a degree of consternation among some of his Socialist counterparts, particularly the French prime minister Lionel Jospin who had a more traditional attitude toward social democracy. Many European Socialists did not take kindly to being lectured by someone with little experience of how Europe managed its affairs. Blair, however, drawing encouragement from his domestic election success, believed he could persuade his new colleagues to come around to his point of view. He was particularly confident that he might make an ally of Gerhard Schröder, the leader of Germany's opposition Social Democrats who was developing a reputation of his own as a modernizer.

A few days later, Blair again managed to upstage his new European allies when they met in Amsterdam on June 16 for the Inter-Governmental

Conference. The mayor of Amsterdam had the rather unusual idea to give the fifteen attending leaders new seven-speed bicycles to race through the city streets. While the more portly leaders, such as Germany's chancellor Helmut Kohl, politely declined the invitation, Blair made sure he was first across the finish line. The popular British press could not restrain their delight. "Blair Leads From the Front," the headlines read. Tony Blair had made his mark in Europe.

The highlight of Blair's first weeks in office, however, came at the end of the month when Bill Clinton arrived in London to pay tribute to his political "little brother." Blair was eager to discuss the priority he intended to give the transatlantic alliance, and Clinton was afforded every possible privilege to underline the importance Blair gave to their political friendship. Clinton was invited to address the British cabinet, the first American president to do so since Richard Nixon. At the end of Clinton's speech, the new ministers gave him a standing ovation. Blair and Clinton then retired to the prime minister's private quarters, where they discussed various international issues, including Northern Ireland, the withdrawal of NATO peacekeepers from Bosnia, and the upcoming handover of Hong Kong to China. They compared notes on their respective election strategies and, as one Clinton aide put it, spent time "simply shooting the breeze."

Later in the afternoon, amid bright sunshine, Clinton and Blair participated in a decidedly relaxed press conference in the garden of Number 10. Clinton did his best to compliment his host, expressing his envy both at the 179-seat majority Blair had achieved at the election and the fact that the new British prime minister was so youthful. "I'm sick of it, because he's seven years younger than I am and he has no gray hair," Clinton joked. Becoming more serious, Clinton paid tribute to the "unique partnership" that existed between the United States and Britain. "Over the past fifty years our unbreakable alliance has helped to bring unparalleled peace and prosperity and security. It's an alliance based on shared values and common aspirations." In response, Blair outlined the policy that would underpin his difficult balancing act of maintaining a close working relationship with Europe while also making sure that the Atlantic alliance did not suffer as a consequence. "Britain does not need to choose between being strong in Europe or being close to the United States of America," said Blair, "but that by being strong in Europe we will further strengthen our relations with the U.S." In the years that lay ahead, this delicate balancing act would be tested to the limit.

Two

ENEMY TARGET

ONE OF THE FIRST visitors to be received at Downing Street by the new prime minister was Sir David Spedding, the head of Britain's Secret Intelligence Service. "C," as he was known among his colleagues, had spent most of his career fighting Middle Eastern terrorism. The fifty-four-year-old spy's most memorable achievement had been to thwart a plot by the Palestinian terrorist mastermind Abu Nidal to assassinate the queen during an official visit to Jordan in 1984. Spedding, an urbane, Oxford-educated Englishman, had forsaken a promising career as a historian to join the Secret Service, and was appointed director-general in 1994. Sir David had been called to Downing Street to educate the new prime minister in the global threats to Britain's security.

When Tony Blair became prime minister, he possessed few of the attributes usually associated with a war leader. Unlike Winston Churchill, Britain's most famous wartime commander, Blair had no military experience. As a schoolboy, he had mocked the Combined Cadet Force, where British adolescents are taught the basic skills of soldiering, and as a young politician, he had favored a number of antiwar organizations, such as the Campaign for Nuclear Disarmament, a powerful pressure group. Blair's lack of military experience was reflected throughout his cabinet; none of Labour's front bench had any military experience. Indeed, during the long years of opposition, Labour had acquired a reputation for being weak on defense and lacking the will to defend Britain's national interests overseas. Apart from his preelection conversations with Charles Guthrie, the chief of the defense staff, Blair had very little understanding about military strategy or handling threats to the Western alliance.

Spedding brought with him briefing documents from senior intelligence officers, who were experts in their fields. Blair learned of the heavy responsibility his office carried when Robin Butler, the cabinet secretary, gave him instructions on how to use the secret codes that would launch the Trident nuclear missile system. Blair had displayed his quick mastery of his nuclear brief during a meeting of the Defence and Overseas Policy Cabinet Committee. Although the discussions involved complex and secret issues on Britain's nuclear deterrent and the loading of missiles and warheads, the military were impressed by Blair's grasp of detail and his contribution to the discussions, which they thought was "impressive and helpful."[1]

Spedding first explained to Blair how the intelligence establishment operated; he then set out the specific threats his officers were acting against. Blair was made fully aware of the close cooperation that existed between the British and American intelligence agencies, and how the CIA and SIS shared information and operations. Spedding listed the priority areas that occupied most of the time and resources of the intelligence community.

Spedding, an Arabist by training, had spent most of his career in the shadow of the Cold War. Since his appointment in 1994, he had been responsible for overseeing a radical reappraisal of the intelligence community's priority targets. During the Cold War, most of the organization's resources had been directed specifically at containing the threat posed by the Soviet Union. This included trying to discover the likely target range and trajectory of Soviet nuclear missiles, monitoring political intrigues at the Kremlin, and trying to contain the Soviets' efforts to spread their influence around the world, particularly in the Middle East and Africa. By the mid-1990s, the intelligence priorities had undergone a radical transformation. The newly created Russian Federation was still kept under close observation, but it no longer posed a direct threat to Britain's security.

By the time Blair came into office, the intelligence community's focus had altered significantly. A great amount of its resources was directed against so-called rogue states, such as Iraq, Iran, Libya, Syria, and North Korea, which were suspected of either helping to train and support Islamic terror groups or attempting to develop weapons of mass destruction. The collapse of the Soviet Union meant that significant quantities of state-of-the-art nuclear material and expertise had found their way to the black market, and a great amount of effort was expended in trying to prevent this material from falling into the wrong hands. British intelligence was particularly concerned that, following the success of the Aum Shinrikyo sect in staging a sarin gas attack on the Japanese underground in March 1995,[2] Islamic terrorist groups might try to acquire nuclear, biological, or chemical weapons. By the spring of 1997, Spedding had given instructions that the primary intelligence priority was to keep a watchful eye on rogue states, to prevent the proliferation of weapons of mass destruction, and to prevent such weapons from falling into the hands of Islamic terror groups.

At the head of Spedding's list of rogue states was Saddam Hussein's Iraq.[3] More than six years had passed since the end of the 1991 Gulf War, and the UN had still not managed to persuade the Iraqi dictator to dismantle his weapons of mass destruction arsenal. Under the terms of UN Resolution 687, the American-led coalition had agreed to bring hostilities to a halt in return for Saddam's promise to disarm. But by the time teams of UN weapons inspectors began arriving in Iraq, President George H. Bush, who had led the coalition, was in the midst of a presidential election campaign. Saddam, who had proved himself to be a skillful manipulator of international public opinion, was well aware that there was little chance of another international military coalition being assembled to confront him. He took advantage of Bush's preoccupation with the election to obstruct the inspectors.

Despite a brief breakthrough in 1995, when Saddam's two sons-in-law defected to Jordan and revealed details of the Iraqi dictator's illegal weapons programs, by 1997 the UN's efforts to get Saddam to comply with his disarmament obligations had reached stalemate. Tony Blair was under pressure from human rights groups, and many members of his own

Labour Party were waging a vociferous campaign to lift the rigorous UN sanctions that had been imposed on Iraq following the 1990 invasion of Kuwait. Intelligence reports showed clearly that Saddam was selling vital medical and humanitarian supplies on the black market while using the profits to sustain his regime. Even so, serious cracks were beginning to appear in the policy of "containment" that Clinton had imposed against Iraq, as many of Washington's former allies, including France and Germany, argued strongly in favor of having the sanctions lifted.

Spedding told Blair that despite the growing clamor for sanctions against Iraq to be lifted, British intelligence and the CIA remained deeply concerned about Saddam's illicit weapons arsenal. Although the evidence provided by Saddam's sons-in-law suggested the Iraqi dictator had abandoned his attempts to build an atom bomb, grave concerns remained about his chemical and biological weapons capabilities. Both American and British intelligence were convinced that Saddam was still hiding "some chemical weapons agents, munitions, precursor chemicals and production equipment," and that Iraq was "capable of regenerating a chemical weapons capability in a matter of months."[4] There were also significant numbers of Iraqi missiles that were unaccounted for.

The United States and Britain were the only two countries at the UN that continued to argue in favor of maintaining sanctions against Iraq and of forcing Saddam to comply fully with the ceasefire terms he had agreed to at the end of the Gulf War. Frustrated by the lack of progress, the American and British governments authorized their respective intelligence agencies to arrange a coup in Baghdad that would remove Saddam from power.[5] In the mid-1990s, both the CIA and SIS worked closely with different Iraqi exile groups, but their attempts to stage a coup came to nothing. An attempt by Ahmed Chalabi's Iraqi National Congress (INC) to overthrow Saddam in 1995 failed when Washington pulled its backing at the last moment. Another attempt by an Iraqi exile group, the Iraqi National Accord (INA), which was planned with the help of British intelligence in the summer of 1996, similarly ended in disaster when Saddam's agents uncovered the plot and executed the ringleaders.[6]

Iraq was not the only major threat that Blair was briefed about by Spedding. The other area of pressing concern was the activities of A. Q. Khan, the Pakistani nuclear scientist who had built his own uranium-enrichment facility. "After Iraq, our biggest worry was Khan, and the illegal trade was our primary concern," said one of Blair's senior aides. "We had a great deal of information of the trafficking in technology and equipment, and all our efforts were devoted to trying to prevent this material from falling into the wrong hands."[7]

Khan's work enabled Pakistan to test its first nuclear device in 1998, and the reports received by British and American intelligence showed that in order to finance his research, Khan was prepared to sell his technological expertise to other states, including Libya and Iran. Like Iraq, Libya was subjected to wide-ranging UN sanctions because of Colonel Gadhafi's refusal to hand over two Libyans suspected of masterminding the 1988 bombing of a Pan Am jumbo jet over the Scottish village of Lockerbie, with the loss of 270 lives. Although Gadhafi had indicated that he was interested in reaching a rapprochement with the West, there were incomplete intelligence reports that the Libyan leader was attempting to develop nuclear and ballistic missile programs.

Iran was another country that was giving the international intelligence community reason for concern. After Ayatollah Ruhollah Khomeini seized control during the 1979 Iranian revolution, Tehran had been on a collision course with the United States and the West and had been responsible for the abduction of American and British subjects in Lebanon during the 1980s. The intelligence assessment that Blair was given indicated that Iran had developed a missile system—the Shahab 3—with a range of nearly eight hundred miles, sufficient for attacking Israel. In addition, Iran was known to be developing its own production and processing facilities for nuclear material, with much of the technology coming from A. Q. Khan's research laboratory, via Libya. North Korea was also interested in selling ballistic missile systems to rogue states, including Iran and Libya. In 1997, it was believed that North Korea's efforts to develop its own nuclear weapons system had been shelved after the United States negotiated with the North Koreans to suspend plutonium production.

Regarding the international terror network, the primary focus of Spedding's briefing to Blair was on the activities of Osama bin Laden's al-Qaeda (the Base) organization.[8] A former veteran of the mujahideen campaign to drive the Russians out of Afghanistan in the 1980s, bin Laden had returned home to his native Saudi Arabia after the Russians were finally defeated in 1989. Expelled in 1991 for plotting to overthrow the Saudi royal family, he had sought refuge in Sudan, where he set up a number of training camps for his followers to learn modern terrorist techniques. Bin Laden's main objective was to drive American and other foreign forces out of Saudi Arabia, where they had been based since the end of the Gulf War. The American military bases had been set up to protect Saudi Arabia's vital oil reserves from another attack by Saddam, but bin Laden believed that the presence of foreign "infidels" on the sacred land that had once been inhabited by the Prophet Mohammed was sacrilegious, and he was determined to wage a violent terrorist campaign against them.

In August 1996, bin Laden issued his own fatwa, or religious ruling, calling on Muslims to drive American soldiers out of Saudi Arabia. The rambling document condemned the Saudi monarchy for allowing the American army there. It celebrated a suicide truck-bomb attack that bin Laden's followers had carried out the previous June against a U.S. Marine compound in Dharhan, in eastern Saudi Arabia, which had killed 19 Americans and wounded 372. Although bin Laden claimed he carried out the attack, U.S. intelligence reports suggested that it was principally— perhaps exclusively—the work of an Iranian-backed group of Saudi Arabian dissidents called Saudi Hezbollah. *The 9/11 Commission Report,* which later examined the bombing, concluded that "while the evidence of Iranian involvement is strong, there are also signs that al-Qaeda played some role, as yet unknown."[9]

Bin Laden's organization had previously been implicated in a car-bomb attack on a Saudi-U.S. joint facility in Riyadh in November 1995 and a plot to blow up a dozen U.S. airliners over the Pacific Ocean. Other known al-Qaeda terrorist activity included setting up a cell in the Kenyan capital, Nairobi, from which they supplied arms to Somali warlords fighting U.S. peacekeepers. Al-Qaeda military trainers claimed credit for shooting down two Black Hawk helicopters in Mogadishu, which eventually led to the withdrawal of U.S. troops from Somalia. Bin Laden's organization was also implicated in the 1993 bombing of the World Trade Center in New York.

Apart from conducting terror attacks against American and Saudi targets, al-Qaeda representatives attempted to purchase what they believed was enriched weapons-grade uranium, which was later found to be fake. Even so, al-Qaeda was not discouraged. Asked why they wanted to acquire such material, one of bin Laden's aides replied: "It's easy to kill more people with uranium." [10]

When bin Laden was based in Sudan, his organization made contact with a senior Iraqi intelligence officer. Reports picked up by the CIA and passed to British intelligence suggested that bin Laden had asked for space to establish training camps in Iraq and for help in procuring weapons, although there was no evidence that Iraq responded to the request. [11] There were further reports of bin Laden attempting to make contact with Iraqi intelligence, and the precise nature of the relationship between Saddam Hussein and al-Qaeda was to become a subject of intense interest and speculation within the Atlantic intelligence community. By the time Blair came to power, bin Laden had been forced to leave Sudan after he was involved in a failed assassination attempt against Egypt's president Hosni Mubarak. Seriously short of funds, and with his training apparatus in disarray, bin Laden was forced to regroup before he could plan any further terror attacks.

Blair was deeply affected by the bleak intelligence assessment that Spedding had provided, and resolved to demonstrate strong leadership when it came to confronting rogue states and the more pressing issue of WMD proliferation. He expressed this deep concern a few months later, during a conversation with Paddy Ashdown, the Liberal Democrat leader. Blair confided to Ashdown in November 1997 that he had been studying the intelligence on Saddam's weapons capability and was troubled by what he had learned. "I have now seen some of the stuff on this," said Blair. "It really is pretty scary. He (Saddam) is very close to some appall-

ing weapons of mass destruction. I don't understand why the French and
the others don't understand this. We cannot let them get away with it."
Blair wanted to have the evidence published, just as President John F.
Kennedy had done during the Cuban Missile Crisis in 1962, and Blair
put pressure on President Clinton to follow suit.[12]

Having absorbed the details of Spedding's intelligence briefings, Blair
set to work on reorganizing Britain's armed forces. Blair was determined
to distance himself from the pacifism and defeatism that had tainted the
Labour Party's previous approach to defense issues, and he wanted to
ensure that Britain was properly equipped to face any possible challenge
during his term. Blair had impressed Charles Guthrie, the chief of the
defense staff, when the two had met at Claridge's Hotel while Blair was
still leader of the opposition. Guthrie, a gruff, intelligent man who had
served as an officer in the SAS, the British Army's elite special operations
unit, gradually warmed to Blair, and encouraged his colleagues to overcome the military's historic suspicion of Labour governments. In the same
way that Britain's intelligence priorities were changing, Guthrie thought
it was essential to reorganize Britain's armed forces. "We needed to complete the transformation from having an army equipped to fight the Cold
War in Europe to developing it into an expeditionary force that could be
deployed around the world at any time," he said.[13]

Blair encountered another formidable political adversary at the Foreign Office, where Robin Cook had just taken up residence. Cook, a
prickly, supremely confident man, came from the traditional left of the
Labour Party and saw himself as a potential successor to Blair, as indeed
did Gordon Brown. Cook was determined to make an impact on the new
government's conduct of foreign policy. Cook wanted to add a moral dimension to Britain's foreign policy and move away from the cynical realpolitik that he believed had characterized the Conservatives' approach to
foreign issues. On May 12, Cook summoned a select group of the media,
academic experts, and diplomats to the Foreign Office to deliver his mission statement for the future. Cook declared that he wanted Britain "to
once again be a force for good in the world." Human rights would be
placed "at the heart" of everything he did, and he lectured that British
foreign policy "must have an ethical dimension and must support the

demands of other people for the democratic rights on which we insist for ourselves."[14] The new foreign secretary wanted to impose strict controls on the sale of British arms overseas. Cook made no mention of the United States in his speech, a fact that was not overlooked by the American Embassy in London. His high moral tone was reflected in his aides' description of the speech as Cook's "ethical foreign policy," a term that would haunt him in the years to come.

Blair was not pleased with Cook's mission statement, which he felt was naive and unrealistic.[15] He was concerned that Cook's restrictions on arms sales would alienate British arms companies. Blair's principal foreign policy advisors in Downing Street—Jonathan Powell, his chief of staff, and John Holmes, his foreign policy advisor—both believed that Cook had gone too far, with Powell actually exclaiming "What a load of crap!" when he read the text of Cook's speech. Blair waited until the autumn before he delivered his official riposte to Cook.

In a speech at the annual banquet given by the lord mayor of London on November 11, Blair stated the importance he placed on maintaining a strong relationship with Washington. "When Britain and America work together on the international scene, there is little we cannot achieve," he said. "Our aim should be to deepen our relationship with the U.S. at all levels. We are a bridge between the U.S. and Europe—let us use it. By virtue of our geography, our history, and the strengths of our people, Britain is a global player. We need strong defense. . . . It is an instrument of influence. . . . We must not reduce our capability to exercise a role on the international stage."

In politics, actions often have more resonance than words, and Blair gave an early indication of his no-nonsense approach to taking on international terrorists when he authorized an SAS snatch squad to seize a brutal Serb war criminal in early July 1997. Blair took the decision after meeting up with President Clinton during a NATO summit in Madrid. The two leaders had attended the summit to discuss NATO's expansion to include newly liberated Eastern European states such as Poland, Hungary, and the Czech Republic. After the summit ended, Blair invited Clinton to his hotel room to discuss the continuing problems Western peacekeepers faced in Bosnia. It was now a year since the Dayton Peace

Accord had brought the civil war to an end. As part of the deal struck at Dayton, Bosnian Serb war leaders such as Radovan Karadzic, who had been responsible for the horrors of ethnic cleansing that had claimed tens of thousands of innocent lives, agreed to withdraw from public life. But a year later, the Bosnian Serb strongmen were still strutting around their ministate with impunity, striking fear into the local population and threatening the uneasy peace.

Blair had been briefed by Sir David Spedding on the joint effort by British intelligence officers and the military to hunt down and capture known Bosnian Serb war criminals. Blair then gave specific orders to Spedding that any Serb leader accused of committing war crimes should be apprehended and sent to The Hague to stand trial before the International War Crimes Tribunal.[16] Blair understood that the lack of clarity that had affected Britain's previous involvement in Bosnia needed to change, and by giving clear, concise orders he hoped to send a message to the Bosnian Serbs that in the future, they would be held accountable for their actions.

British intelligence officers who had undergone intensive language training were sent to infiltrate the Serb-held districts and find out where the main culprits were hiding. Although they were unable to locate the whereabouts of Karadzic and other top leaders, by the time Blair met up with Clinton in Madrid, British intelligence had been able to identify several key suspects. The two leaders agreed that if they failed to act quickly to curb the activities of the Bosnian Serbs, there was a strong likelihood that the conflict would be rekindled, and that British and American troops engaged in peacekeeping duties would become embroiled in a bloody civil war. SIS officers on the ground reported that they had found several suspects who would be easy targets for an SAS assault team. One of them was Simo Drljaca, who had overseen ethnic cleansing operations in the northwest Bosnian town of Prijedor.

After consulting with Clinton, Blair ordered the SAS into action. The plan was for the assault team to apprehend two Bosnian Serb suspects who would then be flown out of the country in American Black Hawk helicopters. The next day, two SAS teams moved into action. In the first raid, their target, a hospital administrator who had previously run the notorious Omarska concentration camp outside Prijedor, surrendered without a fight. But when they approached Drljaca as he sat having breakfast beside a Balkan lake, the Serb reached for his gun and managed to shoot one of the British soldiers in the leg before being gunned down. After just over two months in office, Blair had experienced his first kill.

THE MOST IMMEDIATE TERRORIST threat that faced Britain when Tony Blair became prime minister came from the Irish Republican Army, or IRA. For more than thirty years, successive British governments had suffered from the seemingly endless cycle of violence in Northern Ireland. Rival gangs of Catholic Republicans and Protestant Unionists had indulged in an orgy of violence in the province of just 1.6 million people. The conflict amounted to a de facto civil war, and by the mid-1990s it had claimed an estimated three thousand lives and left thousands of others injured or maimed. On occasion, the violence had spread to the British mainland, where gunmen from the Provisional wing of the IRA had conducted a bloody campaign of bombings and political assassination. In 1985, the IRA had staged one of its more spectacular attacks, in which it very nearly succeeded in killing Margaret Thatcher and several leading members of the government when it bombed the Brighton hotel where they were staying for the Conservative Party's annual conference.

Blair regarded the Northern Ireland conflict as both an affront to his own strong Christian beliefs and an ugly stain on Britain's international reputation, and he recognized that it was in urgent need of attention. In the past, Labour had been inhibited from acting as an honest broker in the dispute because of the hard left's overt support for a united Ireland, irrespective of the wishes of the Protestant majority in the north. After he became party leader in 1994, Blair slowly moved the party to a more pragmatic position. "Even before the general election I had taken a very keen interest in what was happening in Northern Ireland," Blair later recalled. "I hadn't done anything particularly dramatic other than shifting my own party's position away from one of pushing for a united Ireland. That was really because I had a sense that, if I was going to play a part in the negotiations, I should come to it with relatively clean hands."[17]

In his conversation with Clinton after becoming prime minister, Blair said that Northern Ireland would be one of the most important priorities of his premiership, news which Clinton received warmly.[18] It was a significant political gamble for Blair to undertake, particularly as the risk of failure far outweighed the prospects for success. Ever since William Gladstone had attempted a Herculean effort to resolve "the Irish Question," successive generations of politicians, from Lloyd George to Margaret Thatcher, had tried and failed to make progress. Even with his landslide victory under his belt, most political consultants would have warned Blair to keep well away from the province, as there was little to be gained but rejection and public opprobrium.

Some of the foundations for bringing the violence to an end had been laid before Blair came to office. When Margaret Thatcher was prime minister, British intelligence had picked up soundings that there was an influential group within the leadership of the IRA that was beginning to despair of achieving its stated goal of creating a united Ireland through violence alone. A dialogue was opened between SIS officers and IRA commanders. The key figures on the IRA side were Gerry Adams and Martin McGuinness, the leaders of Sinn Fein, the IRA's political wing. Both men had seen active service with the IRA, and Adams continued to serve on the organization's Army Council.[19] By the early 1990s, they were frustrated by the lack of progress their terror campaign brought, and were looking for ways to enter into a political dialogue with the British government.

Bill Clinton had taken a keen interest in the Irish problem. With Sinn Fein dropping heavy hints that they could deliver an IRA ceasefire, Clinton was ideally placed to bring pressure to bear on them to engage in the political process, as the Republicans drew much of their financial support from Irish-Americans. Clinton and John Major worked closely to break the impasse, although there were occasional tensions between the two men, such as over Clinton's decision to invite Adams and McGuinness to Washington, giving rise to suspicions that Clinton was too eager to impress the Irish-American voters. Clinton allayed some of Major's fears when in 1995 he became the first serving American president to visit Belfast, Northern Ireland's capital.

Clinton, however, was regarded as being "too green," i.e., too supportive of the Irish nationalist drive for a united Ireland, to have any realistic prospect of breaking the impasse. "The fundamental flaw of the Clinton administration was that they did not regard Sinn Fein as terrorists," said a former senior Downing Street official who worked with both John Major and Tony Blair on resolving the Northern Ireland dispute. "They had very good relations with Sinn Fein and Gerry Adams, who they almost treated like a freedom fighter rather than a murderer. But their contacts with the Protestant Unionists were virtually nonexistent."[20] Partly this was the Unionists' fault, because, unlike Sinn Fein, they didn't have an influential lobby in Washington. John Major tried to redress the balance by arranging for David Trimble, the Unionist leader, to visit Washington, but his visit had only a marginal impact, and by the time Major left office, the negotiating process was paralyzed. Major was limited in how far he could go in making concessions toward Sinn Fein because of the pressure from the right of his own party.

In Northern Ireland, the only tangible achievement of the Clinton and Major years was to get Sinn Fein to arrange a temporary ceasefire (both Clinton and Major indulged the Sinn Fein leaders Gerry Adams and Martin McGuinness in the fiction that their organization was separate and distinct from the IRA command, whereas both men sat on the IRA's governing body). On August 31, 1994, the IRA announced a three-month ceasefire. This was in response to Major's statement in the Downing Street Declaration of December 1993 that the U.K. government had no "selfish strategic or economic interest" in Northern Ireland, a rather quaint formulation for reassuring Irish Republicans that Britain no longer retained any colonial aspirations.

Major's attempts to get the IRA to commit to a permanent ceasefire, however, ultimately ended in failure when the two sides were unable to reach an agreement over the decommissioning of the IRA's stockpile of guns and ammunition. Major wanted the IRA to disarm fully before Sinn Fein took its place at the negotiating table for a new constitution for Northern Ireland; the IRA wanted to see tangible political progress being made before they gave up their weapons. Given the divisions within the Republican movement over whether or not it should enter into a dialogue with the British in the first place, and its long-standing belief in British treachery, it was not long before the ceasefire was revoked. At 7.01 p.m. on Friday, February 9, 1996, it ended dramatically when the IRA detonated a massive bomb at Canary Wharf, a modern financial complex in eastern London, murdering two people.

Blair had supported Major's Northern Ireland initiative, although he was privately critical of Major's tactics. Soon after his election as Labour leader in 1994, Blair appointed Mo Mowlam as shadow Northern Ireland secretary. He told her, rather indelicately, that Labour's policy would be "so far up Major's arse that he can never accuse us of not being behind him."[21] If this was Labour's public stance, in private Blair was more critical of the way the talks were being handled. He thought that Major had been unrealistic in insisting that the IRA disarm before it could participate in negotiations, and he thought that Major could have put more pressure on the Unionists.[22] In public, however, Blair was supportive of Major's efforts, and resisted pressure from within his own party to criticize the way the Conservative government was handling the peace process. In recognition of the Labour leader's support, Major authorized his staff to keep Blair and Mowlam fully briefed on developments, and even allowed them access to confidential documents.

Blair maintained a dialogue with the Clinton administration on Northern Ireland while liaising closely with Major. He was greatly assisted in this by Jonathan Powell. Before joining Blair's team, Powell had developed an impressive network of contacts in the United States while working as a political secretary at the British Embassy in Washington. Powell worked closely with Nancy Soderberg, whom Clinton had brought in to work exclusively on Ireland, as did Mo Mowlam, although Powell and other Downing Street officials involved in the talks did not have a high regard for Clinton's officials. "We felt Soderberg was naive and out of her depth," said one of Blair's close advisors. "In some respects, the Clinton crowd were a liability, particularly the way they dealt with Sinn Fein. The reality was that we had to try and sort out this mess in spite of their interventions."[23] Discussions on Northern Ireland featured prominently when Blair met with Clinton in Belfast in November 1995, and again when they met at the White House in April 1996, when Clinton said that, if Blair became prime minister, he would have a unique opportunity to make progress in the province, one that he should seize with both hands.[24]

When Blair became prime minister, it was generally recognized both in Whitehall and Ulster that he was far better placed than Major to move forward with the peace process. "By the time Major left, everything was paralyzed," said a senior Downing Street official involved in the negotiations. "When Blair arrived, he had far more freedom of movement and the ability to make a fresh start."[25] On May 16, 1997, Blair signaled his determination to revive the peace process when he flew to Belfast. Much was made of the fact that he had an Irish-born and Protestant-raised mother, that his wife was a Catholic, and that, as a child, he had spent many happy family holidays in Donegal. Blair, though, was keen to make his mark on the entrenched positions of the Unionists and Republicans.

The main purpose of his Belfast visit was to reassure the Unionists that they had "nothing to fear" from a Labour government. In a speech delivered at the unlikely setting of the Royal Ulster Agriculture Show, Blair declared that any change to the status of Ulster would only be accomplished with the consent of the people. "Northern Ireland is part of the United Kingdom because that is the wish of the majority of people who live here," he said. "It will remain part of the United Kingdom for as long as that remains the case. The principle of consent is and will be at the heart of my government's policies. . . . A political settlement is not a slippery slope to a united Ireland," he said.[26] But Blair made it clear to the Unionists that their traditional negative response to most suggestions that could pave the way for a resolution would no longer be tolerated. It was time, said Blair, for the Unionist majority to face up to the legitimate aspirations of those who sought a united Ireland through political means.

Having tried to reassure the Unionists, Blair attempted to persuade the Republicans that he was keen to address their aspirations, too. If the Republicans were prepared to renounce terrorism, they would be invited to join the political process aimed at establishing the principle of power-sharing in the province. Unlike Major, Blair made no overt reference to the IRA's weapons stockpiles. So long as Adams and McGuinness were prepared to give a commitment that they no longer sought to drive the British out of Northern Ireland through murder and bombs, they would be welcome to join the process. So far as Blair was concerned, the past was the past, and his priority was the future. "The settlement train is leaving," he told the leaders of the Republican movement. "I want you on that train. But it is leaving anyway and I will not allow it to wait for you. You cannot hold the process to ransom any longer. So, end the violence now."[27]

Blair was determined to restore the ceasefire that had lasted for seventeen months under John Major and to make it permanent. He was rewarded when Sinn Fein announced the resumption of a ceasefire two months after his Belfast visit, although there was no guarantee how long it would last. During the late summer of 1997, Blair had private misgivings about the Republicans' sincerity in committing themselves to the peace process. "If you ask me if the Republicans have definitely decided to give up violence for good, the answer is probably no," he said. "But I do think that the more they are drawn into the political process the harder it gets for them to return to violence."[28] Persuading Sinn Fein to reenter the negotiating process was Blair's chief aim, and he was determined to steer clear of what he believed was Major's mistake in turning the issue of decommissioning the IRA's weapons stockpiles into a point of principle. His instructions to Mo Mowlam were simply to get Sinn Fein back to the negotiating table. Once that had been achieved, Blair was confident he could deliver the rest.

The extraordinary self-confidence that Blair displayed in his approach to the Northern Ireland conflict was an early indication of how Britain's new prime minister would approach the security challenges that lay ahead. The fact that he had an overwhelming majority in the House of Commons—a luxury that was never afforded John Major—undoubtedly encouraged his belief that he might succeed where so many others had failed. But he was also motivated by a burning moral certainty that his involvement in Northern Ireland was a force for good in a dispute where evil often had the upper hand. "There is no doubt that from the moment that Blair entered Downing Street he truly believed that he could make an impact and get people talking," said one of his Downing Street aides. "He felt very strongly that the horror of Northern Ireland had gone on for far too long and that it was high time that something was done to bring people to their senses."[29]

John Major had appointed George Mitchell, a former U.S. senator, to chair all-party talks on a new constitutional framework for Northern Ireland. Mitchell had carried on with his work after the IRA broke the ceasefire with the Docklands bombing. After Sinn Fein announced the resumption of the ceasefire on July 16, they accepted the principles of nonviolence that Mitchell had laid down as a precondition to entering the talks. Adams and McGuinness accepted Mitchell's principles in September and entered the negotiations. David Trimble, the leader of the Ulster Unionist Party, also agreed to enter the talks, although the hardliner Rev. Ian Paisley, the leader of the Democratic Unionist Party, boycotted the process.

The reality of the mission that he had undertaken was driven home to Blair when he invited the Sinn Fein leaders Gerry Adams and Martin McGuinness to visit Downing Street in December. As the Downing Street gates swung open, a crowd of protesters shouted "murderers" and "shame" as the two men were admitted. Six years previously, Downing Street itself had been subjected to a mortar attack orchestrated by the IRA. Now two of its most notorious activists were entering the prime minister's official residence to discuss peace terms. Aware of the political passions the visit had engendered, Blair opted to conduct the official handshakes in the privacy of the cabinet room. As the Sinn Fein delegation settled into their chairs around the coffin-shaped cabinet table, Adams wondered out loud: "Is this where Michael Collins met Lloyd George in 1921?" Collins had been the last Sinn Fein leader to visit Number 10. He had returned home with the peace treaty that would give much of Ireland independence, except for the six counties of Ulster that were to remain under British sovereignty. Collins was denounced as a traitor and shot dead soon afterwards.

It was the first time that Blair had come face to face with men who had blood on their hands, but such was his determination to reach a settlement. He told Adams and McGuinness that he would do everything in his power to reach an agreement. Then he gave them a hard stare. "But if you ever do a Canary Wharf on me, I will never talk to you again."[30]

Within days of the historic political breakthrough signified by Sinn Fein's Downing Street visit, the whole process was in danger of collapsing after a prominent Protestant terrorist was murdered inside Belfast's Maze prison by an offshoot of the IRA, the Irish National Liberation Army (INLA). Protestant loyalists were quick to retaliate. The same day, a hotel in the Catholic area of the city was riddled with gunfire, killing one man and wounding four others. On New Year's Day, a Catholic was shot dead, which was followed the next day by an attack on a Protestant home. The province was rapidly degenerating into its familiar cycle of tit-for-tat killings, and David Trimble was coming under intense pressure from his Unionist supporters to withdraw from the peace talks. The day was eventually saved when Mo Mowlam took the unprecedented step of visiting the Maze prison herself to reassure the Protestant inmates—who exercised a great deal of influence over the Unionist leadership—that they had nothing to fear from the negotiating process. Mowlam won them over, and the message was duly passed back to the leadership that they should not withdraw.

Blair was learning fast about the realities of dealing with the troubled province and the issues of terrorism. He resolved to try to reach an agreement as soon as possible before the process could be wrecked by another bout of internecine conflict. After consulting with Clinton and Bertie Ahern, the Irish *taoiseach* (prime minister), Blair endorsed George Mitchell's decision to set a deadline for the negotiations to be completed by Maundy Thursday in April 1998. Easter had particular significance for the Republicans; they regarded themselves as the political heirs to those who led the Easter Rising of 1916, the failed Irish rebellion against British rule. The April timetable was ambitious. While the various parties had been negotiating for nearly two years, many substantive issues were still unresolved, and the participants continued to regard one another with deep mistrust. When Gerry Adams, for example, tried to engage Ken Maginnis, one of the Unionist delegates, in conversation during a break in negotiations, Maginnis walked away, muttering: "I don't talk to fucking murderers."

The negotiations moved slowly, and with only a few hours to go before the midnight deadline expired, Blair's aides encouraged him to play what they referred to as "the Clinton card." Clinton's officials had kept in touch with Mitchell's attempts to reach an agreement, and retained strong links with Sinn Fein. Clinton had built up a good understanding with Adams and McGuinness, although the 1996 Docklands bombing had brought home to him the reality of the organization he was dealing with. Blair, though, was reluctant to bring Clinton into play until he had all the other participants committed to an agreement. It was not until the early hours of Good Friday morning that all the other players in the talks—Catholics, Protestants, Irish, and British—reached a deal they could all agree on.

This was the moment Blair had been waiting for. "Get Clinton," he told his aides. It was ten to one in the morning in Washington, but Clinton believed that he could use his smooth-talking telephone manner to persuade the reluctant Sinn Fein duo of the merits of signing the peace deal. Mixing threat with blandishment, Clinton warned the Sinn Fein leadership that they would find themselves isolated if they were blamed for wrecking the agreement. One of Sinn Fein's main concerns was to secure the release of all the Republican prisoners who had been jailed for committing terrorist crimes, and Blair managed to sooth their anxieties by bringing forward the three-year deadline for their release. Clinton re-emphasised the point that Sinn Fein had a deal that they could sell to their supporters—i.e., the IRA. Within a few hours, Sinn Fein acknowledged that it would agree to the terms, and the Good Friday Agreement, as it soon became known, was born.

Blair was exhausted but jubilant. He phoned his wife, Cherie, who was already in Spain for a family holiday, and told her: "We're there."[31] There were some last-minute hiccups before the deal could be publicly announced, such as the refusal of Trimble's Ulster Unionists to allow Sinn Fein into the new Northern Ireland assembly before it had fully disarmed. Blair got around this last obstruction by writing Trimble a letter in which he personally ensured that IRA decommissioning would take place as soon as the agreement had been accepted in the referendum that was due to take place in June (71 percent voted in favor). Blair's letter swung the deal, and all the participants sat around the same table and put their names to the deal. Relations between the Unionists and Republicans had not thawed to the extent that David Trimble was prepared to shake Gerry Adams's hand, but even so, the fact that they had been able to forge an agreement in the face of hostility from all sides was a remarkable achievement. As Blair's party prepared to leave Belfast, he received a call from Buckingham Palace. Her Majesty the Queen wished to convey her congratulations to the prime minister for getting closer to an end of the Troubles than five previous occupants of Downing Street.[32] In Washington, Clinton was also pleased with the outcome. He later wrote in his autobiography: "Good Friday, April 10, was one of the happiest days of my presidency."[33]

Blair's involvement in Ulster was an important rite of passage. There was undoubtedly a degree of opportunism in his engagement in the process, an understanding that his strong domestic political position, allied to the fact that he carried no ideological baggage on the Irish question, placed him in a unique position to effect a radical change in the political landscape. But it took great courage for Blair to become so personally associated with the success or failure of the enterprise. His success showed the world that he could achieve where others had failed, and it demonstrated his strong sense of moral purpose. He had enmeshed himself deeply in an issue that involved terrorism, where human life was directly at stake, and his determined approach would characterize his dealings with similar challenges in the future.

Blair also learned a lot about dealing with the White House. Bill Clinton, who had assisted him greatly in his campaign to become prime minister, had been closely involved in the negotiating process, but from Blair's point of view, not all of the American president's interventions were positive. Downing Street regarded many of Washington's actions as unhelpful, and the pro–Sinn Fein bias of the Clinton camp only served to exacerbate the Unionists' bunker mentality. "It is fair to say that we managed to do a deal in spite of Clinton's interventions," said a Blair aide who was closely involved in the negotiations. "Clinton's intervention with Sinn Fein was helpful, but it was not crucial."[34] The Clinton camp, not surprisingly, took a different view, accusing Blair of making too many concessions to the Unionists.[35] Blair knew that he had a close ally in Bill Clinton, but whether he was a reliable ally was a question that, for the moment, Blair decided not to ask.

Three

TAKE AIM

———— ◆ ————

SADDAM HUSSEIN WAS PREPARING to make a comeback. More than six years had passed since he had suffered a devastating defeat in the Gulf War, and his position as Iraq's powerful dictator still remained unchallenged. In the intervening years, he had survived a widespread revolt against his rule by his Kurdish and Shiite Muslim subjects and at least two coup attempts that had been funded and organized by the American and British intelligence agencies. He had overcome the damaging effects of the defection to the West of his two sons-in-law, who revealed hitherto top-secret details of his weapons of mass destruction programs to Western intelligence. And he had managed to endure the crippling consequences of the most wide-ranging UN sanctions the world had ever seen. Now Saddam believed the time had come for him to reassert his authority and demonstrate both to his own people and to the outside world that the "Butcher of Baghdad" remained a force to be reckoned with.

By the spring of 1997, Saddam was convinced that the UN Security Council no longer had the political will to maintain the sanctions that had devastated the Iraqi economy and seriously undermined Iraq's military prowess. Saddam had shown great cunning in his attempts to manipulate world opinion. He had been masterful at playing the various members of the Security Council against each other, mainly by rewarding countries such as France and Russia, that were prepared to be accommodating to Baghdad, with lucrative oil and arms contracts. Saddam had become adept at playing the international media, so by the summer of 1997, most news reports on Iraq tended to concentrate on the civilian suffering caused by the sanctions rather than the billions of dollars Saddam and his immediate family were making from illicit trading on the international oil black market.

Saddam was preoccupied both with the continuing effects of the UN sanctions and the teams of UN arms inspectors that had been in Iraq since the end of the Gulf War to hunt down and destroy Iraq's WMD arsenal. By the summer of 1997, he felt confident enough in his own domestic position, and in his ability to split the Security Council, to launch himself on a collision course with the UN in an attempt to get the sanctions lifted and the inspectors withdrawn. Saddam realized that support for the sanctions was waning among three members of the Security Council—Russia, China, and France—all of whom had developed substantial trade ties with Baghdad since the end of the Gulf War. According to the report compiled by the Iraq Survey Group, which was set up after Saddam was overthrown in 2003 to investigate his WMD arsenal, "under Saddam's orders, the [Iraq] Ministry of Foreign Affairs formulated and implemented a strategy aimed at these UNSC (United Nations Security Council) members and international public opinion with the purpose of ending UN sanctions."[1] Between them Russia, France, and China accounted for 55 percent of the illicit oil vouchers Saddam used to bribe foreign governments to do his bidding.[2] In July 1997, *Forbes* magazine ranked Saddam fifth in its annual survey of the world's richest, with a personal fortune estimated at $5 billion.[3]

Only the United States and Britain, the two countries that had led the coalition to liberate Kuwait in 1991, remained steadfast in seeking to maintain the sanctions against Iraq. They were the only ones prepared to deploy their fighter planes to patrol Iraq's no-fly zones that had been set up by the UN to protect the Kurdish and Shia population from attack by Saddam. With a change of government in Britain and the election of a relatively inexperienced new prime minister, Saddam calculated that this would be an ideal opportunity for him to test the UN's resolve.

While in opposition, Tony Blair's Labour Party had adopted an ambivalent policy toward Iraq. In 1991, under Neil Kinnock's leadership, it had publicly supported the Gulf War and had generally approved of the British government's steadfast position on enforcing the UN resolutions that required Saddam to disarm. Blair himself had maintained this position after becoming party leader. Blair and his key advisors were determined to bury Labour's image as the party of unilateral disarmament, a party that was more prone to appeasement than confrontation. Blair was driven by his personal conviction that there was moral justification for taking a firm stand against those who desired to do harm in pursuit of their own political and nationalistic goals. This moral certainty may well have compelled Blair to overcompensate for Labour's historic aversion to military conflict. At times, such as in his dealings with Saddam Hussein, and later with Serbia's Slobodan Milosevic, Blair seemed determined to take an uncompromising position, leaving him isolated from Britain's traditional allies, particularly in Europe.

Many Labour politicians and party activists—arguably, the majority—were unhappy about the sanctions against Iraq. They supported the view that the sanctions were responsible for causing a humanitarian disaster in Iraq. The left-wing Scottish MP George Galloway campaigned actively to have the UN sanctions lifted, and he visited Baghdad regularly, meeting with senior Iraqi officials, including Saddam. There was a growing view in some diplomatic and media circles that the sanctions were counterproductive, allowing Saddam to survive in power while subjecting his people to the collective punishment of shortages in basic food and medical supplies. In October 1997, the UN Food and Agriculture Organization and the World Food Program published the findings of a study that stated that the sanctions "significantly constrained Iraq's ability . . . to import sufficient quantities of food to meet needs. As a consequence, food shortages and malnutrition became progressively severe and chronic" in the 1990s. No mention was made of the fact that Saddam himself bore responsibility for the ruination of his country. His regime only spent a small fraction of its vast wealth on the needs of Saddam's people.

In early June 1997, Saddam deliberately sought to provoke the security council when he ordered his officials not to cooperate with the UN weapons inspection teams that had recently returned to Iraq. The Iraqi action was a clear breach of the various UN resolutions that provided the mandate for the inspections. Richard Butler, the abrasive Australian diplomat who had recently been appointed head of the UN Special Commission on Disarmament (UNSCOM), did not hesitate to report the Iraqi action to the Security Council. As Saddam had anticipated, the Security Council was divided on how to respond. The United States and Britain argued in favor of strengthening the sanctions by imposing visa restrictions on Iraqi officials to prevent them from traveling abroad and by suspending indefinitely the regular six-month review of Iraqi sanctions. Initially, France and Russia objected, arguing that the existing sanctions against Baghdad were sufficiently punitive. It required a great deal of political and diplomatic pressure from President Clinton and Madeleine Albright, the secretary of state, to persuade the recalcitrant Russians and French to back the new resolution. At one stage in the negotiations Clinton telephoned Russian president Boris Yeltsin to remind him of his "responsibilities" to the international community.[4] Eventually, the Russians and the French signed the new resolution, but only after American and British diplomats agreed to delay implementation of the new sanctions for four months.

If Saddam was disappointed with the outcome, he could draw some satisfaction from knowing that the resolve of the Security Council was growing weaker each day. Undeterred by the threat of new sanctions, on June 22, 1997, Saddam convened a joint meeting of the Revolutionary Command Council and the Baath Party, Iraq's main governing bodies. "Iraq has complied with and implemented all relevant resolutions," declared a communiqué that was personally authorized by Saddam. "We demand with unequivocal clarity that the Security Council fulfills its commitment towards Iraq . . . The practical expression of this is to respect Iraq's sovereignty and to fully and totally lift the blockade on Iraq."[5]

As if to underscore Baghdad's intransigence, a few days later, Tariq Aziz, Iraq's deputy prime minister and Saddam's official spokesman, said that Baghdad could not guarantee the inspectors unrestricted access to all the sites they wanted to visit. Although the Security Council insisted that the inspectors had the right to enter any site in Iraq that they suspected might conceal banned weapons, Aziz declared that Iraq reserved the right to refuse access to sites that affected "national security or the safety of President Saddam Hussein."[6]

Tony Blair had already received from SIS chief Sir David Spedding a detailed intelligence briefing on Saddam and the recent history of Britain's involvement in containing the Iraqi dictator. But this was the first time he had been required to deal directly with Saddam and his schemes. Blair later confided that his resolve to stand up to Saddam derived from the early intelligence briefings he had received from Spedding. "Strangely enough, it was reading the intelligence soon after I became prime minister," he said. Blair read about "the threat from rogue states and about weapons of mass destruction getting into the hands of terrorist groups."[7] Blair had not paid much attention to these issues before becoming prime minister, and he found them so alarming he determined that they become an important part of his foreign policy. One of his close aides recalled that when Blair saw the intelligence, he went to great trouble to find out more. It was an example of Blair's "politician's instinct to see the coming issue."[8]

Blair gave instructions to the Foreign Office to take a hard line at the UN Security Council, insisting that there was no question of the sanctions being lifted so long as any doubt remained about Saddam's WMD arsenal. "When we got to look at what had happened since the Gulf War, we quickly came to the conclusion that Saddam had been allowed to get away with too much for far too long," said one of Blair's close foreign-policy aides.[9] Blair and his advisors felt that Saddam should have been dealt with as far back as 1992, when he first attempted to obstruct the work of the UN weapons inspectors.

During that period, Saddam had taken advantage of the first President Bush's reelection campaign as a good time to make trouble. When Bill Clinton assumed office, he thought the Saddam issue was leftover business from his predecessor.[10] But by June 1993, he was forced to reevaluate after Iraqi intelligence agents were found to be behind a plot to assassinate former president Bush during a visit to Kuwait. Clinton ordered a cruise missile strike against Baghdad in retaliation. Even so, containment was the policy pursued by the Clinton administration during its first term; so long as the sanctions were in place and the UN inspectors continued with their work, they thought, the threat posed by Saddam would be contained.

Later in Clinton's presidency, Washington's attitude toward Saddam hardened after the defection of the Iraqi dictator's sons-in-law in 1995. Their subsequent debriefing by the CIA and SIS revealed that Saddam could not be trusted. In private, so long as Saddam remained in power, Clinton and his officials had no intention of lifting the sanctions. To do so would enable him to rebuild his power base and threaten the region. In March 1997, Madeleine Albright, Clinton's new secretary of state, confirmed Washington's current tough line on Saddam when she told an audience at Washington's Georgetown University, "We do not agree with the nations who argue that if Iraq complies with its obligations concerning its weapons of mass destruction, sanctions should be lifted. Our view, which is unshakable, is that Iraq must prove its peaceful intentions . . . And the evidence is overwhelming that Saddam Hussein's intentions will never be peaceful."[11]

In her memoirs, Albright denied that her comments at Georgetown represented a change in American policy, claiming they were a reaffirmation of former president Bush's assertion that sanctions would never be lifted so long as Saddam remained in power. She did concede, however, that the first Clinton administration had "taken a slightly different approach," leading Saddam and the Iraqi people to understand that if they complied fully with the UN inspectors, the sanctions would be lifted.[12] That was certainly Saddam's understanding, and the Iraqi leader was determined to challenge this policy shift. In his mind, there was nothing to be gained for Iraq by cooperating with the UN weapons inspectors. The only way for Saddam to get the crippling effects of the sanctions lifted was for him to strike his own deal with the UN.

The British prime minister thought that the Iraqi people should be encouraged to believe that the sanctions would be lifted, but only after Saddam had fully complied with his disarmament obligations. Blair was, however, insistent that Saddam should not be allowed to escape his international duties, and throughout the summer and autumn of 1997, the prime minister remained resolute in forcing Saddam to comply with the wishes of the UN inspectors. Saddam was playing a clever game, and making good use of his French and Russian allies to try to make a deal whereby he would agree to continue to allow the inspectors to do their work in return for the sanctions being lifted. Both Washington and London argued that the formula should be the other way around, with sanctions lifted only after the inspectors had completed their work and given Iraq a clean bill of health, and not before. Saddam's tactics put Clinton and Blair in a quandary, particularly because Clinton had no desire to take military action against Iraq. And Britain simply did not have the military power to confront Saddam on its own, even if Blair had wanted to.

In his conversations with Paddy Ashdown, the Liberal Democrat leader, in November 1997, Blair expressed his concerns about the dilemma Clinton faced. "He said that he had spoken to Clinton several times during the day. Clinton is trying to avoid military action, but doesn't know quite how to do it." The prime minister told Clinton that "it was vital that we drew attention now to why the UN weapons inspectors were there. The world was being exposed to Saddam's viewpoint and had been allowed to forget the reasons for bringing them in the first place."[13]

Saddam understood fully the difficulties he was causing at the Security Council, and ordered his military commanders to make life as difficult as possible for the inspectors. On one occasion during an UNSCOM inspection, an Iraqi official grabbed the controls of an UNSCOM helicopter, almost causing it to crash, in a clumsy attempt to prevent the inspectors from photographing a sensitive site. The Iraqis blacked out the cameras that were supposed to monitor sensitive weapons sites, and moved restricted equipment without informing UNSCOM as they were supposed to do.[14] In October, Tariq Aziz brought matters to a head when he announced that no more Americans would be allowed to work with the inspection teams, and a few days later, the remaining American scientists were expelled. The Iraqis argued, with some justification, that UNSCOM had been infiltrated by the CIA and other Western intelligence agencies, and the "inspectors" were more interested in spying on the Iraqi regime than searching for hidden WMD.[15]

The Iraqi action put Clinton and Blair on the spot. Clinton's only recall of this crisis in his memoirs is in this passing observation: "I ordered the USS *George Washington* group to the region, and a few days later the inspectors returned."[16] It was not quite that simple. The presence of the American battle group in the Gulf certainly signaled Washington's intent to use force. Most of those involved in the crisis realized it was an empty threat because Clinton had no intention of actually going to war with Baghdad; he only planned to send American war planes to bomb specific Iraqi targets, if necessary. To get the inspectors readmitted, Clinton and Blair needed the support of the Security Council. To this end Madeleine Albright then undertook an intensive period of diplomacy that took her throughout Europe, the Gulf states, and Southeast Asia.

In Britain, Albright met with Robin Cook, the foreign secretary. Cook still prided himself on having added an "ethical dimension" to Britain's foreign policy, and he was supportive of Albright's determination to bring Saddam to heel. Cook resigned in 2003 in protest against Blair's decision to join the United States in the war to overthrow Saddam, but in 1998, he was fully supportive of Washington's determination to enforce UN resolutions on Iraq. Albright was impressed with Cook and wrote admiringly, "The British Foreign Secretary had red hair, expressive eyebrows, a well-trimmed beard, and a well-deserved reputation as a brilliant debater and wit. Cook helped ensure Great Britain's position as a stalwart ally in backing an appropriately tough line toward Iraq. We were both determined to keep the pressure on until Iraq met its obligations to disarm."[17] Cook himself informed the House of Commons that, according to UNSCOM reports, "Iraqi stocks of VX nerve gas keep increasing and . . . Saddam Hussein can currently produce sufficient anthrax for two missiles a week."[18]

Tony Blair added his voice to the deepening international concern about Saddam's activities. On November 10, 1997, Blair told the annual Lord Mayor's Banquet in London that the "question of relaxing sanctions" could only be addressed after Saddam had allowed the inspectors to complete their work. And Blair's speech contained a veiled threat to the Iraqi dictator. "The government's determination to stand firm against a still-dangerous dictator is unshakable," he said. "We want to see a diplomatic solution and will work with others to achieve this . . . But Saddam should not take this as a sign of weakness. He has made this fatal miscalculation before."[19]

The November crisis was finally resolved thanks to the intensive diplomatic efforts on the part of Albright, who managed to persuade Yevgeny Primakov, the Russian foreign minister and a former KGB station chief in Baghdad, to put pressure on Saddam to readmit the inspectors. Even at this stage, the Russians were deeply skeptical about the need to keep the inspectors in Iraq. Primakov told Albright bluntly that Moscow thought America and Britain were guilty of exaggerating the threat Saddam posed. Moscow was in favor of establishing a comparatively loose inspection regime whose standards the Iraqis would be able to meet, in return for which the sanctions would be lifted.[20] The Russians and the French were driven by the economic necessity of seeking to recoup the huge sums they were still owed by Baghdad for past commercial transactions—mainly arms sales. The sums ran into billions of dollars, and Primakov was frank in admitting that if the sanctions were lifted, "the Iraqis would sell oil and repay us; with sanctions, they sell oil and use the sanctions as an excuse not to pay us."[21]

Albright was unimpressed by this brazen declaration of Russian self-interest, and she told Primakov that there was no question of the sanctions being lifted until Saddam had fully complied with the UN's requirements. If the Russians wanted their money back, their best course of action was to persuade Saddam to disarm as soon as possible. Other countries might be suffering from "sanctions fatigue," but the United States and Britain remained determined to force Saddam to fulfill his obligations to the UN.

Primakov duly passed this message to Saddam, and the Iraqis reluctantly agreed to allow the inspectors to return unconditionally. Nevertheless, Saddam intimated that he was not going to tolerate the presence of the inspectors forever. The crisis had been put on hold rather than resolved. Tony Blair acknowledged this when he addressed the House of Commons later that month. "It is absolutely essential that [Saddam] backs down on this," he said. "If he does not, we will simply face this problem, perhaps in a different or far worse form, in a few years time."[22]

At this juncture, the policy of the British government was focused on persuading Saddam to cooperate fully with the inspectors. Were military action to take place, it would be in the form of air strikes against Iraqi sites suspected of involvement in Saddam's WMD projects. Tony Blair and his ministers did not at this time regard military action as being aimed as Saddam's removal.[23] Even so, Blair's early interventions on the long-running Saddam situation demonstrated a moral resilience that would underpin his future dealings with the Iraqi dictator. "Right from the beginning of his premiership, Blair was aware of the fact that Saddam was dangerous and had to be dealt with," said one of Blair's senior Downing Street officials. "There was a feeling that we had been going round in circles for years with Saddam, and we were getting nowhere. No one was talking about invading Iraq at that time, but there was an awareness that Saddam could not be allowed to get away with it. In that respect, Blair has been utterly consistent in his Iraq policy from the start."[24]

All the issues that were to result in the Iraq War in 2003 were present in the diplomatic crisis of November 1997 and early 1998. The response of the American and British governments laid the foundations for the joint military action that would remove Saddam from power six years later. The American and British governments were isolated at the Security Council over their resolve to tackle the Iraqi dictator on his WMD programs, while Russia and France continued to argue in favor of lifting the punitive sanctions before Saddam had fully complied with the UN resolutions. The most significant difference between the approach to Saddam in late 1997 and the spring of 2003 was that, unlike his successor, President Clinton was not prepared to use military force on a scale that would resolve the problem permanently.

While Clinton was criticized by leading members of the Security Council for being too tough on Saddam, his domestic critics were telling him he was not being tough enough. In December, William Kristol, one of the founding members of the Project for a New American Century and a leading neoconservative, devoted an entire edition of the *Weekly Standard*, the movement's ideological organ, to this subject: "Saddam Must Go—a How-to Guide." Paul Wolfowitz, another leading neocon who was working at the Johns Hopkins School of Advanced International Studies, contributed one of the articles, in which he suggested that Clinton's most important foreign policy legacy would be to have let "this tyrant grow stronger."[25]

The following month, on the eve of Clinton's State of the Union address, Wolfowitz drafted an open letter to Clinton on behalf of the New American Century board; along with Wolfowitz, the eighteen signatories included Donald Rumsfeld, Richard Perle, John Bolton, and Elliott Abrams, who would all hold high-ranking government positions when President George W. Bush assumed office in January 2001. Wolfowitz argued that the policy of containment that had been implemented against Saddam since the end of the Gulf War was no longer working. As a consequence, "we may soon face a threat in the Middle East more serious than any we have known since the end of the Cold War." The letter called on Clinton to change course, and to make Saddam's overthrow official American policy. "The only acceptable strategy is one that eliminates the possibility that Iraq will be able to use or threaten to use weapons of mass destruction. In the near term, this means a willingness to undertake military action, as diplomacy is clearly failing. In the long term, it means removing Saddam Hussein and his regime from power. We urge you to articulate this aim."[26]

TONY BLAIR COULD NOT have chosen a worse time to make his first visit to Washington as prime minister. Just as he and Clinton were wrestling with the dilemma of how to deal with Saddam, the scandal of the American president's affair with Monica Lewinsky, a twenty-four-year-old White House intern, erupted. Clinton's presidency had been plagued by allegations of sexual impropriety. At the time the Lewinsky scandal broke, Clinton was the subject of a lawsuit filed by Paula Jones, who claimed that she had been the victim of sexual harassment by the president while he was governor of Arkansas. As part of the legal process in the Jones case, Clinton had been ordered to disclose whether or not he had indulged in relationships with women other than his wife. Testifying under oath, Clinton had answered bluntly: "None." If true, the Lewinsky affair meant that the president had committed perjury, an offense for which he faced impeachment by Congress. In addition, Clinton was beleaguered by another investigation, conducted by Independent Counsel Kenneth Starr who was looking into allegations that Clinton had been involved in a fraud involving the construction of the Whitewater property complex in his home state.

The furor that engulfed Clinton over his private life in early 1998 was deeply embarrassing for Tony Blair, who had invested much political capital in making Clinton his most important international ally. Apart from their close cooperation on issues such as Northern Ireland and Iraq, the two men sought to promote a new political philosophy known as the Third Way. When Clinton had visited Blair at Downing Street after his election victory, the president and the prime minister had celebrated "a new generation of politicians and a new generation of leadership." Clinton saw Blair's victory as an endorsement of the new left-of-center politics that he had advocated in the United States, and he wanted to develop an international network of Third World leaders. Sidney Blumenthal, Clinton's special assistant and a pivotal figure in building his relationship with Blair, summed up the atmosphere when he wrote: "With Blair's election in 1997, Clinton felt that he himself was leading an international movement."[27]

Blair readily agreed to Clinton's suggestion that they should seek to extend the success of center-left political thinking to encompass other leaders, such as Portugal's António Guterres, Wim Kok of the Netherlands, and Brazil's Henrique Cardoso. The aim of the Clinton-Blair initiative was to replace the Socialist International, an increasingly irrelevant organization for like-minded socialist groups for much of the twentieth century. In September 1997, Blair and his wife hosted Bill and Hillary Clinton at the Le Pont de la Tour, one of London's most fashionable restaurants, where they spent the evening discussing education and welfare.

As Hillary Clinton later recalled, "we decided to initiate a discussion among our advisors to explore common ideas and strategies."[28] Both the State Department and the Foreign Office were against the idea, arguing that an exclusive dialogue between the United States and Britain might cause offense to other friendly nations. The bond between the Blairs and the Clintons had become so strong that they were able to overcome the objections of the professional diplomats.

In November, the Blairs hosted Hillary Clinton and a group of White House policy advisors at Chequers, the prime minister's official country residence. The purpose of the meeting was to explore common ideas and strategies that would enable them to win the battle of ideas with the right. Blair greeted the American delegation in blue jeans, a signal that he wanted the discussions to be informal. Blair summed up what he thought was the main dilemma facing himself and Clinton. "The similarities are more striking than not. But something is missing from the picture. We win power, but not the battle of ideas. The right wins, even though they're not in power. Unless we define our new type of politics, people will become disillusioned with us."[29]

The Clinton camp had high hopes for this new transatlantic dialogue, which they saw as the perfect platform for developing and exporting a new political strategy. Sidney Blumenthal, who led the American delegation, regarded the meeting as "the beginning of an international Third Way." So far as Blumenthal was concerned, "the Anglo-American special relationship had never before been politically parallel. This parallel gave Clinton's presidency a new sense of coherence and depth. Moreover, Blair's success dramatically altered the international stage on which Clinton operated. The prime minister was an ally like no other through all sorts of difficulties and challenges, from foreign crises in the Balkans to the domestic one over Clinton's possible impeachment."

The dialogue about the Third Way was a welcome distraction for Clinton from his endless policy battles with the Republican-dominated Congress, while for Blair it was a wonderful opportunity to make his mark on the Washington political establishment. Third Way conferences and discussions continued for the remainder of Clinton's presidency, although the initial excitement over the project gradually waned the more Clinton became embroiled in his domestic travails. The problem of Third Way politics for both Clinton and Blair was that few people outside their circle had a clear understanding of what it meant. At one meeting, there were discussions on subjects such as "how to combat inequality and insecurity in the labor market" and another on "One Nation, building cohesive and inclusive societies, tackling social exclusion."

For all the talk, little was achieved, apart from massaging the egos of those who participated. One of Blair's harsher critics sarcastically welcomed his participation in the seminars "for the very good reason that, since the prime minister believes in the Third Way, it is important for him to find out what it is."[30] Adherents of the Third Way probably knew more about what it did not stand for than what it did. It rejected the traditional extremes in the politics of Western democracies—the free-market, minimal government of the right, and the tax-and-spend state-interventionist approach of the left. The Third Way had to do with community, opportunity, rights, responsibilities, and social inclusion, and sought to refashion domestic economies to meet the many challenges of globalization. Blair's policy unit in Downing Street produced a pamphlet called *The Third Way, New Politics for the New Century*, which tried to explain the core ideology. Blair's willingness to indulge Clinton's Third Way vision resulted in some unflattering descriptions appearing in the American media. The veteran American commentator Joe Klein remarked on Blair's "magisterial vacuity,"[31] while the *New York Times* columnist Maureen Dowd accused Blair of "cloning himself from a clone."[32]

After the Chequers meeting, Blair was invited to make a reciprocal visit to Washington the following February. By that time, Clinton was fighting for his political life after his affair with Monica Lewinsky was made public in late January 1998. For someone who prided himself on his personal morality and fidelity, Blair adopted a surprisingly relaxed attitude to Clinton's private indiscretions. However much Blair sought to strengthen his political alliance with Clinton, he was aware that, for all the American president's undoubted political skill, there was, as he remarked to one of his advisors, a "weird bit" to him.[33]

With the Northern Ireland peace process entering a critical stage, and Saddam causing trouble for the weapons inspectors, Blair thought it was important to declare openly his support for Clinton, even though such a gesture was not popular with the British people (an opinion poll showed that 48 percent of voters disapproved of Blair offering Clinton his personal support). On January 27, the day after Clinton's affair became public, Blair called the White House to tell the president "that he had been following events and that he was thinking of him."[34] Despite the public show of support, Blair and the British ambassador in Washington, Sir Christopher Meyer, thought his planned visit for the following week might have to be postponed, especially as some of Clinton's closest aides were predicting his possible impeachment. After careful consideration, Blair decided that it was better for the visit to go ahead.

The day before leaving for Washington, the Foreign Office, at Blair's request, published a dossier detailing the latest intelligence findings on Iraq's WMD capability. Blair had been pressing the intelligence chiefs to produce a dossier since the previous autumn, when Saddam's mistreatment of UN weapons inspectors had reopened the Iraq debate. By January, Saddam was again making life difficult for the inspectors. First, the Iraqis prevented inspectors from visiting "presidential sites"—palaces and other government complexes suspected of harboring secret equipment. The Iraqi authorities then blocked a number of surprise inspections. Finally, Saddam demanded a three-month moratorium on all such activities and a six-month deadline for lifting sanctions, regardless of Iraq's disarmament status.

The rhetoric from both sides in the dispute was becoming more heated, and there was a growing belief in Washington and London that some form of military action would be required if Saddam did not back down. In late January, Blair publicly denounced Saddam as "an evil dictator." After publication of the dossier, Blair said Saddam was a threat to world peace. The dossier generated headlines in the British press to the effect that Saddam's WMD arsenal was powerful enough to wipe out the world's population twice over.[35] It stated that UN inspectors had been unable to track down four thousand tons of chemical warfare materials—enough to fill thousands of poison-gas bombs. More than six hundred tons of materials for making VX nerve gas were unaccounted for. Saddam had the ability to produce enough spores of deadly anthrax each week to fill two missile warheads. To emphasize the imminence of the threat, George Robertson, the defense secretary, appeared on television to illustrate the deadly potential of the Iraqi poisons. Holding up a glass of water, he said, "If this was VX, it could probably kill the whole of London."[36]

Blair's decision to publish an intelligence dossier on Iraq was a new departure for a British prime minister. Blair wanted the British public, as well as his own party, to see the same material that he was receiving on a daily basis from his intelligence chiefs, just as President Kennedy had done over the Soviet missiles in Cuba in 1962. By doing so, he established the precedent that would be followed in September 2002, when the British government published another, far more controversial intelligence dossier in the buildup to the Iraq War. Indeed, some of the findings in the 1998 dossier were, like the 2002 document, subsequently found to have been embellished.

After the start of the Iraq War, Lord Butler, a retired senior British civil servant, was asked by Blair to head an inquiry into British intelligence on Iraq's WMD programs. His report concluded that, contrary to the claims made in the dossier, much of Iraq's WMD capability had already been destroyed by the UN inspection teams. For example, an assessment by the Joint Intelligence Committee (JIC), the body that prepared the main intelligence reports for Downing Street, stated on February 4, 1998, that the UN inspection teams "have succeeded in destroying or controlling the vast majority of Saddam's 1991 weapons of mass destruction capability."[37] Similar conclusions had been reached with regard to Saddam's chemical and biological weapons programs. This meant that the 1998 dossier, like its 2002 successor, provided a misleading assessment of the threat Saddam posed to the outside world.

Blair believed the dossier was necessary "to educate the public" and to counter the growing effectiveness of the anti-sanctions propaganda that Saddam was successfully spreading. Baghdad organized regular press trips for Western journalists to see the devastation that seven years of sanctions had inflicted on Iraq, and the subsequent reports increased the political pressure on the United States and Britain to ease the sanctions' burden. By releasing the document on the eve of his first visit to Washington as prime minister, Blair was hoping to shift attention away from the tawdry details of the unfolding Lewinsky scandal to more pressing affairs.

Clinton's reception of Blair was nothing short of spectacular. Clinton had long planned to use the occasion to celebrate the triumph of Third Way politics. It was also an opportunity to strengthen the transatlantic alliance, particularly at a time when Saddam was causing havoc at the Security Council. And the somewhat over-the-top spectacle that he arranged for Blair provided a welcome distraction from the sordid revelations of the Lewinsky saga.

Blair was not a head of state like Clinton, but the American president laid on a welcome that was fit for the queen. The nineteen-gun salute at the White House was two shots short of the twenty-one that would have greeted a visit by Queen Elizabeth II. The White House proudly announced that on February 5, there would be the biggest banquet since President Richard Nixon had lavishly entertained the Chinese in 1972. The dinner that was held on the first night of the Blairs' visit was one of the most glittering events in Washington's social calendar, an occasion to rival anything seen since the days of John F. Kennedy's Camelot presidency. The best table settings were displayed for Blair, including Eisenhower gold-base plates, Reagan china, and Kennedy Morgantown crystal. The vermeil-and-silver candelabra held gold-tapered candles that cast their flickering light on Clinton's select guests, a curious mélange of Washington's political elite and Hollywood personalities.

Barbra Streisand gave Blair a reassuring cuddle, while Harrison Ford enjoyed his first visit to a White House function. Such unlikely luminaries as Steven Spielberg, Warren Buffet, Tom Hanks, and John F. Kennedy Jr. rubbed shoulders with each other. Stevie Wonder enchanted Cherie Blair with an authentic rendition of the couple's favorite song, "Mon Cherie Amour," and was later joined by Elton John on stage for a duet. Washington's society columnists had rarely seen such a feast. All the snide comments about Blair being a Clinton clone were put to one side as the awestruck commentators reported that the cost of the food, wine, and service for the evening was estimated at $200 per person, not including the flowers, place cards, invitations, and cocktails. Blair had barely been prime minister for nine months, but he was feted as though he was a world leader of immense stature rather than a relative novice on the world stage.

When it came to the speeches, Blair did his host proud. Before making the journey, Blair had discussed in detail how he was going to handle the delicate question of Clinton's private life, which he felt sure would come up. Blair told his advisors that he had warmed to Clinton during their discussions of Northern Ireland and respected his intelligence. "I take people as I find them, and I like them," Blair told his officials.[38] Downing Street and the White House negotiated how Blair should handle the Lewinsky allegations. It was agreed that Blair's line should be "The elected president of the United States does not lie to his people." Blair was encouraged by the fact that the American people were more condemnatory of their media for indulging in the frenzy over the allegations than they were of their philandering president. As Barbra Streisand remarked to Blair at the White House banquet, "We elect a president, not a pope."

This was the line that Blair adopted when he got up to make his banquet speech. "I know I'm not alone in supporting you," Blair told the star-studded audience. "I know the American people support you." He was proud to call Clinton a good friend. He paid a personal tribute to Hillary Clinton, who had given a stoic defense of her husband on American television the previous week. Blair said she was "admired the world over for her dignity and grace, qualities she had displayed again over the past few days." Blair was echoing the comments his wife had made earlier that day at a lunch hosted by Hillary Clinton, when she remarked, "I just want to say how much I personally—and, I believe, the people of Britain—admire Hillary. She is a role model for many women. I feel enormous sympathy for the dignified way she has carried out her duties. I admire especially that she has withstood recent tribulations with such strength and dignity." Clinton was deeply touched by Blair's show of solidarity, and said so. "I think that people who stand up and say things they believe, when it would be just as easy to walk away, show a certain kind of character," said Clinton. "And I'm very grateful that Tony Blair has done that."

The personal bond between the Clintons and the Blairs was undoubtedly strengthened by the prime minister's unequivocal demonstration of loyalty. The day after the banquet Blair and his team attended a four-hour seminar on the Third Way, which, after all, had been the original pretext for the summit. Clinton invited his leading experts in the field, including Joe Nye, dean of the Kennedy School at Harvard; Andrew Cuomo, an urban development expert; and the ubiquitous Sidney Blumenthal. On Blair's team were Professor Tony Giddens, his favorite advisor; Gavyn Davies, one of Britain's leading economists; and David Miliband and Geoff Mulgan from the Downing Street policy unit.

The main business of the visit was concluded the following day, when Clinton and Blair gave a joint press conference before Blair boarded a Concorde for the flight home. The White House had been dreading the press conference, for it gave the press corps a rare opportunity to interrogate the president on the latest twists and turns in the Lewinsky saga. Clinton and Blair wanted to talk about political issues, such as the conclusions of their Third Way discussions, Northern Ireland, Bosnia, and Iraq. But it was inevitable that questions about Lewinsky would come up, and the White House aides were concerned that Blair not say anything to embarrass Clinton. The pre–press conference hysteria in the Clinton camp was so great that one of the president's advisors, Rahm Emanuel, turned to Blair shortly before the press filed in and muttered: "You! Don't fuck this up." According to another Clinton staffer, Paul Begala, "Blair sort of looked at his aides, looked over at Clinton, and they both burst out laughing."[39]

Clinton need not have worried. Blair was steadfast in his support for the American president. When the inevitable question came up, Blair was unequivocal. "I've worked with the American president for some nine months as British prime minister. I have found him throughout someone I could trust, someone I could rely on." Clinton himself, though looking nervous, fended off questions about his private life by stating simply that he could not comment in public on the inquiries taking place. But he was clearly moved by Blair's open display of support, and as they left the press room, Clinton whispered in Blair's ear, "I'm going to make sure you're proud of what you did in there." James Steinberg, Clinton's deputy national security advisor, turned to Sir Christopher Meyer, the British ambassador, and said: "We owe you big-time."[40]

Blair's unqualified support for Clinton not only helped to strengthen the bond between the two men, it helped to buttress Blair's self-confidence. Until this moment, he had lived in the shadow of his more powerful and more famous ally. Now Blair had demonstrated that he was his own man, who could make his own judgment calls, even when his close advisors were urging caution. One of the two telephones on Blair's desk in Downing Street was marked simply "Washington," and the prime minister used it a good deal. After the success of this trip it was used mainly to discuss issues such as Iraq and Northern Ireland. The latter was where Clinton's "payback" came into play, and the American president used his influence as best he could to unlock the Northern Ireland peace process, particularly by putting pressure on Sinn Fein.

Iraq was high on the agenda during the bilateral meetings that took place during Blair's February visit, and the summit ended with an unequivocal declaration of intent by both men to stand up to Saddam. During the press conference, Blair announced the deployment of further British fighter planes to the Gulf. "If the [UN] inspectors are prevented from doing their work," he said, "then we have to make sure, by the military means of which we are capable, that, in so far as possible, that capacity ceases." A few days later, after Blair had returned to London, Clinton declared that "if Saddam does not comply with the unanimous will of the international community, we must be prepared to act . . . and we are."

One important side effect of Blair's Washington visit in February 1998 was that it sowed the seeds of disquiet in some European capitals about Blair's determination to build a strong relationship with Washington. Britain held the six-month presidency of the European Union, and Blair was criticized for not seeking a wider consensus on Iraq—i.e., including the French in the consultations with Washington (at that time, German chancellor Helmut Kohl was in favor of strong action). When Blair spoke in Washington, he spoke on behalf of Britain rather than the Europeans. Blair and Clinton were wary of France's machinations at the Security Council on Iraq, and Blair's support for Clinton increased the ever-present sense of suspicion in Paris about "les Anglo-Saxons." It was a rift that was to become deeper.

. . .

SADDAM'S CONTINUED OBSTRUCTION OF the UN weapons inspectors severely tested the patience of both Washington and London, and plans were drawn up for a series of air strikes against Iraq in the spring of 1998, code-named "Operation Desert Thunder." Washington wanted to act in concert with both Britain and France, but even at this stage, U.S. officials were expressing their doubts about President Jacques Chirac's position. Technically, the issue of Saddam's noncompliance with the inspectors was a matter for the UN, but with France, Russia, and China vacillating over whether the sanctions regime should be maintained, the Americans and British believed that, based on the ceasefire resolution Saddam accepted at the end of the Gulf War, they retained a mandate to take military action against Iraq. Robin Cook, the British foreign secretary, later claimed that he had seen a memo in January 1998—before Blair's visit to Washington—in which Blair pledged his support to Washington even if a further UN resolution was "unachievable."[41]

The crisis was averted when Kofi Annan, the UN secretary-general, flew to Baghdad in late February for talks with Saddam. The key issue that needed to be resolved was the UN's insistence that its inspectors be allowed access to Saddam's "presidential sites," where there were suspicions much of the proscribed equipment was concealed. Saddam refused to back down, claiming that to do so would be an insult to the "honor" of the Iraqi presidency. The Iraqis wanted to know when the UN would lift the sanctions. After several days of discussions, Annan reached a deal with Saddam whereby the inspectors would be allowed to make "visits," rather than "inspections," to the "presidential sites." In return, Saddam believed, he had won a commitment from Annan that the sanctions would be lifted if Iraq complied with a new round of inspections.

The report of the Iraq Survey Group (ISG) would later show that Saddam's strategy at this juncture was to get the sanctions lifted and then to re-create Iraq's WMD capability to a level that it had enjoyed before the Gulf War. In the meantime, "he sought to balance the need to cooperate with UN inspections—to gain support for lifting sanctions—with his intention to preserve Iraq's intellectual capital for WMD."[42] To this end,

Saddam was prepared to cooperate with Annan. The combination of Saddam's shrewd diplomacy at the UN, combined with his cat-and-mouse tactics with the UN inspectors, meant that Western intelligence agencies faced a daunting task in trying to evaluate the precise nature of Saddam's WMD capability. Their primary sources of information throughout the 1990s were the UN inspectors themselves, some of whom, as Saddam correctly deduced, were actually working for the American, British, and Israeli intelligence services, not to mention the Russian and French intelligence services that had an interest in Saddam's military capability.

Although in early February 1998, British intelligence had reached the assessment that "the vast majority of Saddam's WMD capability" had been destroyed,[43] within the Western intelligence community persisted nagging doubts that Saddam had managed to fool the inspectors and was continuing to conceal elements of Iraq's WMD infrastructure. The suspicions of Western intelligence were fueled to some extent by the revelations of Saddam's two sons-in-law, Hussein Kamel al-Majid and Saddam Kamel al-Majid, when they defected in late 1995. Hussein Kamel, the head of Iraq's weapons procurement program, was fully debriefed by the CIA, SIS, and UNSCOM, and he provided details of Saddam's WMD program, which had not been disclosed to the UN and were hitherto unknown to the UN inspection teams. This included the location of hidden chemical weapons plants and front companies assisting with Saddam's weapons procurement and Iraq's secret VX nerve agent program. Hussein Kamel's most startling revelation was that Saddam had been within three months of testing an atomic bomb at the start of Operation Desert Storm in January 1991.

These revelations severely dented the confidence of both Western intelligence and the UN inspectors, who thought that they had identified and destroyed most of Saddam's WMD programs. The information provided by the sons-in-law enabled UNSCOM to take further action to destroy Saddam's WMD, which formed the basis of the February 1998 British intelligence assessment that most of it had been destroyed. The fact that Saddam had been so successful in concealing his WMD operations from the UN in the past, the suspicion that he would resume production as soon as sanctions were lifted, and the knowledge that he had used these weapons in the past against Iran, resulted in the Western intelligence community—France included—forming the view that Iraq still retained elements of its WMD capability. As Lord Butler concluded in his report on British intelligence on Iraq, there were "growing suspicions and concerns" within the intelligence community of "Iraq's chemical, biological, and ballistic missile programs, which were exacerbated and reinforced by Iraqi prevarication, concealment, and deception."[44] Saddam was playing a dangerous game of bluff, and there was a mounting determination in Washington and London to bring the game to an end.

Annan's intervention removed the immediate threat of military action, but no one in Washington or London had much faith that the deal would hold. "We saw it as just another time-wasting ploy by Saddam," said a senior Blair aide. "Annan had done his best, but we knew in our hearts that it was simply delaying the inevitable."[45] Blair told the House of Commons that only the threat of force had persuaded Saddam to back down, and that Blair would have supported the United States if military action had proved necessary. In an interview at the end of February, Blair paid tribute to Clinton's tough stance on Iraq. "It is important," he said, "that we have an American administration and an American people who are not isolationist but will take on responsibilities . . . Thank heavens that the Americans are there and willing to stand up and be counted."[46]

Blair had been sufficiently concerned about the possibility of renewing hostilities with Saddam that he had sought parliamentary approval for military action. By tradition, the British prime minister did not need the approval of Parliament; military action was normally authorized on the government's own authority, with the monarch providing the final assent. Blair, however, wanted to give added legitimacy to any action he might take. Only two dozen Labour MPs voted against action. There was then no hint of the dangerous parliamentary revolt from the backbenches that would cause Blair so many difficulties in the buildup to the Iraq War five years later. Even so, in seeking parliamentary approval for military action against Iraq, Blair had set an important precedent, one that he would be obliged to respect.

While the British and American governments were preoccupied with Saddam, another, and far more lethal, terrorist threat was coalescing in the Middle East. By early 1998, Osama bin Laden had been for nearly two years based in Afghanistan, where he had formed a close alliance with the Taliban, the Islamic fundamentalist movement that had taken control of most of the country. Although bin Laden had a strained relationship with the Taliban leadership, who objected to some of his political statements, he was able to buy their support with the strong financial assistance he received from his supporters in Saudi Arabia and elsewhere. Bin Laden was operating with the tacit approval of Pakistan's military intelligence, and the combination of substantial funds and powerful backers enabled him to rebuild his terrorist infrastructure following his hurried departure from Sudan. Unlike his operations in Sudan, where his efforts were mainly directed at providing funds, training, and weapons for like-minded terror groups, such as the Somali warlords, in Afghanistan bin Laden's aim was to build an organization that was capable of planning, directing, and executing its own operations.[47]

As part of his efforts to turn al-Qaeda into a global terrorist network, once he had established himself in Afghanistan, bin Laden sent out feelers to the Iraqi regime, offering cooperation. Initially his overtures were rejected, but in March 1998, Iraq invited two al-Qaeda members to Baghdad to meet with Iraqi intelligence. In July, an Iraqi delegation traveled to Afghanistan to meet first with the Taliban and then with bin Laden. A CIA intelligence report said that one, or perhaps both, of these meetings was arranged through bin Laden's Egyptian-born deputy, Ayman al-Zawahiri, who had his own ties with the Iraqis.[48] The timing of Iraq's overture to bin Laden was most likely a response to the mounting diplomatic pressure Saddam was encountering at the UN, although the precise nature of his contacts with bin Laden was not known.

Prior to the contacts with Iraq, in February 1998, the forty-year-old bin Laden and al-Zawahiri arranged from their base in Afghanistan for the London-based Arabic newspaper *Al-Quds Al-Arabi* to publish a fatwa, issued in the name of the World Islamic Front. A fatwa is normally an interpretation of Islamic law by a respected Islamic authority, but neither bin Laden nor al-Zawahiri could lay claim to being scholars of Islamic law. In their statement, which was similar to the one bin Laden had issued in August 1996, after his arrival in Afghanistan, they claimed that

America had declared war against God and his messenger. They called for the murder of any American, anywhere on earth, as the "individual duty for every Muslim who can do it in any country in which it is possible to do it."[49] Three months later, bin Laden elaborated on these themes when he was interviewed by ABC. He claimed that it was more important for Muslims to kill Americans than to kill other infidels. "It is far better for anyone to kill a single American soldier than to squander his efforts on other activities," he said. And asked whether he approved of terrorism and of attacks on civilians, he replied: "We believe the worst thieves in the world today and the worst terrorists are the Americans. Nothing could stop you except perhaps retaliation in kind. We do not have to differentiate between military or civilian. As far as we are concerned, they are all targets."[50]

Bin Laden directed his threats almost exclusively at the United States. None of bin Laden's early terrorist attacks involved British targets or interests, and for this reason, Tony Blair and his intelligence chiefs did not regard the emergence of bin Laden and the formation of al-Qaeda as a pressing priority. SIS, whose mandate is limited to protecting Britain's national interests, assets, and citizens, was monitoring bin Laden's activities, but at the time it was believed that bin Laden did not constitute a direct threat to Britain's national security.[51] "Bin Laden simply was not at the forefront of our minds," said a close Blair aide. "We were kept informed of what was going on in the Middle East and Africa, and we were aware that it was potentially a very dangerous organization. But, frankly, we had more pressing matters to consider, such as sorting out Iraq."[52]

British intelligence began to take bin Laden more seriously as a threat toward the end of 1998, when the Joint Intelligence Committee informed Downing Street that bin Laden "has a long-standing interest in the potential terrorist use of CBR (chemical, biological, and radiological) materials, and recent intelligence suggests his ideas about using toxic materials are maturing and being developed in more detail . . . There is also secret reporting that he may have obtained some CB (chemical and biological) material—and that he is interested in nuclear materials. We assess that he lacks the expertise or facilities even to begin making a nuclear weapon, but he may seek to make a radiological device"—i.e., a dirty bomb.[53]

By contrast, in the United States the CIA had made the threat posed by bin Laden a top priority since 1996, when a special unit of a dozen officers was set up "to analyze intelligence on and plan operations against" him.[54] The CIA initially worked on the assumption that bin Laden was merely financing terrorist attacks. It was not until 1997, after he had relocated to Afghanistan, that the agency discovered bin Laden had a "military committee" that was planning operations against U.S. interests worldwide and was actively trying to obtain nuclear material. A plan was devised, with the cooperation of Afghan tribal leaders funded by the CIA, to capture bin Laden and hand him over for trial either in the United States or in an Arab country. Planning for the operation reached an advanced stage, but it was eventually called off in May 1998 over fears that it would involve civilian casualties and the concern that "the purpose and nature of the operation would be subject to unavoidable misinterpretation and misrepresentation—and probably recriminations—in the event that bin Laden, despite our best intentions and efforts, did not survive."[55]

American concerns over bin Laden's personal well-being were not reciprocated. At 5.35 a.m. on August 7, 1998, Sandy Berger, the national security advisor, woke President Clinton with the news that almost simultaneous suicide truck bomb attacks had been carried out against the American embassies in Nairobi, Kenya, and Dar es Salaam, Tanzania, killing 224 people—12 of them Americans—and wounding 5,000 others. American intelligence had been monitoring an al-Qaeda cell in Nairobi for nearly one year, and within twenty-four hours it was confirmed that bin Laden was responsible for the attacks. Blair, who was on holiday in France with his family, immediately sent a letter "expressing his condolences and sympathy" to Clinton and to the Kenyan and Tanzanian governments.

The following day, George Tenet, the director of the CIA, convened an emergency meeting of key intelligence officials to discuss Washington's response. Tenet came to the meeting equipped with information that terrorist leaders were planning to meet at a camp near Khowst, in Afghanistan, to plan future attacks. Bin Laden was due to attend. The CIA described the area as a military compound occupied by Islamic fighters. The meeting reached a consensus that the camp should be attacked with Tomahawk cruise missiles. It was also decided to attack a Sudanese pharmaceutical plant al-Shifa. Soil samples taken by the CIA suggested that the plant, which was financed by bin Laden, was being used to produce a precursor ingredient for VX nerve gas. A suggestion that cruise missiles be fired at a Sudanese tanning factory that was owned by bin Laden as a purely commercial concern was dropped because Clinton saw no point in killing anyone who was not directly involved in bin Laden's operations.

On August 20, U.S. Navy vessels in the Arabian Sea fired a barrage of seventy-five cruise missiles, and though they hit their intended targets, neither bin Laden nor any other terrorist leader was killed. The attack on al-Shifa demolished the plant, but provoked a heated response from the Sudanese government, which claimed that the complex manufactured nothing more sinister than veterinary antibiotics.

Before ordering the attacks, Clinton called Blair from the Oval Office to tell him about the proposed action. Blair had been briefed by Vice President Al Gore that an air strike was imminent. After the attacks were launched, Blair immediately issued a strong statement of support. While Clinton agonized over how to respond to the bomb attacks in Africa, Blair had been dealing with the aftermath of a bomb attack in Omagh, Northern Ireland, that had killed twenty-nine people and injured four hundred. The bombing had been carried out not by the IRA but by a breakaway group that called itself "the real IRA" and rejected the Good Friday Agreement that had been signed the previous April. Blair identified a clear link between the Omagh atrocity and the attacks against the United States. "The atrocities in Nairobi, Dar es Salaam, and Omagh have shown the pain that terrorism can bring to innocent people," he said. "I support this action. Terrorists the world over must know that democratic governments will act decisively to prevent their evil crimes."[56]

The only European leader who publicly supported Clinton's retaliatory strikes against Afghanistan and Sudan was Tony Blair, and his unwavering support for the United States caused much consternation among both his European allies and his own supporters in Britain. There was particular concern that Clinton had only launched military action to divert interest away from his personal difficulties over the Lewinsky scandal. Clinton, who was staying at his summer retreat at Martha's Vineyard while planning for the retaliation strikes, had finally revealed the truth about his infidelity with Lewinsky to Hillary and their daughter, Chelsea, on August 15, prior to giving his grand jury testimony to Kenneth Starr, the independent counsel. By his own admission, during the buildup to the August 20 attacks, Clinton was "alternating between begging for forgiveness and planning the strikes on al-Qaeda."[57] Two days before the air strikes took place, Lewinsky gave her testimony to a Washington grand jury and Clinton made his televised confession of his "inappropriate relationship" with her.

Blair rejected the accusations that Clinton had ordered the retaliation attacks to distract attention from the Lewinsky saga. He continued his unequivocal support of Clinton despite the fact that several senior British officials had severe reservations about bombing Sudan. The official justification used by Downing Street to defend the action was similar to that which Margaret Thatcher had given in 1986, when President Reagan launched air strikes against Libya, and again in 1993, when Clinton launched cruise missiles against Iraq in retaliation for the failed assassination attempt on former president Bush. "Everyone knew that what Clinton was doing was wrong—bombing that plant—but we knew that supporting him was right," said one of Blair's aides.[58]

Blair gave a steadfast defense of his support for the U.S. action when questioned about the bombing in the House of Commons a few months later. "The U.S. told us at the time of the strike on al-Shifa that it had compelling evidence that the plant was being used for the production of chemical weapons materials," he said. He pointed out that great care had been taken to ensure "no one was killed in it," and reaffirmed his commitment to take tough action against those who perpetrated acts of international terrorism. "We gave a very clear signal—and I think the right one—to those who engage in international terrorism that we are prepared if necessary to take action in retaliation."[59]

Despite these public shows of support, Blair had his misgivings about Clinton's private proclivities and about his American ally's ability to survive in office. As a more detailed account of the extent of Clinton's infidelity began to emerge through the late summer of 1998, Blair had doubts about the wisdom of allying himself so closely with the American president. At first, Blair found it hard to comprehend Clinton's obfuscation of his sexual misdemeanors. "It was all rather embarrassing," recalled the Foreign Office representative who had to brief Blair on the Lewinsky scandal. "I had to tell him what Clinton was supposed to have done and when sex was sex and when it wasn't. He couldn't believe it. I thought to myself, 'He doesn't understand the details of these things.' "[60] Among his colleagues, Blair simply shrugged off Clinton's immoral behavior. "That's Bill for you," he would remark.[61]

A few days after the bombings, Bill and Hillary Clinton flew to Northern Ireland to meet the survivors of the Omagh bombing and bereaved relatives. They were accompanied by the Blairs and walked through the devastated town center, where they inspected the damage and talked to the large crowds that had gathered to meet them. No mention was made in public of the retaliation bombing raids, nor of Clinton's personal difficulties, although Hillary Clinton seemed noticeably happier in the company of Cherie Blair than that of her husband. Clinton and Blair concentrated their energies on making sure the bombing did not derail the Good Friday Agreement, which was about to enter a critical phase. They made a joint appeal to the province's leaders to keep faith in the peace agreement they had signed the previous April, and to work toward a lasting reconciliation between the two war-torn communities.

With Clinton distracted by bin Laden and Lewinsky, and Blair devoting much of his time to trying to secure a lasting peace in Northern Ireland, there was still the problem of Saddam Hussein. By early autumn, the agreement that Kofi Annan had negotiated with Saddam in the spring was starting to unravel as Iraqi officials continued to make the UN inspectors' task difficult. Clinton wanted to avoid a military confrontation with Baghdad and encouraged the inspectors not to be too provocative. This prompted Scott Ritter, the chief UN inspector, to resign in protest at political interference from Washington and London. Before departing, Ritter claimed that Saddam could have as many as three nuclear weapons ready for use.

In August, Saddam provoked another clash with the UN by demanding that UNSCOM complete its work as soon as possible. In October, the Republican-dominated U.S. Congress, dismayed by Clinton's disinclination to confront Saddam, voted the Iraqi Liberation Act into law, in which it pledged $97 million to Iraqi opposition groups working to overthrow Saddam. The legislation was partly inspired by the neocon movement in Washington, which was running a sustained campaign to persuade Clinton to launch a military and diplomatic offensive that would result in Saddam's overthrow. The Iraqi dictator responded the following month by suspending all cooperation with UNSCOM. Baghdad and Washington were now firmly set on a collision course, and when the inspectors were withdrawn in November, the Pentagon and Britain's Defence Ministry began drawing up plans for joint Anglo-American air strikes against Baghdad. To prepare British public opinion for the looming confrontation with Iraq, on November 12, Blair released a three-page briefing note to the House of Commons, entitled "Iraq's Weapons of Mass Destruction." A distillation of the dossier released the previous February, the new document included photographs of presidential palaces and other suspected sites, and repeated the British intelligence assessment that Saddam was continuing to conceal elements of his WMD program.

The Pentagon's plan to attack Iraq consisted of bombing 250 key military targets. The air strikes were due to start on November 14, but it was called off at the last minute—the bombers were already airborne—after Kofi Annan persuaded Saddam Hussein to give the inspectors one last chance. Acting on the advice of George Robertson, the defense secretary, Blair was strongly opposed to calling off the air strikes, arguing that Saddam's offer was meaningless. But Washington wanted to see precisely what concessions Saddam was offering.

Blair's suspicions proved to be correct. When American officials studied Saddam's letter to Kofi Annan, they found it was "riddled with more holes than a Swiss cheese."[62] Washington wanted to reschedule the air strikes for the following day, but this time Blair intervened to persuade Clinton that it would reflect badly on them if, having publicly stated that they wanted to give diplomacy one last chance, they immediately reneged on their promise. Clinton agreed, somewhat reluctantly, and Richard Butler returned to Baghdad with his inspectors to report back to the UN about whether or not Saddam was cooperating. Within days, Butler found that the Iraqis were still being obstructive, and this time the Clinton administration decided that air strikes were inevitable. They were to take place between Clinton's prearranged trip to Jerusalem and the start of Ramadan, the Muslim holy month of fasting.

On December 11, while on his way to the Middle East on Air Force One, Clinton phoned Blair and informed him of the forthcoming attack. Blair fully endorsed Clinton's decision, and pledged British military support for the air strikes. On December 15, on the flight back from Jerusalem, Clinton worked out the final details for the attack on Iraq the next day. American aircraft, with limited British support, would bomb about 250 Iraqi targets that were suspected of concealing aspects of Saddam's secret WMD program. Significantly, no other country was prepared to back military action against Saddam. Gerhard Schröder, the recently elected German chancellor, gave lukewarm support. But elsewhere in Europe, the proposed action evoked a hostile response, particularly from France, where President Chirac argued—as he would four years later—that Saddam had to be given more time, and that the sanctions should be gradually lifted to allow Iraq to rebuild its infrastructure.

At 11 p.m. Baghdad time, on December 16, Operation Desert Fox was launched when the first salvoes of Tomahawk cruise missiles were fired against Baghdad. Two hours later, Royal Air Force Tornado bombers joined U.S. fighter bombers against key Iraqi installations. Although the American planes flew most of the sorties, the Tornadoes made a significant contribution. This was the first time that Blair had been directly involved in military action, and the first hours of it affected his composure. Earlier in the day, when he had convened a meeting of the cabinet's Defence and Overseas Policy Committee to secure British agreement for the attacks, he had impressed his colleagues with his coolness. When asked to authorize the action, Blair simply said: "OK, that's it." When the action actually started, Blair was with his wife in their flat above Downing Street, entertaining friends to dinner. When his aides informed him that the first Tornadoes had taken off, the possible loss of British servicemen weighed heavily on his mind. He relaxed only after he was informed that all the British pilots had returned safely to base.

The bombing continued for four more days before Clinton and Blair called a halt to hostilities. American and British warplanes had flown about 650 sorties and attacked more than 200 strategic Iraqi targets. Initial intelligence reports suggested that the bombing raids had put the Iraqi WMD program back two years, although the Iraqis claimed that many of the bombs and missiles had missed their targets. The bombing raids also created a diplomatic vacuum that Saddam would be free to exploit. Now that the Americans and British had carried out their retaliation attacks, Saddam believed he was under no obligation to readmit the inspectors. And with France, Russia, and China all opposed to maintaining the strict sanctions against Iraq, there were many lucrative loopholes that Saddam could exploit to finance his regime. The French Foreign Ministry was almost incandescent in its condemnation of the military action. "France deplores the escalation which led to the American military strikes against Iraq and the grave human consequences which they could have for the Iraqi people." So far as Saddam was concerned, the bombing had helped him achieve his objectives—the end of inspections and the end of the sanctions.

Operation Desert Fox was launched on the same day as the announcement that the House of Representatives would conduct impeachment proceedings against the president. As a result, the December attack on Baghdad became known as "Monica's War." For many in America, and elsewhere, there were striking parallels between the action against Iraq and a recently released satirical movie *Wag the Dog*, in which a beleaguered American president tries to draw attention away from a sex scandal by declaring war on Albania.

As with the bombing of Afghanistan and Sudan the previous August, Blair was dismissive of any suggestion that Clinton had ordered the attack out of political expediency. He was also very sensitive to claims that he was Clinton's "poodle." "I was very, very insistent myself that this action was right," an indignant Blair declared on British television the day the bombing ended. "To those people who say, 'Well, the timing of this was geared to internal affairs [in the U.S.]', I find that grotesque and I find it offensive . . . I myself was insistent that we made sure the action was taken as quickly as possible."[63] Blair gave a robust defense of his action in the House of Commons shortly after the action commenced. Operation Desert Fox, he said, had two objectives. "To degrade the ability of Saddam Hussein to build and use such weapons of mass destruction, including command and control and delivery systems, and to diminish the threat he poses to his neighbors by weakening his military capability." Although Blair insisted that at this point the objective was not to remove Saddam from power, "no one would be better pleased if his evil regime disappeared as a direct or indirect result of our action."[64]

The problem for both Clinton and Blair following the December attacks was that they had few other options for dealing with Saddam. They had taken a moral stand in confronting the Iraqi dictator, but lacked any other means of enforcing his compliance with the UN. There was no discussion of launching a full-scale military invasion of Iraq to remove Saddam, particularly as the Pentagon and Downing Street claimed that the bombing raids had destroyed much of Iraq's remaining WMD capability. In the early months of 1999, Blair worked hard to persuade the UN to pass a new resolution against Iraq, but the strong objections of the French and Russians, and, to a lesser extent, the Chinese, meant that progress was painfully slow.

For the next three years, Clinton's much-vaunted policy of "containment" against Saddam would be gradually eroded to the point where the Iraqi dictator had almost made the sanctions redundant. The failure of the UN Security Council to confront Saddam after Operation Desert Fox made a deep impression on Blair, who became disillusioned with the ability of the UN to deal with rogue states and the threat of WMD proliferation. In order to provide a legal justification for their action, Washington and London had been forced to rely upon UN Resolution 687, which had set out the ceasefire terms for ending the Gulf War in 1991. It would set a precedent for future military confrontations with Iraq. "Blair lost faith in the UN as a body as a result of what happened over Iraq in 1998," said one of his close Downing Street aides. "We realized that containment was failing. We wanted the inspectors back and Saddam to comply. The fact that the UN was unable to act showed that there were fundamental flaws in its structure. We all realized that if we had to take action of this nature in the future, we could not rely on the UN for support."[65] For Blair, Saddam's continued defiance made the Western alliance look weak and ineffectual, and he resolved to make sure that in the future the Iraqi dictator be held accountable for his actions.

Four

MISSION ACCOMPLISHED

IN THE EARLY HOURS of January 15, 1999, an elite unit of Serbia's feared paramilitary police entered the Kosovan village of Racak. They had been sent to the village, fifteen miles south of the regional capital, Pristina, on a revenge mission at the orders of the Serbian president Slobodan Milosevic. The previous week, in a well-planned ambush, members of the Kosovan Liberation Army (KLA), a guerilla group waging a bitter battle for independence from Serbia, had killed three Serb policemen. Two days later, in another raid, they had killed another Serb official. Having carried out their attacks, the KLA then quietly disappeared into the surrounding countryside. The provocation was too much for Milosevic, who was determined that Kosovo should remain an integral part of greater Serbia. When the Serb paramilitaries arrived at Racak, they rampaged through the village, ransacking houses and terrorizing the villagers as they searched for the KLA gunmen. Unable to track down the fighters, they rounded up as many men and boys as they could find from the village. These men and boys were then led up a steep hill on the outskirts of the village and executed with a single bullet to the back of the head, their bodies left in a pile for the villagers to collect and bury. The final death toll was estimated at fifty-four.

Less than a month after concluding military action against Saddam,

Tony Blair found himself embroiled in another international crisis. Tensions between the Serbs and Kosovans had been building for most of the past year, and various diplomatic attempts by the Western alliance—France, Germany, Britain, Russia, and the United States—to halt the conflict had achieved little. Serbia was determined to maintain its control over Kosovo, even though nearly 90 percent of the population was comprised of ethnic Albanians, who were equally determined to declare their independence. During the 1990s, a succession of former Yugoslav republics—Slovenia, Croatia, and Bosnia—had declared independence from the Serb-dominated federal government in Belgrade, plunging the region into a bloody civil war that lasted two and a half years, in which two hundred thousand people were killed and almost two million left homeless. Hostilities were finally brought to an end in November 1995, when President Clinton brought the leaders of the warring factions together at the U.S. airbase in Dayton, Ohio, and held them there until they reached an agreement. Under the terms of the General Framework Agreement, Bosnia, the main battleground of the conflict, remained a single state but was divided into two almost equal parts—a Muslim-Croat federation, and a Serb republic.

The Dayton Agreement succeeded in bringing the conflict in Bosnia to an end, although the last convulsions of the Bosnian civil war had put relations between Washington and London under severe strain. President Clinton's initial reluctance to become involved in the conflict had derived from the first Bush administration's view, articulated by James Baker, the secretary of state, that "we don't have a dog in that particular fight," meaning that the travails of Yugoslavia after the collapse of the Iron Curtain was solely a European issue. Clinton's pollsters told him that the American public had little interest in a conflict that was taking place in a part of the world few of them had heard of.

As the conflict spread, however, the scale of the humanitarian crisis had forced the White House to act. Warren Christopher, the U.S. secretary of state, had a succession of meetings with European leaders, including Douglas Hurd, the British foreign secretary, at which he outlined Washington's proposal to lift the UN-sponsored arms embargo that had been applied in 1991 against all the Yugoslav republics. Christopher argued, with some justification, that the arms embargo discriminated against the Bosnian Muslims, engaged in a desperate battle for survival against the Serbs, who could draw on the massive stockpile of weapons and ammunition they had inherited following the dissolution of Yugoslavia. The Major government opposed this proposal in the belief that lifting the arms embargo would simply result in the Balkans being flooded with weaponry, thereby prolonging the hostilities.[1] The British government was persuaded by Hurd that diplomacy was the best solution, and the war was allowed to drag on with the loss of tens of thousands of lives before Clinton was finally able to force the warring parties to sign the Dayton Agreement.

Blair had shown no active interest in the Bosnian civil war, and the Labour Party had largely supported the Conservative government's position. Blair did, however, learn the lessons of the conflict once the fighting had ended, and read up on the UN reports of the 1995 massacre of thousands of Bosnian Muslim civilians at Srebrenica by the Serbs while the Dutch peacekeepers who had been sent to protect them simply fled. Bosnia had been included in the foreign policy "seminars" that Blair had attended prior to his election, and he reached the conclusion that the Bosnian tragedy had been allowed to happen because of a failure of nerve by Britain and its allies, and he vowed that a similar mistake should not be made in the future. "Frankly, we were appalled at the cowardice of the Tories," said one of Blair's key Downing Street advisors. "It was a moral thing with Tony. He believed very strongly that Britain should be a force for good in the world, whether it was the Middle East, Kosovo, or Africa. In this respect, he was an old-fashioned Labour internationalist."[2]

Slobodan Milosevic returned from Dayton like a conquering hero and peacemaker, arguing that he had succeeded in bringing the war to an end while ensuring the Serb population of Bosnia would remain safe under his protection. The lifting of sanctions enabled Belgrade to rebuild after years of economic repression. The end of the war saw a resurgence in political activity in the Serb capital, but when opposition groups posed a genuine threat to Milosevic's authority, he defrauded them of victory by intimidating candidates and making nationalistic appeals to the rural, uneducated electorate. Kosovo remained an important part of Milosevic's claim as the defender of greater Serbia. Although Serbs constituted around 10 percent of the population, Milosevic saw it as Serbia's duty to protect them from the majority ethnic Albanians. From late 1996 onwards, tensions in Kosovo had been rising as the Kosovan Liberation Army (KLA) had begun to procure weapons and organize itself to wage guerilla war for Kosovan independence.

When Milosevic ordered the reprisal raid against Racak, he had no doubt calculated that he would be able to take advantage of the same international disunity that had enabled the Serbs to wage their military campaign in Bosnia unhindered for so long. He would certainly not have been aware of the more robust approach of the Blair government. From the summer of 1998, Downing Street was arguing strongly in favor of the possible use of force if Milosevic tried to ignite another civil war in the Balkans. Blair's view was that "the only thing that would change Milosevic's actions will be (military) actions in and over Kosovo itself."[3] The U.S. State Department also noticed a change in style in Downing Street, with the Blair government moving toward a more active policy than had existed under John Major. "The British no longer had to be dragged along to confront the Serbs," said one senior U.S. State Department official. "We saw a completely different attitude."[4] Blair's interest in Kosovo grew after he had concluded the Good Friday Agreement in April 1998, and he soon came to see Slobodan Milosevic in the same light as Saddam Hussein—a bully and an evil dictator who must be called to account for his actions.

Blair was content to take a back seat and allow Robin Cook, the foreign secretary, to handle the Kosovo crisis. Here, after all, was a clear-cut test case for his much-heralded "ethical" approach to foreign policy. Blair was still involved with Iraq and with the political fallout from the recent resignation of Peter Mandelson, his close personal friend and one of the architects of New Labour, who had been forced out of office in the midst of the Iraq bombing campaign, following damaging revelations about his private finances. Cook himself had suffered more than his share of political obloquy during the preceding eighteen months, starting with his public separation from his wife at Heathrow Airport just as they were about to embark on a family holiday. Cook had been forced into announcing his separation from his wife, Margaret, in August 1997, after the *News of the World* told Downing Street that it was about to publish details of his affair with his secretary, Gaynor Regan. For the next year, Cook endured a series of savage attacks from his estranged wife, who depicted him as an emotionally stunted serial adulterer who drank heavily at times of stress. Kosovo presented an important opportunity for Cook to rebuild his reputation.

There was a strong and immediate reaction to the Racak massacre as Western leaders sought to impress upon Milosevic that they would not tolerate further acts of Serb brutality in Kosovo. The previous autumn, as Milosevic had first begun to raise the specter of ethnic cleansing in Kosovo, Britain had played a leading role in the International Contact Group, alongside the United States, Russia, Germany, France, and Italy. In October 1998, this unique cooperation had resulted in UN Security Council Resolution 1203, which warned of an imminent human catastrophe in Kosovo. The resolution insisted that all Kosovan refugees be allowed to return to their homes. Richard Holbrooke, the U.S. envoy who had successfully negotiated the Dayton Agreement, met with Milosevic and agreed on a ceasefire, to be monitored by unarmed civilians, although some British officials were concerned that Holbrooke's agreement with Milosevic was not strong enough. "It was too imprecise," said General Sir Mike Jackson, who was to take command of NATO forces in Kosovo. "It gave Milosevic too much room for maneuver. We also had the distinct feeling of American reluctance to become too deeply involved."[5] The Racak massacre showed that Milosevic was not intimidated by the threat of retaliatory military action by NATO.

General Wesley Clark, the NATO commander, was dispatched to Belgrade with Klaus Naumann, the German chief of NATO's military committee, to warn Milosevic that any further attacks would be regarded as a clear breach of the UN resolution, and not tolerated. They demanded immediate access to Racak for investigators from the International War Crimes Tribunal that had recently been established in The Hague, the Dutch capital. According to Naumann, Milosevic was uncooperative. When the NATO team confronted him with the evidence of the Racak massacre, the Serb president denied it. "He said again that Serb forces do not do this, that they fought cleanly." Milosevic rejected NATO's right to interfere in the Balkans. "Milosevic said that NATO might be the world's most powerful alliance, but we had no right to bomb Serbia, and if we did we would be war criminals."[6]

After meeting with Blair and George Robertson, the defense secretary, at Downing Street, Robin Cook told the House of Commons that the Racak attack was "a war crime." A few days later, the British foreign secretary flew to Belgrade to confront Milosevic personally. He delivered what he described as a "final ultimatum" to the Serb president: Milosevic must accept a Western-sponsored peace plan or risk NATO air strikes. After the meeting, Cook declared that Milosevic "undertook to study the proposal very carefully." Milosevic's response was to send another Serb paramilitary force to the Kosovan village of Prekaz, where they hunted down and killed Adem Jashari, a KLA leader, and murdered more than fifty members of his family and clan who were found hiding with him.

Milosevic had no intention of complying with either the UN or NATO. He was encouraged by what he regarded as the West's weak response to Saddam's defiance of the UN the previous December. Operation Desert Fox had lasted a mere seventy-two hours, caused Saddam no great hardship, and the UN inspectors had not been allowed back. Milosevic was prepared to suffer a few days of NATO bomb sorties if it meant that he would be given a free hand in Kosovo. NATO was celebrating its fiftieth anniversary, and yet it had never been involved in offensive operations. Just as Saddam had calculated that he could take advantage of splits at the UN Security Council, Milosevic thought that any attack on Belgrade would split NATO.

Several NATO states, including Greece and Italy, were against military action, and there were tensions developing between Washington and Europe over plans to strengthen European military cooperation. On December 4, 1998, the British and French governments had signed the St. Malo Agreement, where both countries agreed to plan and execute a combined response to international crises. Blair saw this as a means of providing Europe with the ability to make a more telling military contribution to future international crises, but many in Washington regarded it as an unwelcome challenge to NATO, which they believed should fulfill that function. Apart from seeking to capitalize on these rifts within NATO, Milosevic was counting heavily on the support of Russia, the figurehead of the Slav "fraternity," which he assumed would not allow the West to attack its Slavic allies in Serbia.

Against this fraught background, Robin Cook, the British foreign secretary, and Madeleine Albright, the U.S. secretary of state, sought to make one last effort to reach a peace agreement on Kosovo. Britain and France agreed to chair peace talks amid the tranquil setting of the eighteenth-century hunting lodge and presidential summer palace at Rambouillet. The talks started on February 6, 1999, but little progress was made. The Kosovan delegation was divided over how far they should go in pressing for complete independence from Belgrade, while the Serbs were determined to maintain control over Kosovo and to take action to root out the KLA "terrorists."

Albright managed to persuade the Albanian delegation to sign on to an agreement whereby they would enjoy self-government under NATO protection so long as the KLA disbanded. The Serbs, however, were adamant that they would not accept an international military presence in Kosovo. So far as Milosevic was concerned, the KLA was a terrorist threat that only the Serbs could handle. As Albright recalled in her memoirs, the Serb position was "we will have nothing to do with an outside military force. We will deal with the terrorist threat in our own way. And it will not take long."[7] Cook worked closely with Albright at Rambouillet, but the negotiations were primarily driven behind the scenes by the United States. Albright's primary concern was to prevent Moscow from intervening directly on behalf of Serbia, and she got an undertaking to that effect from Igor Ivanov, the Russian foreign minister. The Russians were insistent that they would not agree to air strikes against Serbia, and that NATO, whose mandate was to defend Europe, had no right to attack a sovereign state. Even so, Ivanov, who was exasperated by Milosevic's delaying tactics, indicated that he thought the threat of force might be necessary to achieve a political settlement.[8]

From mid-February, President Clinton was noticeably more engaged in the process after the U.S. Senate voted against removing him from office over the Lewinsky affair. Now that the failure of the Rambouillet talks increased the likelihood of war, Tony Blair also became more involved in directing British policy. Throughout the buildup to the war, Blair had taken a bullish line among his close colleagues, telling them that Milosevic had to be shown "some steel." But as it became clear that military conflict was inevitable, Blair was less comfortable with his stance, confiding to a close ministerial friend, "This is not a war I wanted."[9]

By mid-March, the refugee situation in Kosovo was deteriorating rapidly, as the Serb harassment prompted a further twenty-five thousand Kosovans to flee their homes. American and British intelligence reported that the Serbs were planning a spring offensive against large KLA units and command centers during a two-week period in March, which no doubt explained Milosevic's extreme reluctance to allow NATO troops into Kosovo. Such an offensive would inevitably involve civilian casualties and the displacement of hundreds of thousands of people.

A steady parade of foreign dignitaries from a variety of nations, including Russia, Greece, France, Britain, and the United States, passed through Belgrade in an attempt to persuade Milosevic that his refusal to compromise would only lead to war. But as Igor Ivanov reported after his visit to Belgrade, he found "only idiots who are ready to go to war."[10] On March 19, President Clinton convened a meeting at the White House to discuss the mounting crisis. George Tenet, the CIA director, informed Clinton that, as predicted, the Serb offensive had begun and succeeded in forcing many KLA units to withdraw. Civilians in Kosovo were highly vulnerable to Serb attacks, and the only realistic option available in defense of Kosovo's civilian population was to launch NATO air strikes against Serb positions. Such attacks might weaken the Serb president, but it was unclear how long he could hold out. At this stage, no one at the White House was advocating the use of ground troops in Kosovo to halt the Serb offensive. But after the horrors of Bosnia, Clinton was determined that Milosevic should not be allowed to run amok in the Balkans. "In dealing with aggressors in the Balkans, hesitation is a license to kill," he declared.[11]

The final attempt to avert conflict came on March 22, when Holbrooke visited Belgrade to persuade Milosevic to do a deal. He told the Serb leader that the NATO bombing of Serbia would be "swift, severe, and sustained," but still Milosevic refused to budge. When Holbrooke reported Milosevic's intransigence back to Albright, the secretary of state ordered him to return. So far as Washington was concerned, Milosevic's decision to launch his spring offensive in Kosovo left it with no option other than to respond; the longer the Serb dictator's feared paramilitary police were allowed to rampage through Kosovo the more innocent lives would be lost and families made homeless. A few hours later, on the evening of March 23, NATO secretary-general Javier Solana ordered General Wesley Clark, the NATO commander, to launch air strikes at Serb positions. For trying to maintain good relations with Moscow, the timing of the raids could not have been worse, as Yevgeny Primakov, the Russian prime minister, was flying to Washington at the very moment that Clinton gave his assent for the air strikes to commence. Al Gore, the U.S. vice president, was delegated to inform Primakov, who responded by ordering his plane to turn around and fly him back to Moscow.

Both Blair and Clinton were reluctant warriors at the start of the Kosovo conflict. After it became clear that Albright's diplomatic efforts were going nowhere, Clinton still needed convincing that military action was necessary. Albright had to use all her skills of persuasion to justify the need for NATO air strikes. "If we don't respond now, we'll have to respond later," she told Clinton shortly before the conflict began. "Milosevic has picked this fight. We can't allow him to win." [12] The British Embassy in Washington reported back to Downing Street that Clinton was still looking for some sort of compromise that would avoid the necessity of military action. [13] In addition, Blair's advisors were telling him that several leading European countries, including Germany and Italy, were deeply skeptical about the need for war and whether military intervention by NATO would actually succeed in halting the ethnic cleansing and killing of innocent civilians in Kosovo.

Blair had his own doubts about using military force, but these were more about whether or not a bombing campaign against the Serbs would work. In conversations with General Sir Charles Guthrie, the chief of the defense staff, prior to the war, Blair was constantly seeking reassurance that NATO air strikes would achieve the political objective of forcing Milosevic to abandon his ethnic cleansing program and accept the Rambouillet Agreement. But Guthrie could give no such assurance and informed the prime minister that once the conflict began they would be entering uncharted territory.[14] Even so, Blair was adamant that Milosevic should not be allowed to reintroduce the horrors of ethnic cleansing to Europe, nor succeed in his open defiance of NATO. One of Blair's close advisors suggested that he might be going out on a limb in his determination to stand up to Milosevic's bullying tactics, and that he might be better advised to work with Clinton and the Europeans on a compromise. But Blair would have none of it. "If there's going to be a fudge, I'm not going to be part of it," he indignantly replied. Blair was preparing to take Britain to war in Europe for the first time since 1945.

Blair's moral conviction was evident in the speech he made to a packed House of Commons the night the bombing started. "We have made a very plain promise to the Kosovar people," said Blair. "To walk away now would not merely destroy NATO's credibility. More importantly, it would be a breach of faith to thousands of innocent civilians whose only desire is to live in peace and who took us at our word: to protect them from military suppression." Blair recited a list of the agreements that the Serbs had betrayed, and drew attention to the two thousand Kosovars who had already been killed and the tens of thousands who had been driven from their homes by the Serbs' ethnic cleansing. "We must act to save thousands of innocent men, women, and children from humanitarian catastrophe, from death, barbarism, and ethnic cleansing by a brutal dictatorship. We have no alternative but to act and act we will."[15]

Blair was to express similar sentiments on the eve of the Iraq War in 2003, but in the early spring of 1999, his words had an almost missionary zeal that jarred many of his supporters and some of his European allies. Blair sought to justify his actions on the compelling moral argument that it was the duty of a civilized democratic country like Britain to prevent evildoing, and Milosevic's attempt to terrorize the indigenous Albanian population of Kosovo into leaving their homes was, to his thinking, a clear-cut case of tyrannical behavior that could well result in genocide. His own Labour Party, however, was less convinced, and expressed doubts about the legitimacy of interfering in the affairs of a sovereign country without international backing. Russian president

Boris Yeltsin's threat to use his veto meant that there was no chance of
the UN Security Council passing any resolution that justified military
action against the Serbs. "To be honest, the legal issues were not at the
forefront of our minds," said one of Blair's senior Downing Street advisors. "We could not go to the UN because of the Russians, but there was
a strong feeling within NATO that the Western alliance could not stand
idly by. Our view was that there was an overwhelming humanitarian
necessity to act, and act we did."[16] Robin Cook, the foreign secretary,
asked the legal team at the Foreign Office to justify British involvement
in military action against Kosovo. Their arguments were accepted by
the attorney general.

NATO OPENED THE MILITARY campaign against Milosevic on the
evening of March 23, 1999, with an intense seventy-two-hour aerial
bombardment of key Serb military and communications sites. Both the
Foreign Office in London and the State Department in Washington took
the view that an intensive bombing campaign would force Milosevic to
accept the deal outlined at Rambouillet. At this stage, no proposals were
put forward for military intervention on the ground in Kosovo, as both the
White House and the Pentagon were confident that the overwhelming
firepower of the bombing campaign would bring Milosevic to his senses.
There was some disquiet in London that most of the military action
would be undertaken by American bombers, and that the British government would have little control over the conduct of the campaign, but
Blair's main concern was to make sure that Washington was involved in
the conflict from the outset. "Even after the failure of Rambouillet we
sensed this reluctance by the Americans to get involved," said one of
Blair's key aides. "We felt that the credibility of NATO was on the line,
and it was crucial that Clinton was on board."[17]

From the start, the bombing campaign did not go as planned. On the
first night, on March 24, NATO warplanes and cruise missiles targeted
forty Serb sites, including military bases and air defense installations. But
the Serbs proved to be wily adversaries. Many of the military bases had
been cleared of key equipment—it was feared a NATO mole had tipped

off Milosevic about the likely targets. Serb commanders deliberately did not activate their air defense systems in a way that would allow NATO's sophisticated missile systems to "lock on" and destroy them. During the first night of the bombing campaign, the Tornado bombers of the Royal Air Force failed to hit a single target. Combined with the Pentagon's insistence that its planes keep above cloud cover for safety, the initial NATO air attacks achieved little.

Milosevic, meanwhile, was able to exploit NATO's exclusive reliance on airpower to achieve its objectives by increasing his campaign of ethnic cleansing in Kosovo. Before the bombing campaign began, the Serb offensive had already driven a hundred thousand Kosovars from their homes. The figure grew rapidly as the air war continued. Milosevic was intent on achieving four goals: the complete destruction of the KLA, the restructuring of Kosovo's ethnic balance in favor of the Serbs, the terrorization of the remaining members of the Albanian population, and the creation of a humanitarian crisis that would divide the region. Milosevic skillfully used the effects of the bombing campaign in Serbia to rally support, and the Serbs exploited the killing of civilians by NATO bombers for their own propaganda purposes.

At the start of the conflict, Blair took an intense interest in the military campaign, demanding that he personally authorize all the targets for that night's sorties, and asking searching questions of the military planners. He would wait anxiously each day to find out if all the British pilots had returned safely to their bases. Because of this micromanagement of the conflict Blair began to realize that airpower alone was not going to halt the mounting humanitarian crisis that was being created by Milosevic's ethnic cleansing.

Both Blair and Clinton had made it clear at the outset of the war that they had no intention of deploying ground troops. In his televised address to the American people on the day that the air strikes were launched, Clinton had explicitly stated, "I do not intend to put our troops into Kosovo to fight a ground war." This statement had been drafted by Sandy Berger, Clinton's national security advisor, who argued that the Republican-dominated U.S. Congress was deeply opposed to committing American troops to an open-ended intervention in Kosovo. In his parliamentary address, Blair had made similar comments, telling MPs, "We do not plan to use ground troops in order to fight our way into Kosovo. No one should underestimate the sheer scale of what is involved in that action. We would be talking about one hundred thousand ground troops, even more."[18]

Blair and Clinton's public admission that they were not prepared to use ground troops played to Milosevic's advantage, confirming his suspicions that NATO did not pose a serious threat to his campaign of ethnic cleansing in Kosovo. By the first weekend of the campaign, Blair was informed by Guthrie that the bombing campaign was not succeeding and Milosevic was intensifying his "final solution" in Kosovo. The narrow roads leading out of Kosovo had been transformed into desperate rivers of humanity, and Blair, Cook, Robertson, and Guthrie, the group that bore ultimate responsibility for prosecuting the war, had to persuade the Macedonian government to accept the victims of Milosevic's ethnic cleansing.

The war was turning into a public relations disaster for both the British and American governments. While NATO bombers struggled to find their targets, the television pictures concentrated on the plight of the thousands of Kosovars who were being driven from their homes by the Serb paramilitaries. Blair sought to rally support by making an emotional address on British television, in which he insisted that the bombing campaign "was simply the right thing to do" to "defend our fellow human beings." Aware that his critics were questioning the effectiveness of the bombing campaign, Blair declared, "To those who say the aim of the military strikes is not clear, I say it is crystal clear. It is to curb Milosevic's ability to wage war on an innocent civilian population."[19]

Blair and Cook came under pressure from some colleagues who were still not satisfied by the legal justification for the war. During a cabinet discussion soon after hostilities commenced, one minister demanded to know: "How is it any country can take military action against a sovereign state and fellow members of the UN without the approval of the Security Council?"[20] George Robertson, the defense secretary, conceded that it would not be a "casualty-free conflict," but stressed that the main purpose of the war was to prevent a human catastrophe. If Milosevic "stopped his violence towards the Kosovan Albanians, we will stop the action against him."[21]

By contrast, President Clinton gave every appearance of not being concerned by the human catastrophe that was unfolding in the Balkans. When Blair phoned Clinton on the first weekend of the conflict to discuss progress, he found the American president making preparations for an afternoon of golf. Clinton told Blair that he needed more public backing from Europe's leaders to enable him to broaden the air campaign. Mike Short, the American general in charge of the bombing, wanted to launch a devastating bombardment of the Serbian capital, Belgrade, which, he argued, would "make Milosevic's eyes water." But there was little support for such action in Europe, where the high level of civilian casualties that would incur was regarded as morally unacceptable. Blair himself was not ready to countenance saturation bombing of Belgrade. "What if we cut off power to a hospital," he fretted. "Then we'll be accused of killing babies."[22]

Blair agreed to assist Clinton in persuading the Europeans to remain supportive of the campaign. Clinton and Blair phoned each other every day as they attempted to resolve the humanitarian crisis that was spiraling out of control in Kosovo. On March 30, nearly a week into the war, Clinton convened a meeting of his senior officials and advisors in the Oval Office to assess the progress. He told his political advisor Sidney Blumenthal that, in his view, Britain "was firm and would be staunch to the end." Clinton had told Blair that the bombing had to continue and that there could be no pause, not even for Easter, which fell in the first weekend of April. "We need to ramp up operations," he told Blair on April 1.[23] Blair asked Javier Solana, the head of NATO, to broaden the bombing targets, while Clinton managed to persuade the Italian prime minister, Massimo d'Alema, to drop his request to halt the bombing entirely. Clinton was determined to maintain national and international unity; otherwise, he felt he would be playing into Milosevic's hands.

The situation on the ground in Kosovo was only getting worse. By the first week of April, virtually all of Kosovo's Albanian population was in hiding or in flight. In scenes reminiscent of the Holocaust, desperate columns of bedraggled Albanian refugees were being herded onto trains and trucks and shipped out of their homeland to an uncertain fate. The images had a profound impact on Blair, who for the first time in his career suffered intimations of his own political mortality. "This could be the end of me," he confided to one of his close aides during the Easter holiday.[24]

The contrast between Blair's predicament in 1999 and the previous year, when he was celebrating the historic achievement of the Good Friday Agreement in Northern Ireland, could not have been starker. He spent the weekend giving a series of media interviews in which he pledged his determination to resolve the crisis. "This is no longer just a military conflict," he declared. "It is a battle between good and evil, between civilization and barbarity."[25] In a television interview, he insisted that the air strikes would continue with "iron resolve." And he made a pledge that Clinton had so far avoided. "We will not let you down," he told the Kosovars. "We will make sure that you are able to return to your homes, and live in peace."[26]

It was increasingly apparent that NATO was unable to take effective action to halt the ethnic cleansing without deploying significant ground forces. As General Wesley Clark later conceded, "The air campaign began with enough forces to punish the Serbs, but it lacked the mass and capabilities needed to halt the ethnic cleansing."[27] In Washington, Clinton was privately expressing his exasperation that he had been persuaded to rule out the possibility of sending American troops into Kosovo, and pressured Sandy Berger to go on American television to say publicly that all options remained open. But Clinton did not want to open a public debate among the allies over ground troops, which he felt would expose weaknesses within the NATO alliance.

Blair, meanwhile, was becoming more convinced than ever about the need to deploy ground forces. He spent the Easter holiday at Chequers, closely analyzing the course of the war and, isolated from the day-to-day distractions, was determined to take personal charge of the conflict. "It was one of those rare moments in his premiership when he focused single-mindedly on just one issue," said one senior official.[28] He summoned Charles Guthrie and George Robertson for detailed discussions on the strategic options available. Blair now understood fully that it had been a fundamental error to rule out the use of ground troops, which broke the first rule of warfare: keep the enemy guessing. Milosevic knew that if he could withstand the air bombardment for a few weeks, he would get his way in Kosovo. During the Chequers meeting, Blair and Guthrie agreed that, unless NATO could seriously threaten the deployment of ground troops, Milosevic would not be brought to heel. Guthrie pointed out in detail the huge difficulties this entailed, including Washington's adamant opposition to sending American troops into Kosovo. Blair concluded that there was simply no alternative, and he wrote a long letter to Clinton, setting out the arguments in favor of military intervention.

In mid-April, Blair dispatched Paddy Ashdown, the former leader of the Liberal Democrats, on a four-day tour of the region to give him a detailed assessment of how the war was progressing. Ashdown had been an outspoken critic of Serb aggression during the Bosnian civil war, and his report on Kosovo provided Blair with a stark reality check. "You think you are winning this war. I think you are losing it," wrote Ashdown. He reported that the military were confused about what was expected of them, and that there was little immediate prospect of the Kosovan refugees being allowed to go home. "This is the first war in history that is being fought for refugees," he concluded. "If they don't go back, we have lost." [29]

In what was rapidly developing into the most serious crisis Blair had faced since becoming prime minister, he received welcome support from Margaret Thatcher, who had been an ardent campaigner for military intervention during the Bosnia conflict. "Thatcher was very supportive of Tony over Kosovo," said one of Blair's closest political aides. "She told him that she knew all about the loneliness of leadership and she gave him a lot of support." [30] In late April, she made a speech in which she was deeply critical of "eight long years of Western weakness" in the Balkans. Comparing Milosevic's Serbia with Nazi Germany, she said the West must be prepared to deploy ground troops to ensure that "a truly monstrous evil" was destroyed. "Trying to fight a war with one hand tied behind your back is the way to lose it," she declared. [31]

Blair emerged from his week's break at Chequers determined to change the course of the war. Clare Short, his temperamental international development secretary, flew to Macedonia where she took decisive action to alleviate the burgeoning refugee problem. Alastair Campbell, Blair's feared but effective press secretary, arrived in Brussels to advise NATO's press team about winning the propaganda war. On April 20, Blair himself traveled to Brussels to discuss strategy with General Wes Clark. Clark, a silver-haired West Point graduate and Rhodes scholar, was regarded with some suspicion at both the White House and the Pentagon, where he was seen as being too "political."[32]

Like Blair, Clark had reservations about waging war through airpower alone, and hoped that Blair would be able to bring pressure on the Clinton administration to amend its strategy. The first question Blair asked when he met Clark was, "Are we going to win?" To which Clark replied, "Yes, Prime Minister, we are going to win." For a moment, both men looked hard at each other before Blair said, "Good, because the future of almost every government and leader in Europe depends on our success here." Blair was overstating his case for dramatic effect, but the point was not lost on Clark. "Tony Blair was representing Europe. He was saying what Washington had not: that we must win," Clark later wrote. And the most pressing question that Blair had to ask of the NATO commander was, "Are we going to win without ground troops?" Clark was candid, stating that he could not guarantee victory with airpower alone, to which Blair responded, "Will you get ground troops if you need them?"[33]

Clark knew that Blair wanted to begin preparations for a ground war, but that the Pentagon was firmly opposed to any expansion of the military campaign. The Pentagon staunchly resisted the notion of a ground war that could produce many casualties and that had no clear exit strategy. Consequently, the Pentagon blocked a request by Clark early in the war for Apache ground attack helicopters to be deployed to seek out and destroy the Serbs' heavy military installations. The military planners in Washington argued that such a deployment would result in U.S. troops being used to support the Apache air strikes. If Clark was going to overcome the institutional resistance of the Pentagon, he needed to support Blair's determined leadership on the issue.

A few days later, Blair and General Sir Charles Guthrie flew to Washington for a dinner planned long before the Kosovo crisis, to celebrate NATO's fiftieth anniversary. Cook had already been to Washington to talk to Madeleine Albright about whether she would be willing to support a more robust approach with ground troops, to the war. Her parents had fled their native Czechoslovakia from the Nazis and Albright was seen as the administration's hawk. Cook wanted Albright to enlist the support of William Cohen, the U.S. defense secretary. Although she would explore the possibility of deploying ground troops, she was skeptical about how much influence she would have at the Pentagon. She suggested that the British might have more luck if they lobbied their case directly with the president.

By the time Blair arrived in Washington on April 23, the ground troops issue threatened the biggest crisis in NATO's history. At the heart of this dispute was the British suggestion that NATO forces could enter Kosovo in a "semipermissive" military environment, as opposed to the "permissive" one that Washington was prepared to accept. A "permissive" environment is one where the enemy has capitulated, and NATO's forces would be able to enter unopposed, which was the only ground option that Clinton was prepared to consider. But Blair was concerned that in the absence of a tangible threat of ground troops, the war could drag on indefinitely, with Milosevic refusing to surrender. The British wanted troops to enter Kosovo in a "semipermissive" environment, which Blair argued would allow NATO to avoid an endless bombing campaign and show Milosevic that he intended to do whatever was necessary to win.

General Hugh Shelton, the U.S. chairman of the Joint Chiefs of Staff, was contemptuous of the notion that it was possible to enter Kosovo while hostile forces were still present, without taking the necessary precautions. "You do not get semishot," he said when told of the British plan.[34] Shelton was backed by Cohen and Clinton. In order to enter Kosovo, a huge land force would be required—prewar NATO planning estimates put the figure in excess of one hundred thousand, and most of the troops would be American soldiers. Even so, Cohen believed that both the Pentagon and NATO should draw up plans for a ground offensive as a precaution, especially since it was unlikely that NATO ground forces could be sent into Kosovo before early July.

When Blair arrived in Washington, Britain was the only country fully committed to the ground option. Germany and Italy were against it, and the French would support it only in the unlikely event that it was authorized by the Security Council. The fiftieth anniversary summit to celebrate NATO's achievement in winning the Cold War and maintaining the peace in Europe was in danger of being ruined by a squabble over ground troops, a dispute that would only play into Milosevic's hands. As Madeleine Albright conceded in her memoirs, "What saved us in the end was largely the relationship between President Clinton and Prime Minister Blair."[35]

Before the summit got going in earnest, Blair and his delegation were invited to the White House together with Madeleine Albright and Sandy Berger. According to Albright, Blair was "Churchillian" in expressing his determination to prevail in Kosovo. The British were prepared to put more than fifty thousand troops—half the British army—into Kosovo. Cohen, the U.S. defense secretary, reminded Blair that the use of American troops would be "an almost impossible sell" to both the American people and Congress. Blair countered that the alliance still needed to start thinking about troops, if for no other reason than they would be needed to police the region once the conflict was over. NATO needed "to start planning for success," said Blair. Clinton watched the exchanges somewhat detached. Clinton's only significant contribution to the discussion was to voice his concern about Moscow's reaction to the use of ground forces. "I'm worried about the Russians," he said.[36] Clinton was still holding out for the possibility that Russian president Boris Yeltsin could negotiate a deal with Milosevic.

Sandy Berger was hardest on Blair, telling him that talk of committing troops would be read as a sign that the air campaign had failed. Aware that he was not making much headway, Blair sought an opportunity to talk to Clinton in private, away from his advisors. Too polite to ask the president's advisors to leave the room, Blair asked Clinton the location of the restroom. Picking up on the signal, Clinton volunteered to show him the way. The two did not reappear for half an hour, during which time they managed to come up with a formula that saved the NATO summit from an embarrassing split. While Blair agreed not to publicly raise the issue of ground troops, Clinton agreed to allow planning to begin for a ground deployment in Kosovo in case the bombing campaign proved to be insufficient. Clinton and Blair then agreed to lobby their fellow NATO leaders individually in favor of their plan.

The following day, Blair flew to Chicago to give the most important speech of his career, on foreign defense policy, a speech that would become the benchmark for Blair's response to numerous security challenges that he would face during his premiership. Until now, Blair had not seriously addressed foreign and defense policy issues. He chose his invitation to address the Chicago Economic Club on April 22 as the platform to expound his worldview. His plan to write the speech himself was abandoned because of the turmoil in Kosovo, and Jonathan Powell, his chief of staff, approached Professor Laurence Freedman, a British expert on defense studies, to help draft the script. Freedman set out five criteria for international intervention. Combining academic arguments with common sense, Freedman argued that the first criterion should be "Are we sure of our case?" followed by: Have all the diplomatic options been exhausted? Can the military operation be prudently undertaken? Is there a will to hold out for the long term if required? And are there national interests involved?[37] Blair tidied the speech during the flight to Washington, and added his own moral dimension to Freedman's draft.

Blair outlined what was to become known as the "Blair doctrine" when he made his speech at Chicago's Hilton Hotel. In his new "doctrine of the international community," he attempted to outline the moral reasoning behind NATO's action in Kosovo. It would later serve as Blair's justification for backing the United States in the war on terror. In Kosovo, said Blair, the world was witnessing "awful crimes that we never thought we would see again—ethnic cleansing, systematic rape, mass murder . . . This is a just war, not based on territorial ambition but on values." Blair justified NATO's action on the basis that the West could not afford to "turn our backs on conflicts and violations of human rights" when there was a genuine fear that they might spill across international borders. In Milosevic's case, not to act now would only result in the West spending "infinitely more blood and treasure to stop him later." The other dimension to taking firm action that needed to be considered was the deterrent effect on other dictators. If NATO were able to stop Milosevic in Kosovo, it would send a warning to other dictators—such as Saddam Hussein. So far as Blair was concerned, the international community could no longer regard "acts of genocide" as a "purely internal matter."[38] Blair was the only leader of the nineteen-member alliance to set out a cogent defense of NATO's action, and by doing so he had set a template by which the West's response to future challenges would be determined.

Blair professed himself delighted with the speech and particularly with the reception it received in both the American and British media. In London, the *Financial Times* declared that "Britain yesterday emerged as NATO's most hawkish country on the issue of introducing ground troops . . . an option resisted by most other members."[39] The American media, meanwhile, was quick to exploit the glaring gap between Blair's position and that of the American president. The *Wall Street Journal* drew a contrast between the determination shown in Blair's position on Kosovo and "a reluctant White House." The *New York Times* hailed Blair as "King Tony," and the *Los Angeles Times* remarked that "Britain's Prime Minister is emerging as the alliance's most outspoken hawk." Blair's appearances on a number of American talk shows, such as *Meet the Press* and *Larry King Live*, drew plaudits from Clinton's Republican opponents, who delighted in the embarrassment Blair's uncompromising views had caused the American president.

The speech was less well received among Blair's own officials and the White House. The Foreign Office in London complained that it knew nothing of the speech until it had been delivered, and expressed its concern about international law and the position of the UN. Blair's speech had turned the doctrine of the inviolability of national sovereignty, the fundamental principle that governed the UN, on its head. The White House, too, was less than impressed with Blair's visionary ideas. Sandy Berger was unhappy with the notion of producing a humanitarian rationale to justify intervention, while Clinton himself was upset about Blair's public comments on ground troops. Blair had been aware that he risked upsetting Clinton over the Chicago speech. Blair had had an argument with Alastair Campbell, his press secretary, on the flight to Washington, over whether or not he should even raise the issue of ground troops. But he decided to press ahead, well aware that he was going out on a limb. "Clinton is firmly opposed to ground troops: how are we going to pull all of this together?" he asked Sir Christopher Meyer, the British ambassador to the United States.[40]

If Blair was having difficulty persuading the Clinton administration of the validity of his argument, he would have had no such problem with the powerful neoconservative lobby in Washington, which was already mounting a staunch campaign in favor of expanding the military operations. Led by the Republican Arizona senator John McCain, a powerful lobby was coalescing among Washington's neocon elite to send American troops into Kosovo to bring a halt to the ethnic cleansing. Among those who supported greater American involvement were key figures from previous Republican administrations, including Jeane Kirkpatrick, Caspar Weinberger, Zbigniew Brzezinski, Henry Kissinger, and Richard Perle.

An editorial in the *Weekly Standard*, the official organ of the neocons, published in Washington a few days before Blair arrived, made virtually the same arguments as the British prime minister did in favor of deploying ground forces in Kosovo. "The bare minimum that the United States and NATO must achieve in the coming weeks is the removal of all Serb forces from Kosovo," it said. "Driving Serb forces out of Kosovo is now going to require U.S. and NATO ground troops. It is irresponsible for the president and his advisors to continue ruling out the ground option, and it is simply unforgivable that the administration has refused even to begin preparing for such a deployment. Mobilization for a ground war will take weeks. The longer Clinton waits, the better Milosevic's chances to win."[41] Blair could not have put it better himself.

The arguments used by many leading Republicans to justify expanding the military campaign in Kosovo were remarkably similar to those Blair had used in his Chicago speech. In late April, Kissinger declared, "NATO cannot survive if it now abandons the campaign without achieving its objective of ending the massacres." Brzezinski agreed, stating, "It is no exaggeration to say that NATO's failure to prevail would mean both the end of NATO as a credible alliance and the undermining of America's global leadership." For the leading neocon ideologues, Robert Kagan and William Kristol, the fundamental issue at stake in Kosovo "was the kind of world we want to live in—where peace and civilized behavior reign, especially in strategically vital parts of the world, like Europe . . . Are these American interests that are worth pursuing or not?"[42]

In Houston, Texas, Governor George W. Bush, a politician relatively unknown on the international stage, added his voice to the Republican campaign to expand the war. In an interview published by the Associated Press in early May, Bush criticized Clinton, saying it was a mistake for the president to say "right off the bat" that he would not "use land troops" in Kosovo. Echoing almost word for word what Margaret Thatcher had said in her speech in London, Bush claimed Clinton's statement said, " 'We're coming to fight you with one hand.' I happen to think it's important for Milosevic to hear one voice, and that we're serious . . . We need to have one objective in mind and that is to achieve the goals and to do so ferociously. It's an awesome responsibility to be commander-in-chief . . . but the commander-in-chief has a responsibility, once the troops are committed, to win."[43] This was a rare statement on foreign policy from the man who would later succeed Clinton as president, and, unlike Clinton, Bush fully endorsed Blair's uncompromising position. At this point in Bush's political career, however, with the American presidential election still more than a year away, few outside Republican circles knew much about the Texas governor, apart from the fact that he was a son of a former president. Certainly, at this point, Blair would have been blissfully unaware that, two thousand miles away, in Texas, he had an unexpected ally in his own campaign to persuade Clinton to change course in the war in Kosovo.

After Chicago, Blair returned to Washington to attend the conclusion of the NATO summit. The deal Clinton and Blair had struck in the unlikely confines of the White House restroom ensured that their plan was acceptable to the nineteen member states. NATO reaffirmed its insistence that the Serbs had to be removed from Kosovo and the refugees brought back as soon as possible. Precisely how this was to be achieved was left unsaid, although Javier Solana, the organization's secretary-general, said that a review would be conducted of all the military options, a clear indication that the deployment of ground troops was now being considered. Nevertheless, Blair was made aware of the deep antipathy of many NATO leaders who were firmly set against putting "boots on the ground" in Kosovo. Gerhard Schröder, the German chancellor, was particularly dismissive of Blair's entreaties, telling him that the British "liked fighting" while the Germans had become "fundamentally pacific" since 1945. As one NATO official commented at the end of the summit, "There is only one person arguing for ground troops and that is Tony Blair."[44]

Blair and his party had a private dinner with the Clintons at the conclusion of the summit. Clinton confessed that he was becoming increasingly frustrated by how the war was progressing, and for the first time in his talks with Blair, he dropped a heavy hint that he might be prepared to support ground troops. The next day, Blair returned home to Downing Street unsure of whether he had won the argument with Clinton. Although Blair had failed to win NATO approval for a full military deployment, he had made the key decision-makers aware of the risk that the war might be lost. Blair fretted that he may have pushed Clinton too hard. He feared that by upstaging Clinton he had made the president look weak, and that Clinton would be "even more reluctant" to make a commitment to troops because it would look as if "he had been 'bounced' by me."[45]

The worsening refugee crisis in Kosovo persuaded Blair and his wife, Cherie, to fly to Macedonia to see for themselves the tide of human misery that had been created by Milosevic. At Bradze, on the Kosovo-Albanian border, Blair came across a line of ten thousand people who had arrived overnight. The very old, the sick and disabled, newborn babies in their mothers' arms, all cowered in the blistering heat. Wiping angry sweat from his brow and neck, Blair exploded, "This is obscene. It's criminal. Just criminal. How can anyone think we shouldn't be stopping this."[46] The trip confirmed Blair's belief in the righteousness of his cause.

After Macedonia, Blair flew to Bucharest, where, in his address to the Romanian parliament, he drew a direct comparison between the plight of Kosovo's Albanians and the treatment of European Jewry in the Second World War. In a rare moment of hubris, Blair also compared himself to William Gladstone, the ultimate Victorian moralist of international affairs, who, he declared, was "one of my political heroes." Blair's increasingly messianic belief in the war raised eyebrows among his close political advisors in Downing Street. Sir Richard Wilson, the cabinet secretary, in mid-May noted the intensity of Blair's commitment to resolving the dispute by military force. When Wilson asked him rhetorically what his likely reaction would be if Clinton told him there was no option other than a diplomatic solution, Blair immediately replied, "I will not do it."[47]

The only tangible development to emerge from April's NATO summit in Washington was an escalation of the air war to target Belgrade itself. Clinton, Cohen, and Shelton were still convinced that Milosevic could be forced to back down if a sustained bombing campaign was given long enough to work. Blair had dropped his opposition to attacking civilian structures because of the adverse publicity it would attract, but by late April, the British government was so desperate for success that it effectively ceded control of the air war to Washington. To circumvent NATO's cumbersome planning structure, where all nineteen member states had to authorize proposed bombing targets, the Americans set up their own targeting team, which no longer provided the other NATO countries— including Britain, Washington's closest ally—with details of its plans.

On May 7, the difficulties of waging war by airpower alone were brought home in graphic detail when a U.S. B-2 stealth bomber accidentally bombed the Chinese embassy in Belgrade. The Americans had targeted the Hotel Yugoslavia, the base of Arkan, the well-known Yugoslav war criminal. Both the White House and Downing Street sent hurried notes to Beijing, apologizing for the error, but the bombing was yet another public relations disaster that played into the hands of those who opposed the war. In the House of Commons, NATO became an object of ridicule when one MP pointed out that "the greatest military alliance in the world cannot shoot straight."[48] To prove the point, the following day NATO bombs killed eighty Kosovan refugees at the village of Korisa.

Relations between Clinton and Blair became increasingly strained the longer the war continued. In mid-May, Blair made his second visit to the "front line" to meet Kosovan refugees in Albania, where the British prime minister met with refugees who claimed that they had been abused and beaten by the Serbs. Blair again compared the plight of the Kosovars with that of the Jews in the Holocaust. In Washington, Clinton was becoming vexed as Blair's hard-line approach continued to dominate the headlines. In one lengthy telephone conversation, the president suggested that the prime minister "pull himself together" and halt the "domestic grandstanding" that, Clinton said, was threatening to tear NATO apart.

Blair was under mounting pressure at home as well. Sir Richard Wilson, the cabinet secretary, felt compelled to caution the prime minister that the conflict could still go "badly wrong" and that Blair had placed himself in a "very dangerous" position. Wilson based his comments on the fact that the war was being conducted without UN consent and in a manner for which NATO had not been designed. NATO had been constructed for the defense of Europe, and it was ill equipped for offensive operations such as those being conducted in Kosovo. As the bombing raids showed no sign of delivering victory, Wilson confided to his colleagues that the war could destroy Blair's premiership. Blair himself was coming to a similar conclusion, and again voiced the concern to his aides that "This could be the end of me."[49] A coalition of British war-opponents from the Tory right took the pragmatic view that it was not in Britain's national interest to wage war in the Balkans. The hard left of the Labour Party denounced the NATO bombing raids as war crimes.

The pressure on Blair resulted in some heated exchanges with Clinton. A lead article in the *Financial Times* on May 17 was deeply critical of the American president's apparent inability to commit ground troops. "Mr. Clinton's prevarication about offering the U.S. troops that are vital to a successful outcome has left time on Mr. Milosevic's side," it read.[50] The *New York Times* castigated Clinton for not demonstrating stronger leadership. According to one Downing Street aide, the White House "went ballistic" the morning the *New York Times* piece appeared. Sandy Berger called London to complain that the article was the work of Alastair Campbell, Blair's redoubtable spin doctor.

A few hours later, Clinton phoned Blair and went into one of his infamous rages. "It was a Sunday evening in Downing Street and there weren't many people around," recalled one of Blair's aides. "Clinton started talking as though he was reading from a prompt card. Then he went off the script and started talking about how much pleasure it must give us in Britain to read all the negative headlines he was receiving in America.

And then he just lost it. The language he used was really quite colorful." The conversation lasted ninety minutes, and Clinton berated Blair for not doing more to control his spin doctors. "Get your people under control," Clinton screamed at Blair. "This briefing has got to stop." The main object of Clinton's ire was Campbell, who, fortunately for Blair, was not in the room.[51]

Clinton lectured Blair that it was not helpful for the transatlantic alliance for Britain to air its differences with Washington in public; their differences must be kept private. Washington was happy to have Britain as an ally, but only so long as Britain followed Washington's agenda. Clinton told Blair that he was personally hurt by the adverse criticism. "I am sure it gives you and your people a lot of pleasure to see me down," he said, making a thinly veiled criticism of Alastair Campbell. Blair required all his persuasion skills to calm down the enraged American president, and managed to conclude the conversation by making Clinton focus on the task in hand. "We've got to get this sorted," Blair told Clinton. "We can't let this drag on."[52]

The row with Clinton marked a watershed in Blair's relations with the president. As the conflict progressed, Blair became more and more frustrated with what he regarded as Clinton's refusal to commit himself to a firm course of action. Blair's disillusionment with Clinton was all the stronger for the fact that they had developed such a close working relationship in the past. Clinton had been a role model for Blair's New Labour election machine, and the two men had worked closely on promoting the "Third Way" political agenda. Now Blair regarded Clinton in a different light. He saw Clinton's inability to decide whether Kosovo was an opportunity to rise above his battles with his domestic critics or a political liability. The Downing Street camp formed the view that Clinton had been demoralized and weakened by his yearlong impeachment battle over the Lewinsky affair. Throughout the conflict, Clinton appeared to be more concerned with what his focus groups were telling him than the mounting humanitarian tragedy unfolding on Kosovo's borders. As one of Blair's top military officers during the war later commented, "Blair never entertained the same confidence about Clinton after the war as he did before it."[53]

The tension between Blair and Clinton was not helped by the fact that the White House did not keep Downing Street fully informed of its conduct in the war. "The Americans were not being straight with us about the impact the bombing was having on the war, which led us to conclude that it was worse than was, in fact, the case," said a key Downing Street aide. Washington invested a great deal of effort in persuading Russian president Boris Yeltsin to bring pressure to bear on Milosevic. In many respects, Washington regarded Russia as being of equal importance to Britain in resolving the Kosovo conflict. Blair's public gestures of defiance and saber rattling helped to maintain pressure on Belgrade, but in terms of getting the message through to Milosevic that this was a conflict he could not win, Russian involvement was crucial. On the same day the NATO summit ended in Washington, President Yeltsin called Clinton to discuss their strategy on Kosovo. Yeltsin had already appointed Viktor Chernomyrdin, his pro-Western former prime minister, as his special envoy to the Balkans. He worked closely with Strobe Talbott, U.S. deputy secretary of state, and Martti Ahtisaari, the Finnish president. Blair was not directly involved in this joint diplomatic initiative, although the Foreign Office received regular briefings. Washington wanted Moscow to make it clear to Milosevic that he could not rely on Russian support, and that the Russians would not intervene if NATO launched a ground invasion.

Blair was wary of Clinton's collaboration with Moscow, and suspected that he might cut a deal which would end hostilities without resolving the Kosovo issue. In early May, Blair sent Cook to Washington. One of Blair's close advisors recorded his reaction to the suggestion that Clinton might do such a deal. "If he does that, that's it. I'm finished with him."[54] While Clinton concentrated much of his effort on cajoling the Russians to exert their influence on Milosevic, Blair invested all his diplomatic effort on assembling an invasion force for Kosovo. On May 17, Robin Cook flew to Brussels in an attempt to persuade the other NATO members that a force could be deployed in Kosovo before the Serb forces had surrendered. He met stiff resistance from the Italians and Germans, with Gerhard Schröder publicly stating that talk of ground troops was "unthinkable." Meanwhile, Guthrie and other senior British officers were cautioning Blair against half measures. In Guthrie's view, the Serbs were overrated as soldiers and could be easily defeated in a summer campaign. But to achieve that, an army in excess of one hundred thousand would be necessary, and a decision would have to be taken soon if a force was going to be deployed in the summer of 1999.

In late May, Blair ordered the activation of a plan drawn up for British commanders to send a NATO force into Kosovo. Another plan to invade Serbia itself was considered far too dangerous. With few of Blair's European partners willing to support the plan, the British prime minister declared himself ready to provide the lion's share of the proposed force. Britain was prepared to commit fifty thousand of its troops—effectively, the entire combat army and, without doubt, the largest British force assembled since 1945. This was an enormous gamble on Blair's part. It demonstrated that he had the courage to back his moral conviction that the war was justified. But it also showed a recklessness that a more experienced politician might have avoided. William Cohen, the U.S. defense secretary, was stunned when George Robertson, his British counterpart, informed him on May 27 that Britain was ready to commit so many troops to the Kosovo campaign. Clinton was impressed by Blair's determination, and assured him that if a ground invasion became necessary, the United States would give its full support.

The invasion of Kosovo was not necessary after all. On June 2, Viktor Chernomyrdin and Martii Ahtisaari traveled to Belgrade to present yet another ultimatum to Milosevic. Chernomyrdin informed Milosevic that Moscow was fully backing NATO's demand for the withdrawal of all Russian troops from Kosovo and for the refugees to be allowed to return to their homes. None of the NATO leaders had any realistic expectation that Milosevic would agree. So, it was with considerable surprise and relief that Blair, who was attending a meeting of European leaders in Berlin, received the news that the Serb parliament had accepted NATO's demands. At first, Blair and his colleagues were suspicious. Was this just another delaying tactic by Milosevic? Blair wanted verification of Milosevic's intentions before he would accept that the conflict was over. When Joschka Fischer, the German foreign minister, produced a bottle of champagne to celebrate, Robin Cook insisted on diluting his with orange juice.

He would only drink an undiluted toast when the first Kosovar refugee returned home.

Blair's instincts proved right. When General Sir Mike Jackson, the British commander in charge of the NATO invasion force, met with Milosevic's generals to discuss the Serb withdrawal from Kosovo, the talks broke down over the Serbs' demand to maintain a military presence in the province. NATO bombing continued for another two days, until June 9, when Milosevic ordered his generals to agree to NATO's demands for a complete Serb withdrawal from Kosovo. The UN then passed Security Council Resolution 1244, which authorized the deployment of NATO troops in Kosovo to supervise the return of the refugees. The conflict was effectively at an end. There was one last hiccup when three hundred Russian troops, taking advantage of the NATO force's hesitation in entering Kosovo, took control of the international airport at Pristina, the Kosovan capital. "Operation Agricola," as it was called, was due to start at dawn on June 11, but it was delayed for twenty-four hours because Wesley Clark wanted U.S. Marines, who were still in Greece, to be part of the invasion force. Clark ordered Jackson to remove them by force, but Jackson, thinking it madness to take on the Russians, passed on his concerns to Guthrie, who then passed them on to Blair. The prime minister agreed that it was in no one's interests to "start World War Three," and Jackson was ordered to remove his men. George Robertson telephoned Clark and informed him that if he issued the order to attack the Russians, Britain would veto it.

The end of the Kosovo conflict was a momentous, and seminal, event in Blair's political career. Never before had he deliberately placed himself in such a vulnerable position in pursuit of his principles. He had found himself isolated within the Western alliance, isolated within his own party, and had stretched his hitherto close relationship with the White House to a breaking point. As his biographer Anthony Seldon wrote, the Kosovo conflict "took him to the very brink of his self-belief and his ability to endure stress. He had never before felt so much weight on his shoulders."[55] Although the end of the conflict came as a great relief, Blair was in no mood to celebrate his personal victory. "I feel no sense of triumph. We end it with no sense of rejoicing," Blair said when he addressed the media outside Downing Street the following day. "Nothing we can say or do can compensate for the loss of the loved ones killed in this conflict . . . War is never civilized. The innocent die as well as the guilty. But war can be necessary to uphold civilization. Good has triumphed over evil. Justice has overcome barbarism. And the values of civilization have prevailed."[56]

Blair remained convinced that the genuine threat of a NATO invasion force entering Kosovo was the deciding factor in persuading Milosevic to capitulate. Certainly that was the widely held view among British diplomats. "The Americans were very reluctant to accept the fact that had it not been for the threat of ground troops Milosevic would never have capitulated," said a senior Downing Street advisor. "By the time Chernomyrdin arrived in Belgrade, the Russians were convinced that NATO was about to launch a ground offensive. They told this to Milosevic, and they also told him that, if this happened, they would not intervene. This was undoubtedly the tipping point in the war, when Milosevic realized that the game was up."[57]

Downing Street's view was not shared by the Clinton administration. In his memoirs, Clinton wrote that, while Sandy Berger was examining the possibility of sending in ground troops in support of a NATO force "if it became clear that the air campaign wasn't going to prevail," the American president "still believed the air war would succeed."[58] When Milosevic finally gave in, Clinton had no doubt that "the punishing bombing raids on the Serbs finally broke Milosevic's will to resist."[59] Clinton cites the eminent British military historian Sir John Keegan in defense of his argument that the bombing campaign, allied with Russian diplomacy, won the war. "The success of the air campaign in Kosovo marked a new chapter in military history," Clinton concluded.[60] Although the war succeeded in its primary objectives of forcing a Serb withdrawal from Kosovo and ending the ethnic cleansing, it could not be described as an unqualified success. When NATO forces finally entered Kosovo, they found that most of the Serbs' military infrastructure remained intact; most of NATO's bombs had missed their target. The refugee crisis caused by the war made more than a million people homeless, and a year after hostilities ceased, at least two hundred thousand Kosovars had still not returned to their homes.

Blair had learned many important lessons both about himself and his allies, which would determine his approach to future world crises. His relationship with Clinton would never be the same. On a personal level, the two men would remain friends, even after Clinton had left office, but Blair would never be able to trust the American president as a reliable ally. Blair had seen the reality of the so-called special relationship between Britain and America and found that the White House could ride over British interests. Blair had also found that his much-vaunted European allies were at best fair-weather friends, keeping a watchful eye on the political lifeboats to ensure their own survival if events became too tempestuous.

Even so, the experience strengthened Blair's belief in himself and his world outlook. The Chicago speech had set a template for Blair's approach to global troubleshooting. When, for example, in the summer 2000, a UN peacekeeping force in the African republic of Sierra Leone was threatened by a superior rebel force, Blair did not hesitate to send British troops to defend the government. Blair later justified British intervention on grounds similar to those he had set out in Chicago. "On Sierra Leone there were those who said: what's it got to do with us? But I am sure that Britain's and Europe's long-term interests in Africa are best served if we intervene . . . to do what we can to save African nations from barbarism and dictatorship. And be proud of it."

But it was in Kosovo that Blair learned the art of statesmanship. He learned how to manage the competing expectations of different world leaders. The conflict exposed deep divisions within NATO, particularly with the Americans, who had carried out the overwhelming majority of the bombing sorties, and the Europeans, in particular the French and Germans, who insisted on being involved in NATO's decision-making process without committing themselves militarily. But the biggest lesson Blair learned was about his own ability and judgment. He had led the way over Kosovo, and in his mind, he had triumphed. He had achieved victory despite the doubts expressed by his allies in Washington, his neighbors in Europe, and his colleagues in London. He had emerged from the war stronger and more confident, and determined to demonstrate his newfound prowess on the world stage.

But the maturing of Blair as a world leader was, as he later admitted, a painful experience. Kosovo was "very, very difficult," he recalled in a British newspaper interview two years later. "Kosovo was more difficult even than people thought at the time. For a time I was very, very isolated on that. I felt I was quite a long way out at the end of the branch. The country was obviously asking, why are you doing this? Our allies were very nervous about the question of ground troops, which I was convinced we had at least in principle to be prepared to use to get Milosevic to back down." For all the difficulties he encountered, however, Blair was clear in his own mind that the war was a just cause. On one level, said Blair, it was possible to argue that the war "was an act of self-interest, in the sense that I think had we not intervened in Kosovo there would have been serious consequences for Europe as a whole. But I'm frank about it, that's not what really motivated me during it . . . To allow genocide to happen right on our doorstep and do nothing about it would have been criminal on our part."[61] Doing the right thing was central to Blair's core belief. If he believed in the necessity of taking a certain course of action, he would do it, irrespective of the political consequences.

Five

CHANGING THE GUARD

———— ◂▸ ————

TONY BLAIR WAS ONE of the first world leaders to telephone his congratulations to George W. Bush after the U.S. Supreme Court finally declared him the winner of the 2000 U.S. presidential election. Most commentators had predicted that Al Gore, Clinton's former vice president, would win a narrow victory, which, in terms of ballots cast, would indeed have been the case had Gore managed to find the five hundred plus votes he needed to carry Florida. If Gore had succeeded in fulfilling Democrat expectations, then his victory margin over Bush would have been larger than Kennedy's over Nixon in 1960. But in mid-December, Blair was presented with the delicate task of conveying his congratulations to a new Republican president of the United States.

Ironically, on the day that the Supreme Court announced its decision, Blair was attending an address given by President Bill Clinton at Britain's Warwick University. Bill and Hillary were spending two days with the Blairs, staying the night at Chequers as part of their farewell presidential tour of Europe. Over dinner, Blair had quizzed Clinton about Bush and how he should deal with him. "Be his friend," Clinton replied without hesitation. "Be his best friend. Be the guy he turns to." Fortunately for Blair, he and Bush had a mutual acquaintance who had been able to break the ice beforehand. Bill Gammell, who ran a successful oil and gas exploration company, had been at school with Blair and knew Bush through the oil business. When it became clear that Bush was a real contender for the White House, Downing Street asked Gammell to put in a good word for Blair, to which he readily agreed. Gammell visited Downing Street and told Blair that Bush was straightforward and that, in spite of the negative headlines he was attracting, the prime minister would be able to work with him. Thus, when Blair called Bush soon after the Supreme Court judgment had been announced, the new American president's first words to the British prime minister were: "I believe you know my friend Bill Gammell."[1]

Blair had made a point of keeping his distance from both candidates during the 2000 presidential election campaign. The British prime minister did not want to repeat the offense John Major's government had caused Clinton when the British Conservative Party had worked with the Republicans to dig up compromising information about the American leader. Although Blair had met Al Gore, he had not built the same close relationship with him as he had done with Clinton. The Gore campaign had made a conscious decision to distance itself from Clinton, whom they regarded as damaged goods because of the Lewinsky affair. "Gore did not want to be seen as 'Clinton Two,' and we respected that," said a key Blair advisor. "And we were not very close to Gore anyway. We found him a bit distant."[2] Gordon Brown, the chancellor of the Exchequer, kept in touch with Bob Shrum, one of Gore's campaign advisors, while Philip Gould, Blair's private pollster, worked closely with Stan Greenberg, who had the same job for Clinton. Blair himself took a far more pragmatic view of the election. His primary concern was that he would be able to do business with the new occupant of the White House, whoever that might be.

Even so, Blair would have been aware that the main campaign slogan of the Bush camp was ABC—"Anything But Clinton." Certainly it was easier for Blair to establish some common ground with Clinton, the Oxford-educated Rhodes scholar, as distinct from the governor of Texas. But during their first telephone conversation on December 14, Bush made it clear that he did not have any problem with Blair's friendship with Clinton. Bush was going to run the White House his own way and it would bear little resemblance to Clinton's presidency. Blair was deeply relieved after his first telephone contact with Bush, even though the call ended with Blair none the wiser as to how his relationship with the new president was likely to develop.

"There was undoubtedly a degree of nervousness in Downing Street when Bush came in," said one of Blair's senior Downing Street officials. "But Blair was very upfront with him and made no bones about the fact that he was friends with Clinton and intended to remain so. But he said he looked forward to working with the new president, and that he looked forward to a good relationship. It was a bit like walking on eggshells to start with. After all, here was a Republican president in the White House, and the big question was how would he get on with a Labour prime minister?"[3]

Although Blair had kept his distance from the presidential election campaign, his advisors had taken the necessary precautions to prepare for the likelihood of a Bush victory. Sir Christopher Meyer, the British ambassador to Washington, had initiated contact with Bush in 1998, when he visited him at his Texas ranch. British diplomats pride themselves on being ahead of the game, and Meyer had been tipped that George W. Bush was considering the presidency. Meyer visited Bush again in 1999, soon after Bush had given his backing to Blair's campaign for a ground invasion of Kosovo. Meyer reported back to Downing Street that, although Bush lacked experience on foreign issues, he was street-wise, a shrewd political operator, and put a high price on loyalty. According to Meyer, who had taken up his post in Washington in 1997 when Clinton was still president, Downing Street, rather than the Foreign Office, had controlled relations with Washington ever since Blair was elected. Indeed, on his appointment, Meyer had been somewhat indelicately ordered by Jonathan Powell, Blair's chief of staff, to "get up the arse of the White House and stay there."[4] Even so, the British Foreign Office was aware that Blair's close association with Clinton might become a handicap if Bush won the election, and intense efforts were made to find out how the Bush camp really viewed Blair. Meyer personally raised his concerns with two of Bush's key aides—Karl Rove, his campaign manager, and Condoleezza Rice, his foreign affairs advisor. They reassured Meyer that they did not regard Blair's closeness to Clinton as a problem. On the contrary, he was informed that the steadfast displays of loyalty that Blair had shown Clinton—even during the humiliation of the impeachment proceedings—was something that Bush admired and, so far as Bush was concerned, he and Blair were starting with a clean slate.[5] As the election drew closer, Meyer repeatedly warned Downing Street during the summer and autumn of 2000 not to make Al Gore the only bet and to take Bush's chances seriously.

As a precaution, Blair's advisors invited the elder George Bush to pay a courtesy call on Downing Street while on a private visit to Britain in the late summer of 2000. The visit of the former American president, together with his son's confirmation as the official Republican candidate in the election, gave Blair the pretext he was looking for to make contact with George W. Bush. Blair wrote him a note saying how much he had enjoyed meeting his father, wished him well during the rigors of the election campaign that lay ahead, and expressed the hope that he would be able to meet the governor in person later in the year. Bush was delighted by Blair's overture and sent back a similarly anodyne reply. The Bush camp floated the idea of him visiting Europe before the November election, but the idea was dropped because of the negative press he received in Europe during the election campaign.

With Bush's victory confirmed, Blair's priority was to arrange a face-to-face meeting with the new president at the earliest available opportunity. Robin Cook, the foreign secretary, was dispatched to Washington in early January to meet Colin Powell, who had been appointed in place of Madeleine Albright at the State Department. Although Cook got along well with Powell, his meeting with Dick Cheney was more strained, and he came away with the distinct impression that not everyone in the new administration was well disposed toward the Clinton-loving Labour government in London. Cook's visit was quickly followed by Jonathan Powell and John Sawers, two of Blair's key Downing Street aides, who had a series of unpublicized meetings with key officials in Bush's new administration. While Powell and Sawers were doing the rounds, Meyer was pressing Condoleezza Rice for a firm date for Blair to meet with Bush. "We knew most of the people in the Bush team. The problem was that we did not know much about Bush himself," said one of Blair's aides.

"Personal relationships count for so much at this level, and we didn't know whether it was going to be possible to transfer the closeness that had existed between Blair and Clinton to Bush."[6]

President Jacques Chirac, in his capacity as acting president of the European Union, became the first European leader to meet the new president. The meeting, which took place in the French embassy in Washington, only lasted ten minutes, but it nevertheless served to increase the sense of neurosis that appeared to have taken over Downing Street. When Meyer again asked Rice to set a firm date, he was told that Bush's next major meeting with a foreign leader would be with President Vicente Fox of Mexico. Only then would the president be able to see Blair. Eventually, they agreed that Bush and Blair would have their first face-to-face meeting on February 23.

Apart from getting to know the new president, Blair was keen to discover precisely how the new administration intended to handle its relations with the rest of the world, what policies it would pursue, and how Britain and British interests would come together. During the campaign, Bush had avoided taking strong positions on foreign policy subjects that tended to divide Republicans. No one was sure whether Bush would follow in his father's footsteps in pursuing a multilateral foreign policy or side with his more isolationist cabinet members. As Bush assembled his foreign policy team, there was consternation in Downing Street, and a degree of confusion, about the attitude of the Bush presidency toward a number of issues. As one senior Bush administration advisor later conceded, "The whole approach of the new administration to foreign policy was pretty schizophrenic. One minute it seemed as though the White House would be heading towards a new area of isolationism, the next it wanted to lead the free world. It was really difficult for people outside the White House to work out what was going on."[7] One of Blair's senior Downing Street officials said, "Condi Rice had written articles that said they were not interested in nation-building, or getting involved in the world outside America. We didn't want Bush to be like Clinton after Somalia. It was not obvious to us that they would engage in the outside world."[8]

There were those, such as Paul Wolfowitz, the new deputy defense secretary, who took the view that in the aftermath of the Cold War,

America should use its position as the world's only superpower to be a force for good in the world, with the important caveat that America should only use its influence when it was clearly in its interests to do so. Wolfowitz, a veteran of the Reagan and first Bush administrations, was regarded as the ideological standard-bearer of the neoconservative intellectual movement associated with the Project for the New American Century, which was lobbying hard for the new president to undertake a number of radical foreign policy initiatives.

In their book *Present Dangers: Crisis and Opportunity in American Foreign and Defense Policy*, published in April 2000, Robert Kagan and William Kristol, two key founding members of the project, set out an ambitious program for dealing with the threat posed by such disparate countries as China, Russia, North Korea, Iran, and Iraq. China was "fast emerging as the greatest threat to American interests" while the "new realism" of Russian leaders offered both "dangers and opportunities" to the United States. In one chapter, Richard Perle, another veteran Reaganite, warned that Saddam Hussein was about to break free from the international constraints imposed on him at the end of the 1991 Gulf War and that, unless a concerted effort was made to remove him from power, "he will soon acquire weapons of mass destruction and fundamentally alter the strategic balance of the Middle East." Iran was regarded as "a supporter of terrorism, a destabilizing influence in the Middle East, and a potential nuclear power." North Korea was simply "very dangerous." According to the neocon worldview, previous American governments had a lamentable record in preventing the proliferation of weapons of mass destruction and long-range missiles, and plans for building a missile defense system to protect the United States from such attacks had been undermined by "disastrous inadequacy." The only references to Britain in this seminal work on neoconservatism was a critique of Britain's failure to confront Hitlerism in the 1930s. Britain's value as a key American ally in the twenty-first century was not considered a subject worthy of serious discourse.[9] Nor did the neocons show much interest in Blair, even though the worldview he espoused in his Chicago speech bore many similarities to neocon thinking. "He just wasn't really on our radar," said Bill Kristol.[10]

The neocons were just one among many powerful political lobby groups vying for influence in Washington, but many of their views would later inform the policies adopted by the Bush administration. Wolfowitz was to spend the next four years working for Donald Rumsfeld, who was returning to the job of defense secretary after twenty-four years. Rumsfeld, together with Dick Cheney, another veteran of a succession of Republican administrations, adopted a more self-interested view of the world than the neocons. Like the neocons, Cheney and Rumsfeld were in favor of asserting American supremacy, by military means if necessary, and ensuring that no other power emerged that would challenge American preeminence. But unlike the neocons, who possessed an almost missionary zeal to reform hostile and threatening regimes into democratic, pro-American governments, Rumsfeld did not want the U.S. military to become an international police force. There was yet another faction, led by Colin Powell and the State Department—and, to a lesser extent, the CIA—that still believed in the value of working closely with America's allies and giving due respect to long-standing international treaties and institutions.

Known collectively as "the Vulcans," the group of individuals that Bush had brought together to advise him on key areas of foreign policy brought much experience as well as ideology to the new administration. For all their differences, they were unanimous on one fundamental principle. "All the Vulcans believed that American ideals and power are, on the whole, a force for good in the world."[11] Certainly they made a deep impression on Blair and his officials at Downing Street, who duly noted that the Bush team was of a far higher caliber than its predecessor. "It was obvious to us that, with people like Powell, Rice, and Rumsfeld, this was a much more impressive group," said one Blair advisor.[12] The challenge facing Blair was to work out which of these competing factions had the ear of the president at any one time, and on which issue. The other difficulty Blair faced in befriending the new administration is that the more hawkish members of the administration, such as Vice President Dick Cheney, had close and long-standing ties with the British Conservative Party and were suspicious of Blair's left-of-center politics.

The one enigma among this high-powered galaxy of politicians appointed to key posts in the new Bush government was Dr. Condoleezza

Rice. Born in 1954 and raised in Birmingham, Alabama, under the shadow of segregation, Rice would emerge as Bush's most trusted foreign policy advisor and would act as his gatekeeper. An accomplished pianist, Rice often said that she had to be "twice as good" just to keep pace with her peers. A protégée of George Shultz, who had served as Ronald Reagan's secretary of state in the 1980s, and Brent Scowcroft, who had been the elder Bush's pragmatic national security advisor, Rice worked as a Soviet affairs advisor on the elder Bush's National Security Council. After Clinton's election in 1992, she returned to Stanford University in California, where she became the youngest, first female, and first nonwhite provost. She had worked as chief foreign policy advisor throughout Bush's presidential campaign. She became such a permanent fixture in the presidential inner circle that "the president and the first lady had in a sense become her family."[13]

Downing Street was aware that Rice had publicly criticized the Chicago speech Blair had made during the Kosovo conflict. Rice had opposed Blair's arguments for committing troops to Kosovo in the spring of 1999, although she supported the principle of tackling Milosevic. In a newspaper interview, she once recalled how, when she was a child in Alabama, one of her kindergarten classmates had been killed in a racial confrontation at a church, an incident that had left a deep impression on her. "I appreciate how far America has come, and that we are now a functioning multiethnic democracy. The reason to take on Milosevic was that he challenged what may be the most important principle for Europe going forward, which is that multiethnic groups can live together without threat to minorities."[14]

During the presidential election, however, both Rice and George W. Bush caused alarm in Downing Street when they suggested that American troops serving with the NATO peacekeeping force in Kosovo and Bosnia should be withdrawn. They argued that the Clinton administration had been "crisis-driven," with no proper strategic planning. They were particularly scathing of Clinton's dealings with Europe, where protracted negotiations often resulted in an unhappy compromise, as was demonstrated by Clinton's record in the Balkans. On issues such as missile defense, the International Criminal Court, the Kyoto Protocol, and

Iraq and Iran, Bush had little patience with the views of many European countries. Bush's view of the Europeans was that they were unwilling to recognize the importance of force in international relations and all too ready to appease dictators and weapons proliferators rather than confront them.[15] It was unclear precisely how the new administration viewed Britain, which traditionally had a foot in both camps. On Iraq and Kosovo, Blair had behaved in a very un-European manner, in that he had seen force as a first, not last, resort. But on other issues, such as Kyoto and the International Criminal Court, Blair's views were more in line with continental Europe than America. By criticizing Clinton's policies, Bush and Rice were, by implication, criticizing Blair, so the more Bush attacked Clinton, the more uncomfortable Blair felt.

In their increasingly frantic efforts to unravel the conflicting signals emanating from the Bush camp, Blair's Downing Street staff paid particular attention to an article Rice wrote for the January/February 2000 issue of the journal *Foreign Affairs*, called "Promoting the National Interest." Written when the election result was still unknown, Rice took issue with the Clintonian view that "the national interest is replaced with humanitarian interests or the interests of the international community." She was not interested in the multilateralism that was central to Blair's thinking. According to Rice's worldview, America should not get itself involved in humanitarian missions in far-flung lands: the Somalia debacle was a case in point. Rice used the same reasoning to justify her opposition to American involvement in the Kosovo crisis. In the future, she declared, a Republican administration would proceed "from the firm ground of the national interest, not from the interest of an illusory international community." So far as the new Bush administration was concerned, nation-building was not on their agenda.

In many respects, Rice's article reflected some, but by no means all, of the views espoused by neocon thinkers such as Kristol and Kagan. She set out two basic principles that she believed should underpin the foreign policy of a future Republican administration. The first was to ensure that "America's military can deter war, project power, and fight in defense of its interests if deterrence fails," and the other was "to promote economic growth and political openness by extending free trade and a stable international monetary system to all committed to these principles." Where Rice differed from the neocons was in her disinclination to let America take the lead in promoting democracy throughout the world. The neocons believed that if America took the lead in encouraging democracy, the world would be a safer place. This view derived from the success that had been achieved in countries as disparate as South Africa and Taiwan, where, the neocons were quick to point out, the successful transformation of those countries into internationally recognized functioning democracies had been accompanied by their governments disarming their weapons of mass destruction programs.[16]

Rice's view, as expounded in the *Foreign Affairs* article, was that it was not America's job alone to campaign for the spread of democracy, but that it should work closely with its Western allies to achieve these objectives. "Powerful secular trends are moving the world toward economic openness and—more unevenly—democracy and individual liberty," she wrote. So far as Rice was concerned, "the United States and its allies are on the right side of history." To ensure that the momentum for change was maintained, America should strengthen its ties with "the western hemisphere, which has too often been neglected as a vital area of U.S. interest."[17]

Bush prided himself on the quality of the people he had gathered around him, even if they did not necessarily agree with his viewpoint or the decisions he made. Donald Rumsfeld, for example, had clashed on various occasions with the elder George Bush, and Bush loyalists blamed Rumsfeld, when he was Gerald Ford's chief of staff in 1975, of depriving the elder Bush of the chance to run for vice president. But George W. Bush's primary aim was to build the strongest team available to him. And if Bush had wanted a quiet life, he would not have made Colin Powell his secretary of state. Powell was the scourge of the hawkish wing of the Republican Party, the architect of the "Powell doctrine," the result of his painful experience as a young army officer in Vietnam, which advocated the use of military force only when it was directed at securing identifiable and indisputable national interests.

At a White House press conference given shortly after he had appointed Rumsfeld to the Pentagon in late December 2000, Bush acknowledged that there were a number of strong personalities in his foreign policy team. "General Powell's a strong figure, and Dick Cheney's no shrinking violet, but neither is Don Rumsfeld, nor Condi Rice," he remarked. "I view the four as being able to complement each other. There's going to be disagreements. I hope there is disagreement, because I know that disagreement will be based on solid thought." Bush's approach to managing his headstrong cabinet was based on three principles: build a strong team, outline a clear vision and agenda, and stick to whatever position you take. Bush proved to be particularly stubborn when it came to implementing this last requirement, as his erstwhile allies were to discover in the buildup to the Iraq War.

British officials observed the assembly of the Bush administration with a sense of confusion, and a deepening concern that the cozy relationship between London and Washington during the Clinton presidency was about to unravel. The early indications emanating from Washington did nothing to put the Blair camp at their ease. Rice had already ruffled feathers in London by suggesting that, if elected, Bush would withdraw American troops serving with the NATO peacekeeping force in Kosovo. The new Bush team was determined to press ahead with the controversial National Missile Defense (NMD) system, which the Pentagon claimed would be able to protect the U.S. mainland from a limited strategic ballistic missile attack from a rogue state. The system relied heavily on radar tracking devices, and for Britain, its development would mean the construction of massive early-warning systems at the Fylingdales radar station in Yorkshire, on the eastern coast of Britain. There were grumblings among the more hawkish members of the Bush cabinet about the likely impact on NATO of Europe's attempts to build its own defense force, as proposed by Blair and Chirac during the 1998 St. Malo Anglo-French summit, which the White House regarded as a direct challenge to America's position as the world's sole superpower.

Bush's advisors wanted the new administration only to pursue policies that were directly in America's interests. Their main concern in early 2001 was how to tackle Russia and China, which they regarded as posing the biggest threat to American hegemony in the twenty-first century. Consequently, many of the issues that had absorbed the Clinton presidency, such as the Middle East and Northern Ireland, were downgraded. Washington privately informed Jonathan Powell, Blair's chief of staff, that they had little interest in continuing U.S. involvement in the Northern Ireland peace process, which they considered an exclusively British affair. The attitude of the new administration did not do it any favors during its first encounters with Washington's allies. George Robertson, the former British defense secretary who had been appointed NATO secretary-general in August 1999, took exception to Donald Rumsfeld's tone when they first met at a meeting of European defense ministers in Germany. Robertson's attempts at small talk got him nowhere, and he soon found himself being interrogated by Rumsfeld on European objections to the NMD project. Robertson later told his colleagues that Rumsfeld talked to the defense ministers as though he were shouting at neighbors over a garden fence.[18]

Blair invested an enormous amount of effort in planning his trip to meet Bush. He was well aware that Britain was very much the junior partner in the transatlantic relationship, and that an isolationist White House was perfectly capable of pursuing its foreign policy goals without British assistance. How well the alliance prospered in the years ahead would come down to the personal chemistry between Blair and Bush. If Blair could establish a strong personal bond with Bush, the rest would take care of itself. Sir Christopher Meyer, the British ambassador, privately coached Blair on how to deal with Bush. He told the prime minister that he should "play to his strengths, be informal, practical, and direct, and it'll work."[19] Blair tried to set the right tone for the trip by publicly stressing the importance of the transatlantic alliance. Europe and America needed to work closely together because "only bad people . . . the Saddam Husseins of the world" benefited when "we are apart." Blair's officials briefed British journalists that "we are proud to be America's closest allies" and that "we in Britain are uniquely placed to bring the United States and Europe together in a way that is to our mutual benefit."[20] As if to emphasize the point, shortly before Blair left for Washington, British and American warplanes bombed Iraqi military targets outside Baghdad.

Unbeknown to Blair, the new administration had already formed the view that Britain was likely to be its most important European ally. "We saw Britain in a different light to the rest of Europe," said a senior Bush aide. "To start with, Britain and America had this close relationship that went back to World War Two. Then on many of the key issues, such as Iraq and Kosovo, Britain was more in tune with thinking in Washington than it was with Europe. Therefore it made sense to continue doing business with a tried and tested ally."[21] Compared with Blair's efforts to befriend the new administration, the other European leaders were not exactly welcoming. French president Jacques Chirac was haughtily dismissive of the Republicans' isolationist tendencies, and openly critical of Bush's proposed missile defense system. Nor did Germany's Gerhard Schröder make any significant effort to embrace the new American government.

If Blair was aware of the Bush administration's welcoming disposition, he was disinclined to take it at face value. Such was his obsession with making the right impression on Bush that he had several discussions about what sort of present the British delegation should give the new president. Bush was known to be an admirer of Winston Churchill, and Blair's staff suggested presenting the president with a bust of the great British wartime leader. Blair, however, was concerned that the bust chosen was not of sufficiently high quality to adorn the Oval Office. Eventually, it was decided to borrow a bust sculpted by Sir Jacob Epstein in 1946 from the government's art collection, which was loaned to Bush for the duration of his presidency and was given pride of place in the Oval Office. In the meantime, Downing Street had a copy made of the final draft of the 1941 Atlantic charter and of a manuscript of suggested amendments handwritten by Churchill. Britain's famous war leader was to be a permanent fixture at the Bush White House.

Blair was to meet Bush at Camp David, the president's country retreat in Maryland. Before going to Camp David, Blair stopped in Washington, where he had a distinctly frosty encounter with Vice President Dick Cheney. Like Rumsfeld, Cheney was an experienced Washington operator who had most recently served as defense secretary under the first President Bush during the Gulf War. After the easygoing meetings Blair had enjoyed with Clinton, he found his first meeting with the high-ranking member of the new Bush administration an intimidating experience. "Cheney was not very clubbable," explained one of Blair's senior aides. "He liked to keep his own counsel, and he made no great effort to put people at their ease. We felt he was trying us out to see whether we were going to be a reliable ally or a liability."[22]

Accompanied by Lewis "Scooter" Libby, his chief of staff, Cheney pressed Blair hard on a number of issues. The main topics of discussion were National Missile Defense, Russia, the Balkans, and the Middle East. On Iraq and the Balkans, the British and Americans were basically in agreement. Cheney stressed how important the missile defense project was to Bush, even though its implementation was likely to destroy the long-standing Anti-Ballistic Missile (ABM) Treaty, the international framework for arms control that had been set up during the Cold War. Cheney wanted British support for the project, which presented Blair with a formidable political challenge, given that the proposed "son of Star Wars" system had already been heavily criticized in Europe for being both unnecessary and unworkable. Cheney also pressed Blair hard on the European defense initiative, leaving the British prime minister in no doubt that the new administration regarded the Anglo-French initiative as a dangerous development that could undermine the future effectiveness of NATO. Blair attempted to impress Cheney by extolling the virtues of Vladimir Putin, who had recently succeeded Boris Yeltsin as Russia's president and whom Blair had identified as someone that the West could do business with. But Cheney, a veteran of the Cold War, was unimpressed, and the Blair delegation came away from the meeting somewhat downcast. Cheney had left Blair with the distinct impression that, as an instinctive conservative with a realistic view of America's predominant world position, he had little time for the opinions, or contribution, of a left-leaning Labour leader from a small country in Europe. It was a view that would inform Blair's attitude in his future dealings with the American vice president.

Blair later blamed the difficulties he experienced during his first encounter with Cheney on the opposition Conservative Party, which retained close ties with the Republicans. "They've had poison poured in their ear by the present Conservative Party going over there and saying this is all about ripping apart NATO," he complained in a newspaper interview the following month. "Well, if we don't get involved in European defense, it will happen without Britain. Then those people who really may have an agenda to destroy NATO will have control of it."[23]

If Blair was downhearted after meeting Cheney, his spirits rose the minute he stepped off the U.S. Air Force helicopter at Camp David for his first face-to-face meeting with George W. Bush. Blair had been there many times before and was familiar with the surroundings, a rural idyll of wooden lodges and pine trees surrounded by guard posts bristling with communications antennae. Bush went out of his way to make Blair feel welcome, immediately informing him that he was the first world leader to visit the presidential retreat under the new administration. The atmosphere was deliberately informal, with Bush greeting Blair in chinos. Sir Christopher Meyer, the British ambassador, had tutored Blair on the need to be informal, and he quickly adjusted to the Bush camp. The proceedings began with a working lunch. The agenda had been carefully scripted beforehand by American and British officials, to ensure that the talks focused on issues that were of mutual concern and that any policy differences had been ironed out beforehand.

Bush set the tone by addressing Blair simply as Tony, and without indulging in small talk, the two men immediately set to work discussing a number of sensitive issues. The headline issues concerned America's determination to press ahead with the National Missile Defense (NMD) program, and the future of NATO. Blair found Bush a lot more accommodating than Cheney, and a deal was hatched whereby Blair would support the American initiative in return for Washington giving its approval to Europe's plans to set up its own defense force, on the clear understanding that such a force would neither undermine nor act independently of NATO. It was the defense deal that made all the headlines when the two men appeared at a joint press conference at the end of the twenty-four-hour summit, with both the *New York Times* and the *Washington Post* remarking that Mr. Bush's endorsement of Blair's plans for a European defense force could have been written by Downing Street.

Iraq was another important issue that was discussed at Camp David. Blair had been frustrated over Saddam's continued refusal to comply with the UN since the 1998 bombing raids during Operation Desert Fox. But as Clinton entered the twilight of his presidency, there was no compelling political will in Washington to tackle the Iraqi dictator, so by the time Bush came to power, Saddam's regime had spent nearly two years subverting the UN sanctions and using its illicit profits from oil smuggling to begin rearming. British diplomats had worked hard at the UN to secure a new Security Council resolution—Resolution 1224, which was passed in late 1999—that set up a new structure for weapons inspections. But the resolution was passed in the face of stiff opposition from the French, who were building up lucrative trading ties with Baghdad in spite of the continued existence of UN sanctions. And in the absence of much political will in Washington toward the end of the Clinton presidency to force Saddam to comply with the new inspections, the Iraq issue was allowed to drift to the extent that by early 2001 Saddam's regime was able to circumvent the sanctions almost at will.

At this stage, the Bush administration did not show much interest in tackling Saddam, even though some of the more hawkish members of the new government regarded Saddam as unfinished business from the previous Bush administration. During the meetings that British officials had with Condoleezza Rice prior to Blair's visit, the Americans stressed that they were looking to neutralize the situation in Iraq, and were not looking for confrontation. This was the line that Bush adopted with Blair at Camp David. Their objective was to tighten the sanctions against Baghdad and force Iraq to readmit UN weapons inspections. There was no agreement, even an understanding, about getting rid of Saddam, and hardly any mention was made of the Iraqi leader in the subsequent media briefings. "The main obsession of the Bush administration at Camp David was with their proposals for missile defense," said one of Blair's advisors at Camp David. "So far as Iraq was concerned, they simply wanted to find a way to stabilize the issue so that it did not dominate the agenda. To us Rice seemed far more concerned about China than the Islamic world."[24]

The sensitivity surrounding Iraq on both sides of the Atlantic was highlighted a few days after the summit ended, when Richard Perle, who was regarded as one of Bush's key defense policy advisors, declared, "The

Bush administration recognizes removing Saddam is the only way to solve the problem. I fully expect the U.K. will support and be part of it." Perle's remarks were immediately rejected by Geoff Hoon, who had replaced George Robertson as British defense secretary. "It isn't U.K. policy. Regime change has not been part of U.K. policy so far. We'd never argue the objective of our policy should be the removal of Saddam as such."

The main working sessions over, Blair's party was invited to relax at the more informal location of Laurel Cabin, Bush's private residence at the retreat, to allow the two sides to become better acquainted. By now, Blair had changed out of his suit into jeans, to match Bush's more informal style, and the two leaders went for a much-photographed walk in the woods during which they set the seal on the exclusive relationship that would have such a profound bearing on each man's personal and political destiny. Before setting off on their two-mile jaunt, Bush, wearing a brown leather bomber jacket and accompanied by his spaniel, Spot, stopped for a moment outside another cabin, called Holly. "This is where Prime Minister Winston Churchill, the first visitor to Camp David, stayed and it is a huge honor for me and Laura to welcome the current prime minister and his wife here." Asked how the two leaders were getting on, Bush replied simply: "Pretty darn good."

The day ended with Tony and Cherie Blair joining Bush and his wife, Laura, for a private dinner. If the prime minister was deeply satisfied with the way the meeting had gone, Mrs. Blair was less convinced. Cherie had found it harder to adjust to the new political climate in Washington. Not only had she developed a close personal relationship with former first lady Hillary Clinton, she had actively supported many of the social policies that had been advocated during their discussions on the politics of the Third Way. The Bush administration had made no secret of its disdain for Clinton's political style, and during its first few months in office seemed to go out of its way to overturn Clinton's political legacy, such as withdrawing U.S. participation from the Kyoto Protocol on global warming. Even so, Mrs. Blair put on a brave face and did her best to match her husband's enthusiasm for the Bushes, and after dinner, the two couples rejoined their aides in the Camp David cinema for a viewing of the Hollywood comedy *Meet the Parents,* starring Robert De Niro.

The summit was hailed as a triumph by both Bush and Blair. By the time they emerged before the cameras for their first joint press conference, they had taken the opportunity to look relaxed and comfortable in each other's company. Blair appeared in an open-necked shirt, while Bush wore a bomber jacket. The president was lavish in his praise for his British ally. He publicly praised Blair's charm, and the importance of the transatlantic alliance. Britain, said Bush, was "our strongest friend and ally," and Mr. Blair was a "pretty charming guy." The relationship between the United States and Britain was "an alliance that has made a huge difference in the world," he continued. "Ours will be a strong and good personal relationship and an alliance that will stand the test of time." Bush was keen to stress the personal dimension of the relationship he had developed with Blair. "He put a charm offensive on me and it worked," he said. Now, when he phoned Blair in the future, "there'll be a friend on the other end of the phone." The only awkward moment came when Bush was asked whether he and Blair had a personal interest in common. "Well, we both use Colgate toothpaste," the president replied, to Blair's obvious embarrassment. "They're going to wonder how you know that, George," Blair replied self-consciously. The toothpaste was provided to all the rooms at Camp David, and Bush thought he was making light of the question. As a consequence, the much-vaunted summit of the American and British leaders became known as the "Colgate Summit."

For Blair, the outcome of the Camp David talks could not have been better. His fear that his long-standing friendship with Bill Clinton might work to his detriment with the new administration had proved to be unfounded. Moreover, Blair had discovered that Bush was someone he enjoyed doing business with. Unlike dealing with Clinton, who always had one eye on his focus groups and the opinion polls, Bush liked to tackle an issue head-on, work out a solution, and then stick to it. On the flight home, Blair expressed his respect for the new American president, telling the accompanying group of British journalists that Bush was "impressive," was "really on the ball," and that he was "extremely bright." Blair told his aides that he was particularly impressed with Bush's mastery of a subject and his ability to grasp the key issues. This was an unfamiliar portrait of an American politician who had been cruelly lampooned in both America and Europe as a tongue-tied buffoon. It had been best articulated by the late-night talk-show host Jay Leno who, during the presidential election, had described the Bush-Cheney ticket as "the Wizard of Oz ticket"—one needed a brain, and the other a heart.

"We felt a sense of euphoria after that first meeting," explained one of Blair's advisors who accompanied him to Camp David. "It was crucial that Blair establish a close personal relationship with Bush, but we really had no idea whether it would come off. Bush had got a very bad press both in Europe and America during the election campaign, and we didn't really know what we were dealing with." What little they did know about Bush was that first impressions were important—"he made his mind up about people very quickly, as Jacques Chirac found to his cost," said Blair's aide. "Blair immediately made a favorable impression on him."[25]

"We found that Bush was very straightforward," said another close Blair aide. "You could put an argument to him in very strong terms and he will listen to you and then he will make his decision. He is also very canny. He lets people think he's a fool because it suits him. He is a warm person with a self-deprecating sense of humor, and he is always teasing those around him, including Blair." The Blair team came away from the summit impressed by Bush's intelligence and his self-confidence. "He had this really powerful team of foreign policy advisors around him, but he was not intimidated by them. The most striking thing for us was to find that Bush was nothing like the public image that had been created of him. He was smart and capable, and it was a great relief to all of us to find that he was someone we could work with."[26]

The challenge Blair faced was to work out exactly where Bush stood in relation to the highly opinionated and polarized team of advisors and officials that held key positions in his administration. Was Bush an internationalist, like Colin Powell, his secretary of state, or was he an old-fashioned Republican isolationist, like Cheney and Rumsfeld? Or did he share the utopian vision of the neocons who sought to exploit America's superpower status in order to mold the world in its image? Blair was none the wiser as to where Bush stood, and working out whose counsel the president was acting upon would be one of the more difficult challenges Blair would face in his dealings with Bush, particularly after 9/11.

Blair and Bush had established a good working relationship, but that did not mean that the Bush camp was not to pursue policies that made Blair uncomfortable. Blair's tacit support for NMD left him isolated from the rest of Europe, which preferred to stand by the disarmament provisions of the 1972 ABM Treaty rather than embark on another arms race. "Our view was very pragmatic," said one of Blair's negotiators. "We took the view that the British people would welcome the idea of having a system that would protect us from foreign attack, from a country like Iran or something like that."[27] Blair's concession to the Americans that the proposed European defense force would remain under NATO command upset the French, and the French defense ministry issued a statement in which it reaffirmed its commitment to a separate command structure for the so-called Euro Army.

During the next few months, as the Bush administration sought to distinguish itself from the Clinton era, it continued to announce policy decisions that provoked international criticism and a degree of hostility, starting with Bush's confirmation in March that the United States would not sign the Kyoto agreement. When Washington's chief representative at the talks tried to defend her position, declaring, "The Bush administration takes the issue of climate change seriously and we will not abdicate our responsibilities," she was booed by the other delegates and ministers. Similarly controversial decisions were taken on issues such as international law, disarmament, and free trade. No matter how controversial Washington's policy statements appeared, Blair studiously declined to criticize his new ally in public. In a British newspaper interview in March, Blair, fresh from his Camp David bonding session, declared: "I've been as pro-America a prime minister as is possible to have. There is not a single issue I can think of in which we haven't stood foursquare with America."[28]

Blair was unique among European leaders in refusing to criticize Washington in public, a lesson he had learned from the strains that had been placed on the transatlantic alliance during his disputes with Clinton over the conduct of the Kosovo War. Blair was determined to maintain his self-appointed position as the bridge builder between Europe and America. But it was not an approach that found much support among his European colleagues. Bush's insistence on developing the NMD program at the expense of the ABM Treaty, together with his refusal to sign the Kyoto Protocol, caused much disgruntlement in both Paris and Berlin. During a United States–European Union summit at Göteborg in June, Chirac and Schröder forcefully articulated their displeasure with the Bush administration. In private, Schröder vented his frustration with Blair's bridge-building activities. The problem with Blair's bridge, said Schröder, was that the traffic seemed to be going in only one direction.

There were undoubtedly occasions when Downing Street might have felt the same. But Blair preferred to stress the positives of his relationship with Bush, and could point to his tangible success in persuading the new American president to engage in a dialogue with the new Russian president, Vladimir Putin. Bush had been fascinated by Blair's enthusiasm for Putin during the Camp David talks, even though Cold War veterans of the administration, such as Cheney and Rumsfeld, remained skeptical of Russian motives. Bush, however, followed up on Blair's suggestion that Washington should explore the opportunities offered by the arrival of a new face at the Kremlin. The Bush administration had been lukewarm toward Moscow when it first came to power, giving the impression that it wanted to cut Russia down to size. The Russians, after all, presented the biggest obstacle to Bush's NMD scheme, and the more hawkish members of the administration were determined that their pet project should not be undermined by Russian support for the ABM Treaty. In March, Washington had risked a serious diplomatic breach with Moscow after it expelled fifty Russian diplomats whom it accused, correctly,[29] of being spies. Putin, who had spent most of his career working as a KGB officer in Eastern Europe, was talked out of responding to Bush by Blair during a European Union–Russia summit in Stockholm. Blair assured Putin that the United States did not intend a broader political message. At the same time, Blair continued his efforts to persuade Washington that Putin was serious about bringing Russia closer to the West.

Blair's quiet diplomacy paid off when Bush met Putin in the Slovenian capital Ljubljana in mid-June. The two men hit it off in spectacular fashion. Bush looked into the eyes of the former KGB adversary and "got a sense of his soul." At one point, Putin deliberately appealed to Bush's strong Christian conviction by showing him a crucifix his mother had given him that he had once lost and then found. "I sensed that we had the cross in common," said Bush. At the end of their meeting, Bush heaped praise on the Russian president, whom he described as a "paragon." He was a "remarkable and trustworthy" leader "who loves his country." He spoke of Russia as a "partner and ally," which in time could become a "strong partner and a friend." Bush's enthusiasm for Putin was not the result simply of Christian bonding. The meeting began a dialogue that would enable the United States to withdraw from the ABM Treaty the following year without causing an international crisis. The Russians, moreover, responded to the American challenge by negotiating significant cuts in both countries' strategic nuclear weapons arsenals. Bush's successful engagement with Putin was a diplomatic triumph for Blair, and a reproach to both Chirac and Schröder, who had studiously kept their distance from the Russian leader. The breakthrough certainly helped to refute Schröder's sarcastic remark that all the traffic on Blair's bridge went in one direction.

THE ONE SUBJECT THAT hardly featured in Blair's dialogue with Bush during the first half of 2001 was al-Qaeda and the terrorist activities of its leader, Osama bin Laden. Both Blair and Bush expressed their concerns about rogue states and the proliferation of nuclear weapons, but with the exception of Iraq, most of the Bush administration's early efforts were concentrated on implementing the NMD program. The subject of al-Qaeda had been included in a briefing that George Tenet, the CIA director, provided at a breakfast meeting during Blair's Camp David summit with Bush. "There was a general discussion about terrorism and al-Qaeda," said one of Blair's advisors. "But at this stage, Blair's main concern in this area was rogue states and the proliferation of WMD. Al-Qaeda was not seen as the great looming threat during the first half of the year. From what Tenet told us, it was simply a cause for concern."[30]

Blair was interested in the wider issues of Islamic terrorism, but al-Qaeda did not pose a direct threat to Britain. His focus was directed at dealing with rogue states such as Iraq, Iran, Libya, and North Korea, and preventing Pakistan from exporting its recently acquired nuclear technology to these rogue states.

In early 2001, Sandy Berger, Clinton's national security advisor, provided his successor, Condoleezza Rice, the customary handover briefing in which he told her that "she would be spending more time on terrorism and bin Laden than any other issue."[31] Tenet had made much the same point during his first briefing to Bush, Cheney, and Rice at Blair House, opposite the White House, just a few days before Bush's inauguration. Tenet highlighted al-Qaeda as one of three major threats to American security. Bin Laden's organization, said Tenet, posed a "tremendous threat" against the United States that had to be considered "immediate." There was no doubt that bin Laden was going to strike at U.S. interests in some form, but it was not clear when, where, or by what means. Tenet informed Bush that President Clinton had authorized no fewer than five separate intelligence orders to try to disrupt and destroy al-Qaeda. The other two threats facing the United States were identified by Tenet as the proliferation of weapons of mass destruction and the rise of China as a military power. Iraq was barely mentioned and did not feature as prominently on Tenet's list of threats.

Clinton said he personally emphasized the importance of the al-Qaeda threat when he met the then president-elect on December 19, 2000, at the White House. "I told him that based on the last eight years, I thought his biggest security problems, in order, would be Osama bin Laden and al-Qaeda; the absence of peace in the Middle East; the stand-off between nuclear powers India and Pakistan; and the ties of the Pakistanis to the Taliban and al-Qaeda . . . I said my biggest disappointment was not getting bin Laden . . . He listened to what I had to say without much comment, then changed the subject to how I did the job."[32]

Despite Tenet's graphic warnings about bin Laden, most of the Bush administration's effort against al-Qaeda until 9/11 was left in the hands of the departmental specialists, with no one taking overall responsibility, with the result that policy was implemented haphazardly. Paul O'Neil, the U.S. treasury secretary, even suspended American participation in international efforts to target al-Qaeda's financial resources. Whether it was because of the new administration's visceral unease about anything associated with the Clinton era, or because it was preoccupied with other policy issues, the Bush White House did not fully grasp the enormity of the threat posed by bin Laden's organization.

As Bush himself later admitted, before 9/11, bin Laden was not his focus or that of his national security team. "I knew he was a menace, and I knew he was a problem. I knew he was responsible, or we felt he was responsible, for the previous bombings that killed Americans." Throughout the summer of 2001, Rice's team at the National Security Council worked on developing a plan to eliminate al-Qaeda, but no formal recommendations were ever presented to Bush directly. "I know there was a plan in the works . . . I don't know how mature the plan was," said Bush. "I was prepared to look at a plan that would be a thoughtful plan that would bring him to justice, and would have given the order to do that. I have no hesitancy about going after him. But I didn't feel that sense of urgency, and my blood was not nearly as boiling" as it was after the 9/11 attacks.[33] In fact, throughout the summer of 2001 Condoleezza Rice had been overseeing a plan to revive a CIA plan to arm the Northern Alliance in Afghanistan to enable it to destroy al-Qaeda's infrastructure. A National Security Presidential Directive was due to go before Bush on September 10, 2001. But the details of these intelligence operations were not passed on to Downing Street. "We had a rough idea that they were working on various plans to capture bin Laden, and our intelligence people were also working on the same objective," said one of Blair's intelligence advisors. "But as no one knew where bin Laden was, we could not really take them seriously."[34]

The only point upon which Bush and his national security team were absolutely clear was that whatever action they took against bin Laden's al-Qaeda network, it would be markedly different from that of Clinton. The Bush team believed Clinton's response to bin Laden and to international terrorism, especially since the bombings of the American embassies in Kenya and Tanzania in 1998, had been so weak as to be provocative, a virtual invitation to launch another strike at the United States. "This antiseptic notion of launching a cruise missile into some guy's, you know, tent, really is a joke," Bush remarked. "I mean, people viewed that as the impotent America . . . It was clear that bin Laden felt emboldened and didn't feel threatened by the United States."[35]

Bush was referring to the bombing raids Clinton had launched against Sudan and Afghanistan in retaliation for the 1998 Africa bombings. In his testimony to the national commission set up to investigate al-Qaeda and the 9/11 attacks, Berger defended the bombings on the grounds that it was the "one time we had predictive, actionable intelligence as to bin Laden's whereabouts."[36] Whatever Bush said in public about Clinton's attempts to deal with bin Laden, he knew both from the private briefings he personally received from Clinton before his inauguration, and from other intelligence briefings his officials received, that the Clinton administration had engaged in a complex, but ultimately futile, quest to hunt down bin Laden. This continued right up to the moment that Bush won the 2000 presidential election. "Throughout this period, we were aware that the Republicans felt that Clinton was not really dealing with the issues, and that America's response to these terrorist attacks amounted to nothing more than a pinprick against the terror organizations," said a Downing Street official.[37]

After the embassy attacks, bin Laden continued to conduct terrorist operations that accounted for the deaths of about fifty American citizens. However, attempts to follow up the August 1998 cruise missile attacks with further military action against bin Laden's infrastructure were dropped on the advice of William Cohen, the defense secretary, and General Hugh Shelton, the chairman of the Joint Chiefs of Staff. They regarded the targets as nothing more than "jungle gym" camps that were not worthwhile targets for expensive missiles. Clinton was also aware of the negative publicity such attacks created, particularly after the international criticism he received over the bombing raids on Iraq in 1998 and Kosovo in 1999. If Clinton authorized more attacks against bin Laden and they missed their target, then they would most likely enhance bin Laden's stature and win him new recruits.[38]

Clinton primarily persuaded countries such as Pakistan and Saudi Arabia to put pressure on the Taliban to expel bin Laden from Afghanistan. In November 1999, Washington succeeded in persuading the UN to impose sanctions on the Taliban regime. On several occasions, Clinton received intelligence reports that claimed to have identified bin Laden's whereabouts, and in late December 1998, Clinton had actually signed a Memorandum of Notification, authorizing the CIA to assassinate bin Laden if his capture was not judged feasible.[39] But a planned attack against bin Laden's house in the Afghan city of Kandahar was called off for fear of inflicting heavy civilian casualties. Other attempts to target bin Laden directly were called off because U.S. intelligence did not have sufficient information to precisely pinpoint his whereabouts.

Despite the considerable resources Clinton invested in tracking down bin Laden, al-Qaeda remained a serious terrorist threat. It is now known that the seeds of the 9/11 attacks were sown during a meeting bin Laden held with his senior aides at Kandahar in the spring of 1999. The proposed targets included the White House, the U.S. Capitol, the Pentagon, and the World Trade Center. Although the precise details of the plot were unknown to U.S. intelligence agencies, there were reports of possible attacks being prepared by bin Laden throughout 1999. They included a threat to blow up the FBI building in Washington and to attack a flight out of either Los Angeles or New York. At the end of 1999, there were plans by al-Qaeda to conduct terrorist attacks against the United States during the millennium celebrations. The enhanced counterterrorism operations set up by Clinton in response to the Africa embassy bombings meant that many of these plots were uncovered and the perpetrators arrested. The first serious attempt by al-Qaeda to launch a direct terror attack against the United States did not come until January 2000, when one of bin Laden's teams attempted to attack a U.S. warship off the Yemeni port of Aden. The attack failed when the suicide boat sank. They were more successful nine months later, when, on October 12, 2000, al-Qaeda operatives, using a small boat laden with explosives, attacked the U.S. Navy destroyer, the USS *Cole*, as it lay at anchor in Aden. The blast ripped a hole in the side of the *Cole*, killing seventeen members of the ship's crew and wounding at least forty others.

In the immediate aftermath of the attack, which took place during the final stages of the 2000 presidential election campaign, President Clinton was hampered from taking immediate retaliatory action by the lack of firm evidence that bin Laden was responsible for the attack. As Clinton himself told the 9/11 Commission, before he could "launch further attacks on al-Qaeda in Afghanistan, or deliver an ultimatum to the Taliban threatening strikes if they did not immediately expel bin Laden, the CIA or the FBI had to be sure enough that they would 'be willing to stand up in public and say, we believe that he (bin Laden) did this.' " By the time Clinton left office, the intelligence agencies had strong suspicions but had reached "no conclusion . . . that it was al-Qaeda."[40] The attack on the USS *Cole* was discussed in December, when Bush met with Clinton for a two-hour, one-on-one discussion of national security and foreign policy challenges. Clinton told Bush, "One of the great regrets of my presidency is that I didn't get him (bin Laden) for you, because I tried to."[41]

In late January 2001, after Bush officially arrived at the White House, the CIA briefed senior officials in the new administration on al-Qaeda and the attack on the USS *Cole*. This included the "preliminary judgment" that al-Qaeda was responsible, with the caveat that no evidence had yet been found that bin Laden himself ordered the attack. Richard A. Clarke, who had served as Clinton's counterterrorism chief and was, by his own admission, "obsessed" with bin Laden,[42] had retained his position following the Bush handover on the recommendation of Condoleezza Rice. He continued to pursue his obsession by trying to persuade Bush's team to respond to the USS *Cole* attack. Clarke was convinced of al-Qaeda's culpability, even though the CIA could not provide the evidence to support his claim. Clarke was convinced that al-Qaeda had a number of "sleeper" cells in the United States that were preparing to attack the White House.

At the time of the attack on the USS *Cole*, Bush had said in an interview with CNN, "I hope we can gather enough intelligence to figure out who did the act and take the necessary action. There must be a consequence."[43] In the absence of firm evidence of bin Laden's involvement, Bush was reluctant to act "lest an ineffectual air strike just serve to give bin Laden a propaganda advantage." For the United States to act effectively against the Taliban, ground forces would need to be deployed.[44]

Rather than retaliate directly for the attack on the *Cole*, the new administration intended to adopt a new, more aggressive strategy against al-Qaeda. By June, Rice had drawn up the first draft of a new presidential directive, which was described as an "admittedly ambitious" program for confronting al-Qaeda. The goal was to "eliminate the al-Qaeda network of terrorist groups as a threat to the United States and to friendly governments." Clarke claimed the directive was a reworked version of proposals he had made to the new administration in December 2000. He asked to be moved from his counterterrorism post, claiming that the Bush administration was not "serious about al-Qaeda."

Blair was aware of the general threat posed by bin Laden and al-Qaeda, and had condemned al-Qaeda's attacks against American facilities. But Washington's war against al-Qaeda was, at this stage, very much an American affair, and Downing Street's involvement was at best peripheral. The Foreign Office was active in supporting Washington's diplomatic efforts to persuade various governments to apply pressure on the Taliban to expel bin Laden from Afghanistan. But Britain was not involved in planning the covert operations to capture or kill bin Laden, and on several occasions was not even informed that they were taking place.[45] Britain's main contribution was to assist Washington with its intelligence-gathering activities, particularly with its efforts to locate bin Laden's hideaway and monitor al-Qaeda's attempts to procure WMD. While, in Washington, Richard A. Clarke was talking in apocalyptic terms about al-Qaeda, British intelligence took a more measured view of bin Laden's terrorism potential. "In London, there was no Richard A. Clarke running around the place telling us we had got it all wrong on al-Qaeda," said one of Blair's aides.[46] In January 2001, SIS provided Downing Street with an intelligence assessment of bin Laden's activities in which it claimed "the actual threat (posed by al-Qaeda) does not match the media hype." While bin Laden was known to want to acquire WMD, and had the funds to do so, SIS did not regard al-Qaeda as a direct threat to Britain. "Their resources and targets tend to be abroad rather than in Britain, so the risk of attacks using toxic materials has always been greater overseas."[47]

Rather than targeting bin Laden, Blair concerned himself with tackling those states and individuals that might provide bin Laden with the

WMD he so desperately sought. In this respect, for the first few months of Bush's presidency Blair concentrated his energy on maintaining the tough sanctions against Iraq until Saddam Hussein had fully complied with his disarmament program. British and American warplanes continued to patrol the no-fly zones in northern and southern Iraq, while British diplomats worked hard with their American counterparts to get new resolutions introduced at the UN Security Council, often to no avail. The Iraq issue had been discussed during Blair's Camp David summit, and Bush was determined to stiffen the sanctions against Baghdad. Both men agreed that the current sanctions were not working, and Bush had told Blair he wanted to warn Saddam not to test Washington's will. The subject was frequently discussed during Rice's almost daily telephone conversations with David Manning, who replaced John Sawers as Blair's foreign policy advisor in the summer of 2001. But progress was slow. "Pre-9/11 Washington's main fixation was missile defense and China. Nothing else seemed to matter," said a Blair aide.[48] As with the plan to eradicate al-Qaeda, the Bush administration would act on Iraq when it was ready.

Apart from the intermittent intelligence briefings on al-Qaeda and bin Laden, Blair received a constant stream of intelligence reports on the proliferation of WMD. The reports relating to Iraq were particularly alarming. In May 2001, SIS reported to Downing Street: "There is evidence of increased activity at Iraq's only remaining nuclear facility and a growing number of reports on possible nuclear-related procurement. We judge but cannot confirm that Iraq is conducting nuclear-related research . . . and could have longer-term plans to produce enriched uranium for a weapon. If successful, this could reduce the time needed to develop a nuclear warhead once sanctions were lifted."[49] The report noted that Saddam had recalled Iraq's nuclear scientists, and was attempting to purchase uranium ore from Niger, which had been one of Iraq's main suppliers in the 1970s when Saddam first embarked on his attempts to build an atom bomb. SIS identified similar patterns of activity in Saddam's biological and chemical programs, and concluded that Iraq "retains equipment and materials" for biological weapons, and "retains some production equipment, stocks of CW (chemical weapons) precursors, agent, and weapons." SIS's most confident reports concerned Saddam's ballistic missile program, where "we know that Iraq is developing longer-range systems, possibly up to 2,000 km," which would enable Saddam to fire WMD at targets such as Israel and NATO bases in southern Europe.[50]

In the spring of 2001, however, Blair had other matters to contend with as he prepared to seek reelection for a second five-year term as prime minister. While he had undoubtedly grown in stature as a world statesman during his first four years in office, his domestic popularity had eroded. Many traditional Labour voters were disillusioned over the government's failure to deliver on a wide range of social domestic issues. Blair was accused of being more concerned with winning a second term in office than with the policies he had been elected to implement, such as the wholesale reform of Britain's crumbling public services and transportation system. The election, which had initially been planned for May, had already been postponed because of a nationwide outbreak of foot-and-mouth disease that had decimated Britain's cattle industry. With this coming after a nationwide protest the previous autumn over soaring gas prices blamed on government stealth taxes, Blair's reputation for managerial efficiency had taken a battering. Even so, owing more to the paucity of the opposition than his own popularity, on June 8, 2001, Blair secured a second landslide victory.

While Blair's victory had been widely predicted, the appointments he made the morning after the election had not. Blair had always had a strained relationship with Robin Cook, who came from the traditional left of the Labour Party and who, a decade earlier, had seen himself as a future party leader. As Blair's stature in world affairs increased, so Cook's had waned. He had enjoyed a revival in his standing during the Kosovo crisis, where his personal commitment to halting the humanitarian disaster in Kosovo was genuinely appreciated by Blair. But Cook, though a highly intelligent man, was not popular with his colleagues in the Foreign Office nor with the new Bush administration. Never one to keep his opinions to himself, Cook had been highly critical of Bush's refusal to sign the Kyoto Protocol. He had also publicly questioned the wisdom of Bush's NMD project. The more hawkish members of the Bush camp were already suspicious of having a left-leaning government in London as a key ally, and Cook's public pronouncements did nothing to allay their fears.

Having done at Camp David the hard work of persuading Bush that he was a trusted ally, Blair could not run the risk of keeping Cook at the Foreign Office. Cook's ambition of becoming Labour's longest-serving foreign secretary was lost the morning after the election, when he was called to Downing Street and told by Blair that he was being moved from the Foreign Office to the less high-profile position of leader of the House of Commons. Cook was replaced by Jack Straw, the former home secretary. Blair was not prepared to take any risks with his alliance with George Bush.

Blair next met Bush when the president visited Chequers for an overnight stay with the Blairs on July 19. By now, Bush knew that he was dealing with someone who would be Britain's prime minister for the rest of his first presidential term. Bush had been encouraged by his meeting with Putin the previous month, and was confident that he could clinch a missile defense deal by the end of the year. Blair had worked hard behind the scenes to bring Bush and Putin together, and credited himself with the success of Bush's meeting with Putin the month before. The main subjects of discussion at Chequers were Russian-related issues, such as how Moscow was likely to respond to Washington's NMD program and the preparations being made for the accession of the former Soviet Baltic republics to NATO. According to a senior Blair aide present at the talks, Iraq and al-Qaeda "barely featured." This was also the first time that David Manning, Blair's new foreign policy advisor, met with Rice. An indication of how far Blair had risen in Bush's regard in the six months the two leaders had been working together was seen the following day, when Bush and Blair gave a joint press conference at an RAF base before flying off to a G8 summit in Genoa. "The thing I appreciate about the prime minister is that he is willing to think anew as we head into the future," said Bush.

Not everyone in the Blair household, however, made the same impression on the American president. The previous night, over dinner at Chequers, Cherie Blair, who was making a name for herself as a human rights lawyer, directly challenged Bush's views on the death penalty. Judicial executions, she said, were an immoral violation of human rights and an affront to the fundamental principles of justice. Even though Blair shared his wife's opinion, he was far too diplomatic to say so himself. When he was later asked about the exchange, Blair referred to the iron rule about his dealings with the White House. "The thing about private conversations," he said, "is that they stay private."[51]

PART TWO

Six

APOCALYPSE

———————◆———————

AT LUNCHTIME ON TUESDAY, September 11, 2001, Tony Blair was sitting in a hotel suite in Brighton, putting the finishing touches to a speech that he was due to deliver later that afternoon at a conference of the Trades Union Congress. After his reelection the previous June, Blair was determined to press ahead with his reform program for Britain's public services, and union support was crucial if his policy were to succeed. He was working on the text with Alastair Campbell, his press secretary, when the television in the adjoining room began to broadcast pictures of the first plane crashing into the Twin Towers in New York. At first, Blair and his advisors were not sure what had happened, and the prime minister continued to work on his speech. It was only after the second plane hit the Twin Towers that the full enormity of what was happening on the eastern coast of the United States because clearer. Blair abandoned his speech and sped back to Downing Street for emergency talks with his senior colleagues and Britain's security chiefs.

While Blair was in Brighton, his officials in Downing Street were desperately trying to make contact with President Bush. The American president was visiting the Emma E. Booker Elementary School in Sarasota, Florida, to promote his education agenda when the attacks took place. Like Blair, Bush did not react immediately to the first attack on the Twin Towers, thinking it might be an accident. He did not fully grasp the enormity of what was taking place until he was informed by Andrew Card, his chief of staff, that a second hijacked plane had hit the South Tower. The later broadcast television footage of Bush sitting in the schoolroom, his hands neatly folded on his lap as he listened intently to what Card was saying, has become one of the enduring images of the 9/11 attacks. In an interview with Bob Woodward, the veteran *Washington Post* investigative reporter, Bush later said that he immediately understood the implications of the attacks. "They had declared war on us, and I made up my mind that moment that we were going to war."[1]

Fearing further attacks, Bush's security team wanted to fly the president to a secret destination as soon as possible, but before boarding Air Force One, Bush made a brief public statement. He was cautious, describing the morning's events as "an apparent terrorist attack," and vowed to deploy the full resources of the federal government to find "those folks who committed this act. Terrorism against our nation will not stand." Bush was then swept away in his motorcade to the local airport, where Air Force One was waiting to fly him to Offutt Air Force Base in Nebraska, the base of Strategic Command, which controls the nuclear weapons arsenal of the United States. It has a specially constructed nuclear bomb–proof shelter to protect the president. Before boarding the flight, Bush told his Secret Service agents to "be sure to get the first lady and my daughters protected."

With Bush on his way to Nebraska, Dick Cheney assumed control of the White House. Bush was in constant contact with Cheney from Air Force One, telling him simply, "We're at war."[2] Cheney himself had been taken by his Secret Service team from his West Wing office to the Presidential Emergency Operations Center, the emergency bunker beneath the grounds of the White House, which had been built during the Cold War. By now, a third American airliner had crashed into the Pentagon. Rumsfeld had been giving his daily intelligence briefing in his office when the hijacked plane struck the western face of the Pentagon. Rumsfeld's immediate response had been to rush to the scene of the devastation and help with the rescue effort, and his security detail had to persuade him to leave the area.

The attack on the Pentagon, together with the news that a fourth air-craft, believed to be headed toward the White House itself, had crashed in the Pennsylvania countryside, led Cheney to conclude that the terror-ists were attempting to decapitate the entire U.S. government. He con-tacted Bush on Air Force One and almost ordered him not to come back to Washington. Bush stopped for a brief layover in Louisiana, where he gave a less than convincing performance as he read another statement that was meant to reassure the American people. Looking red-eyed and mispronouncing several words, Bush did not come across as a confident commander-in-chief. "Make no mistake. We will show the world we will pass this test," he said, before continuing his journey to Nebraska.

During the chaotic aftermath of the 9/11 attacks, Blair had only the briefest contact with the American president. Before returning to Down-ing Street, he managed to get a telephone call through to Bush on Air Force One. "When we got through to Air Force One, we found that the president was rather disoriented, as we all were," said a senior Downing Street official who listened in on the conversation. "Bush was not sure if the attacks were going to continue, or what was going on. Blair was still stuck in Brighton and we needed to make sure that our own security ar-rangements were in place in case al-Qaeda was planning an attack against us as well."[3]

Bush was preoccupied with his security considerations, and Blair was on his own in deciding how Britain should respond to the biggest peace-time attack on the United States since Pearl Harbor during the Second World War. The decisions he would make in the next few hours as the world digested the enormity of the attacks in the United States would not only determine Britain's response, they would define his premiership. "Sometimes things happen in politics, an event that is so cataclysmic that, in a curious way, all the doubt is removed," Blair said when later recounting his immediate reaction to 9/11. "From the outset, I really felt very certain as to what had to be said and done."[4] An insight into pre-cisely how Blair was thinking in the hours immediately after the attacks was provided in the short speech he made to the Trades Union Congress before boarding the train back to London. Looking visibly shaken, he told the union officials that "there have been the most terrible, shocking events in the United States of America in the last hours . . . We can only imagine the terror and carnage there, and the many, many innocent people who have lost their lives. This mass terrorism is the new evil in our world today."

In Iraq in 1998, and in Kosovo the following year, Blair had drawn on a deep moral conviction to determine his actions. Unlike many European leaders, when dealing with threats to international security, Blair was inclined to confront issues directly rather than try to seek a compromise solution. And in his reaction to the 9/11 attacks, Blair was convinced from the outset that the perpetrators of the attacks should be confronted by whatever means necessary. Blair used the fifty-minute train journey from Brighton to London to collect his thoughts, to work out how Britain should best respond and how to handle Bush. "On the train . . . I could see what the terrorists would want was not merely to cause carnage by the original terrorist act, but to set in motion a series of events, including setting the Muslim world against America."[5] On arrival in London, Blair was met by a police escort that swept him into Downing Street, where he immediately convened a meeting of his top officials and intelligence chiefs.

The meeting took place at Cabinet Office Briefing Room A, or COBRA, the windowless, white-walled bunker deep beneath Whitehall, which is where the British government retreats in times of national emergency. The main purpose of the meeting was to assess the immediate threat posed to Britain, and afterwards Blair decided that he should immediately make a statement in support of the United States. In what was undoubtedly a visceral response to the attacks, Blair declared his intention to stand "shoulder to shoulder" with America. "This is not a battle between the U.S. and terrorism, but between the free and democratic world and terrorism. We, therefore, here in Britain, stand shoulder to shoulder with our American friends in this hour of tragedy, and we, like them, will not rest until this evil is driven from the world." Within hours of the 9/11 attacks, Blair had decided that Britain's fate was to be inseparably linked to the United States in the war against international terrorism. "When you look back, it was the obvious thing to do," said one of Blair's close aides. "I am sure the United States would have reacted in the same way if the terrorists had staged their attacks against Britain."[6]

As in Washington, the main concern in London in the hours immediately following the attacks was whether there would be further attacks against prominent targets. The Joint Intelligence Committee (JIC) was the body responsible for liaison between Downing Street and the British intelligence agencies, which provided Blair with his weekly intelligence reports. It had reported on July 16 that the al-Qaeda network, operating from bases in Afghanistan and beyond, was in the "final stages" of preparing a terrorist attack on the West. The JIC fulfills a similar function to the CIA in preparing the president's daily brief, a summary of the latest key intelligence findings.

The information that was passed to Blair by JIC on al-Qaeda at that time contained the latest intelligence assessments from the CIA.[7] As the *9/11 Commission Report* would later show, from the spring of 2001, the CIA was receiving a growing number of reports that al-Qaeda was planning a big attack. In May, the FBI had interviewed a "walk-in," a person offering to reveal information about bin Laden's activities, who claimed that there was a plan to launch attacks on London, Boston, and New York. According to George Tenet, the CIA's director, by July 2001 his organization was receiving so many warnings of a planned al-Qaeda attack that his organization's warning system "was blinking red."[8] At this stage, though, the CIA believed the most likely location for such attacks would be on the Arabian peninsula, or in Israel.

The JIC had advised Blair that the most likely targets would be Americans or Israelis. The main threat to British interests was "collateral damage in attacks on U.S. targets." As Parliament's Intelligence and Security Committee (ISC), which was asked by Blair to look into the intelligence available to him prior to 9/11, later concluded, the JIC assessment on al-Qaeda was "not a stark warning of immediate danger to the U.K."[9] On this assessment, Britain's intelligence services were proved to be correct.

But Blair was taking no chances. Throughout the rest of the day, Downing Street remained concerned that al-Qaeda would launch attacks against British targets. Westminster, Whitehall, the City, and Canary

Wharf, the new financial district in eastern London, were all identified as possible targets, as were the country's nuclear power stations. Contingency plans for terrorist attacks on Britain were implemented with immediate effect. City Airport, located a few miles from the Canary Wharf complex, was closed, and other commercial air traffic was diverted from flying over London. Admiral Sir Michael Boyce, who had replaced Charles Guthrie as chief of the defense staff, was authorized to give the order to shoot down any civilian airliner that breached the no-fly zone over London. Bush had given the same order to American fighter planes from Air Force One.

One of the biggest problems Blair had to consider with some urgency was to work out precisely how to tackle al-Qaeda, which soon emerged as the most likely culprit of the atrocity. Unlike the United States, where the CIA had set up a special bin Laden unit to track al-Qaeda's activities, the British authorities had not previously paid the same degree of attention to al-Qaeda. John Scarlett, the head of JIC, even suggested that there was a remote possibility that a far-right American militia group, such as the one responsible for the 1995 Oklahoma bombing, had carried out the attacks. Although Blair himself had taken a keen interest in nuclear proliferation and rogue states such as Iraq and Libya, he knew less about bin Laden, al-Qaeda, and the Taliban, as these were not subjects that took high priority in his weekly intelligence reports from JIC.[10] Downing Street's attitude toward al-Qaeda pre-9/11 was summed up by one of Blair's top aides, who remarked, "We thought that the Americans were rather obsessed with al-Qaeda, and that by keeping going on about it they were giving bin Laden a high profile that merely served to encourage him to undertake further acts of violence."[11] As the ISC investigation would later reveal, Downing Street was not helped by the fact that British intelligence had underestimated the threat bin Laden posed to Western security. "The scale of the threat and the vulnerability of Western states to terrorists with this degree of sophistication and a total disregard for their own lives was not understood," the report concluded.[12]

Blair ordered his intelligence experts to draw up a briefing document that provided a detailed explanation of al-Qaeda, its methods and objectives. The British government was playing catch with the world's deadliest terrorist organization. Downing Street was equally ignorant of the long-running civil war in Afghanistan, the organization of the Taliban and why it had developed such close ties with bin Laden. A copy of a recently published book on the Taliban by Ahmed Rashid was purchased and passed around among the Downing Street staff, which read it with avid interest.

The other issue that preoccupied Blair was how Bush and the United States would react to the attacks. With only intermittent communication possible with the distraught American president, Blair fretted that Washington would lash out indiscriminately at targets in the Middle East without having fully thought through the implications. One of Blair's ministers later recalled that for the first two or three days after 9/11, Blair was worried that Washington would launch an "immediate, inappropriate, and indiscriminate response."[13] The fact that Dick Cheney—regarded by some Downing Street officials as the éminence grise of the Bush administration—was running the White House did little to ally their anxiety. In the eight months since the Bush administration first assumed office, it had demonstrated impatience, bordering on contempt, for international institutions such as the UN, which it felt put intolerable constraints on America's national interests. On issues such as NMD, the Kyoto Protocol, and trade, Bush had ridden over the sensibilities of other allies and nations. Throughout the afternoon, Blair repeated time and again, "How is Bush going to react? What will he do?"[14] Was Bush going to "jump out of the international system" and go his own way in favor of unbridled revenge against his enemies, or could he be persuaded to work with NATO and the UN? Downing Street felt it was unlikely that Bush would strike at bin Laden himself, because Blair's officials were well aware that both British and American intelligence had no idea of his whereabouts. "We knew the Americans had been planning to take out bin Laden. But if their plans had been any good, they would have taken out bin Laden straight after 9/11. The fact that they didn't suggested to us that the plans were not very good," one of Blair's senior Downing Street advisors later recalled.[15]

While Bush was hidden away in Nebraska, Blair busied himself with contacting other world leaders, and during the evening, he spoke to German chancellor Gerhard Schröder, French president Jacques Chirac, and Russian president Vladimir Putin. The German and French leaders were unanimous at this stage in their support for America. For them, the 9/11 attacks were an outrage, a terrible act against humanity, not just against America. The French newspaper *Le Monde* even went so far as to declare in its front-page headline, *"Nous sommes tous des Américains!"* Putin was also very supportive. Mindful of his own fight against Islamic-sponsored terrorism in Chechnya, Putin was forthright in condemning the attacks. As Blair himself later recalled, "We supported America . . . We had no doubt at all that we had to get out there together and stand with America, get the menace and deal with it."[16] When the calls were completed, Blair realized there was little more he could do until he could consult with Bush, which he hoped to do the following morning. No one was in any doubt about the challenge they faced, least of all Blair.

In Nebraska, President Bush was gradually coming to terms with the implications of the attacks. Using the air base's video-conference facilities, Bush convened the first meeting of the National Security Council at 3.30 p.m. George Tenet, the CIA director, confirmed that bin Laden was almost certainly behind the attacks. Three known al-Qaeda operatives had been on American Airlines Flight 77, which had crashed into the Pentagon. One of the hijackers, Khalid al-Midhar, had even been on the FBI's domestic watch list. It was clear that there had been a major failure within the American intelligence community. Bush was becoming increasingly restless that he was far removed from the heart of government and, against the advice of his Secret Service team, insisted that he return to the White House as soon as possible.

Bush arrived back at the White House at 6.30 p.m. and wanted to give a speech that night to the nation, to reassure the American people. An initial draft of the speech contained the phrase "This is not an act of terrorism. This is an act of war." But Bush asked for it to be removed, because he wanted his message to be one of reassurance, not provocation. Even so, the seven-minute speech Bush made from the Oval Office later that evening contained a phrase that would define the American government's response to the 9/11 attacks and its conduct of the war on terror: "We will make no distinction between those who planned these attacks and those who harbor them." The sentence encapsulated what was to become the new Bush doctrine, one of the most significant foreign policy shifts Washington had taken in years. Echoing President Ronald Reagan's famous "You can run, but you can't hide" warning to a previous generation of Islamic terrorists, Bush was making a declaration of intent not only to pursue the terrorists responsible for the 9/11 attacks, but any country suspected of giving them support. Since the 1980s, the State Department had published an annual list of countries it suspected of sponsoring and supporting terror groups. Up to that point, these countries had been subject to economic, diplomatic, and military sanctions. From then on, they would be prime targets in the Bush administration's war on terror. That night, Bush wrote in his diary, "The Pearl Harbor of the 21st century took place today."

Bush started the following morning with an intelligence briefing from Tenet. Reports had arrived from Afghanistan overnight, stating that the terrorist attacks of the previous day had been planned for nearly two years. This and other intelligence proved conclusively, so far as Tenet was concerned, that al-Qaeda was responsible for the attacks. Bush told Tenet to start work on a plan to get bin Laden. Bush then convened a meeting of the National Security Council in the cabinet office. He had come to the conclusion that the time for reassuring the American public was past, and what was now required was action. So long as Washington developed a logical and coherent plan, Bush was confident that the rest of the world would "rally to our side." At the same time, he was determined not to allow the threat of terrorism to alter the way Americans lived their lives. "We have to prepare the public without alarming the public," he said.[17]

After the NSC meeting, Bush convened a meeting of the half-dozen key aides who would form his war cabinet and would be the principal architects of America's war against international terrorism. Among them was Colin Powell, who had been in Peru when the attacks happened. Powell had not been consulted about the apparent radical change in foreign policy, which the president had announced the previous night, and was anxious to ensure the administration picked the right target when it came to retaliation. Powell was already focused on Afghanistan and Pakistan. Afghanistan was effectively controlled by the Taliban, an extreme

Islamic fundamentalist group that had seized power in 1996 and had given refuge to bin Laden after his expulsion from Sudan. Pakistan's powerful intelligence service, the ISI, had helped create the Taliban and establish its power. Powell believed his first task should be to carry the president's message—you are either with us or against us—to Pakistan and the Taliban. Bush was insistent that he wanted a list of demands to be put to the Taliban. Handing over bin Laden was not good enough. At the very least, he wanted the entire al-Qaeda infrastructure thrown out of Afghanistan.[18]

Even at this early stage in planning Bush's response to 9/11, the more hawkish members of the administration were arguing in favor of broadening the forthcoming military campaign well beyond the confines of the Taliban and bin Laden. At that first war cabinet meeting, Rumsfeld asked whether the focus should be confined to al-Qaeda or broadened to cover terrorism more generally. "It is critical how we define goals at the start, because that's what the coalition signs on for," he argued. Powell responded by saying that while the goal was terrorism in the broadest sense, the priority should be to focus "first on the organization that acted yesterday." Rumsfeld's more expansive position was supported by Cheney. "To the extent we define our task broadly," he said, "including those who support terrorism, then we get at states. And it's easier to find them than it is to find bin Laden." The conversation concluded with Bush saying, "Start with bin Laden, which Americans expect. And then, if we succeed, we've struck a huge blow and can move forward."[19]

Later that day, at another meeting of the NSC, Rumsfeld revived the discussion by openly raising the question of whether Iraq should be included in the war aims. On the afternoon of September 11, when, with dust and smoke still filling the Pentagon's operations center, he had discussed with his staff the prospect of going after Iraq as a response to the terrorist attacks. According to Bob Woodward, Rumsfeld wrote himself a memo that stated: "hit S.H. (Saddam Hussein) @ same time—not only UBL (bin Laden)."[20] Rumsfeld asked Paul Wolfowitz, his deputy, to look into evidence about a possible link between Saddam and bin Laden. Rumsfeld also raised the subject directly with Bush at the NSC the following afternoon, when he asked if the terrorist attacks did not present an "opportunity" to launch a military offensive against Iraq. Powell immediately objected. "Any action needs public support. It's not just what the international coalition supports; it's what the American people want to support. The American people want us to do something about al-Qaeda."[21] Within twenty-four hours of the 9/11 attacks, deep divisions over how America should respond were emerging at the White House, divisions that would have a crucial bearing on Washington's prosecution of the war on terror.

Tony Blair had a more detailed discussion with Bush on Wednesday. Blair had met with his own war cabinet in the COBRA bunker, and the main topic of conversation was how he should handle the Americans. Blair had to take Clinton's advice and "get close" to Bush. If the future war on terror was going to be the defining event of Blair's premiership, the same was true of Bush's presidency, and there was genuine concern in London that Washington would simply go its own way, irrespective of the catastrophic consequences that this would have for the transatlantic alliance. After the meeting, Blair continued to worry about his phone call to Bush, and he wanted to be absolutely clear in his own mind about what action should and should not be taken in response to the 9/11 attacks. He had received the overnight intelligence brief on al-Qaeda and bin Laden, but still did not feel on top of the subject.

Unlike Bush, who had received numerous briefings on the al-Qaeda threat since he won the 2000 election, for Blair this was relatively new territory. To make sure he fully understood all the issues relating to al-Qaeda, Blair took advantage of the time difference between London and Washington to organize an emergency seminar on bin Laden. Sir Richard Dearlove, the head of SIS; John Scarlett, the JIC chairman; and other experts from the Foreign Office and Ministry of Defence came to Downing Street to help Blair grasp the enormity of the challenge he faced. The meeting was scheduled to last for just forty-five minutes, but Blair was so fixated on the issue that it went on for nearly two hours. By the end of it, Blair felt he understood fully what was at stake, and was better prepared to receive the all-important phone call from the American president.

"Tony Blair had an intuitive instinct for spotting issues important to him," Sir Richard Wilson, Blair's senior civil servant in Downing Street, drily observed.

Bush phoned Blair at 7.30 a.m. Washington time. Blair was gratified that Bush's first call to a foreign leader that morning was to Downing Street. Blair expressed his "shock and horror" at the attacks of the previous day, pledged his "total support" to the president, and said he assumed Bush was considering an immediate response. "Obviously, you know, we're thinking about that," Bush replied. Most European governments—including Blair's Downing Street staff—were fearful that Bush would be under irresistible political pressure at home to retaliate immediately with a military strike. Blair, however, had come to a different conclusion, confiding to an advisor his belief that American public opinion would give Bush breathing space and adequate time to prepare. Bush reassured Blair by telling him that he did not want to "pound sand with millions of dollars in weapons" just to make himself feel good. "That was basically Bush's message from the outset," said a senior Downing Street official. " 'We are not going to pound sand.' Bush said it over and over again during our conversations with him in the days after 9/11. Once the dust had settled after the attacks themselves, Bush was cool and calm and said he was going to find out precisely who was responsible, before he did anything. At no point did Bush give us the impression that he was going to lash out wildly."[22]

Bush's remarks were a clear dig at Clinton's tactics during his presidency, but Blair, who had supported Clinton's bombing of Iraq in 1998, did not take offense. Instead, the two leaders agreed it was important first to move quickly on the diplomatic front to capitalize on the international outrage to the attacks. If they got support from NATO and the UN, they would have the political and legal framework to undertake military action. Jeremy Greenstock, Britain's ambassador to the UN, worked through the night in New York on a resolution reaffirming the right of countries to respond to terrorism "as they saw fit." Lord Robertson, the NATO secretary-general, was working to get an agreement for Article Five of the NATO charter to be invoked, declaring that the attack on the United States was an attack on all the members of the NATO alliance. Before ending the conversation, Bush and Blair returned to the question of a military response. Blair told Bush that he had to make a choice between rapid action and effective action. And effective action would require preparation and planning. Bush agreed. Again, he said he didn't want to fire missiles at targets that did not matter. Bush concluded the conversation by reiterating the message he had broadcast to the American people the previous night, that the United States would make no distinction between the terrorists responsible for 9/11 and the governments that harbored them. Bush stressed that he had no interest in a short-term, gratuitous response to 9/11. This was going to be a long haul, a "mission for a presidency."[23]

Although Blair and Bush came from very different political backgrounds, there were many areas where they saw eye to eye, and where Blair found himself in agreement with the Bush doctrine. "They finished each other's sentences," said a senior administration official who sat in on the Bush-Blair meetings. "They each had the ability to get inside each other's minds, and they helped each other to develop their long-term strategy."[24] Blair had been frustrated by Clinton's disinclination to take effective military action. He was well aware that Operation Desert Fox in 1998—where a great deal of Iraqi sand had been bombed to little effect—had failed to halt Saddam Hussein's defiance of the UN, and that Saddam had taken advantage of the steady erosion of the UN sanctions regime to rebuild his power base in Baghdad. It was Blair's belief, contrary to what Clinton claimed, that Slobodan Milosevic would never have capitulated over Kosovo in the summer of 1999 had NATO not threatened a ground invasion. In both these conflicts, Blair had shown a willingness to act without the official endorsement of the UN, although this came after every diplomatic avenue had been fully explored. When there was a clear-cut threat to the security of the Western alliance, Blair, unlike many of his European allies, had no qualms about using all the means at his disposal to defeat the enemy.

Britain had a long-standing policy of taking a robust attitude toward "rogue" states, going back to the 1980s. Under Margaret Thatcher, Britain had cut diplomatic relations with Libya, Syria, Iraq, and Iran for their involvement in international terrorism. Britain had fully supported the implementation of UN sanctions against Libya, over Colonel Gadhafi's refusal to hand over two Libyans suspected of involvement in the 1988 bombing of Pan Am Flight 103 over the Scottish village of Lockerbie, with the loss of 270 lives. Iraq had been the target of similar sanctions because of Saddam's continued noncompliance with the Gulf War ceasefire terms that required the Iraqi dictator to dismantle his WMD programs. Together with the United States, during the 1990s, first under John Major and then under Tony Blair, Britain had campaigned rigorously for the retention of the sanctions against Iraq in the face of stiff opposition from other Security Council members. This policy, combined with Blair's personal interest in the proliferation of WMD, meant that it was unlikely that he would raise strong objections to forcing such rogue states to drop their support for international terrorism. Like Bush, Blair was driven by a deep moral conviction in the justice of his cause and, once he had decided on a course of action, devoted all his energy to achieving his declared goal.

By resolving to give Washington his unqualified support Blair was making a personal commitment to the transatlantic alliance. Previous Labour prime ministers had been exceedingly cautious in committing Britain to an open-ended military alliance with Washington. But unlike Harold Wilson, the Labour prime minister who in the 1960s had supported President Johnson in the Vietnam War without providing any military support, Blair had no interest in qualifying his support for the United States. As American rescue workers labored their way through the smoldering rubble of the Twin Towers, there was a massive groundswell of sympathy and support throughout Britain for America's plight. The only dissonance in Britain came from hard-left anti-Americans and Muslim extremists who expressed the view that America "had it coming." So far as the majority public mood was concerned, however, Blair knew that the British people were squarely behind America, for the moment, at least.

"From the day of the attack, the prime minister was quite emphatic about what he wanted to do," said one of Blair's key Downing Street aides. "He was determined that the U.S. must not feel that it was on its own, and that it had friends that would stand by it. We were well aware that how America responded to these attacks would define its relations with the rest of the world, and Blair believed that it was crucial that we were part of that decision-making process."[25] For Blair, an attack on America was the same as an attack on Britain, and in such circumstances it was the indisputable duty of an ally to stand firm, irrespective of the consequences. "If Britain had been attacked by al-Qaeda on 9/11 instead of the U.S., we would have expected America to come to our defense," said a Blair advisor. "The unreserved support that we gave Washington was the same that we would expect from Washington if Britain came under attack. It's what being an ally is all about."[26]

Nevertheless, many of Blair's Downing Street staff continued to worry about the influence that the more hawkish members of the administration, such as Rumsfeld and Cheney, would exert over Bush. From his dealings with Clinton during the Iraq and Kosovo crises, Blair had much experience of trying to influence the formulation of policy at the White House, even if his interventions were not always welcomed by the incumbent. At the height of the Kosovo crisis, Blair had written Clinton a long, personal letter outlining his arguments for deploying ground troops. Now, following his telephone conversations with Bush, he resolved to do the same in attempting to influence America's response to 9/11.

Blair retreated to his "den," his private office in Downing Street, to write a note to Bush setting out his thoughts on how the West should react to the attacks. In the first of what would become a lengthy stream of correspondence from the prime minister, similar to the letters Churchill had sent Roosevelt during the Second World War, Blair argued that the first priority should be to tackle al-Qaeda and the Taliban. There was no mention of Iraq, even though Saddam Hussein's regime was Blair's personal bête noire of rogue states. Shaping world opinion was crucial in Blair's estimation. Blair said that a dossier should be presented outlining the evidence linking al-Qaeda to the 9/11 attacks. It should provide information about the terrorist camps in Afghanistan as a way of drawing attention to the role of the Taliban regime in nurturing the terrorist network. An ultimatum should be delivered to the Taliban, while at the same time intense diplomatic efforts should be made to persuade Iran and Pakistan, countries which both had close ties to the Taliban, to cooperate with the West. Blair was in favor of supporting the Northern Alliance in its fight against the Taliban. Finally Blair raised an issue of the utmost sensitivity. In order to solidify support in the Arab world for the war on terrorism, it was important to make a concerted effort to restart the peace process in the Middle East.[27] Blair was directly linking the long-standing Israeli-Arab dispute to the war on terror. It was not a view that would attract much support in either Washington or Israel. His handwritten note ran to five full pages. After Blair was satisfied with his draft, it was typed up and faxed to Bush.

Work began immediately on putting together an international coalition. In Washington, Powell was given the main responsibility for sounding out potential partners, while Bush, following his lengthy conversation with Blair, phoned the leaders of France, Germany, Canada, and China. Bush's call to Putin was made at Blair's behest. At this stage, despite what his critics would later claim, Bush's main interest was in organizing a multinational response to 9/11. "My attitude all along was, if we have to go it alone, we'll go it alone, but I'd rather not."[28]

Meanwhile, at NATO's headquarters in Brussels, George Robertson was working hard to persuade the nineteen member states to invoke Article Five of its founding charter, its collective defense clause. Robertson later recalled that only two members of the alliance expressed reservations about invoking the article: one over fears that to do so might make all NATO member states the target of al-Qaeda attacks, while the other was concerned about giving the Americans "an open checkbook." Robertson stressed that the discussion was initiated at his request, not by Washington. "It was a dramatic act of solidarity," said Robertson. "Even then we felt that if there was going to be an attack on Afghanistan, we would need a broad coalition." The North Atlantic Council, NATO's governing body, convened at 8 p.m., and by 9.20 p.m., the resolution invoking Article Five was passed. The alliance had undertaken to do something it had never done before, to fight to defend the United States rather than have the United States fighting to defend Europe. This was a valiant gesture— the Germans even promised to implement a tax increase to pay for improved global security. Yet the Europeans were to be left feeling deeply disappointed by Washington's failure to acknowledge their historic act of support. "The U.S. made a mistake in not taking up our offer of support," said Robertson.[29] A similar gesture of support was made at the UN in

New York, where the Security Council, at France's initiative but backed by Britain, passed Resolution 1383, which offered the United States any assistance necessary.

WITHIN TWENTY-FOUR HOURS OF the 9/11 attacks, the fault lines were starting to appear between the United States and the rest of the world, which would later create deep divisions, particularly between Washington and Europe, over how to conduct the campaign against international terrorism. There was widespread support for a campaign against the Taliban and al-Qaeda, neither of which enjoyed much sympathy prior to the attacks, and both NATO and the UN had not hesitated to demonstrate their solidarity with America. But the Bush administration had given the distinct impression prior to the 9/11 attacks that they had little faith in the effectiveness of such institutions to deliver tangible results, and the isolationist trend that so worried Tony Blair was plainly evident as Bush and his senior advisors debated their response.

Despite Bush's comment that he would prefer to work with an international coalition, the body language emanating from the White House suggested the opposite. Bush was very clear in his own mind that he did not want to risk future delays or diminish U.S. control by accepting too much international assistance. "There was this very strong feeling that we had been attacked and that we had the right to act in self-defense," said a senior Bush administration official. "And we did not want the UN to dictate terms to us."[30] Bush was determined to wage the war on terror on his terms, and not those of the UN, NATO, or any other international institution. At a war summit convened at Camp David at the end of the week, Bush told his key aides that he did not want other countries setting terms or conditions for the war on terrorism. "At one point," he said, "we may be the only ones left. That's okay with me. We are America."[31] Bush's attitude would be spelled out in his speech before a joint session of Congress on September 20. "Every nation, in every region, now had a decision to make. Either you are with us, or you are with the terrorists . . . [This] country will define our times, not be defined by them. As long as the United States of America is determined and strong, this will not be an age of terror; this will be an age of liberty." This was America's war.

If Bush's declaration of intent caused consternation among America's allies, the attitude of his officials toward their European counterparts increased the growing sense of resentment that their offers of help and support were being ignored. At the first high-level briefing provided by Washington to NATO defense ministers after 9/11, Paul Wolfowitz ruled out using any international or NATO structures. He made clear that Washington was not planning to rely heavily on European forces, either, instead noting that the effort "would be made up of many different coalitions in different parts of the world."[32] Donald Rumsfeld was equally dismissive of the gestures of support, particularly from Europe. In his formulation, "the mission needs to define the coalition, and we ought not to think that a coalition should define the mission."[33] His comments provoked an angry response from Javier Solana, the former NATO secretary-general, who had become the European Union's foreign policy chief. "The alliance should determine the mission, and not vice versa," he declared, while complaining that NATO had "invoked its most sacred covenant" and yet was totally ignored by American war planners.[34]

Bush's unilateralist response reflected the deep-seated misgivings of many Republicans about the effectiveness of international institutions in dealing with threats to American security, particularly such institutions as NATO, which had been set up to fight the Cold War. "The American military had an awful experience with NATO during Kosovo," said a senior White House advisor. "The military was almost begging us not to make them go through NATO."[35] Some of Blair's aides were sympathetic to the American position on NATO. "It was all very well invoking Article Five, but when it came to practical offers of help, there were not many European hands being raised at NATO headquarters," a Blair aide said.[36] The only world leader who seemed to have any degree of influence on the inner deliberations of the Bush White House was Tony Blair. The question, asked as much in Downing Street as elsewhere, was just how much notice would Bush take of the advice proffered by his British ally?

By September 2001, Downing Street had worked out the positions of the various factions competing for the ear of the president, and the degree of influence the neocons could bring to bear on Bush. "We quickly realized that Bush himself was not a neocon," explained one of Blair's senior Downing Street aides. "He would listen to what they had to say, but he would make the decision himself. We did not see Rumsfeld as a neocon either. He was an old-fashioned Kissinger realpolitik guy." Despite their political differences, Blair believed that there was common ground between him and Bush. "It was a very curious journey that brought Bush and Blair together," explained the Downing Street aide. "Blair is an internationalist and Bush is an isolationist. But even though we were coming at it from different points of view, it all changed after 9/11."[37]

Before 9/11, Condoleezza Rice had written frequently that America should look after itself and "not run around the world trying to change things." After the attacks the Bush White House realized it had no alternative. In Downing Street, "we realized that we shared the common goal of wanting to spread our values around the world," the aide continued. "Blair is an old Labour internationalist who wants to be a force for good in the world. Perversely, this fits in with the neocon view of the world. It was a case of old-fashioned Labour internationalism meets right-wing neocons. In the sense that he wants to make the world a better place, Blair is a neocon himself."[38]

Blair's experience of having dealt with Clinton over Kosovo proved invaluable in handling Bush. "We had learned the lesson that you need to be very careful dealing with a superpower," said one of Blair's most trusted confidants. "We had got to the position where we had lots of influence in Washington and, on a personal level, we were very close. We had learned that they did not like having disputes in public, and that the Americans did not like to feel that they were being made to do something against their will. They always want to give the impression that they are leading the way, and that whatever they do, they do it for their own best interests." Certainly Downing Street was very sensitive to the accusation that Blair's influence over Bush was minimal, and that he was nothing more than Washington's "poodle," who could be counted upon to do its bidding, irrespective of the consequences. "It is very unfair to say that Blair did not have any influence on Bush. He had a lot of influence on events after 9/11. It's just that he chose not to make it public."[39]

One development that certainly assisted Blair's dealings with the White House during this crucial period was his personal disenchantment with what he regarded as the flawed institutional framework of the UN. "Blair had become disillusioned with the UN long before 9/11," said a senior Downing Street official. "The UN's failure over Iraq and Kosovo had made him realize that so long as you have vetoes from five countries, it is impossible to get anything done."[40] Bush's willingness to listen to Blair's advice—even if he did not act on it—was treated with suspicion by other members of the Bush war cabinet. Vice President Cheney, in particular, was wary of Blair and insisted on being present every time Bush met with the British prime minister. "Blair found it very hard to get on with Cheney," said a long-standing Downing Street foreign policy advisor. "Cheney is not very clubbable, and has a very laconic manner, and does not say more than he has to. Blair found him rather sinister."[41] Cheney, who was regarded by many as the conscience of the Republican Party with regard to foreign policy, had long-standing links with the British Conservative Party, and was not ideologically well-disposed toward Blair's New Labour Party. After 9/11, Blair and Bush had a video conference every week on a special link set up between the White House and Downing Street to discuss progress on the war on terror and other related issues. "Cheney would always be there, listening in on the conversation, but not contributing very much at all," said a Downing Street aide.[42]

Cheney was arguably the most isolationist member of Bush's war cabinet, who believed that the institutions and alliances "built to deal with the conflicts of the twentieth century may not be the right strategies and policies and institutions to deal with the kind of threat we face now." The UN had "proven incapable of meeting the challenge we face in the twenty-first century, of rogue states armed with deadly weapons, possibly sharing them with terrorists." So far as Cheney was concerned, subordinating U.S. national security interests to the need for international consensus was a "prescription for perpetual disunity and obstructionism." When presented with imminent threats, waiting for allies could even be dangerous.[43] Such views made Cheney a formidable obstacle that Blair needed to overcome if he was to succeed in bringing his influence to bear on the crucial decisions Bush had to make in deciding how to fight the war on terror.

Nor was Cheney the only member of Bush's inner circle who had reservations about the value of the transatlantic alliance in fighting the war on terror. Donald Rumsfeld, the secretary of defense, was another political heavyweight who was not temperamentally disposed to take advice from outsiders. "Rumsfeld liked to keep his cards close to his chest and keep everyone guessing about what he was up to," said one of Blair's Downing Street staff. "But it was not just us who were trying to find out what was going on. It was just the same for the White House!"[44] British attempts to find out what Rumsfeld was thinking were not helped by the fact that he had a strained relationship with Geoff Hoon, the British defense secretary who had replaced George Robertson. Hoon, a lawyer by training, was "socially diffident," according to his officials, and had difficulty establishing a good working relationship with Rumsfeld, whose personality he found overwhelming.

Fortunately for Blair, the relationship between Jack Straw, the foreign secretary, and Colin Powell was far less problematic. Straw, a former left-wing student firebrand and long-serving Labour Party apparatchik, had acquired a reputation for being a wily operator, skillful at ensuring that his image remained unsullied by negative publicity, even when his policies aroused considerable controversy.

The other important relationship between British and American officials after 9/11 was that between Sir David Manning, who had replaced John Sawers as Blair's foreign policy advisor in Downing Street, and Condoleezza Rice. Manning, who had previously been British ambassador to Israel and the European Union, had first met Rice when she accompanied Bush to a dinner at Chequers the previous July. The cerebral Manning had got on well with Rice—"a marriage made in heaven," is how one aide described their respect for each other[45]—and had been invited to Washington by Rice "to do the rounds" in September. On the evening of September 10, Manning and Rice had dinner at the British embassy in Washington, hosted by Sir Christopher Meyer, the British ambassador, where they discussed various issues, most prominent among which was peacekeeping in the Balkans. International terrorism was never mentioned during the evening.

BLAIR DID NOT SPEAK again to Bush for two days, until Friday, September 14. By the time he spoke to the American president, Blair had addressed an emergency session of a packed House of Commons. In his speech, Blair warned that the plans currently under consideration could result in a change in what he described as "the present world order." Countries such as Afghanistan, Iraq, Iran, Syria, and Libya, which were suspected of harboring or supporting international terrorist groups, would have to choose between terrorism and the West. Bush would make the same assertion in his address to Congress the following week. The risk of nuclear, biological, and chemical attacks from terror groups, Blair said, justified extending the war on terrorists to the states that enabled them to flourish. Jack Straw weighed in to the debate with a robust defense of the policies that Britain was about to adopt. "To turn the other cheek would not appease the terrorists, but would lead to a still greater danger," he said, and then drew comparisons with the disastrous attempts to appease Europe's rising dictators during the 1930s.[46] Straw's words bore an uncanny resemblance to comments that Bush would later make to justify the tough line he adopted following the 9/11 attacks: "I do believe there is the image of America out there that we are so materialistic, that we're almost hedonistic, that we don't have values, and that when struck, we wouldn't fight back."[47]

The leadership qualities Blair displayed in the critical days after 9/11 had a profound effect on the White House, even among those members of the Bush cabinet who had been cool toward the British prime minister. "His contribution was immense," said a senior White House aide who attended many of the subsequent meetings between Blair and Bush. Blair's unequivocal stand in support of Washington was warmly received at both the State Department and the Pentagon, even though these institutions would soon be involved in a bitter power struggle over the formulation of America's policy on the war on terror. "Blair became a central figure for us after 9/11," said a senior State Department official. "His instincts could not be faulted. He knew precisely how to reach out to the American president and the American people in their hour of need."[48] A similar view was expressed by a senior Pentagon official. "He was a key player. Across the whole of our government everyone was concerned about what he had to say. All the senior figures in the administration came to hold him in high regard."[49]

When Blair next spoke to Bush, the president opened the conversation by thanking Blair for the huge outpouring of support America had received from the British people. He thanked Blair for his five-page memo, which he said "mirrored" his own views. Since their last conversation, Bush had been involved in detailed discussions over how to wage an effective military campaign against al-Qaeda. The only country he was prepared to consider as a close ally in what would be an American-led campaign was Britain. During a meeting with Donald Rumsfeld, Bush had said that the British really wanted to participate. "Give them a role," he instructed his defense secretary, adding, "Time is of the essence."[50] Bush had reflected on how he intended to conduct the campaign, and he reassured Blair that his primary intention was to go after al-Qaeda and the Taliban. Only when that objective had been achieved would the war on terror be extended to tackle rogue states. Bush described the forthcoming campaign as a series of circles emanating from a pebble dropped in the water. "We focus on the first circle," Bush told Blair, "then we expand to the next circle and the next circle."

Iraq was not mentioned during the conversation, but Blair understood perfectly well where Bush was headed. Blair stressed the need to give the Taliban a strongly worded ultimatum, and the two men then discussed the reaction of other world leaders to the crisis. Blair said the ultimatum would need careful consideration. The main demands should be that the Taliban surrender bin Laden and his key lieutenants, shut down the training camps, and allow international monitors into Afghanistan to check that the demands had been met. Blair and Bush then discussed how to build an international coalition against terrorism. They discussed their respective conversations with other world leaders, and agreed that Pakistan would be a key player. British intelligence had long suspected

Pakistanis of playing a vital part in the proliferation of illegal nuclear weapons, and Pakistani intelligence was known to have close ties to al-Qaeda and the Taliban. Colin Powell had already spoken to General Pervez Musharaf, the Pakistani leader, and won his backing for firm action against the Taliban and al-Qaeda, and Bush told Blair that he expected Musharaf's full cooperation.

Blair raised another issue with Bush that was close to his heart: the importance of making a concerted effort to restart the peace process in the Middle East as a means of solidifying support in the Arab world for the war on terrorism. Even at this seminal stage, Blair was convinced that the Middle East peace process was directly linked to the war on terror. He believed that the failure of the Israelis and Palestinians to reach a peace settlement meant that terror groups throughout the Arab world had no difficulty in recruiting volunteers to do their dirty work. The peace process had effectively died during the closing months of the Clinton presidency, when Yasser Arafat, the president of the Palestinian Authority, had refused to sign a peace agreement with Ehud Barak, the Israeli prime minister, after weeks of very difficult negotiations at Camp David in late 2000. The failure of the negotiations had resulted in the Palestinians launching a second intifada, or uprising, against Israel's continued military occupation of the Palestinian territory captured during the 1967 Six-Day War.

The Bush administration blamed Arafat for the collapse of the talks, and refused to meet with him after the Israelis claimed that Arafat was personally responsible for ordering suicide bomb attacks against Israeli civilians. Blair, on the other hand, was more sympathetic to the Palestinians. It was said that Blair lost more sleep at night worrying about the plight of Palestinian children than any other international issue. Blair hoped that by linking a Middle East peace settlement to the wider war on terror he could persuade the Bush administration to resurrect the process that had come so tantalizingly close to resolving the conflict at Camp David. Bush was noncommittal, saying that he would talk to Ariel Sharon, who had replaced Barak as Israel's prime minister, and impress upon him the importance of seizing the moment in the Middle East. Blair concluded the conversation by offering Bush a piece of advice that derived from his own experience during the Kosovo conflict: "You've got to decide what you're going to do and then you've got to focus very single-mindedly on it." Bush said he agreed "one hundred percent."[51]

After Blair, the only other world leader Bush called that day was Ariel Sharon. But advice was all that Blair could give at this stage, and his was just one of many powerful voices, especially within the White House, that were competing for the presidential ear as Bush considered how best to respond to 9/11. Many key discussions took place at a meeting of Bush's war cabinet at Camp David during the weekend of September 14–16, at which Blair was neither present nor consulted. Chaired by Bush, the war cabinet consisted of Vice President Dick Cheney, Secretary of State Colin Powell, Secretary of Defense Donald Rumsfeld, National Security Advisor Condoleezza Rice, CIA director George Tenet, and Andrew Card, Bush's chief of staff. The weekend began with briefings from Tenet, Robert Mueller, the FBI director, and General Hugh Shelton, chairman of the Joint Chiefs of Staff. The discussions focused on the various intelligence and military options available for attacking al-Qaeda and the Taliban. This led to a more wide-ranging discussion of the difficulties faced in dealing with the politics of the region, particularly Afghanistan and the surrounding countries, the shaping of a coalition, the need to think unconventionally about fighting the war, and whether Iraq should be included in the war's first phase.

During the Camp David discussions, Bush displayed the characteristics that would become the benchmark of his presidential style. As he later explained, Bush knew he had limited experience with national security issues, and resolved to listen carefully to the advice of his war cabinet before making a decision. "One way you're not impulsive is to make sure you listen," he said. "If I have any genius or smarts, it's the ability to recognize talent, ask them to serve, and work with them as a team."[52] As Bush listened to the advice of the war cabinet, he made several contributions that indicated how he intended to retaliate. The ideal result from the forthcoming campaign, said Bush, would be to kick terrorists out of places like Afghanistan, and through that action persuade other countries that had supported terrorism in the past, such as Iran, to change their behavior. Bush stressed that he did not want other countries dictating terms or conditions for the war on terrorism. He repeated Blair's point about giving the Taliban a deadline, as well as an ultimatum. But the more hawkish members of the cabinet were against setting a deadline, as they did not want to impose any restrictions that would hinder the start of military action. Bush, however, wanted "to give the Taliban a right to turn over al-Qaeda; if they don't, there have to be consequences that show the United States is serious."[53]

Bush expressed strong reservations about bringing Iraq into the terror equation at this juncture. During the morning discussions, both Rumsfeld and Paul Wolfowitz, his deputy who had accompanied him to Camp David, argued strongly in favor of launching military action to remove Saddam Hussein from power. Rumsfeld was first to raise the issue at Camp David, although he had already mentioned Iraq in previous conversations with some of the other war cabinet "principals." He noted there would be a big buildup of forces, with not too many good targets in Afghanistan. If the United States were serious about terrorism, at some point it would have to deal with Iraq. Wolfowitz was even more adamant, at one stage even interrupting his boss to make a point, which caused an awkward silence, as Bush expected only the principals to speak for their respective departments. Wolfowitz argued that the real source of all the trouble and terrorism was probably Saddam, and the 9/11 terrorist attacks created an opportunity to strike. According to Wolfowitz, Saddam was a dangerous leader bent on obtaining and probably using weapons of mass destruction. Even though there was no evidence to support the claim, Wolfowitz argued that Saddam was most likely guilty of carrying out the 9/11 attacks.[54]

The main opposition to the Iraq faction came from Powell, who argued that while there was widespread international support for action against al-Qaeda, it would dissolve if Washington decided to bring Iraq into the equation. "If you get something pinning Sept. 11 on Iraq, great . . . let's put it out and kick them at the right time. But let's get Afghanistan now. If we do that, we will have increased our ability to go after Iraq—if we can prove Iraq had a role." Although Bush let the conversation continue, he said that he had strong reservations about Iraq. He was concerned about two issues. "My theory is you've got to do something and do it well and that . . . if we could prove that we could be successful in this theater, then the rest of the task would be easier. If we tried to do too many things—two things, for example, or three things—militarily, then . . . the lack of focus would have been a huge risk." Bush's intervention effectively ended the discussion about Iraq—for the time being. He received support from Dick Cheney, who argued it was not the right time to tackle Saddam. Cheney did, however, express his deep concern about Saddam and that he was not ruling out going after Saddam at some point in the future. During the afternoon session, Bush took an ad hoc vote on whether to include Iraq in the first stage of the war on terror. Cheney, Powell, Tenet, and Card all voted against, while Rumsfeld abstained.[55]

A few days later, on Thursday, September 20, Blair flew to New York to attend a memorial service at St. Thomas's Church in Lower Manhattan for the victims of the 9/11 attacks, and then flew to Washington to see Bush. Blair was still unsure how Bush intended to respond, and was eager to hear what conclusions Bush had reached after the Camp David summit. Blair had spent much of the intervening period talking to a number of world leaders about building international support for action against al-Qaeda. On September 19, he visited Gerhard Schröder in Berlin, who, while sympathetic to the Americans, could offer nothing more than political support. He then flew to Paris for breakfast with President Jacques Chirac, whom he found surprisingly supportive. "We're with you all the way," Chirac reassured him. Blair even managed to talk to President Mohammed Khatami of Iran, the first time a British prime minister had spoken to the leader of Iran since the overthrow of the Shah in 1979. Blair told Khatami that it was important not to see the conflict as a struggle between Islam and the West but between civilization and terror. Khatami, who did not hold the Taliban in high regard, offered his support. Blair later said his conversation with Khatami was one of his most exciting moments, post-9/11. When he later informed Bush, the American president was flabbergasted. "You mean you actually *talk* to those guys?" he exclaimed. The fact that Blair had conversed with Khatami demonstrated his usefulness to Bush: he could talk to people who had been off-limits to Washington.

Blair's visit to Manhattan so shortly after the attacks made a deep impression on Americans. During the service at St. Thomas's, Blair read a
passage from the end of Thornton Wilder's *Bridge of San Luis Rey*, a novel
that discusses the cruelty of sudden death and describes love as "the only
survival, the only meaning." In his address to the congregation Blair
moved many of those present, including Kofi Annan, the UN secretary-
general, and former president Bill Clinton, when he said, "Nine days on,
there is still shock and disbelief. There is anger, there is fear, but there is
also, throughout the world, a profound sense of solidarity, there is courage, there is a surging of the human spirit." Sir Christopher Meyer, the
British ambassador, read a message from the queen, which contained
the words "grief is the price we pay for love," subsequently engraved into
the masonry of the church.[56] Blair's visit prompted the *Washington Post* to
rate Blair alongside Rudolph Giuliani, the New York mayor, as "the only
other political figure who broke through the world's stunned disbelief."[57]

From New York, Blair flew to Washington, where he was driven directly from Andrews Air Force Base to the White House. On arrival,
Blair and his entourage were taken to the Blue Room for informal drinks,
where Bush took him to a window overlooking the Washington Memorial. Blair was still unsure of Bush's plans. As Meyer later recalled, "We
finally got to the White House after this very emotional morning in New
York. One of the issues was, were the Americans going to use 9/11, quite
apart from hunting down al-Qaeda, to go after Iraq as well? Tony Blair's
view was, whatever you're going to do about Iraq, you should concentrate
on the job at hand, and the job at hand was get al-Qaeda. Give the Taliban an ultimatum, and everything else was secondary to that." Bush told
Blair, "I agree with you that the job at hand is al-Qaeda and the Taliban.
Iraq we keep for another day."[58] Bush then spent twenty minutes outlining the orders he had issued to the NSC a few days previously.

Blair's gamble in giving his unqualified support to Bush in the immediate aftermath of the 9/11 attacks seemed to be paying off. The deep
forebodings of his advisors in Downing Street and at the Foreign Office
about how Bush would react had proved to be unfounded. Had Bush's
war cabinet been more determined at Camp David to press for an immediate attack against Iraq, Blair would have been placed in a very dif-

ficult position both with his European allies and with his own supporters in the Labour Party. But Bush had independently reached the same conclusion as Blair, and the historic alliance between Britain and the United States was strengthened as a result. Irrespective of the political differences between a center-left British prime minister and a right-wing Republican American president, when it came to dealing with threats against the Western alliance, their instincts bore a remarkable similarity. Blair's constant stream of advice to the White House, in the form of telephone calls and memos, was by no means the decisive factor in formulating American policy. As Bush made clear at Camp David, he was prepared to listen carefully to advice, but it was the president who made the final decision. In that context, Blair's own confidently expressed opinions served to reinforce the president's views. Even so, it helped Blair that nearly all of the principals in the Bush war cabinet—with the exception of Donald Rumsfeld—had themselves drawn similar conclusions.

Bush was grateful for the unquestioning support that Blair had given the United States and the American people, and he went out of his way to show his appreciation. Later that evening, Bush was to address the joint session of Congress, and over dinner, Blair's aides marveled at how relaxed Bush appeared in view of the fact that, in a few hours, he was going to make the most important speech of his life. After dinner, Bush invited Blair and his wife to the White House residence. On the way there, Blair asked Bush directly if he felt apprehensive about his imminent speech. "Well, actually I'm not that nervous about it because I know what I want to say, and I know what I am saying is right."[59] When the time came for Bush to leave the White House, he invited Blair to travel with him in the president's car to Capitol Hill, a rare honor. Once in the Capitol, he accompanied Laura Bush and Rudolph Giuliani, the New York mayor, to the VIP seats in the "heroes" gallery of the House of Representatives. As they made their way along the balcony, they were greeted with thunderous applause. Bush's speech was punctuated by thirty-one standing ovations. In it, he officially named bin Laden and al-Qaeda as parties responsible for the 9/11 attacks. "Our war on terror began with al-Qaeda, but it does not end there," said the president. Bush set down another key plank of his policy for battling international terrorism.

"Either you are with us or with the terrorists." He also paid a handsome tribute to his British ally. "I'm so honored the British prime minister has crossed the ocean to show his unity with America . . . Thank you for coming, friend." The audience responded by giving Blair another thunderous standing ovation.

Seven

DECLARATION OF WAR

THE WAR ON TERROR began officially on the night of Sunday, October 7, 2001, when U.S. military forces, with British support, launched a devastating aerial bombardment against thirty-one al-Qaeda and Taliban targets in Afghanistan. U.S. aircraft and cruise missiles carried out the bulk of the bombing. The aircraft consisted of twenty-five F-18 strike jet fighters from the aircraft carrier USS *Missouri* and fifteen B-1 and B-52 bombers from the U.S. military base on the British-controlled island of Diego Garcia, in the Indian Ocean. Three cruisers and one destroyer from the U.S. Navy fired a salvo of fifty cruise missiles, which were also launched from Britain's nuclear-powered submarines HMS *Triumph* and HMS *Trafalgar*. The missiles and bombs were aimed at the Afghan capital, Kabul, and a command base at Kandahar airport, the spiritual home of the Taliban in southern Afghanistan. Air strikes were also directed at Osama bin Laden's training camps, including those near Jalalabad, in the east of the country, together with a number of Taliban bases.

The declared aim of the aerial bombardment was to bring about the collapse of the Taliban regime, which, in turn, it was hoped, would lead to the capture or death of bin Laden and his inner circle. Once the bombing campaign had achieved its objectives, the plan was for hundreds of American and British special forces to link up with the Northern Alliance and other anti-Taliban groups and assist them in attacking the Taliban. They would take part in search-and-destroy missions, and would attempt to capture bin Laden and Mullah Omar, the Taliban's spiritual leader. Shortly after the air offensive got under way, Blair appeared outside Downing Street to issue a short statement. "The cause is just," he declared. "The murder of almost seven thousand innocent people in America (the correct 9/11 death toll was still not known at this time) was an attack on our freedom, our way of life, and civilized values the world over." He stressed that the attacks were being directed against "places we know to be involved in the al-Qaeda network of terror, or against the military apparatus of the Taliban." Every effort was being made to avoid civilian casualties, he said. The same steely resolve that had seen Blair through the Kosovo crisis was apparent as he embarked on a military alliance that would be the most controversial issue of his premiership. "We will not let up or rest until our objectives are met in full," he declared.[1]

Blair remained in close contact with Bush throughout the preparations for the military offensive against Afghanistan, although Washington made it clear that it would be predominantly an American operation. Bush devoted all his energy to preparing for the military campaign, and Blair's role was to act as a roving envoy, traveling the world to whip up as much support as possible for the forthcoming war on terror. "Bush's priority was to reassure American public opinion," said a senior White House official. "Blair had both the stature and the contacts to do the diplomacy. He was the only world leader that we would trust to do that."[2] The two leaders stayed in regular contact, with Bush keeping Blair informed of the military preparations, while Blair updated Bush on the responses he received from his meetings with various heads of state. On Wednesday, October 3, Bush called Blair to confirm their agreement that the United States could make use of a number of British military assets, including the use of the Diego Garcia base. Apart from the deployment of the nuclear submarines, Britain's contribution to the war in Afghanistan would mainly include the use of Royal Air Force support aircraft, Royal Navy patrols in the Gulf and Indian Ocean, and the deployment of up to one thousand troops—the bulk of which were units of the elite Special Air Service (SAS) and Special Boat Service (SBS). There was also close cooperation on the ground between British and American intelligence officers. "The intelligence cooperation between the two countries was the best in the world," said a senior State Department official.[3]

As the deadline for the commencement of hostilities approached, Blair was anxious to publish a dossier setting out the case for war against al-Qaeda and the Taliban. He had undertaken similar exercises prior to the conflicts in Iraq in 1998 and Kosovo in 1999. On this occasion, however, he met with resistance from America's intelligence agencies that bridled at the idea of publishing top-secret information about its foremost enemy. Blair took the opposite view, arguing that it was important to win over public opinion by presenting it with the facts. Consequently, on October 4, the British government published a dossier titled "Responsibility for the Terrorist Atrocities in the United States." Much of the information contained in the dossier would have been unknown to Blair himself prior to the 9/11 attacks, but having subjected himself to a crash course on the evils of al-Qaeda, he was adamant that the material should be made available to a wider public. Apart from providing evidence that bin Laden was directly responsible for 9/11, it declared that "bin Laden and al-Qaeda retained the will and resources to carry out further atrocities," and that "the United Kingdom and United Kingdom nationals are potential targets."[4]

Blair was informed that the attack on Afghanistan was about to take place as he was being driven to Downing Street from Heathrow Airport after returning from three days of meetings with world leaders. Between seeing Bush at the White House and the start of the war, Blair immersed himself in a whirlwind world tour to drum up international support for the campaign against al-Qaeda and the Taliban. Blair had been told, during his meeting with Bush at the White House in September, that the United States had decided on October 7 as the launch date for hostilities. Bush was anxious to reassure the American public that he was not dragging his feet. Immediate military action against the Taliban, using a combination of intelligence assets, special operations units, and heavy bombing, was the most feasible option available, unlike a military invasion, which would require months of planning. Having been taken into Bush's confidence about America's war plan, Blair assumed the role of messenger, traveling the globe to explain the initial strategy in the war on terror, and to persuade potential allies of the need to support the war aims. In the eight weeks after September 11, Blair had fifty-four meetings with other world leaders, traveling more than forty thousand miles on thirty-one flights.

The prime minister began his international odyssey by flying directly from Washington to Brussels for an EU emergency summit, where he briefed European leaders about Bush's war plan. According to his colleagues, Blair's moral certainty in the justice of the cause, a cause he had helped to shape, and the favorable impression he tended to make on other foreign leaders, helped to strengthen international support for the war in Afghanistan. "During this period, Blair seemed like a man possessed, whose utter conviction in the course he was pursuing enabled him to undertake a punishing schedule," remarked one of his aides.[5] Blair was convinced that military action was the only way to tackle the threat posed by Islamic terror groups which, backed by WMD, constituted the greatest danger to the West since the Cold War.

Blair worked hard at being a "bridge" between America and Europe, studiously relaying to wary European leaders Washington's war plans. In early October, he flew to Moscow to meet President Putin, with whom he had previously established a close working relationship. Blair had nagged the Bush administration to treat the Russians as serious partners, even though the instinct of the more hawkish members of the administration, particularly the Cold War veterans Cheney and Rumsfeld, was to keep the Russians at a distance. But a thaw of sorts had set in between the Bush White House and the Putin Kremlin, following Bush's soul-searching meeting with the Russian leader the previous summer.

On October 4, Blair arrived in Moscow, where he had talks at the Kremlin. He then drove with Putin to his dacha at Gorky, about thirty-five miles from the capital, where the two men had dinner with Putin's wife, Lyudmila, their teenage daughters, Yekaterina and Maria, and the family's pet Labrador. Halfway through dinner, they broke off to answer a telephone call from President Bush. As Alastair Campbell, Blair's press secretary, wryly observed, "We think we can safely say it is the first time ever that a prime minister has taken a call from a U.S. president from the family dacha of a Russian president."[6] When the call was concluded, Blair and Putin went for a walk in the woods for a private conversation away from their aides. Blair then returned to the British ambassador's residence in Moscow, where he told his aides that Putin had pledged to support the action in Afghanistan by providing intelligence and offering the use of former Soviet bases in Central Asia. The quid pro quo for this generous offer was distinctly unappetizing. In return for assisting America's campaign to destroy al-Qaeda, Putin received an assurance that he would be given a free hand to undertake a similar mission against Chechen separatists.

Blair was proud of his diplomatic triumph, although some of the ground work had been laid two weeks previously, when Richard Armitage, the U.S. deputy secretary of state, and Cofer Black, a senior CIA officer, had flown to Moscow and negotiated the terms of the deal. By the time Blair arrived in Moscow, the Russians had already sent a team of experts to the CIA's Langley headquarters to advise the Americans about topography and caves in Afghanistan. And so far as the former Soviet-controlled Central Asian republics were concerned, the CIA had been operating Predator drones—unmanned aerial reconnaissance aircraft—from Uzbekistan for more than a year, as part of its covert operation to track bin Laden. Even so, Blair's officials were delighted with the outcome of the visit, which they regarded as crucial to building an international, post-9/11 coalition. "Blair was central to getting Putin onside for Washington's response to 9/11," said an aide who accompanied Blair to Moscow. "Waging a campaign in Afghanistan was no easy task, and Blair did a lot of very hard work to make the campaign possible. Putin's agreement to let us use bases in Central Asia was crucial to the success of the campaign."[7]

From Moscow, Blair flew to Pakistan to see General Musharraf, by far the most important piece of diplomacy he was to undertake in the buildup to the Afghan war. During the 3,200-mile journey from Moscow to Islamabad, the RAF VC10 carrying Blair's team passed over Afghanistan's forbidding mountain terrain, giving the prime minister a glimpse of the formidable obstacles coalition forces would encounter in their military campaign to destroy al-Qaeda. The meeting with Musharraf was arranged by Charles Guthrie, Blair's former chief of the defense staff, who had studied with the Pakistani leader at the Royal College of Defence Studies in London. Blair had sent Guthrie to see Musharraf after he seized power in a military coup in 1999, to express Britain's unease. As the region's former colonial power and head of the Commonwealth, Britain continued to enjoy strong political and diplomatic ties, and, through Guthrie's efforts, a line of communication had been kept open. After 9/11, Musharraf found himself in an awkward position. He realized the perils he faced if he did not cooperate with Washington on destroying al-Qaeda, but equally he was under fierce domestic pressure from Pakistan's Islamic hardliners to maintain Islamabad's support for the Taliban.

Prior to Blair's visit, Guthrie visited Musharraf and told him of the likely consequences if he decided not to side with the Americans. By the time Blair arrived in Islamabad, Musharraf had already made up his mind, and Blair, who made it clear he was representing Bush, was surprised at his readiness to cooperate. Musharraf said that Pakistan would abandon its support for the Taliban, assist with the capture of the al-Qaeda leadership, cooperate on intelligence, and tighten restrictions along the Afghan border. Although American officials had already made their views known to Musharraf, Blair's diplomacy was undoubtedly important in helping to persuade the Pakistani leader to align himself with the West, a crucial breakthrough in the war against al-Qaeda and the Taliban. "Blair's intervention with Musharraf was even more important than the meeting with Putin," said one of Blair's officials. "At the time Blair went to Pakistan, it was by no means clear where Musharraf was going to come down. The ISI had very close links to bin Laden, and Musharraf was under tremendous pressure not to side with the Americans. Blair's visit was very important in helping Musharraf to make the right choice."[8] From Pakistan Blair flew to India for a meeting with Indian prime minister Atal Bihari Vajpayee. After a visit to India's rival Pakistan, it was deemed necessary to reassure the Indians that Pakistan was not getting preferential treatment because of its strategic importance in the looming war in Afghanistan.

Apart from acting as Bush's ambassador-at-large, Blair needed to work hard to gain domestic support for the war. He spent the last few days of September working on a speech for the annual conference of the Labour Party in Brighton. Even at this early stage in the war on terror, antiwar protesters had planned a four-thousand-strong rally to disrupt the conference, but their protest had to be abandoned because of bad weather. Blair revisited the themes that had formed the basis of the Chicago speech he had made in April 1999, during the Kosovo war. The world had changed dramatically since then, but Blair remained convinced of the value of the international community and the justification of liberal intervention in the affairs of other sovereign nation-states. He used the same arguments to win over skeptical Labour supporters who had ethical objections to the war.

Military intervention, he said, would have stopped the slaughter in Rwanda in 1994, where one million people had died in a bloody war, and he was proud of the fact that ethnic cleansing in Kosovo had been brought to an end in 1999 by the threat of intervention. The same moral need to act, he declared, applied to Afghanistan, where more than four million refugees required food and shelter after being driven from their homes by the Taliban. Indeed, Blair's vision for the post-9/11 world went far beyond the parameters of the war on terror. Once the terrorist "cancer" had been eradicated, he wanted to work for a world better off morally and economically, where new hope would reduce the breeding ground for terrorists. He wanted to help heal Africa, which was a "scar on the conscience of the world," and he wanted to dismantle the "slums of Gaza" by resolving the Israel-Palestine conflict. It is unlikely that Blair's messianic vision would have attracted much support in Washington; Dick Cheney and Donald Rumsfeld, for example, appeared to show little interest in Blair's vision of a new world order during meetings at the White House. But in terms of winning over the doubters in Blair's own Labour Party, the speech was an unqualified success, and he was given a rousing and prolonged standing ovation by the conference delegates.

The Bush administration, meanwhile, was immensely grateful to Blair for the enormous effort he put into winning international support for the campaign in Afghanistan and for articulating the aims of the war on terror. "Blair understood better than anyone else the strategic challenge posed by 9/11 and did not wait for Bush to lay down a strategy," said one of the president's senior officials involved with formulating policy on the war on terror. "He was clear in his own mind about precisely what he wanted to do. He fulfilled a profoundly important role."[9] The State Department was equally more impressed by Blair's commitment to Bush because it understood better than the White House the domestic pressures the war on terror might cause Blair in the long term. "He was not given to any doubts," commented a senior State Department official who was closely involved in the Afghan campaign. "Blair's message to us was clear all along: 'We must win this thing.' Supporting us was never a problem for Blair. It was a problem for the Labour Party."[10] Officials at the Pentagon, who oversaw military preparations for the forthcoming campaign, were prepared to concede the importance of Blair's contribution, even though they remained single-minded in their determination to insist upon complete American control over operations. "It was very important to the American people to know that we were not alone in our time of need," said a senior Pentagon official. "Thanks to Blair, after 9/11 there was this sense of a great coalition, and the American people found it very reassuring that their most important ally was standing close by their side. If that caused us difficulties, then we were prepared to work through those particular difficulties because we understood the value of having an ally like Blair on our side."[11]

The importance of Blair's unstinting efforts to shore up international support for Washington was reflected in the fact that Britain was one of the few countries the Pentagon allowed to make an active contribution to the Afghan campaign. Intelligence was another vital area of cooperation between the United States and Britain on Afghanistan and al-Qaeda. The CIA and SIS had a long history of close cooperation in Afghanistan, going back to the 1980s when they were actively supporting the mujahideen in its efforts to drive out the Soviet armed forces following Moscow's 1980 invasion of the country. More recently, both the CIA and SIS had invested considerable resources in the country to track down bin Laden and disrupt al-Qaeda. "At the time of 9/11, the only intelligence agencies with any real clout in Afghanistan were the Americans and British," said a senior British intelligence officer. "Before 9/11, we were running our own networks of agents, and conducting independent intelligence operations. After 9/11, we basically agreed to work together on the common goal of capturing bin Laden and destroying al-Qaeda."[12]

The CIA, with its superior resources and technological advantage, was in a far stronger position to influence events on the ground. Before 9/11, the CIA had established good relations with the leaders of the Northern Alliance, the main opposition to the Taliban in Afghanistan. Agency officials had worked closely with Ahmed Shah Massoud, the Northern Alliance commander who was murdered by the Taliban two days before the 9/11 attacks took place. Undeterred, teams of CIA agents were back in Afghanistan within days of 9/11, making contact with the Northern Alliance and giving them millions of dollars to finance the campaign to overthrow the Taliban.

America's, or rather the Pentagon's, determination to go it alone in Afghanistan was the cause of the initial rift between Washington and Europe that was to deepen the longer the war on terror progressed. Those European leaders—and they were in a minority—who made tangible offers of military assistance were disappointed that Washington did not take up their offers. There was almost unanimous support throughout Europe both for the UN Security Council resolution that was passed in support of the United States, and also for invoking the mutual defense article in the NATO charter. But once the military campaign was under way, the Pentagon declined to use NATO's coordinated command structure. Instead, during the autumn of 2001, the Pentagon cherry-picked the military resources made available through NATO by its members. But with the exception of Britain's military contribution, most of the help provided by America's would-be allies was negligible. "In retrospect, it would have been better all around if the Pentagon could have found a role for NATO, however peripheral," said one of Blair's advisors. "If they had done something like putting a NATO navy in the Indian Ocean, it would at least have given the other NATO members a feeling of being involved, and then there would not have been this sense of resentment."[13] Some NATO officials, however, conceded that it was unlikely many of the European members would have supported the type of high-intensity war that the Americans planned for Afghanistan. "If the Americans had asked for support, it is questionable whether many of the European allies would have said yes," said a senior NATO official. "Would the Germans and Scandinavians have been there? I very much doubt it."[14]

While the British military was granted the privilege of participating in the campaign, even British officers at times felt that they were being overlooked. The sizeable British military mission that was confined to the headquarters of U.S. Central Command (CentCom) at Tampa, Florida, for the duration of the war complained that they were being excluded by General Tommy Franks, the U.S. commander of the Afghan military campaign, from the main decision-making process. General Sir Mike Jackson, the commander of the British Army, believed that his officers were justified in feeling left out of the decision-making process, but that this was quite understandable. "You have to remember that the Americans were feeling very raw," he said. "They had been hurt very badly and they wanted to hit back. They didn't need a bunch of British officers to hold their hands." Jackson argued that those who criticized the way Washington went about responding to 9/11 did not understand the reality of the relationship between Britain and America. "Did the U.S. do everything we wanted them to? Well, the answer to that is no. But did Britain have influence? Well, the answer to that is yes. The British voice was heard as much as we could realistically expect. We may have been unequal in terms of military capability, but there was a sense of common purpose. I'm not sure the British government would have behaved any differently if the 9/11 attacks had been carried out against the British mainland, rather than against America."[15]

Washington's disenchantment with NATO stemmed from the frustration many American commanders had experienced with NATO's cumbersome bureaucracy during the Kosovo conflict, when targets had to be passed by a committee representing the nineteen member states. The recent enlargement of NATO meant that there were now nineteen voices that needed to be taken into consideration before any plan could be implemented, and the Bush administration was in no mood to get bogged down in bureaucratic wrangling. "Basically, the whole NATO structure was set up to fight the Cold War," said Jackson, who had commanded NATO ground forces during the Kosovo conflict. "During the Cold War, NATO had one plan, which was for the defense of Europe. Now and again it was modified as new weaponry became available, but the aim remained the same. With the end of the Cold War, NATO simply did not have the ability to respond quickly and effectively to new challenges."[16]

Three days into the conflict, George Robertson, NATO's secretary-general, went to the Pentagon to see Donald Rumsfeld and Paul Wolfowitz. Robertson reiterated his earlier offer to put NATO's resources at Washington's disposal. "They were working twenty-two hours a day and they just didn't have the time to think about it," he said. "Rumsfeld said he was happy for NATO to do the humanitarian work, but so far as the fighting was concerned that was an American affair. I do not think it was a conscious act of arrogance or dismissiveness. But I do think the U.S. made a mistake in not taking up our offer of support. They were big enough to do it. The Pentagon is not designed to build multinational military alliances, whereas NATO is. Invoking Article Five was a dramatic act of solidarity by NATO, and it deserved to be taken more seriously by Washington."[17]

THE AFGHAN WAR WAS unlike any conflict Washington had previously fought. The combination of dealing with the mountainous terrain and fighting an enemy that amounted to an amorphous grouping of primitive tribesmen living in caves provided a significant challenge to the resourcefulness and imagination of the Pentagon's military planners. The main battle plan was drawn up by General Tommy Franks, the commander of CentCom. Initially, the plan had been called "Operation Infinite Justice," but this was quickly changed to "Operation Enduring Freedom" after it was pointed out that devout Muslims believed only Allah could provide them with infinite justice. In drawing up the campaign plan, Franks and his planners not only took great care with targeting al-Qaeda and the Taliban, but carefully considered the history of military operations in Afghanistan and the wider political and religious implications for the region. In order to avoid upsetting local tribesmen, it was stressed that this was not to be an invasion, but rather a military operation to assist indigenous Afghans to overthrow the brutal Taliban dictatorship that had seized control of their country. America and its allies would work with the Afghan people to achieve their goal. "Looking back, it really was a very remarkable operation," recalled a senior British officer responsible for drawing up plans for Britain's contribution to the conflict. "Here you had the world's most sophisticated military machine sending its officers to war on the backs of donkeys."[18] And even though Britain's involvement in the campaign was modest by comparison with the American deployment, it was highly valued. Said a senior Pentagon official, "The professionalism of British soldiers—particularly the special forces— is always something you want to have on your side, and the intelligence cooperation was the best in the world in terms of active support."[19]

Not surprisingly, the American and British campaign plans for Afghanistan set out virtually identical war aims. The American plan, which Franks explained to President Bush on September 21, envisaged that "U.S. Central Command, as part of America's Global War on Terrorism . . . would destroy the al-Qaeda network inside Afghanistan, along with the illegitimate Taliban regime that was harboring and protecting the terrorists." The British campaign, which was code-named "Operation Veritas," set as its objectives the capture of bin Laden and other al-Qaeda leaders, the prevention of further attacks by al-Qaeda, ending Afghanistan's status as a refuge for terrorists, their training camps and infrastructure, and the removal of Mullah Omar and the Taliban regime.[20]

The desire to show that the military offensive was directed solely at al-Qaeda and the Taliban and not the Afghan people meant that U.S. planners were limited in their target selection. Although thirty-one targets were selected for the first-wave attacks on October 7, most of them were located in remote areas, well away from large population centers. The targets included the al-Qaeda brigade, early-warning radar, some command facilities used by al-Qaeda and the Taliban, Taliban military aircraft, airports and runways, and several surface-to-air missile sites. The ten-year-old son of Mullah Omar, the head of the Taliban, was reported to have been killed in the first night of the bombing, and a single missile was fired on the village of Sansegar, destroying the mosque where Omar had started his movement in 1995. As with the bombing campaigns against Iraq and Kosovo, both Washington and London had to contend with the negative publicity caused by claims that innocent civilians were being killed by the air strikes.

The biggest propaganda threat they faced came from bin Laden himself, who had made his own arrangements to counter the American offensive before hostilities began. A videotape that had clearly been recorded before the 9/11 attacks was delivered by a messenger to the offices of Al-Jazeera Television in Kabul on the day the first bombs hit Afghanistan. Bin Laden was shown sitting in a cave, wearing a military fatigue jacket, with an AK-47 assault rifle at his side. "God has blessed a vanguard group of Muslims, the forefront of Islam, to destroy America," he declared. "May God bless them and allot them a supreme place in heaven." Sitting next to bin Laden was Ayman al-Zawahiri, his Egyptian-born deputy, whom the Americans believed to be the technical mastermind behind the 9/11 attacks. Bin Laden's message said "every Muslim should rush to defend his religion" in a world now divided into "faith" and "infidelity."[21] It was a call for an uprising of the whole Islamic *umma*, or nation, in the face of the threat posed to Afghanistan and the international coalition.

Bin Laden's appearance emphasized—as if anyone needed reminding—that the primary objective of the war on terror was the capture or death of the al-Qaeda leader. To ensure that Washington's military campaign in Afghanistan was not undermined by frequent videotaped taunts from bin Laden and his lieutenants, the Bush administration acted quickly to put pressure on the Gulf state of Qatar, where Al-Jazeera was based, not to broadcast any more tapes delivered by al-Qaeda. The Qataris were persuaded by Washington's arguments that the videos could contain coded messages designed to trigger more terror attacks from al-Qaeda's underground network in Europe and America. To make sure that bin Laden could no longer make use of Al-Jazeera's facilities in Kabul, the U.S. Air Force dropped two smart bombs on the television station's Kabul headquarters.

Once hostilities had commenced, Blair was content to leave operational matters to Geoff Hoon, the British defense secretary, and Admiral Sir Michael Boyce, the chief of the defense staff. Boyce had a good relationship with his U.S. counterpart, General Richard B. Meyers, and Blair's experience in Kosovo had taught him that it was best to leave the operational details of a military campaign to the professionals. Blair was confident that the war would be concluded quickly, and in the meantime, he concentrated on making sure that the international coalition in support of the war held together, while maintaining public support at home. Blair also focused on trying to persuade the wider Islamic world that the conflict in Afghanistan was not a war against Islam but solely against al-Qaeda and the Taliban.

On October 10, Blair set off on a tour of Arab leaders to persuade them that they had nothing to fear from the war on terror. Equipped with a copy of the Koran, which he had studied closely, Blair stressed that he had been at the forefront of the international effort to protect Kosovo's Muslim population from Serb atrocities, and was a vociferous supporter of the Palestinian cause. "What we had to do," he later explained, "was to get across very strongly that this was not about taking on Islam." Blair wanted to discuss with moderate Arab leaders how to "capture some of the ground from the extremists who said they were talking on behalf of Islam, when no sensible Islamic cleric could possibly support such an interpretation of Islam permitting something such as the attack in New York."[22]

Blair received a warm welcome during his first such visit in Oman, a former British protectorate where the sultan remained well disposed toward Britain. After inspecting British troops based in Oman, Blair gave a press conference at which he sought to allay the mounting fears in the Arab world that the attack on Afghanistan was merely the first step in a wider campaign that would target many more countries once the Taliban had been defeated. "No country will be attacked unless there is evidence," Blair declared. His aides briefed British journalists accompanying him on the trip that there was still no evidence linking Saddam to 9/11.[23] In Blair's view, there was no justification for going to war against Iraq. During dinner with the sultan of Oman, Blair took a telephone call from Yasser Arafat, the Palestinian leader, who said he was interested in reviving the Middle East peace process. The following day Blair flew to Cairo to meet with Egyptian president Hosni Mubarak, where the two men had a detailed discussion on Islam and terrorism, and explored the possibility of reviving the Middle East peace talks.

Although Blair's efforts to reassure the Islamic world had Washington's blessing, he was running the risk of straining his relations with the Bush administration. His suggestion that there was no case for going to war with Iraq was certainly at odds with the thinking within some circles of the Bush administration, where the president and his advisors had already begun to encourage the view that the Afghan campaign was merely the start of a much wider war against international terrorism. On October 8, less than twenty-four hours after fighting had commenced, Bush issued a statement declaring that the Afghan War was the "first phase" of a general war against terrorists. Nor did the more hawkish members of the administration have much interest in Blair's comments about reviving the Middle East peace process. They were particularly concerned about his attempts at bridge-building with "marginal" or "rogue states," such as Syria and Libya, which had a long history of sponsoring terrorist groups. Even at this stage, many Middle East leaders were aware of the divide between Blair's somewhat utopian vision for the future of the region and Washington's determination to use its undisputed military power to force its will on the region's more recalcitrant regimes. It was hardly surprising, therefore, when a planned meeting in Saudi Arabia between Blair and Crown Prince Abdullah was canceled at the last minute. The Saudis informed Blair as he was flying to Oman that it would be "too sensitive" for him to be received while a heavy bombing campaign was being conducted against Afghanistan.

By far the most risky intervention by Blair during this period came toward the end of the month, when he met with President Bashar al-Asad, the Syrian dictator. Blair seemed to have convinced himself that the catastrophic events of 9/11 had caused a seismic shift in the world's political alignment, so much so that Syria's Baathists could be persuaded to change their ways. Syria, a key ally of the Soviet Union during the Cold War, had long been a thorn in the side of both Britain and America, which accused Damascus of sponsoring international terrorism. Margaret Thatcher had cut diplomatic relations with Syria in 1986, when it was implicated in a plot to plant a bomb on an Israeli El Al jumbo jet at

Heathrow Airport. Relations had been restored after President Hafez al-Asad, Bashar's father, had sided with the American-led coalition against Saddam Hussein following the invasion of Kuwait. The rapprochement between Syria and the West remained lukewarm, however, and Asad the father had taken an uncompromising attitude toward the Clinton-sponsored Middle East peace talks during the 1990s, rejecting an offer from Israel to return the Golan Heights. With the death of the elder Asad in 2000, Bashar had acceded to the presidency, prompting a degree of cautious optimism that the new Syrian regime might be more accommodating both to Israel and to the West.

Blair set off for Damascus on October 30, hoping to achieve a breakthrough on two fronts. For nearly twenty years, Syria had colluded with Iran to fund and support the radical Hezbollah (Party of God) Shiite Muslim militia in Lebanon, which had been responsible for the abduction of American and British citizens in Beirut during the 1980s. Blair hoped both to persuade Asad to drop his support for Hezbollah and other terrorist organizations and convince him that, in the post-9/11 world, it was in Syria's best interests to take a more realistic approach to its dealings with Israel. Blair believed—irrespective of the distinctly lukewarm interest shown in Washington—that a revival of the Middle East peace process would be intricately linked to the war on terror. If this were the case, then persuading the Syrians to adopt a more positive attitude would constitute a significant breakthrough. Blair had already gotten signals from Damascus that his journey would not be in vain.

The visit began well. Bashar had spent much of his early life in London and had an English-born wife, which made it easy for Blair to break the ice with small talk. But once the two men got down to business, the atmosphere quickly turned sour, with the thirty-five-year-old Syrian leader lecturing the prime minister about the iniquities of the West's policies toward the region. In private, Blair and Asad managed to maintain their composure, with Asad at one point remarking, "You have got your street, and I have got mine."[24] But their differences erupted publicly once Asad began to speak at a joint press conference. To Blair's obvious discomfort, far from condemning the activities of Islamic terror groups and Palestinian suicide bombers, Asad hailed them as "freedom fighters," comparing their efforts with those of General de Gaulle and the French resistance during the Second World War. Asad drew a sharp distinction between resistance and terrorism. "Resistance is a social, religious, and legal right," he declared. Asad then proceeded to condemn the bombing raids on Afghanistan, claiming that hundreds of innocent civilians were being killed by American bombers. Then, just as Blair thought his public embarrassment could not get any worse, Asad went so far as to try to justify the 9/11 attacks. It was wrong, said Asad, for the West to pin the blame for the terrorist attacks on America on bin Laden; rather the West should concentrate its energies on confronting Israel for its "daily terrorism" against the Palestinians. Israel, not bin Laden, bore ultimate responsibility for 9/11.

Apart from the public humiliation he suffered, Blair's visit to Syria presented the harsh reality of one of the more insurmountable obstacles in the way of negotiating a peace settlement. A country that was supposed to be a key player in future peace dialogues was actively supporting Islamic terror groups, had close ties with Iran, and, in open defiance of UN sanctions, was smuggling arms and other equipment for Saddam Hussein's Iraq. Blair's encounter with Asad had helped to confirm the suspicions of those hawks in Washington who saw no difference between Bashar's regime and that of his father. In private, Blair tried to downplay the debacle, insisting that the private talks had gone well.[25] According to Blair, Asad's public comments had been made purely for his domestic audience, which was incensed by the West's bombing of fellow Muslims in Afghanistan. But whatever progress Blair may have made in private, it was completely ruined by Asad's public outburst. Lord Charles Powell, Margaret Thatcher's former foreign policy advisor who helped to arrange the visit, said it had made sense to open a dialogue with Damascus, because Syria would have been an important ally against Iraq. "It was a sensible strategy," he said. "The problem was that Asad simply could not deliver what we wanted."[26]

Nor did Blair have much luck during the rest of his meetings with moderate Arab leaders in persuading them to support Operation Enduring Freedom. From Syria, Blair traveled to Saudi Arabia, where Crown Prince Abdullah finally agreed to grant him an audience. But neither the crown prince, nor King Abdullah of Jordan, whom he met the following day, were prepared to endorse the coalition's bombing raids on Afghanistan.

From Jordan, Blair completed his Middle East tour with a trip to Jerusalem to meet Ariel Sharon, the Israeli prime minister. Sharon had already upset the Bush administration by comparing Israel's plight to that of Czechoslovakia in 1938, when Neville Chamberlain had abandoned the Czechs to Hitler by signing the Munich "Peace in Our Time" Agreement. "Do not try to appease the Arabs at our expense," Sharon had told Bush. "Israel will not be Czechoslovakia." Bush had not taken kindly to being compared with Chamberlain, the architect of 1930s appeasement, and had said as much. Not surprisingly, Sharon had little to offer Blair, who, he thought, spent far too much time with Yasser Arafat. Before meeting Sharon in Jerusalem, Blair had traveled to Gaza to see Arafat—his thirteenth meeting with the Palestinian leader since becoming prime minister, more than any other Western leader. Blair got little out of Arafat, and even less out of Sharon, who arranged for the Israeli air force to launch air raids against Palestinian targets just as Blair arrived for talks.

Blair wanted Sharon to pull back Israeli troops from the four main Palestinian cities that had been reoccupied earlier in the year to counter the second intifada. He also wanted the Israeli prime minister to call a halt to his policy of targeted killings of Palestinian activists suspected of involvement in suicide bombings. Blair's visit could not have come at a worse time, as just a few days prior, Palestinian gunmen had murdered Rehavam Ze'evi, Israel's right-wing tourism minister, in the lobby of a Jerusalem hotel. At their joint press conference, Sharon was almost as dismissive of Blair's entreaties as Asad had been. Responding to Blair's call to abandon targeted killings, Sharon responded rhetorically: "What will bring peace earlier? That they (the Palestinians) kill another thirty, forty, fifty Israeli citizens, or that they be stopped on their way there?" So far as Sharon was concerned, there would be no change in Israeli security policy. "On one thing there will be no compromise, now or in the future," he said, "and that is when it comes to the lives and security of Israeli citizens and the very existence of the state of Israel."

The energy and effort Blair invested in his whirlwind diplomatic engagement with the Middle East during the autumn of 2001 did not result in any tangible reward. It left him exposed to the criticism that he was trying to reach out to leaders who had no desire to be grasped by the prime minister's warm embrace. The constant shuttle diplomacy took its toll on Blair, who at times looked gaunt and exhausted. He lost weight, the result of a demanding exercise regime and an irregular diet. Even so, Blair seemed as though he was in his element. Bush was generally appreciative of Blair's efforts, but there were many in Washington who were at best skeptical about what he could achieve, while others, particularly the neoconservatives, were almost willing him to fail. "Blair saw himself as a counterbalance against the influence of the neoconservatives in the White House," said one of his close aides at the time. "This did not go down well with the neocons, who were working behind the scenes to undermine him. Blair knew he was taking a big risk, but so long as his personal relationship with George Bush was working, Blair believed it was a risk worth taking."[27]

Never one to lack confidence in himself, Blair, the architect of the Good Friday Agreement in Northern Ireland and the liberator of Kosovo, believed his unique powers of persuasion could be deployed to break through the decades of suspicion and mutual antipathy that had blighted previous attempts to bring peace to the Middle East. The problem for Blair was that, unlike Northern Ireland, where successive British governments had been working to resolve the conflict since the mid-1980s, 9/11 found the positions of the various protagonists more entrenched than ever. The failure of Clinton's Camp David Agreement, the second Palestinian intifada, and Sharon's brutal suppression of the Palestinian Authority had seen the warring factions adopt ever more intractable positions.

Blair's willingness to engage with Yasser Arafat was a source of particular irritation in Washington. While Blair was prepared to meet Arafat on the grounds that he remained, whatever his shortcomings, the elected representative of the Palestinian people, the PLO leader was distinctly persona non grata at the White House, so much so that Bush refused even to make eye contact with him when they were in the same room at the UN. Arafat had promised to renounce terrorism, but Sharon showed

Bush Israeli intelligence that proved the Palestinian leader was still involved in terrorist activity.[28] Bush took personal loyalty very seriously, and his disdain so maddened the Palestinian leader that Arafat actually tried to shove himself into the president at the UN meeting in November, and had to be physically blocked by the Secret Service.[29]

Despite Bush's deep antipathy toward Arafat, Washington nevertheless understood that in order to secure the support of moderate Arab states for the war on terror, it was necessary to reengage with the Israel-Palestine issue. On October 2, Bush made a personal declaration in support of the creation of a Palestinian state. "The idea of a Palestinian state has always been part of a vision, so long as the right to an Israeli state is respected." Blair had responded to this gesture by inviting Arafat to Downing Street, where he declared Britain's backing for the creation of an independent Palestinian state. But whereas Blair was serious about trying to achieve this goal while Arafat was still the Palestinians' undisputed leader, many of Bush's closest advisors, who had long-standing links with right-wing Israeli politicians, had no interest in the notion of Palestinian statehood.[30] "We felt Blair was hopelessly optimistic on the Middle East, and far too respectful of Arafat, whom we regarded as the embodiment of the problem," said a senior White House advisor on the Middle East. "For that reason, it had no influence or impact here."[31]

Downing Street, however, remained convinced that resolving the long-standing Israel-Palestine dispute was crucial to winning the war on terror, and that the pressure Blair applied to Bush on this issue was persuasive in getting the president to be more proactive on the Middle East peace process. "Bush had learned the lesson of the Clinton era, that you could not deal with Arafat," said one of Blair's top Downing Street advisors. "Arafat had been offered (at Camp David) a great deal and had turned it down. We were aware of all that. Even so, we felt that the Middle East was crucial, and so we kept nagging the White House to do something about it. Eventually, they saw that there was some merit in our arguments."[32]

Blair kept in constant touch with Bush throughout his various coalition-building expeditions, and was happy to play the role of the presidential messenger while Bush concentrated on planning the military campaign and keeping American public opinion steady after the trauma of 9/11. As Alastair Campbell, Blair's communications director, explained, "This is not about instant wins. It's about a slow understanding of where we are. The most important thing is whether face-to-face, in private, the judgment is made that people are serious about wanting to reengage and rebegin the [peace] process. The prime minister's judgment in each capital he has visited is that yes, it is."[33]

IF BLAIR BELIEVED HIS shuttle diplomacy was necessary and worthwhile, it was not a view shared by the British public. While Blair was busy globetrotting, domestic support for the war in Britain dropped from 74 percent to 62 percent in an opinion poll taken on October 30. British commentators were scathing about his efforts, with Simon Jenkins of the *Times* remarking, "By all accounts, his voyage to the Middle East was brave, miserable and fruitless."[34] So far as the *New York Times* was concerned, "[Blair] has often articulated the goals of the war against terrorism more eloquently than Mr. Bush. He has not only been Washington's partner in facing the wider world, but on many occasions, the world's ambassador to Washington. America should be grateful for both roles."[35] If Blair was flattered by the attention, he would have been aware that praiseworthy editorials from the left-leaning *New York Times* made little impression on the hard-nosed pragmatists running the Bush administration.

Blair's European partners were becoming restless about his self-appointed role as Bush's personal intermediary. The French, ever suspicious about the motives of the British, tried to affect an air of wry bemusement about the British prime minister's activities. "In Afghanistan, the Brits sent a few missiles, but Blair gave the impression he was running the war," commented an official at the Quai d'Orsay, the French Foreign Ministry. "That was his style. We weren't that bothered. We had grown used to it."[36] In fact, the French were very bothered indeed, and President Jacques Chirac sought to have his own independent access to Bush, rather than rely on his British "ally" to speak on his behalf. And while Chirac and Blair vied with each other for access to the White House, the smaller European countries complained that they were not being properly consulted. Matters came to a head in early November, when Blair invited Chirac to dinner at Downing Street to discuss tactics prior to the French president flying to Washington on November 6 to see Bush. Blair suggested that Gerhard Schröder, the German chancellor, should join them, as he had just met with Putin in Moscow. The cozy arrangement quickly unraveled when first Silvio Berlusconi, the Italian prime minister, and then José María Aznar, the prime minister of Spain, found out about the dinner and demanded an invitation. Other European leaders followed suit, so what was originally planned as a cozy dinner for three quickly became yet another unwieldy European summit, with the representatives of the different states jockeying for position and influence.

By early November, Blair was starting to entertain serious misgivings about the conduct of the war, or rather about the Pentagon's insistence on having total operational control over it. The deployment of ground troops had been ruled out by Pakistan, which refused to give access, and so the success of the campaign depended heavily on the ability of the Afghan resistance groups—most notably, the Northern Alliance—to defeat the Taliban. By November, U.S. bombers had virtually run out of targets, while teams of American and British forces were assisting and advising Afghan tribal leaders on how best to achieve their objectives. The main British contribution consisted of the Special Air Service (SAS) and the Special Boat Service (SBS), the two elite special forces units of the British armed forces. They were deployed on the ground in Afghanistan, but were frustrated that they were not being given clear orders from Cent-Com. There was growing disquiet among the British public and in Europe about the Americans' use of cluster and daisy-cutter bombs, which were incurring significant civilian casualties.

It was against this unpromising background that Blair made his next visit to Washington on November 7. Blair had covered a lot of ground on Bush's behalf since the last time the two leaders had met, and he had invested a great amount of his personal political capital in providing what seemed like unequivocal support for the American president. Britain was the only member of the alliance that was making a military contribution to the sharp end of the Afghan war. Blair hoped to receive some form of payback from the White House, if for no other reason than to provide a riposte to those critics at home and abroad who taunted him with jibes that he was nothing more than "Bush's poodle."

Blair found Bush in low spirits. The war was taking far longer than he expected, and he knew that the American public expected a swift and devastating defeat of the perpetrators of the 9/11 attacks. The previous day, Donald Rumsfeld had told a briefing of the Pentagon press corps that it could take several months to clear the Taliban and al-Qaeda out of the network of caves in which they had taken refuge. Blair's visit started with a brief meeting in the Oval Office, and then a joint press conference at which both leaders did their best to boost each other and the antiterrorism cause. The United States, Bush said, had "no better friend in the world" than Britain. "I've got no better person I would like to talk to about our mutual concerns than Tony Blair . . . He brings a lot of wisdom and judgment." Blair responded by thanking Bush "once again for his leadership and his strength at this time."[37]

For all the compliments, however, Bush made it clear that his view of the war on terror was different from that of Blair. Bush believed al-Qaeda would be defeated, "peace or no peace in the Middle East." This was the exact opposite of what Blair had been saying during his tour of the Middle East the previous week, when he had tried to impress on moderate Arab leaders and Israel the fact that the fate of the war on terror and the Middle East peace process were inextricable. Despite the hype that had attended Blair's previous meetings with Bush—including the extraordinary reception he enjoyed when he attended the joint session of Congress—the November meeting brought home to him the limits of his influence in the White House. It was not the first time Blair had been forced to confront the limitations of his position: he had encountered similar problems in the spring of 1999 when he tried to persuade President Clinton to commit ground troops to Kosovo. But in the weeks after 9/11, Blair had gone out on a limb in support of Bush, and had hoped that, as a result, his voice would be heard in the White House.

Blair firmly believed that resolving the Israel-Palestine dispute would benefit the wider war on terrorism, and was keen for Bush to reengage in a process that had been left in abeyance since Clinton left office. Over dinner that evening, Blair pressed hard for Bush to meet Yasser Arafat during the UN General Assembly that was due to take place the following week. The White House had suggested that Colin Powell, the secretary of state, would make a historic announcement that would commit the United States for the first time to the creation of a Palestinian state. But Bush refused to change his mind. So far as he was concerned, Arafat was a terrorist, and nothing could persuade Bush to meet him at the UN.

The meeting lasted six hours, and Blair flew home empty-handed. Not only would Bush not budge on Arafat, but Powell's planned statement at the UN on the establishment of an independent Palestinian state was postponed. In fact, in the days immediately following Blair's visit, leading members of Bush's administration seemed to go out of their way to contradict Blair's view of how the war on terror should be conducted. While Blair devoted all his energy to building an international consensus, Rumsfeld bluntly refuted the idea that anyone could tell America how to conduct the war. Addressing a black-tie dinner of the defense establishment in Washington, Rumsfeld received a standing ovation when he repeated the mantra that defined his attitude to fighting the war on terror. "The coalition must not determine the mission," he declared. America would decide what do to, and if others wanted to join, that was up to them.

The other sensitive area, so far as Blair was concerned, was whether success in Afghanistan would lead to the war being expanded to other countries, such as Iraq. During his period of shuttle diplomacy, Blair had constantly sought to reassure skeptical Arab leaders that Iraq would only be targeted if proof were provided that it was involved in the 9/11 attacks. But the day after Blair returned to London, both Dick Cheney, the U.S. vice president, and Richard Perle, a leading neocon who chaired the Pentagon's Defense Review Board, made public statements predicting that an attack on Iraq would follow the successful conclusion of the Afghan War. When asked specifically about Iraq during an interview for a British newspaper, Cheney replied: "A state that hosts terrorists or provides sanctuary has to accept guilt for their actions as much as the terrorists."[38] And in another newspaper interview, the same day, Richard Perle raised the distinctly alarming prospect of extending the war on terror to cover such disparate states as Lebanon, North Korea, Iran, Yemen, Libya, Sudan, and Somalia.[39] However highly Bush might rate Blair as an ally, it was not enough to prevent influential figures in his administration from doing their best to undermine the British prime minister in public.

Downing Street remained philosophical about the limits of its influence over policy in the White House, particularly so far as the Middle East was concerned. "It would be unfair to say that there was tension between Blair and Bush, although it would be fair to say that there were differences of opinion," explained one of Blair's senior Downing Street aides. "The White House worked closely with us and listened carefully to what we had to say. But we did not expect very much of them at that stage, and we were aware that there were significant differences between us on many issues, especially the Middle East. But we believed strongly that resolving the Israel-Palestine dispute was crucial to resolving some of the issues that played into the hands of the terrorists. We had taken a similar approach in Northern Ireland. We felt that we had to do the right thing so far as the Middle East was concerned, and so we kept nagging away in the hope that one day we might make some progress."[40]

A rift in relations between London and Washington was averted by an unexpected breakthrough in the Afghan conflict. On November 10, the strategically important town of Mazar-I-Sharif in northern Afghanistan fell to coalition forces, quickly followed by the fall of Kabul on November 13. The military successes prompted the collapse of the Taliban regime—as both American and British intelligence had predicted before the war—and thousands of Taliban officials and supporters fled for their lives. Most of them headed south to the Pakistan border and east to the Tora Bora region of the country. Sporadic fighting continued for the rest of the month, until the fall of Kandahar on December 7, which meant that almost the whole country was under the control of the Northern Alliance and its allies. The overthrow of the Taliban had been completed in just two months.

Blair watched the fall of Kabul on television in Downing Street. One of the most extreme and repressive religious systems of modern times had been overthrown, and Blair was particularly struck by the television footage of a few women tearing off their burkas, the traditional veil that Afghan women had been forced to wear by the Taliban. The new rulers on the streets announced that women could go back to work and girls back to school, activities that had been banned by the Taliban. Men would be allowed to shave off their beards. Behind the scenes of joyous celebration, however, the liberators were exacting a terrible revenge on their former adversaries. The streets and ditches around the capital were littered with the bodies of Taliban fighters. The Afghan tribesmen particularly hated the foreign, mainly Arab, fighters who had joined the Taliban, and any of them unfortunate enough to fall into the hands of the liberators were lynched.

Bush and Blair were greatly relieved at the rapid conclusion of the war, which happened at the moment when public opinion both in America and Britain was starting to turn against the campaign. It had been achieved with just a few hundred American and British special forces teams and intelligence officers working with Afghan tribesmen, supported by a devastating aerial bombardment by the American air force. Money proved to be a key component in the war strategy, with the CIA paying out an estimated $70 million to Afghan tribesmen for their loyalty, and to Taliban commanders for defecting. An indication of just how much pressure Blair was under when the war ended was reflected in his somewhat petty decision to publish a "roll call of shame" of British journalists who he claimed had misrepresented the war aims.

A political settlement was quickly reached on the future administration of Afghanistan. On December 5, the four main Afghan factions that had supported the campaign to overthrow the Taliban met in Bonn under the auspices of the UN's special envoy, Lakhdar Brahimi. The factions agreed to set up a power-sharing council with Hamid Karzai, a Westernized Afghan tribesman from the south of the country, heading the council for an interim six-month period until a *loya jirga*, a traditional meeting of the clans, could be convened to confirm a postwar settlement. The rapid political settlement of a country that had been involved in a bitter civil war for more than twenty years was a remarkable tour de force by Brahimi who, apart from winning the consent of Afghanistan's quarrelsome tribesmen, managed to achieve a consensus between America and Europe over the country's future.

Despite this success, there were tensions between Washington and London over the postwar reconstruction of Afghanistan. Blair believed that the coalition had a moral obligation to help the Afghans rebuild their lives after the tyranny of the Taliban, while the Bush administration gave every indication that, with Afghanistan out of the way, it wanted to confront new challenges. The Americans, said Sir Christopher Meyer, the British ambassador to Washington, were "immensely allergic to the notion of either 'nation-building' or 'peace-keeping.' "[41] With Bush seemingly indifferent to Afghanistan's future—so long as it no longer afforded a base for bin Laden and al-Qaeda—Blair took it upon himself to demonstrate to the Afghan people that they would not be forgotten as they attempted to rebuild their country. On January 7, 2002, Blair secretly flew with Cherie to Bagram, the coalition's main operational center, to see Hamid Karzai. The journey was not without risk, as the Taliban were still believed to have ground-to-air missiles that could shoot down aircraft. Blair told Karzai that he could count on his support to ensure "Afghanistan becomes a stable country, part of the international community once more."

The military picture was less clear, and although the major objective of overthrowing the Taliban had been achieved, the other key war aim of capturing bin Laden and the leaders of al-Qaeda had not been fulfilled. Throughout the war, bin Laden had boasted in videotaped messages that he would inflict the same fate on the Americans as he had on the Soviets in the 1980s. But by early November, he realized that the Taliban was a lost cause, and on November 10, two days before the fall of Kabul, a convoy of trucks believed to contain bin Laden was seen heading out of the capital. With the exception of Mohammed Atef, the head of al-Qaeda's military committee responsible for running terror training camps in Afghanistan, who was killed in an American bombing raid on his house three days after the fall of Kabul, most of the al-Qaeda leadership managed to escape. Bin Laden and the bulk of al-Qaeda made their way to the forbidding Tora Bora mountain range in southern Afghanistan, close to the border with Afghanistan. Bin Laden's convoy was spotted in Jalalabad on November 12, but after that he disappeared into the network of caves around Tora Bora, which had been excavated during the war against the Soviets. The CIA estimated there were more than one thousand caves in the area, and that between one thousand to fifteen hundred al-Qaeda fighters had gathered for a last stand against coalition forces. Rather than sending troops to clear them out, American commanders opted to bomb the area with daisy-cutter and bunker-buster bombs.

At some point during the massive bombardment of Tora Bora, bin Laden, America's most wanted man, managed to escape, together with his key lieutenants. Blair and his British commanders were frustrated by the American tactics of relying on airpower and the cooperation of local tribal leaders to destroy al-Qaeda. In November, Blair had offered to deploy six thousand British troops to support American operations to flush out the remnants of al-Qaeda, but the Pentagon dismissed his offer. At CentCom headquarters in Florida, General Tommy Franks decided that it was too risky to put U.S. soldiers on the ground at Tora Bora, preferring to let local Pashtun warlords, who were more familiar with the terrain, do the fighting. They worked with teams of special forces, whose main function was to provide American bombers with the coordinates to carry out their attacks. Intelligence intercepts suggested that bin Laden was still at Tora Bora on December 5, when his ghostly voice was heard on the radio, directing his troops. A few days later, however, bin Laden vanished, assisted by local Pashtun villagers whom he had sensibly bribed prior to the war to guide him out of the country.[42]

Bin Laden was able to escape because American commanders had failed to secure the Afghan border with Pakistan, and because they were not prepared to deploy sufficient numbers of American troops. The Pentagon had given Pakistan's president Musharraf responsibility for sealing the one-hundred-mile border, but the Pakistani military, which had enjoyed close ties with the Taliban and al-Qaeda, made only a token effort, so the siege of Tora Bora proved ineffective because the back door was left wide open. The closest anyone got to capturing bin Laden came when a team of British intelligence officers, working with a sixty-strong unit of Special Boat Service forces, stumbled across information that bin Laden was hiding in a valley close to Tora Bora. They were confident that they could kill or capture him if they were allowed to sweep the valley. But when the British officers, who were working under U.S. command, asked for permission to act, they were told to stand down by their U.S. commanders, who wanted their own Delta Force to conduct the operation. Valuable time was then lost while American commanders debated what the risk of U.S. casualties would be, whether local Afghan fighters should move in first, and how low attack aircraft should fly. The delay enabled bin Laden to escape and left the British special forces team feeling badly let down.[43]

The Americans' failure to achieve the main objective of capturing or killing bin Laden prompted allegations that the Pentagon deliberately did not send sufficient numbers of ground troops to Afghanistan because Rumsfeld and other administration hawks already had their sights set on invading Iraq and wanted to conserve military resources. According to Richard Clarke, the White House's former counterterrorism expert, "The plan for Afghanistan was affected by a predisposition to go into Iraq. The result was that they didn't have enough people to go in and stabilize the country, nor to make sure [bin Laden and his associates] didn't get out."[44] There were suggestions by conspiracy theorists that the Americans had deliberately let bin Laden escape because they were afraid of what he might reveal about his previous dealings with Washington. After all, bin Laden had been a key ally of the CIA during the clandestine war to drive the Soviet Union out of Afghanistan during the 1980s.

British officials, however, took a more sanguine view of bin Laden's escape and the refusal of American commanders to allow British special forces to try to capture the al-Qaeda leader. "It was all very frustrating, but we took the view that it was more cockup than conspiracy," said a senior British intelligence officer who was involved in the hunt for bin Laden. "The Americans had their own plans for dealing with bin Laden, and their own way of doing things. It just turned out that it was not a very good plan. But after Tora Bora I think they learned their lesson."[45] And General Sir Mike Jackson, the commander of the British army, said it was wrong to say that the war was a failure because bin Laden was able to escape. "The war in Afghanistan was not a conventional campaign but it was undertaken with skill, and a lot was achieved in a little time," he said. "If we had caught bin Laden and not got rid of the Taliban we would have failed. If the Taliban had stayed, another bin Laden would have come along, and we would have been back to square one."[46]

In early 2002, the Pentagon finally conceded that it could not rely entirely on local Afghan fighters to eradicate the remnants of al-Qaeda in Afghanistan, and three infantry battalions from the 10th Mountain Division and the 101st Airborne Division were deployed against al-Qaeda. In March, U.S. forces were involved in a bloody battle with an estimated one thousand al-Qaeda fighters who had regrouped in the Shah-I-Kot valley south of the town of Gardez, in another mountainous area close to the Pakistan border. The ferocity with which the al-Qaeda fighters defended themselves led intelligence officers to believe that they were protecting an HVT, or high-value target, perhaps bin Laden. An estimated eight hundred al-Qaeda and Taliban fighters were killed during the American offensive, and the coalition suffered eleven dead— eight of them Americans—and eighty-eight wounded. But when U.S. special forces and intelligence officers finally swept the caves around Shah-I-Kot, there was no sign of bin Laden or any of the al-Qaeda leaders. Bin Laden and al-Qaeda had survived to fight another day.

The overthrow of the Taliban and the destruction of al-Qaeda's operational headquarters had inflicted a serious blow on bin Laden's infrastructure, but the amorphous nature of the organization meant that it was able to continue to function in other parts of the world. President Bush had confided that after 9/11 he kept a personal scorecard of al-Qaeda's top leadership in his desk in the Oval Office, and every time one of them was killed or captured, he would mark it with an "X." At the end of the Afghan conflict, following the dramatic escape of bin Laden and the rest of the al-Qaeda leadership from Tora Bora, sixteen of the twenty-two scorecard pictures remained untouched.

Eight

PREPARE FOR BATTLE

ON TUESDAY, JANUARY 29, 2002, an estimated 52 million Americans tuned in to their television sets to watch President George W. Bush make the annual State of the Union address before the joint session of Congress. The audience was the highest recorded since President Clinton's address to the nation at the height of the Monica Lewinsky sex scandal in 1998. Bush had invited a number of distinguished guests to sit with First Lady Laura Bush in the upstairs gallery. Among them was Hamid Karzai, the new interim leader of Afghanistan who had taken office five weeks earlier. Bush began his forty-eight-minute speech by acknowledging the successful U.S.-led operation to defeat the Taliban, and Karzai's position as the new ruler of Afghanistan. With bin Laden still on the run, no mention was made of the al-Qaeda leader. Instead, the president turned his attention to the future conduct of the war on terror.

The key objective for the United States in the years that lay ahead, he said, was to eliminate the threat posed by terrorist regimes that seek weapons of mass destruction. Bush was determined to "prevent regimes that sponsor terror from threatening America or our friends and allies with weapons of mass destruction." North Korea was a regime that was arming itself with missiles and weapons of mass destruction while starving its citizens. Iran aggressively pursued these weapons and exported terror while an "unelected few" repressed the people's hope for freedom. But Bush saved his strongest condemnation for Iraq, a country that "continues to flaunt its hostility toward America and to support terror." The Iraqi regime had been attempting to develop anthrax, nerve gas, and nuclear weapons for over a decade. "This is a regime that has already used poison gas to murder thousands of its own citizens . . . This is a regime that agreed to international inspections—then kicked out the inspectors. This is a regime that has something to hide from the civilized world." So far as Bush was concerned, states like these, and their terrorist allies, constituted an "axis of evil." If left unchecked, these countries could ultimately provide weapons of mass destruction to terrorists, which could be used to attack the United States and its allies. Bush concluded his speech by declaring, "Our war on terror is well begun, but it is only begun."[1]

Bush's State of the Union address in January 2002 developed the themes that he had articulated during his hastily written television broadcast on the night of September 11, when he had declared that "we will make no distinction between the terrorists who committed these acts and those who harbor them." The "axis of evil" reference, however, together with the fact that Bush made scant reference to the worldwide support America had received after 9/11, increased the resentment in Europe that Washington was determined to go it alone in fighting the war on terror. Until this moment, most European leaders had been broadly supportive of the American campaign, even if they felt slighted that Washington had not been more receptive to their offers of help. No one in Europe seriously doubted that bin Laden's organization had been responsible for 9/11, and there was a consensus that America had every right to prosecute its war against al-Qaeda and those who supported it. Islamic terrorism was, after all, a threat that was not solely confined to America and American interests. Many European governments, particularly France and Germany, had their own experience of dealing with Islamic extremists, and there was a general understanding that coordinated action was required to prevent a succession of 9/11-type attacks against European targets. But the implication in Bush's speech that the war on terror would be expanded to include those countries that, so far as it was known, had no direct involvement in the 9/11 attacks caused deep unease

in many European capitals. They would respond by withdrawing the unequivocal support that they had given Washington so long as the war on
terror was confined to al-Qaeda and the Taliban.

Although North Korea and Iran were named with Iraq as forming an
"axis of evil," there was little doubt either in Washington or elsewhere
that the main focus of Washington's attention was Saddam Hussein's
Iraq. David Frum, the White House speechwriter who was involved in
drafting the address, later explained that when he was asked by Mike
Gerson, the president's chief speechwriter, to work on a draft in late December 2001, he understood his task "was to provide a justification for a
war."[2] Charles Krauthammer, a prominent neoconservative essayist and
columnist for the *Washington Post*, understood perfectly what the president was driving at when he wrote, "Iraq is what this speech was about.
If there was a serious internal debate within the administration over what
to do about Iraq, that debate is over. The speech was just short of a declaration of war." Bush, who seemed unaware of the headlines that the
"axis of evil" reference would generate, was satisfied that the speech
blurred the focus by including North Korea and Iran, as it provided ad-
ditional cover for the secret planning for covert action against Iraq, and
war.[3]

If the "axis of evil" reference came as a surprise to Blair, the warmongering over Iraq did not. Bush had told him over dinner at the White
House on September 20, 2001, that, even though Iraq was not going to
be included in the first wave of attacks, he reserved the right to deal with
Iraq at a later date. The success of the military campaign in Afghanistan,
at least in terms of overthrowing the Taliban, had buoyed Bush's spirits
and given him confidence as a war leader, a quality that had not been
immediately obvious in the aftermath of 9/11. Although bin Laden, the
main culprit of the 9/11 attacks, was still at large, Bush did not want to
be constrained by confining the war on terror solely to al-Qaeda.

As early as September 17, 2001, Bush had told a meeting of the National Security Council in the cabinet room that he suspected that Saddam was directly involved in the 9/11 attacks. "I believe Iraq was
involved," he said, "but I'm not going to strike them now. I don't have the
evidence at this point."[4] It was still unclear whether Bush had any evidence

that Saddam was in any way responsible for 9/11, although advisors such as Paul Wolfowitz, the deputy secretary of defense, were convinced of Saddam's culpability. On the day immediately following the 9/11 attacks, Wolfowitz had openly disputed the CIA's assessment that al-Qaeda was responsible for the attacks. So far as Wolfowitz was concerned, the operation was too sophisticated and complicated for a terrorist group to have pulled off by itself. In his view, al-Qaeda must have had a state sponsor, and he believed that Iraq had helped it. Wolfowitz's opinion had clearly made an impact on Bush's thinking, for later that day he told Richard A. Clarke, the administration's al-Qaeda expert, "See if Saddam did this. See if he's linked in any way."[5]

By January 2002, there was still no evidence directly linking Saddam to 9/11, even though by this time the CIA had been able to sift through copious al-Qaeda notes and computer files that had been captured during the Afghan war. The files showed lots of plans of American nuclear establishments, and how to conduct terrorist operations against America, but nothing had been uncovered that suggested al-Qaeda was working in collusion with Iraq. The most alarming discovery, however, was that al-Qaeda was well-advanced in its plans to develop a dirty bomb, a crude nuclear device made up of radioactive material, such as spent fuel rods and Semtex high explosive. Although such a bomb would not cause the same degree of physical damage as a conventional nuclear weapon, it would have the ability to pollute an area the size of Manhattan with high levels of radioactive poisoning. Such a weapon could be carried around in a suitcase, and a detailed examination of material found in al-Qaeda's network of caves in Afghanistan in late 2001 had uncovered a diagram and assembly instructions for a dirty bomb. The discovery was accompanied by a warning from the CIA that a leading al-Qaeda operative had left Afghanistan during the war carrying a canister of what he claimed was radioactive material.

The dirty bomb discovery in Afghanistan had a profound impact on Bush and Blair. In Washington, Bush had been fretting that a bin Laden agent might detonate a radiological bomb in America in retaliation for Operation Enduring Freedom. Only the previous October, American intelligence had received warnings that Islamic militants were planning another spectacular attack on the United States, one that, in the words of

Condoleezza Rice, would "make September 11 look like child's play, by using some terrible weapon."[6] The attack did not materialize, but the scare made a deep impression on the president. The discoveries made in al-Qaeda's Afghan cave network reinforced the view in Washington that Islamic terrorist groups were determined to acquire WMD. In London, Blair was equally concerned about the discoveries. For several years, the prime minister had highlighted the potential threat posed to Western security by WMD proliferation, and the findings in Afghanistan confirmed his worst suspicions. "Here was tangible proof of what Blair had feared all along," said a senior Downing Street official. "It was an example of what he genuinely feared. If a terrorist group successfully got hold of WMD the consequences were unthinkable. This was not something that had been dreamed up. It was a very real threat. Here it was, and Blair felt very strongly that we had to deal with it. He saw it as one of the great contemporary challenges."[7]

Bush's State of the Union speech was drafted with the recent discoveries made in Afghanistan occupying the thoughts of Washington policymakers, and resulted in the parameters of the war on terror undergoing a radical revision. From now on, the war would not merely be waged against those responsible for attacking America on 9/11, but against any group or country that was deemed to pose a threat against the United States. The policy of preemption had been born. Iraq, which had wantonly defied the international community since the end of the Gulf War in 1991, and was known to have an active interest in developing WMD, was the obvious next target. If anything, the U.S. military's perceived success in the war in Afghanistan had made Washington more, not less, determined to pursue its own unilateralist course of action in the war on terror, as the State of the Union address made abundantly clear. Chris Patten, the EU's external affairs commissioner, expressed the concerns of many in Europe when he remarked that the United States was in danger of going into "unilateralist overdrive."

At the Pentagon, Donald Rumsfeld certainly had no qualms about planning for an exclusively American invasion of Iraq. On February 1, just three days after the State of the Union address, he met with General Tommy Franks to discuss a war plan for Iraq—called Op Plan 1003—

that could be executed as a unilateral, U.S.-only invasion. It envisaged a total force of three hundred thousand U.S. troops—less than the five hundred thousand involved in Operation Desert Storm in 1991. Franks had been working on a war plan for Iraq since November 21, when Bush had asked Rumsfeld to draw up a list of the military options available against Saddam. Although no decision had yet been taken to declare war on Iraq, Bush wanted to know precisely what an invasion would entail, how long the preparations would take, and the likely length of such a conflict. Franks's revised plan, which he had discussed in minute detail with Rumsfeld, was presented to Bush on February 7. The general estimated that the war would last for 225 days, which included the 90 days of preparations and force deployment. Given the time needed to assemble such a force, it would not be possible to begin an offensive until October at the earliest. Taking into account other factors, such as Iraqi weather patterns and the annual training routines of the Iraqi armed forces, Franks advised that the best times militarily to attack Iraq would be from December 1, 2002, through February 2003.[8]

At this point, Blair was not aware of the precise military plans being drawn up in Washington for an America-only invasion of Iraq, but he understood that there was immense enthusiasm within the Bush administration for implementing Washington's official policy of effecting regime change in Baghdad.[9] Sir David Manning, Blair's foreign policy advisor, wrote a memo to the prime minister in early March, warning that Bush was determined to remove Saddam from power, and expressing his concern about the possible power vacuum that such action would create in Baghdad.[10] Sir Jeremy Greenstock, the British ambassador to the UN, had discovered the previous month that the United States was serious about Iraq, and thought it was wrong for Washington to view Iraq in the same context as Afghanistan. "I thought the Americans could not assume that because they had sympathy and support for their action in Afghanistan then they could go and do another country that was on their agenda. Iraq was not in the same basket as Afghanistan. It would be far more difficult to handle."[11]

Blair had entertained similar doubts in the autumn of 2001 and in the weeks following the war in Afghanistan, and expressed his reservations in public. His view was that unless there was clear evidence of Iraqi complicity in 9/11, there was no justification for an attack on Baghdad. By early 2002, British intelligence, like its American counterpart, had found nothing to link Saddam with 9/11. "We had been over everything with a fine-toothed comb and there was nothing to link Saddam to 9/11," said a senior SIS officer.[12]

After the success of the Afghan campaign, Blair renewed his interest in Iraq. Since becoming prime minister, Blair had been committed to dealing with the issues of both Iraq and WMD proliferation. He had readily supported President Clinton in the American-led air strikes on Iraq in late 1998, and had been at the forefront of the campaign at the UN to maintain sanctions against Iraq. Britain and America had been the only two permanent members of the Security Council to vote in favor of Resolution 1284 in December 1999, which proposed a relaxation in the terms of the UN sanctions against Iraq in return for Saddam's full cooperation with UN weapons inspectors. France, Russia, and China, which wanted the sanctions lifted irrespective of whether or not Saddam complied with his disarmament obligations, abstained. British and American warplanes continued to patrol the no-fly zones in northern and southern Iraq, and as recently as August 10, 2001, British and U.S. jets had bombed three Iraqi air defense sites.

Throughout this period, Blair was receiving a steady stream of reports from British intelligence, highlighting its concern about Saddam's WMD. By early 2002, the assessment given by SIS to Downing Street led Blair to conclude that there was a continuing and "clear strategic intent on the part of the Iraqi regime to pursue its nuclear, biological, chemical, and ballistic missile programs."[13] At the same time, British intelligence had uncovered evidence that for nearly ten years, the Pakistani nuclear scientist A. Q. Khan had been selling to rogue states key components for making nuclear weapons. With the discoveries made about al-Qaeda's attempts to develop WMD capability, Downing Street was firmly of the opinion that the threat posed by a rogue dictator like Saddam Hussein, who had willfully defied the international community for eleven years, could no longer be ignored.

"What changed for me with September 11," Blair later recalled, "was that I thought you have to change your mindset . . . you have to go out and get the different aspects of this threat . . . you have to deal with this, otherwise the threat will grow . . . you have to take a stand, you have to say 'Right, we are not going to allow the development of WMD in breach of the will of the international community to continue.' "[14] According to one of Blair's close advisors, the prime minister's resolve on the issue of WMD hardened after the discoveries in Afghanistan. "Blair had been warning people about terrorists linking up with rogue states for years, and then we found all this stuff in Afghanistan. It was a chilling demonstration that this was not an idle threat."[15]

Blair was independently forming a conclusion similar to Bush's on how to conduct the next phase in the war on terror. The most significant issue for Blair was the intelligence reports he was receiving from SIS that indicated that Saddam was actively seeking to develop WMD in defiance of the UN. Given that Saddam had used such weapons in the past against the Iranians and the Kurds, there was every likelihood that at some point in the future he would use them again. By early 2002, it was clear to both the British and the Americans that the sanctions regime against Iraq was collapsing through lack of international support. There were regular flights from Jordan, Syria, and Lebanon to Saddam International Airport, and Saddam's immediate family was estimated to be receiving up to $3 billion a year from their illicit oil-smuggling activities. Blair believed strongly that Saddam should be made to comply with the ceasefire terms he had signed at the end of the Gulf War, and allow teams of UN inspectors to verify that all of Iraq's WMD programs had been dismantled.

The main difference between Blair and Bush in their approach to the Iraq issue was that while the prime minister felt that there should be an international campaign to force Saddam to comply, Bush and most of his war cabinet had little faith in the ability of institutions such as the UN to bring the Iraqi dictator to heel. The hawkish instincts of the Bush administration led it to conclude that the only way to ensure that Saddam did not provide WMD to Islamic terror groups was to secure his removal from power through American force of arms. Regime change in Baghdad had, after all, been official American policy since 1998. In addition, Bush argued that Saddam's support for international terrorist groups made it a legitimate target in the war on terror. Saddam had, over the years, supported a wide variety of terrorists, from Carlos the Jackal, the architect of the OPEC siege in Vienna in the 1970s, to the notorious Palestinian terrorist Abu Nidal. In the absence of any hard evidence, the more hawkish members of the Bush administration continued to insist that Saddam was collaborating with bin Laden's al-Qaeda organization, and that he was somehow involved in the 9/11 attacks, although Downing Street did not believe this was the president's view. "Bush and Rice accepted that al-Qaeda was not involved in 9/11, but some people in Washington refused to accept this as fact," said a Downing Street official. [16]

The most important change in Blair's outlook on Iraq in early 2002 was the realization that taking military action to remove Saddam was a feasible option. Previously, Blair and his key Downing Street advisors had never seriously contemplated a military campaign against Iraq to force Saddam to comply with UN resolutions. Apart from providing warplanes to patrol the no-fly zones, Blair had regarded sanctions and containment as the only policies available for applying pressure on Saddam's regime. But, according to a senior Downing Street advisor, a crucial factor in Blair's thinking was the success of the military campaign in Afghanistan in overthrowing the Taliban. "Although Blair took a keen interest in the Iraq issue before 9/11, it never crossed his mind that a military invasion could be launched to remove Saddam from power," said the official. "He realized after Afghanistan that it was possible to make a difference, and that it was possible to rid the world of rotten regimes. The experience in Afghanistan was a real eye-opener for him." [17]

Regime change was not official British policy as it was in America, and many people in Britain, including the Foreign Office and Blair's Labour Party, would have regarded such a policy as a clear breach of international law. But the fact that regime change in Afghanistan had been effected with relative ease, and with minimal loss of life among the coalition forces, encouraged Blair to believe that a similar course of action—if necessary—could be undertaken in Iraq. For Blair, Saddam's secular tyranny was no worse than the Islamic theocracy that had brutalized Afghanistan, and he did not plan to impede an American-led campaign to rid Baghdad of the Baathist dictatorship. Indeed, Blair was exasperated by the antiwar opposition he was starting to encounter from the left of his own Labour Party. "I can't understand why people on the [political] left oppose it," he would tell visitors to his Downing Street study. "Hasn't the left always been committed to fighting injustice in the world?"[18] Or, as one of his Downing Street advisors put it, "If the Spanish Civil War was being fought today, you wonder whose side the left would be on."[19]

Another key consideration of Blair's in early 2002 was his almost visceral belief that it was the duty of a British prime minister, and also in Britain's long-term national interest, to be steadfast in supporting the United States in times of conflict. Blair believed that he had exerted influence on Bush's policy in the initial phase of the war on terror and that Bush had settled on a rational course of action as a consequence. Blair's opinions had carried much weight in the White House, and his was the main voice that Bush paid attention to that came from outside the White House war cabinet.

There was, nevertheless, a degree of hubris to Blair's view that only he could influence policy in Washington. On several occasions in early 2002, Blair made comments to the effect that he was the only Western leader who could make a positive impact on policy-making in Washington, which, while true, might have been better left unsaid. "Bluntly, I am the one Western leader the U.S. will really listen to," he confided to a friend in March 2002.[20] So far as Blair was concerned, apart from being the most powerful nation on earth, the United States was essentially a force for good in the world, and if he was to have any chance of achieving his stated goals of bringing peace to the Middle East, alleviating suffering in Africa, and tackling global warming, he was far more likely to do so if he worked closely with America.

Blair repeated this view during a rare cabinet meeting to discuss the growing revolt within the Labour Party at the prospect of war with Iraq. Blair's governing style had become almost presidential, and he preferred to work with a close group of confidants and advisors in Downing Street rather than use the cabinet, a more traditional method. This shift was much resented by his Labour Party colleagues. The cabinet met infrequently, and many senior ministers were not informed of important developments in British policy. Consequently, on those occasions that the cabinet did meet, Blair was subjected to scathing criticism from some ministers, particularly those from the left of the party, such as Robin Cook, the former foreign secretary who had become leader of the Commons, and Clare Short, who was in charge of overseas aid. On March 7, seventy Labour MPs signed a Commons motion declaring that British involvement in a war against Iraq would be unwise.

A cabinet meeting was called to discuss the government's Iraq policy. Robin Cook, who was still seething over his peremptory removal from the Foreign Office the previous year, claimed in his memoirs, "For the first time in five years, Tony was out on a limb." Blair was asked tough questions about the legality of such a war, and how his alliance with America would affect Britain's relations with Europe. Patricia Hewitt, a Blair loyalist, lamented that Britain was supposed to listen to U.S. worries about Iraq at the same time that Washington was punishing Britain's steel industry by imposing high tariffs on British exports. "We are in danger of being seen as close to President Bush, but without any influence over President Bush," she remarked.[21] Blair listened attentively to the discussion, but "he was very firm with us about where he saw that Britain's national interest lay," said Cook. Blair told his cabinet colleagues, "We must steer close to America. If we don't, we will lose our influence to shape what they do . . . we cannot oppose the Americans."[22] At this stage, Blair had not committed himself irrevocably to undertake military action with the United States, and had an open mind about how the problem of Iraq would be resolved. "He realized that something had to be done about Iraq, but it was really a question of how Saddam reacted to the new world situation post 9/11," explained one of Blair's aides. "Our view was that it would be up to Saddam how we dealt with Saddam."[23]

The Iraqi dictator did little to discourage the determination of the more hawkish members of Bush's administration to carry out their threat of regime change. In October 2001, Saddam had published a long, rambling letter to the American people in which he condemned the war in Afghanistan, and claimed that U.S. policy was being driven by "Zionism." His suggestion that the American mainland could be subjected to further terrorist attacks particularly played into the hands of those in

Washington who believed that Iraq had been involved in the 9/11 attacks. In November, when the UN suggested that sanctions might be lifted against Iraq if Saddam allowed the UN inspectors to return, the offer was dismissed out of hand. And at the end of the year, an Iraqi government survey that was commissioned on Saddam's orders nominated Osama bin Laden as Iraq's "Man of the Year 2001."

THE INITIAL DOWNING STREET reaction to Bush's "axis of evil" was to try to figure out whether Washington was serious about waging war against North Korea, Iran, and Iraq, all at the same time. Sir Christopher Meyer, the British ambassador, dispatched a "don't panic" missive to the prime minister soon after Bush's speech, advising that the language should not be taken at face value. As he later recalled, the message he sent to London was, "Cool it, no knee-jerk reactions, please. Don't jump to conclusions. Start working immediately with the administration about what the practical consequences were of putting Iran, North Korea, and Iraq in the same box."[24] Colin Powell, the secretary of state, was the first to clarify the president's comments, telling Congress that the United States intended to treat North Korea and Iran differently, and that there were no plans to start a war with either country.

Regarding Iraq, however, Bush and his war cabinet were working hard to put together a plan to achieve regime change in Baghdad. While Rumsfeld and Franks concentrated on refining and reworking the Iraq invasion plan, on February 16, Bush signed a Top Secret intelligence order for regime change in Baghdad. The order gave the CIA the authority to work with opposition groups that sought Saddam's overthrow; conduct sabotage operations inside Iraq; work with third countries, such as Jordan and Saudi Arabia; conduct information operations to distribute accurate information about the regime; run disinformation campaigns to confuse Saddam's regime; disrupt the regime's banking and finances; and disrupt the regime's illicit procurement of material related to its military, especially its weapons of mass destruction. A total of $189 million was approved by Congress to pay for the operation, and fifty intelligence officers were assigned to get the operation up and running.[25] The CIA was also authorized to use lethal force to remove Saddam from power. Bush had given the green light for Saddam's assassination. A measure of Bush's determination to overthrow Saddam was reflected in an article that appeared in *Time* magazine. It reported that Bush had poked his head around the door of Condoleezza Rice's office while she was meeting with three senators and shouted, "Fuck Saddam. We're taking him out."

While the Bush administration was determined to remove Saddam, neither the White House nor Downing Street regarded war as inevitable in early 2002, and no decision to go to war had yet been taken. "Of course we were making plans for military action in Iraq—that's our job," said a senior Pentagon official. "But we make plans all the time. The president wanted to have all the options possible available to him, and military action was just one of them. But it was not the only option."[26] At the same time, officials in London were also working on a range of options. "We were all clear in our minds that Saddam was not implicated in 9/11," said a senior Downing Street advisor. "But by the same token, we knew the Iraq issue had to be resolved one way or another. The sanctions were clearly not working, Saddam was making a lot of money from oil smuggling, and we were receiving intelligence reports that he had revived his interest in acquiring nuclear technology. It was not something we felt we could ignore, even though we did not put it in the same basket as Afghanistan."[27]

Good intelligence would be crucial if a successful conclusion to the campaign against Saddam were to be achieved. The Joint Intelligence Committee stated repeatedly in the regular intelligence assessments it provided to Downing Street on Iraq that the effectiveness of Saddam's wide-ranging security apparatus meant that Iraq was a very hard intelligence nut to crack. A JIC report, published on March 15, 2002, which contained the latest information available to SIS, stated, "Intelligence on Iraq's WMD and ballistic missile programs is sporadic and patchy. Iraq is also well-practiced in the art of deception, such as concealment and exaggeration. A complete picture of the various programs is therefore difficult." However, the report went on to state, "it is clear that Iraq continues to pursue a policy of acquiring WMD and their delivery means. Intelligence indicates that planning to reconstitute some of its programs began in 1995. WMD programs were then given a further boost in 1998 with the withdrawal of the UNSCOM inspectors . . . Iraq is pursuing a nuclear weapons program. But it will not be able to indigenously produce a nuclear weapon while sanctions remain in place, unless suitable fissile material is produced from abroad."[28]

British intelligence believed that Iraq retained "some stocks of chemical agents" and that, if Saddam gave the order, it could produce "significant quantities of mustard gas" and "significant quantities of sarin and VX (nerve agents) within months, and in the case of VX may have already done so." Finally, JIC reported that "Iraq currently has available, either from pre–Gulf War stocks or more recent production, a number of biological agents. Iraq could produce more of these biological agents within days."[29] Post-9/11, and taking into account the alarming discoveries that had recently been made in al-Qaeda's cave network, the intelligence reports Blair received from SIS in the spring of 2002 strengthened his determination to resolve the threat posed by Saddam Hussein's regime once and for all.

While SIS had serious concerns about Saddam's WMD activities, senior British intelligence officers strongly advised Blair not to link Saddam with al-Qaeda. "So far as we were concerned, Saddam and al-Qaeda were two separate and distinct concerns, and we warned Downing Street repeatedly not to confuse the two," said a senior British intelligence officer.[30] The main "evidence" linking Saddam with al-Qaeda concerned a report that Mohammed Atta, the lead hijacker in the 9/11 attacks, had met an Iraqi intelligence officer in Prague. The alleged meeting had been used by American hawks, including James Woolsey, the former CIA director, to argue in favor of military action against Iraq. But by March, SIS had concluded that the report was untrue, and that Saddam was not involved in sponsoring al-Qaeda's terrorist activities.

At the end of February, shortly before attending a Commonwealth summit in Australia, Blair made his most combative statement on Iraq to date, declaring that "those who are engaged in spreading weapons of mass destruction are engaged in an evil trade and it is important that we make sure that we take action in support of it."[31] Blair was testing the water both with his Labour Party colleagues and the rest of the world, and he was quickly reminded of the growing domestic hostility to extending the war on terror from Afghanistan to Iraq. Tam Dalyell, the veteran antiwar campaigner and the unofficial spokesman of Labour's antiwar MPs, issued a stern rebuke. "I am dismayed by the warmongering propensities of a Labour prime minister," he said. "One of the conditions of a just war is that everything possible is done to avoid war." [32]

But Blair had seen the intelligence reports, and he felt that he had no alternative other than to make the public aware of the threat he believed that Saddam's WMD posed to international security. Before leaving Australia, he gave a lengthy television interview to Australian television's *60 Minutes* program, in which he gave a detailed explanation of the conclusions he had reached on the Iraq issue. "Iraq is in breach of all conditions of weapons inspectors," he said. "We know they are trying to accumulate weapons of mass destruction. We know that Saddam has used them against his own people. How we deal with this is a matter we must discuss and find the best way to deal with it." Blair lamented the fact that nothing had been done about al-Qaeda in Afghanistan until after the 9/11 attacks had forced the world to confront the threat posed by international terrorism. "For ten years, Afghanistan was like this but we did not do anything. There would have been no consent to do anything . . . but it may have been better to have had the foresight to deal with it then." Now that the threat in Afghanistan had been dealt with, it was time to address the problem of Iraq. "If chemical, biological, or nuclear capability fall into the wrong hands, then I think we have got to act on it because, if we don't act, we will find out too late the potential for destruction." [33]

A subtle but important realignment was taking place in Blair's arguments on Iraq. His initial concern had centered on Saddam's development of WMD and noncompliance with the UN. Now he was saying that there was the possibility that Saddam's WMD could be given to terrorist groups to attack the West, even though the intelligence reports he received from SIS made no mention of Saddam cooperating with terror groups on WMD. The available intelligence on Saddam suggested that Saddam was developing WMD only for his own use, and the links between Saddam's regime and al-Qaeda were at best tenuous. In the 1980s, when Iraq had a WMD capability, there had not been any suggestion that Saddam allowed terrorist groups access to Iraq's chemical, biological, and nuclear technology. Saddam was far too obsessed with power to share such important technology with others. Among all the intelligence in the Middle East that had been presented on rogue states cooperating on WMD programs, such as the links between Libya, Iran, and Pakistan, there was hardly any mention of any Iraqi involvement.[34] But Blair's assertion that Saddam might offer his WMD expertise to terror groups chimed with the views being expressed in Washington, where a potent cocktail of hawks and neocons was taking the argument one step further, claiming that Saddam's WMD could be used by al-Qaeda to attack America and its allies.

The shift in Blair's position on Iraq certainly helped to reassure Dick Cheney when the vice president visited Downing Street on March 11, six months to the day after the 9/11 attacks. Cheney stopped in London en route to the Middle East where he hoped to gather support among Arab governments for the looming Iraq conflict. As secretary of defense in the first Bush administration, Cheney was personally involved in the assembly of the multinational coalition against Iraq for the 1991 Gulf War. He faced a far harder task this time around, as many of Washington's former allies were disputing the necessity of military action against Saddam. Arrangements were already in place for Blair to meet with Bush at his ranch in Crawford, Texas, in early April, and Cheney took advantage of his London visit to catch up on Blair's current thinking about how to tackle Saddam.

Cheney's two hours of talks with Blair at Downing Street on March 11 demonstrated how far Blair's approach to Iraq had evolved since the autumn of 2001, when he had been insistent that Iraq would only be attacked if there were clear evidence of Baghdad's involvement in 9/11. Now Blair supported Cheney's view that the world faced catastrophe if Saddam provided al-Qaeda with nuclear weapons. Although Blair's public comments were guarded, Alastair Campbell, his communications director, left nothing to the imagination when he briefed the British press after the meeting with Cheney. Campbell said that if al-Qaeda had been equipped by Saddam for its September 11 onslaught on New York, "the result would have been not thousands of people dead but tens of thousands or even hundreds of thousands."[35] Cheney, who remained wary of Blair and his Labour colleagues, was pleasantly surprised by the mood of bellicosity he found emanating from the corridors of Downing Street, where Blair's officials seemed to be overreaching themselves in their desire to appear even more hawkish than their American counterparts.

At the press conference Blair and Cheney gave after their talks, it was the American vice president, not Blair, who talked about Saddam linking up with al-Qaeda. Blair, after all, had been explicitly told by SIS that there was no evidence linking Saddam to bin Laden's organization, and little likelihood of Iraq's WMD arsenal being made available to al-Qaeda. Although Cheney conceded that there was no proof of Saddam's involvement in 9/11, he said America was concerned that Saddam could pass on his WMD technology for a second round of more terrible attacks, costing hundreds of thousands of lives. When asked to respond to the same question, Blair certainly gave the impression that the two men were thinking along similar lines. On the one hand, said Blair, Saddam's WMD posed a threat. On the other, if al-Qaeda had been able to deploy WMD during the 9/11 attacks, the consequences would have been far worse. In public, Blair did not dare to link the two. That was left to Cheney, who helpfully pointed out that information obtained from al-Qaeda's training camps in Afghanistan showed that the terror organization was "aggressively seeking" to acquire WMD.

So far as Blair and Cheney were concerned, Saddam had WMD, bin Laden sought to acquire WMD, and, together, Britain and America would make sure that such an apocalyptic union was thwarted. But by trying to align himself with Washington, Blair was undertaking a high-risk strategy. If his hardline approach would help to guarantee admittance to the inner counsels of the White House's decision-making process, he risked overstating the case for war to an already skeptical British public. Blair was attempting to link his long-standing concern about WMD proliferation to Iraq. Even if Iraq was not likely to lend its WMD technology to terror groups, Saddam's continued defiance of the UN could no longer be tolerated in the post-9/11 world. For Blair, this made it imperative to bring Saddam to heel. If Saddam were allowed to get away with his non-compliance, it would send the wrong message to other rogue states. For this reason the West was justified in making an example of Saddam. In seeking to justify his position, however, Blair was prone to being cavalier with some of the facts.

Blair had done enough to reassure Cheney during their Downing Street discussions that Britain would be a reliable ally in the next phase of the war on terror. Before leaving to meet Bush at his ranch in Crawford, Texas, Blair found it harder to make the case for action against Iraq to the British public. The difficulty he faced was underlined when he had to abandon plans to publish an intelligence dossier on Saddam's WMD, because it did not contain sufficient evidence to support military action. Campbell had already briefed the American media that the British government intended to publish proof that Iraq was building weapons of mass destruction, prompting headlines in reputable American newspapers, such as the *Wall Street Journal*: "Britain Will Claim Iraq Is Constructing Massive Weapons." The Foreign Office, which had overall responsibility for compiling the dossier, was forced to withdraw it, mainly because SIS refused to endorse attempts to link Saddam with al-Qaeda.

Blair now faced mounting criticism at home over his controversial alliance with Bush, although there were signs that his attempts to influence policy in Washington were starting to bear fruit. On the day before he was due to fly to Texas, Bush phoned Blair at Downing Street to inform him that he would be intervening in the growing Middle East crisis to stop the Israelis from making military incursions into Palestinian territories. From the outset of the war on terror, Blair had pressed Bush to become more involved in the region, and at first it seemed that the prime minister's entreaties were falling on deaf ears. But the bloody cycle of violence that erupted in the region in early 2002 compelled Bush to deal with the issue. By the end of March, Israelis and Palestinians were on the verge of all-out war after a Hamas suicide bomber had killed twenty-one Israelis as they celebrated Passover at a seder at the seaside resort of Netanya. Sharon responded by sending Israeli army tanks to bombard Yasser Arafat's headquarters in Ramallah, and it took a series of frantic phone calls from Downing Street to persuade the White House to intervene to stop the Israelis from killing Arafat. Bush realized a dramatic intervention from Washington was required if the cycle of violence was to be brought to an end, and on April 5, he made a speech in which he spoke publicly of America's desire for a two-state solution for the region, a commitment previous American administrations had shied away from. "Blair was very persuasive on the Middle East issue," said a senior State Department official. "We had our differences, but we had a constructive dialogue. Blair was always pushing us to do more, and I think he did influence the president. But there was only so far Blair could push us. The big sticking point is that we made it clear we were not going to talk to Arafat, whom we regarded as a terrorist, clear and simple."[36]

On April 6, Blair flew to Crawford to meet with Bush at the family ranch. Blair traveled with three of his top officials—David Manning, his foreign policy advisor; Jonathan Powell, his chief of staff; and Alastair Campbell, his media advisor. On arrival in Texas, Blair and his family were met by Condoleezza Rice, who had been sent by Bush to escort the Blairs for the short helicopter ride from the airport to Prairie Chapel Ranch, the Bushs' 1,600-acre family retreat. Rice was the only senior member of Bush's war cabinet present at Crawford; significantly, Dick Cheney, who usually liked to sit in on Bush's meetings with Blair, was not present. His Downing Street briefing from Blair had been sufficient to allay any fears he may have entertained about Blair's commitment to the next phase of the war. To make sure that there was no misunderstanding about what was on the agenda, on the eve of Blair's visit Bush gave an interview to British television, in which he remarked, "I have made up my mind that Saddam needs to go. That's about all I am willing to share with you." Pressed by the television interviewer about Saddam's links with al-Qaeda, Bush repeated the answer that had become his primary justification for confronting Saddam. "The worst thing that could happen would be to allow a nation like Iraq, run by Saddam Hussein, to develop weapons of mass destruction, and then team up with terrorist organizations so they can blackmail the world. I'm not going to let that happen." The television reporter then pressed Bush on whether Saddam was the next target in the war on terror, to which Bush replied, in a noncommittal way, "I have no plans to attack on my desk."[37]

Bush had indeed set his mind on Saddam's removal, but at the time of Blair's visit, there were still serious differences of opinion within his administration about how this goal might be achieved. The more hawk-ish members of Bush's war cabinet—Cheney and Rumsfeld—thought defeating Iraq would be a cakewalk, while the doves—such as Powell—argued against taking precipitate action. At this point, the U.S. Joint Chiefs of Staff believed they were engaged in a military exercise simply to scare Saddam.[38] Blair's arrival at Crawford meant that there was an-other voice to be added to the discussion.

Bush was eager to have "face time" with Blair, and so the three Down-ing Street officials were put up in a local hotel near Waco for the night, to enable the Bushes and the Blairs to have dinner alone. Blair, who wore a black suit out of respect for the recent death of the Queen Mother, trav-eled with Cherie and the couple's teenage daughter, Kathryn. It was now just over a year since the two leaders had first met at Camp David, and their shared experience during the challenging months since 9/11 had helped them to form a close personal bond. "Bush is very canny," said a Blair aide who accompanied him on most of his trips to see Bush. "You can put an argument to him in very strong terms and he will listen to you and then he will decide. He lets people think he is a fool because it suits him. But he is a warm person, with a self-deprecating sense of humor. He is always teasing those around him, and Blair was no exception."[39]

Blair was grateful to Bush for his intervention on the Middle East, which gave him sufficient ammunition to deal with rebellious members of his Labour Party who claimed he had no influence over White House policy. Indeed, at Crawford, Blair was more interested in discussing the Israel-Palestine issue than he was Iraq.[40] So far as Blair was concerned, the prior-ity was to stabilize the situation in the Middle East before tackling the issue of Saddam and his WMD. He argued that if Bush could exert pres-sure on Sharon and Arafat, the two sides could be persuaded to resume a peace dialogue. The big sticking point for Bush was Arafat. "The problem for Blair is that by the time they had met at Crawford, the president had lost patience with Arafat," said a senior White House official. "The way to a viable, independent state was being undermined by Arafat's continuing support for terrorism. However, the president had committed himself to a two-state solution, and for that Blair deserves some of the credit."[41]

During his talks with Bush, Blair revisited many of the issues that he had raised the previous autumn. He said he was prepared to support U.S. policy on Iraq, but that he had certain conditions for doing so. He argued that any planning for military action should be conducted at the same time as negotiations to resolve the Israel-Palestine dispute, that every effort should be made to assemble the widest possible international coalition, and that the UN should be involved at every stage. These three conditions were anathema to some of the more hawkish members of the administration, who saw no reason to link Israel and Palestine to the war on terror and were averse to building international coalitions and had nothing but contempt for the UN. According to Blair's advisors, the meeting broke up without reaching any firm conclusion, although Bush told Blair that militarily, the best time to attack Iraq would be in the spring of 2003 or, failing that, the autumn of the same year. Bush showed Blair the latest CIA briefing on Iraq, although Blair had been told in advance that the CIA's information was not as good as that provided by SIS.

"This was a very crucial period in the buildup to the confrontation with Iraq, and it was very important that Britain was in a position to bring influence to bear on Bush's thinking," said a senior Downing Street aide who was privy to Blair's discussions with Bush at Crawford. "It would be very unfair to say that Blair did not have any influence on Bush. Bush listened very carefully to what Blair had to say. He had a lot of influence over the decision-making process. It's just that we chose not to make it public."[42]

Another key Blair official who traveled to Crawford recalled that, while Iraq was discussed, it was by no means at the top of the agenda. "The really important issue we dealt with was the mounting tension between India and Pakistan," the official said. The long-standing border dispute between the two countries had recently flared up and, as both countries were known to have nuclear weapons, there was a genuine fear in Washington and London that the dispute could easily escalate into a nuclear conflagration. "We really thought they were going to have a nuclear war. It came very close," the official recalled. "Iraq would have been a footnote in 2002 if Indo-Pak had gone off." The one constructive decision to emerge from Crawford was to send Colin Powell to Jerusalem. "We agreed that Colin Powell should get on a plane and visit the Middle East to calm things down." All of the British officials who accompanied Blair are insistent that no decision to go to war against Iraq was taken during the Crawford summit. "This idea that Bush and Blair were prepared to invade Iraq during Crawford is complete bullshit," commented one of Blair's senior aides. "Crawford was all about the acute concern felt about India-Pakistan and who should be sent to the Middle East."[43] A few days after Crawford, Colin Powell set off on a troubleshooting mission, but his effort ended in embarrassing failure. The Palestinians continued their campaign of suicide bombings against Israel, and the Israelis responded with their military offensive against suspected militant hideouts in the West Bank.

If Iraq did not top the agenda during the Crawford talks, it was nevertheless the main talking point when the two leaders emerged for a joint press conference. "I explained to the prime minister that the policy of my government is the removal of Saddam . . . we support regime change," said Bush. While this stark message was accompanied with a personal tribute to Blair's personal qualities—"The thing I admire about the prime minister is that he doesn't need a poll or focus group to convince him of the difference between right and wrong"—it did not make it any easier for Blair to explain himself to his cabinet colleagues and the British public, who were convinced Blair had gone to Crawford to sign up for a war to overthrow Saddam. Even if regime change was a long-standing American policy, the tone of Bush's comments jarred on the other side of the Atlantic. The Europeans generally acknowledged that Saddam was a ruthless tyrant, but there was little support for ousting him by force of arms.

Blair appeared to be taken aback by Bush's public commitment to regime change in Iraq, and consequently, his own comments were more measured than they had been when he had met with Cheney in London. On this occasion, Blair confined himself to talking about Saddam's WMD program and his defiance of UN resolutions. While neatly dodging the issue of regime change directly, Blair said, "It has always been our policy that Iraq would be a better place without Saddam Hussein. I don't think anyone can be in any doubt about that." But on the issue of WMD, there was no mention of Saddam or al-Qaeda, only the more logical argument that Iraq should be made to comply with its UN obligations. "You cannot have a situation in which he carries on being in breach of UN resolutions, and refusing to allow us to assess whether and how he is developing these weapons of mass destruction. Now, how we proceed from here, that is a matter that is open for us." While Blair was trying to be diplomatic, Bush was determined that no one should misunderstand where he was coming from. "Maybe I should be a little less direct and be a little more nuanced and say we support regime change."

A number of British commentators later argued that it was at Crawford that Blair took the momentous decision to sign up with the Americans for military action against Iraq, and that all his subsequent comments and diplomatic maneuvers were a cover to disguise his true intentions. This seems highly unlikely, as Bush himself had not worked out precisely how he intended to tackle Saddam. At Crawford, military action was just one option. Another was a modified version of Operation Enduring Freedom, where the CIA, working in conjunction with American and British special forces, had linked up with local Afghan tribesmen to overthrow the Taliban. Some American policymakers believed that there was still a possibility that a similar operation could be conducted against Saddam. Blair's British critics suggested that, after Crawford, he ordered U.K. military commanders to draw up war plans for Iraq, further evidence of his bellicose intent. But General Sir Mike Jackson, the British army commander, said that just because British commanders were working on plans for Iraq did not mean that war was inevitable. "Plans are simply plans, and they don't mean anything until somebody gives the order to implement them," he said. "Given the political climate, we would have been failing in our duty if we had not drawn up contingency plans for Iraq. But that is all they were—plans."[44] Downing Street officials were equally dismissive of the suggestion that Blair was preparing for war from Crawford onwards. "Look, Bush and Wolfowitz were talking about Iraq immediately after 9/11," said a senior Downing Street official, "but that doesn't mean that planning for the war in Iraq started then."[45]

Blair returned home knowing that Bush was determined to deal with Saddam. And Blair resolved that, come what may, he was going to stick close to Washington. Sir Christopher Meyer, the British ambassador, was quite clear in his own mind what the likely consequences were of sticking close to Washington. "As a matter of practical politics, or realpolitik, if you are asked a question, 'Can you disarm Iraq without changing the regime?' your answer would have to be, 'No, of course you can't,' because if Saddam had actually come into compliance 100 percent, as laid down by all these [UN] resolutions, he would have had a personality transplant, a soul transplant. He would not have been Saddam Hussein."[46] After Crawford, Blair took an even closer interest in British intelligence reports on Iraq, and assessments about the likely strength of Saddam's regime. "After Crawford, everything moved into a different gear," said a senior British intelligence officer. "When he got back, he wanted full briefings on everything that was going on with Iraq. He showed an intensity of interest that had not been there before."[47]

On the journey home, Blair stopped off to give a speech at the nearby George Bush Presidential Library and Museum in College Station, Texas. The speech was a distillation of Blair's thinking on the next stage in the war on terror, and contained many of the points he had made to Bush. The speech drew on many of the arguments he had used in Chicago in 1999 to justify international intervention in Kosovo. "I advocate an enlightened self-interest that puts fighting for our values right at the heart of the policies necessary to protect our nations. We must be prepared to act where terrorism or weapons of mass destruction threaten us . . . if necessary, the action should be military and again, if necessary and justified, it should involve regime change."

As he might have expected, Blair did not receive a warm welcome when he returned to London to report on his discussions with Bush to his cabinet colleagues. The essence of Blair's message to the cabinet was, "I do believe in this country's relations with the United States." It was a view that was not universally shared by Labour ministers. One of them warned about the prospect of tensions with Britain's Muslim communities if action against Iraq was not authorized by the UN. Robin Cook argued that the UN must be involved. But Blair shared the White House's skepticism about the UN's ability to deliver. While he regarded the UN as important, he told his cabinet colleagues, "we should not tie ourselves down to doing nothing unless the UN authorized it."[48]

Powerful voices were being raised against the prospect of war outside the cabinet. The Foreign Office argued that other states, such as Syria and Iran, had far worse records as sponsors of terrorism than Iraq, and that North Korea's nuclear program posed a far greater, and immediate, threat to global security. Sir Richard Dearlove, the head of SIS, reflected the views of many in Whitehall when he told a couple of BBC journalists, "When weapons of mass destruction and Islamic terrorism come together, you have a particular potential crisis. By any Cartesian analysis, Iraq does not emerge as the top priority. Syria and Iran are the priorities."[49] Another group of influential British diplomats argued that invading Iraq should take second place to resolving the Israel-Palestine dispute, although they seemed unaware that this was also Blair's personal view. In Europe, many of Blair's allies were unhappy about being excluded from what they regarded as "the council of war" that had taken place in Crawford, and significant sections of the Labour Party and the British media were adopting an increasingly hostile view toward military action in Iraq.

IN BETWEEN BLAIR'S MEETING with Bush at Crawford in April and his next meeting with the president at Camp David the following September, the two worked as closely together as any two leaders of their respective countries had done since Churchill and Roosevelt during the Second World War. There was a strong personal bond between the two men, and mutual respect for each other's political acumen. The transatlantic dialogue between the two leaders was so close that it prompted Colin Powell to say that "they're essentially inside each other's thinking. They complete each other's thoughts."[50] The two regularly paid each other compliments in public. "I like George's directness," Blair commented at one stage. "I like the way he has understood my political problems."[51] Bush responded in kind, remarking that "Americans admire character and courage. And Tony Blair has true character and courage."[52]

American officials who sat in on the frequent meetings and transatlantic videolink conversations between Bush and Blair were impressed with how they worked together to thrash out policy issues. "They developed strategy like a couple of guys who were a doubles pairing in tennis," said a senior

White House official. "One would take the net while the other covered for him, and then it would be the other way around. Bush would make a point, and Blair would develop it, and vice versa. Blair had a huge impact developing policy on the war on terror and articulated issues that were particularly difficult, such as Israel-Palestine. Blair brought intellectual dynamism to many of the issues."[53] Another key Bush aide who attended the meetings agreed that they had formed the closest political bond between an American president and a British prime minister since Roosevelt and Churchill. "As with Churchill and Roosevelt, Bush and Blair were linked by the great strategic challenge of the modern world," said the official. "Blair was the world leader with the most influence on Bush. It was a powerful bond. They explored issues together, often finishing each other's sentences. No one who sat there and listened to them go back and forth could accuse Blair of being a poodle. Blair has been the driving force in the relationship and has played an important role in the evolution of American thinking since 9/11."[54]

Bush administration officials also pointed out that there was a very important difference between Blair's relationship with Bush, and the president's relationship with members of his war cabinet. "The likes of Cheney, Rumsfeld, and Powell could be as opinionated and argumentative as they liked, but at the end of the day, they had been appointed by Bush and they had to do what the president decided," said a senior administration official. "Blair, on the other hand, saw Bush on a more equal footing, as one world leader to another. It was a very significant difference, and meant that, so long as Bush trusted Blair's judgment, the prime minister could bring a lot of influence to bear on the president's thinking."[55]

Blair continued his frequent video conferences with Bush—Cheney was always a brooding presence in the background, rarely commenting—and there was a constant stream of communication between senior officials and advisors in both camps. After Blair, Downing Street's most important interlocutor was David Manning, his foreign policy advisor. Manning, a former British ambassador to Israel and NATO, spoke at least daily with Condoleezza Rice, his American counterpart, to discuss progress. The other important transatlantic link was between Jack Straw, the foreign secretary, and Colin Powell. During the difficult months that preceded the Iraq War, Blair also kept in touch with Bill Clinton, who provided him with an outsider's take on what was happening in Washington.

However much Blair prided himself on the closeness of his relationship with Bush, the British prime minister found himself at the mercy of the bitter power play between rival factions within the White House disagreeing about how to deal with Saddam and about other, wider issues relating to the war on terror, such as the Israel-Palestine dispute. Iraq, more than the Afghan War and the hunt for bin Laden and al-Qaeda, was to be the defining moment of the Bush administration. How Bush dealt with Iraq would fashion the administration's ideological identity. If Powell and those who sought international consensus in support of American policy were to prevail, then the Bush presidency would have lost what the neocons regarded as the opportunity to set a radical new agenda in global politics. But if the isolationist hawks and their neoconservative backers could persuade Bush to tackle Saddam their way, then America's unchallenged military supremacy would be used to create a revolution in how the world dealt with future security challenges.

Blair was more sympathetic toward the Powell camp, if for no other reason than he needed to reassure his domestic critics that whatever action was taken against Iraq was wrapped in a cloak of international legitimacy. Unfortunately for Blair, Powell, who was regarded as an outsider by the hawks and neoconservatives, was frequently outmaneuvered by their more experienced and ideologically committed political rivals. After Crawford, Cheney, in particular, remained suspicious of Blair's influence over Bush, and disapproved strongly of Powell, whom he saw as "Britain's ambassador."[56] He also kept a wary eye on Manning's dealings with Rice.

The issue that caused Blair most difficulty during the summer of 2002 was not Iraq but Israel-Palestine. The plight of the Palestinians touched a raw nerve within the Labour Party, and the argument was constantly advanced that, if Saddam was forced to comply with UN Security Council resolutions, why not Israel, which was still illegally occupying Palestinian land it captured during the 1967 Six-Day War and was widely believed to have developed a nuclear weapons arsenal of its own? Blair was desperate to secure at the very least a ceasefire between the warring factions, and had dwelt on the issue at length at Crawford. Bush had made some encouraging noises both before Blair's visit and during their meeting, and dispatched Colin Powell to the region in a vain attempt to stop the bloodshed. But the initiative quickly lost momentum, not least because Ariel Sharon had influential allies in the White House who made it their business to ensure that Powell's mission was a failure.

After 9/11, Sharon drew a direct parallel between Israel's long-running dispute with the Palestinians and America's war with al-Qaeda. Both countries, Sharon argued, were fighting their own war on terror, and so far as Israel was concerned, Yasser Arafat was no different from Osama bin Laden. Sharon's uncompromising attitude toward the Palestinians was fully shared by the powerful neoconservative lobby in Washington. Many neocons, who themselves were Jewish and held key positions in the Bush administration, had close links with Sharon's Likud Party, which was ideologically opposed to the creation of an independent Palestinian state. "Our views on Israel were poles apart from Blair's," said a senior White House advisor on the Middle East. "Blair just did not understand our concerns."[57]

When Bush finally outlined his proposals for the creation of an independent Palestinian state on June 24, it contained a clause that immediately made it void. "Peace requires a new and different Palestinian leadership so that a Palestinian state can be born," he said, and urged the Palestinians to elect "leaders not compromised by terror," i.e., get rid of Arafat. Bush had finally lost patience with Arafat, but as the veteran PLO leader was the only person with any claim to lead the Palestinians, the absence of a negotiating partner meant that Bush's peace plan had no immediate prospects of success.

The Bush plan was a significant victory for the U.S. hawks, and equally a setback for Blair, who had been trying to persuade Bush to deal with Arafat. But on this issue, Blair's powers of persuasion had made no impression on the president. And the absence of a constructive dialogue between the Israelis and Palestinians meant there was little serious prospect of the murderous cycle of violence being brought to an end. Even so, Blair deserved some of the credit for pushing Bush toward making the historic commitment to the establishment of a Palestinian state in the

first place. "Blair put Bush under a lot of pressure over Israel and Palestine, and it led to the June statement," said a senior Downing Street advisor. "Blair did not get everything he wanted, but it was undoubtedly a
move in the right direction. Bush had learned the lesson of the Clinton
era, that you could not deal with Arafat. Arafat had been offered a great
deal [at Camp David] and turned it down. We were aware of that. Even
so, we felt that the Middle East was crucial and we kept nagging the
White House about it."[58] This view was supported by White House officials. "The president committed himself to a two-state solution, and it
was something that came out of his discussions with Prime Minister
Blair. They had good discussions on that and other issues."[59]

Washington was more successful in defusing the tensions between
Pakistan and India, which by early June had threatened to escalate into a
nuclear conflict. India, provoked beyond endurance by terror attacks carried out by Pakistani-backed Muslim separatists in the disputed region
of Kashmir, had threatened to launch an operation similar to the one the
Americans had conducted in Afghanistan, to destroy militant bases in
Pakistan-controlled territory. The Pakistanis, who were a key Washington ally in the war on terror, had threatened to launch military action
against Delhi if the Indian operation went ahead. "It got to the point
where if either side made a false move, we would have had a nuclear catastrophe on our hands," said a Downing Street official. The crisis was
averted when Richard Armitage, the deputy secretary of state, made an
emergency trip to Delhi and Islamabad and persuaded the two sides to
back down. "Basically, everyone in Washington—the doves, the hawks,
the neocons—agreed that a war between India and Pakistan, while plans
were being made for war in Iraq, would be bad news," said a State Department official. "So, on this occasion, we were actually able to get
something done."[60]

Throughout this period of intense diplomatic activity in the summer
of 2002, Blair continued to pressure Bush to take the UN route on Iraq.
But the constant war of attrition between the rival camps in the Bush
administration seriously jeopardized Blair's chances of winning the argument. In June, Bush seemed to be heeding the counsel of Cheney, the
arch exponent of American unilateralism, when he gave a strident speech

at the West Point military academy, defending America's right to take preemptive action against its enemies rather than abide by the policy of deterrence that had been the bedrock of defense policy during the Cold War. "Deterrence, the promise of massive retaliation against nations, means nothing against shadowy terrorist networks with no nation of citizens to defend," said Bush. "Containment is not possible when unbalanced dictators with weapons of mass destruction can deliver those weapons on missiles or secretly provide them to terrorist allies . . . If we wait for threats to materialize, then we will have waited too long." Bush's comments echoed Blair's speech at College Station, but there was a crucial difference: Blair argued that such action should have international approval; Bush thought America was justified in acting alone.

Blair's mounting concern at Washington's increasingly gung-ho attitude to the war led him to dispatch David Manning to the United States in July 2002 for an emergency meeting with Rice. The shrill tone of some of the rhetoric emanating from Washington was alienating large sections of the British public and the Labour Party, not to mention many governments in Western Europe. Blair believed that there was a real possibility that the Americans would go it alone without UN approval, which would make his position untenable. Blair wrote Bush a letter in which he hinted that, without UN support, Britain would not be able to contribute to the war. Manning took the letter to Washington and reemphasized Blair's dilemma in meetings with both Rice and Bush. The president's response was noncommittal, and Manning reported back that it was still not clear whether Bush had accepted Blair's argument in favor of using the UN.

While Bush deliberated, Blair understood only too well that his whole political future depended on his ability to win the argument in Washington.

Nine

A QUESTION OF RESOLVE

SITTING AT LUNCH IN his private dining room at Number 10 Downing Street in the summer of 2002, Tony Blair made no secret of his determination to confront Saddam. "It is high time that we sorted out Saddam's weapons of mass destruction," he said. "In the post-9/11 world, it is no longer tenable for a brutal dictator like Saddam Hussein to be allowed to develop weapons of mass destruction with impunity while at the same time defying the will of the international community. We have no alternative other than to act." With a few other select journalists, I had been invited to lunch at Downing Street to discuss, among other subjects, the looming confrontation with Iraq. It was a lovely English summer day in late June, and crowds of tourists could be seen from Downing Street's Georgian dining-room window, strolling in the warm sunshine across Horse Guards Parade. Blair did not seem like a man who was wrestling with the most momentous decision of his political career. "Hey, you guys, what's been going on at Wimbledon?" he greeted us cheerily. Blair is a keen amateur tennis player, and took a close interest in the tournament taking place in southwestern London. He had been at meetings all morning, and had not yet had the opportunity to catch up on the day's play. "Head teachers this morning, policemen this afternoon," he said with a hint of weariness. "It all goes with the job."

Over a lunch of fish pie and fresh fruit, I pressed the prime minister on why he appeared so determined to confront Saddam when there seemed to be no evidence to suggest that the Iraqi dictator was involved in the 9/11 attacks. Throughout the lunch, Alastair Campbell, Blair's overly protective press secretary, sat at the end of the table, noting our conversation but making no contribution. He gave the appearance of a particularly savage guard dog that might leap to its master's defense at the slightest hint of provocation. My question elicited a particularly hard glare from Campbell, who seemed to be indicating that Blair had no reason to answer. After casting Campbell a reassuring look, Blair stated simply that he had received "bits and pieces" of intelligence from SIS that suggested there were links between Iraq and al-Qaeda, although nothing that tied Saddam directly to the 9/11 attacks. But that, said Blair, was not the main point. "This is about Saddam and WMD," he said. "He's had them in the past and he's used them in the past. All the evidence suggests he is continuing to develop them, and all the time he is defying the UN. I simply don't think that this is something we can ignore."

Our lunch took place at a time when Blair was involved in an increasingly intense political struggle with Washington to ensure UN involvement in dealing with Saddam. But Blair did not behave like a man with the weight of the world on his shoulders. Rather he was relaxed and jovial, even making jokes about his long-running feud with Gordon Brown, the chancellor of the Exchequer, who at the time was blocking Blair's attempts to get Britain to join the single European currency. Throughout the course of the lunch, Blair gave every indication that he was clear in his mind about what he needed to do, and that nothing was going to stop him from resolving the issue of Iraq and Saddam's WMD.

Blair's single-mindedness would be crucial if he were to ensure that his voice was heard during the summer of 2002 above the acrimonious debate taking place in Washington. While Blair dealt directly with Bush, Jack Straw, the foreign secretary, liaised closely with Colin Powell, encouraging the secretary of state to keep up the pressure on the White House to find means other than military action to deal with Saddam. Straw had personal reservations about both the legitimacy and the necessity of taking military action to overthrow Saddam, a position that would later lead to tensions between Downing Street and the Foreign Office over the handling of the Iraq issue. But at this juncture, Downing Street was grateful that there was another line of communication open, through which Blair's desire to seek an international consensus on Iraq could be transmitted.

Nor was Blair alone in this view. Cheney and his allies continued to argue that Bush should only go through the UN as an exercise to demonstrate the UN's resolve, not to let it control the issue. Other elder Republican statesmen, some of whom had also held important positions in the first Bush administration, cautioned that it was not in America's long-term interests to proceed to the next stage in the war on terror without international support. Both James Baker, the former secretary of state, and Brent Scowcroft, the former national security advisor, advised the president to act with caution. Even Dr. Henry Kissinger, the primary architect of American foreign and security policy during the latter stages of the Cold War, weighed in, criticizing the Bush administration's apparent reliance on military might alone.

By early August, it appeared that the tide was turning in favor of the doves. On August 5, Powell, accompanied by Rice, had dinner with Bush, at which he raised his concerns about the prospect of war with Iraq. "I was upfront with the president, who is the person I'm paid to be upfront with," said Powell. "My caution was that you need to understand that the difficult bit will come afterwards—the military piece will be easy." Powell, who had much personal experience of the region through his involvement in Operation Desert Storm, warned Bush that Iraq would "crack like a goblet, and it'll be a problem to pick up the pieces. It was on this basis that [Bush] decided to let me see if we can find a UN solution to this. Everyone agreed," Powell said. "Don, Dick, and Condi."[1]

During a video conference Bush hosted at Crawford on August 16, the president told the war cabinet that he was supporting Powell's argument that the UN must be consulted, although precisely what role he envisaged for the organization was still unclear. Despite Powell's claim that all the war cabinet agreed with the president's decision, Cheney was furious, and a few days later made a rare public statement on Iraq, in which he made a spirited counterattack on those who urged caution over an Iraq invasion. Speaking at a conference of war veterans at Nashville, Tennessee, Cheney argued strongly in favor of taking preemptive action against Saddam Hussein to stop him from acquiring nuclear weapons. "The risk of inaction is far greater than the risk of action," said Cheney. "What we must not do in the face of a mortal threat is to give in to wishful thinking or wilful blindness." There was little doubt whom Cheney was accusing of "wishful thinking," and his public attack on Powell provided a rare insight into the bitter power struggle that was raging in Washington between the doves and the hawks. Apart from his frustration over Powell's influence over the president, Cheney had been prompted to go public with his views after James Baker launched yet another attack on the Bush administration when he said that a unilateral attack on Iraq would be politically and economically perilous. In response, Cheney cited his own experience during the Gulf War, remarking that "as one who helped put the international coalition together, it would have been infinitely more difficult if [Saddam] had had nuclear weapons. If we did wait, Saddam would become emboldened and it would become harder to get allies."[2] Cheney was also scathing about the prospects of the weapons inspectors returning to Iraq. "A return of inspectors would provide no assurance whatsoever of his compliance with UN resolutions," said Cheney. "On the contrary, there is a great danger that it would provide false comfort that Saddam was somehow 'back in the box.'"

To reinforce his case, Cheney presented his own National Intelligence Assessment—a function normally carried out by the CIA—on Saddam. "Simply stated, there is no doubt that Saddam Hussein has weapons of mass destruction and there is no doubt that he is amassing them to use against our friends, against our allies, and against us," Cheney declared. Neither the CIA nor SIS had ever suggested that Saddam was preparing to attack the United States with WMD, but so determined were the hawks to oust the Iraqi dictator from power that they were not prepared to let simple facts impede their prowar rhetoric. The evidence being provided by Cheney and other members of Washington's prowar lobby prompted Sir Richard Dearlove, the head of SIS, to warn Blair that the case for war was being "fixed" by Washington. After attending a briefing in Washington in the summer of 2002, Dearlove told Blair and his ministers that "the facts and intelligence" were being "fixed around the policy" by George W. Bush's administration. He also told Blair that in his opinion, war with Iraq was "inevitable."[3]

The bitter in-fighting in Washington briefly broke into the open in late August, when Colin Powell, while attending an Earth Summit in Johannesburg, let slip that there were "rifts" at the White House about what to do on Iraq. When a transcript of Powell's comments reached Rice's office in Washington, she called the secretary of state and ordered him to retract his comments, telling him that making public what everyone knew to be the case in private was "not helpful." The following day, Powell dutifully announced that there was no significant difference between his position and Cheney's on going to the UN. The spat between Rice and Powell indicated the true balance of power in the White House, and prompted speculation that Powell would quit his post at the end of the first term. Britain's main ally in Washington was struggling to hold his own.

"It was always very difficult finding out about what was going on with the power battles that were taking place in the White House, and precisely what Cheney was doing," said a senior Downing Street official. "We knew he (Cheney) had influence, but you could never tell how Bush was going to react. We also knew that our voice was listened to in the White House, which is about all we could ask for." Blair had to compete with the other key figures in the administration for influence over the president, although he was aware that it was the president who ultimately decided policy. "Bush always allowed a lot of discussion and allowed everyone the freedom to express their opinions," the aide said. "But he was the one who made the decision, and once he had made the decision, everyone had to jump to it—and that included Cheney."[4]

Blair returned from his summer holiday with his family to discover that the thinking on Iraq had undergone a radical change during the few weeks he had been absent. He had departed for Italy believing that Bush would use the UN to deal with Saddam, but by the time he returned, Cheney's public intervention and the effective campaign being waged by the hawks had led many people to conclude that the "go-it-alone" tendency in Washington once more had the upper hand. During the family holiday in Italy, the looming conflict with Iraq had weighed heavily on Blair's mind. On one occasion, he admitted to one of his houseguests, "This could lose me my job. I may have to pay the price for doing what I think is right."

Blair was taken aback at the way the debate over Iraq had developed while he was away, and sought to have an emergency summit with Bush to find out precisely what was going on. "There was a lot of bellicose talk, and there were a lot of different policy options," said a senior Blair advisor. "There was planning going on for a military campaign. There were also discussions going on about how to have regime change in Baghdad by other means than war. No one view was predominant at that time." Straw was also on holiday during August, and when he and Blair returned, they found that the hawks in Washington had gained ground. "They got back from holiday and said, 'hang on, the public debate has moved on.' Blair thought it essential that he see Bush to have a serious discussion about Iraq."[5]

Straw had twice spoken to Powell during his summer vacation to brief him on the British position, and to find out who was winning the debate in Washington. Straw was anxious to avoid a fissure in U.S.-European relations. Following his dinner with Bush, Powell reassured Straw that an attack on Iraq was not imminent and that the United States wanted to work through the UN. A few days after returning home from his holiday, on September 3, Blair visited his Sedgefield constituency, where he showed he had lost none of his resolve over the Saddam issue. He had taken a bundle of intelligence briefing papers on Iraq on holiday. "He read new evidence about Iraq pretty much every day," said one of his officials. Over drinks with party supporters at Sedgefield's Trimdon Labour Club, Blair told the gathering that America did not want to be "dicked over by Iraq." Earlier in the day, he gave a press conference at which he revealed that he would shortly be publishing an intelligence dossier of evidence on Saddam's WMD. Before that, he would be flying to Camp David for talks with Bush.

Blair flew to the United States on September 7 with the same advisors that had accompanied him to Crawford the previous spring—Manning, Powell, and Campbell. To ensure he remained relaxed during the crucial talks with the American president, Blair packed his favorite guitar. Blair had remained a keen amateur guitarist since playing in his own rock group at Oxford University. Blair continued to string his guitar for relaxation throughout his adult life, particularly in times of stress, and planning for war in Iraq was about as stressful as it gets. Bush was due to address the UN General Assembly on September 12, and this was Blair's last chance to persuade Bush to seek UN backing for any action that might be taken against Iraq. Before leaving for Washington, Blair was asked by a journalist what he thought of Bush. Was the American president an intellectual lightweight? "Look," Blair replied. "That's all wrong. He is very straightforward and open. In fact, he's disarmingly open." Was it true, then, that Blair found it easier to get on with Bush than Clinton? "Of course, Clinton was a friend," said Blair. "But with Bush there is no doubt who makes the decisions."[6]

Blair and his team were somewhat disconcerted to find the brooding figure of Dick Cheney accompanying the president when they arrived in the Catoctin Mountains in Maryland. Cheney and his officials remained opposed to Blair's policy of getting UN backing. Scooter Libby, Cheney's chief of staff, had offended British officials over the summer by making sarcastic remarks about Blair during their discussions on how to tackle Iraq. On one occasion, when Libby disagreed with a proposed course of action, he remarked, "Oh dear, we'd better not do that, or we might upset the prime minister." Cheney still regarded Blair with suspicion, and he asked to be added to the party attending the Camp David summit so that he could keep an eye on the prime minister.

During his summer holiday, Blair had come up with a phrase to explain his view on how Iraq should be dealt with. The issue should go to the UN, but only so long as it was "a way of dealing with the matter rather than a means of avoiding it." By the time he arrived in Camp David, it appeared that Bush—prompted by Powell—had reached a similar conclusion. Blair's meeting with Bush consisted of a series of round-table discussions, most of them held in the Presidential Lodge, the place Franklin D. Roosevelt once described as "the bear's den." Throughout the evening, Bush and Blair broke off for one-to-one talks. They spoke about the military plans for Iraq and the delicacy of forming an international coalition. During the two leaders' absence, the British delegation did their best to convince Cheney that the UN process was worth pursuing. They found it heavy going. "He just sat there throughout like a lump," recalled one of the British delegation. Another Blair aide recalled, "He did not say much. He just listened in on our discussions. He was wary of the whole UN route, but he did not say anything."[7]

The case Blair presented to Bush was straightforward. "Blair told Bush that if you wanted to take the allies with you, then you have to go to the UN," said one of Blair's aides who accompanied him to Camp David. "It was tough for Blair, because we knew there were people in Washington whose view of going to the UN was 'over my dead body.'"[8] If Bush agreed to work for a new UN resolution to authorize the return of weapons inspectors to Iraq, then Blair would be able to overcome opposition to the war in Britain, and rally support among European leaders. There were high expectations in both London and Washington that other major European countries, such as France and Germany, could be persuaded to support military action. There was also a feeling that Iraq should be used as a test case for the effectiveness of the UN in handling challenges to international security. The UN would be given a last chance to resolve the issue of Saddam's WMD. If that did not work, then America could count on Britain's full support for war with Iraq.

At one point, Blair and Bush took a stroll through the woods of the president's mountaintop retreat. As they walked, Bush reflected that exactly a year earlier, he and his foreign policy advisors had been discussing Iraq. Back then, said Bush, the plans were to tighten sanctions against Saddam Hussein. War against Iraq was not on his agenda then, as it was now. Blair agreed that times had changed.

Later, after they returned, Bush, with Cheney sitting beside him, looked Blair straight in the eye. "Saddam Hussein is a threat. And we must work together to deal with this threat, and the world will be better off without him." Bush later recalled that he was "probing" and "pushing" the prime minister. He said it would most likely entail going to war, and that Blair would have to send troops. Without hesitating, Blair replied, "I'm with you." With that simple sentence, Blair committed himself to the most controversial decision of his political career. Bush was relieved. "We want you to be part of this," Bush replied. Blair's resolve made a deep impression on Bush, and significantly improved Bush's position. Blair's commitment meant that if it came to war with Iraq, America would not have to go it alone. As the meeting concluded, Bush remarked to Blair's aides, who were waiting anxiously outside, "Your man has got *cojones.*"[9]

"Our main argument was that we had to stay with the UN," said a Blair aide. "We knew that Bush was committed to regime change, but that was not something we could support publicly for all kinds of reasons. So far as we were concerned, there was a smart way and a dumb way of doing it, and we believed the smart way of doing it was through the UN. There was still no sense then that we were going to storm into Iraq, although clearly there were many options that were open to us."[10]

During the talks with Bush, Blair raised his pet subject, namely pressuring the president to focus on getting a peace settlement on the Israel-Palestine issue in parallel with increasing pressure on Iraq. Blair said that if this could be achieved, there was still hope that some Arab governments might be persuaded to join the international coalition against Saddam. The two leaders also discussed how they were going to get the Russians on board. Mikhail Kasyanov, the Russian prime minister, had told Blair that Moscow wanted a currency deal in return for their support at the UN. Russia was owed an estimated $10 billion by Saddam, and wanted assurances that they would get their money if the Iraqi leader were overthrown. Finally, Bush provided Blair with an outline of Washington's military plans for Iraq. Up to this point, the Ministry of Defence in London had no information about America's proposed battle plans, and had been working in the dark on their own possible war scenarios. British officers had no idea how many British troops, planes, and ships would be required—if at all. It was agreed that Geoff Hoon, the defense secretary, would visit Rumsfeld later in the month to discuss military planning on Iraq. Relations between the two defense secretaries remained problematic. "It was like trying to get two pandas to mate," said an exasperated British defense official.

At the end of their meeting, the two leaders agreed on a joint course of action on Iraq. The main thrust of their policy would be to set a strict new deadline for Saddam to dismantle all of his WMD capability, and to give weapons inspectors unhindered access to any suspect Iraqi site. If Saddam failed to comply with any of these conditions, he would face military action. Having got his way with Bush over the UN, Blair stepped up the propaganda war against Baghdad by making an even more alarming claim about Saddam's WMD capability. According to Blair, Saddam was a "very real threat to Britain." Saddam would soon be able to target Britain if he was allowed to continue obtaining long-range missiles capable of delivering chemical, biological, or nuclear weapons. A similar claim would be made after publication of the British government's long-awaited intelligence dossier on Iraq, even though the intelligence estimates provided to Downing Street by British intelligence were unable to substantiate such alarmist allegations. But at Camp David, Blair was insistent. "The threat is very real, and it is a threat not just to America or the international community but to Britain," said Blair. "If these weapons are developed and used, there is no way that any conflict Saddam initiated using these weapons would not have direct implications for the interests of Britain." Bush officials also helped to raise the stakes in the standoff with Iraq. Shortly before the summit, Rice had warned that the next target for attack "wouldn't have to be New York or Washington. It could be London or Berlin." Bush concluded the press conference with Blair by reiterating the findings of the International Atomic Energy Agency (IAEA) at the end of the 1991 Gulf War that Saddam's secret nuclear program had been within six months of producing an atom bomb. "I don't know what more evidence we need," said Bush. "It threatens the U.S. It threatens Britain. The battlefield has changed. We are in a new kind of war." [11]

Bush administration officials who participated in the Camp David talks said that Washington's reluctance to deal with the UN was overexaggerated. "It became a bit of an urban myth that the administration did not want to go to the UN," said a senior White House official. "We were happy to go to the UN, but we did not want the UN to dictate terms. Our view was, 'we will do what we have to do.'" [12] Even officials at the Pentagon reluctantly accepted that there were benefits to going through the UN. "We had our initial doubts about the UN process, although we eventually came to see some value in it," said a senior Pentagon official. "It is always better to have allies with you in these situations, and by going to the UN, it enabled us to work on building a coalition."[13] Bush administration officials acknowledged that Blair had played an important role in persuading the president to take the UN route. "When ideas were being put forward, if someone said we are doing this because it is important to Blair, then people sat up and took notice. His name topped our list of allies. No one else came close." But State Department officials, even though they pushed for the UN, identified a difference of approach between Washington and London. "Our question was, very simply, have the Iraqis violated the ceasefire resolution?" (agreed upon at the end of the 1991 Gulf War) said a senior State Department official. "In our minds, the answer was very clear—yes. But Blair had to go further and persuade the Labour Party that Iraq posed an imminent threat. That is where the difficulties began."[14]

Despite the personal commitment Blair had received from Bush about the UN, Downing Street still faced a nervous wait until the president made public his commitment during the speech he was due to give at the UN on September 12. For days after the Blair-Bush meeting at Camp David, Sir Christopher Meyer, the British ambassador, made sure that there would be no slippage in the U.S. position before Bush's statement. It was a tense time for all concerned. Even when the president had made his decision, there was always the fear that the neoconservatives would try to drag it back to their position. "Colin Powell was trying to ward off the rats," said a British official.[15] Downing Street's primary concern was whether there would be a last-minute intervention from Cheney to persuade Bush to water down America's commitment to the UN. As Bush's speech went through various drafts, British officials were working overtime trying to find out the contents. "We didn't see the drafts, but we were involved in the drafting process," said Sir Jeremy Greenstock, Britain's ambassador to the UN. "We were active up until the last twenty-four hours, to make sure there was a clear commitment to the UN process."[16]

As Bush made his way to the podium to address the UN General Assembly on September 12, Colin Powell was not sure whether or not the president would commit himself to taking the UN route. Blair was confident he would do so, but still had no guarantees. He watched the address on television in Downing Street, and, momentarily, his worst fears were confirmed as the key sentence went missing. After all the wrangling over the final draft of the speech, the wrong draft was put into the autocue, which omitted the all-important passage. Fortunately for Blair, Bush noticed the omission, and ad-libbed the key sentence. "We will work with the Security Council for the necessary resolutions," he declared. Bush had kept his end of the deal he had struck with Blair at Camp David, but in doing so, he had unwittingly made an error that would have serious implications for the future involvement of the UN in the Iraq issue. In the original draft, Bush was supposed to say that Washington would seek a new UN resolution—singular—on enforcement of weapons inspection. Bush's use of the plural "resolutions" suggested that the UN process would actually be more protracted than Bush himself anticipated. But the semantics of Bush's declaration were lost amid the relief that swept Downing Street after Bush confirmed his commitment to the UN. Later that day, Straw, who was in New York for the General Assembly, saw Bush at a reception. "Jack, you know how much time we spent on getting there, and then the crucial line went missing," said Bush. "I knew the words in my head. I put them back in, but not in the right place."

APART FROM COMPETING FOR influence at the White House, by the late summer of 2002, Blair faced the difficult task of persuading his own Labour Party and the British public to support British policy toward Iraq. Few doubted the brutality of Saddam's regime, but many people in Britain and Europe were far from convinced that the threat Saddam posed to the outside world justified military action. Throughout the summer, Blair had discussed on several occasions the need to produce a dossier based on the intelligence reports that he regularly received on Saddam's WMD capability from SIS. As he had remarked at our lunch, "some of these reports make pretty scary reading." Blair felt strongly that if the essence of the intelligence reports could be made public, people would understand why Saddam posed a threat, and the necessity of taking action to remove it.

Blair later told the Butler inquiry into the use of British intelligence in the buildup to the Iraq War, "I remember that during the course of July and August, I was increasingly getting messages saying, 'Are you about to go to war?' and I was thinking, 'This is ridiculous' . . . I remember, toward the end of the holiday, actually phoning Bush and saying that we have got to put this (the intelligence dossier) in the right place straight away . . . we've not decided on military action . . . he was in absolute agreement . . . So, we devised a strategy, and this was really the purpose of Camp David, where we would go down the UN route, and the purpose of the dossier was simply to say, 'This is why we think this is important, because here is the intelligence that means that this is not a fanciful view on our part, there is a real issue here.' "[17]

The intelligence dossier was commissioned by Blair on September 3, just before he left London to meet Bush at Camp David. During the summer, SIS had received "significant new intelligence"[18] about Saddam's WMD capability from its network of agents in Iraq. While much was made of the fact that SIS, unlike the CIA, had a network of agents working inside Saddam's regime, the reality was that Britain's intelligence chiefs relied on just two main agents and two subsidiary sources for most of its information, and none of them had access to the inner sanctum of Saddam's immediate ruling circle.[19] Consequently, much of the intelligence they passed to their SIS spymasters in London was based on the assumption that Iraq was continuing to develop WMD, an assumption that Saddam himself did nothing to refute.

As part of the process of compiling the dossier, SIS asked its Iraqi agents to update their assessments of Saddam's WMD capability. The reports that they produced led to JIC, the body responsible for compiling the dossier for Downing Street, making a significant change in the assessment it had provided the previous March, shortly before Blair's Crawford visit. The new assessment stated starkly that "Iraq has a chemical and biological capability and Saddam is prepared to use it." While it contained the traditional caveat that "intelligence remains limited and Saddam's own unpredictability complicates judgments about Iraqi use of these weapons,"

244 AMERICAN ALLY

the assessment left Downing Street under no illusion about the seriousness
of the threat posed by Saddam: "Iraq currently has available, either from
pre–Gulf War stocks or more recent production, a number of biological
warfare and chemical warfare agents and weapons."[20]

This assessment was reached primarily on the basis of reports provided
by two SIS agents. Of the two SIS agents, the first, a long-standing British intelligence asset who had provided reliable information in the past,
was not in a position to "confirm from direct experience that Iraq had
chemical weapons," and based his claims that chemical agent production
was taking place solely on the "common knowledge" within his circle
that such activity was taking place.[21]

But it was the second agent, who also had an established relationship
with SIS, who provided the most enticing and worrying new intelligence on Iraq. Relying on information he had obtained from a new
source of his own, he reported that Iraq had acquired mobile laboratories that could be used to make and store biological weapons. The report, which was received by SIS on August 29, also included the claim
that Saddam had dispersed his "special weapons" to storage sites at strategic locations around the country, where they could be placed with
military units and ready to use within forty-five minutes. SIS was particularly excited about the discovery of their new source in Iraq, and
were so convinced of the authenticity of his information that they did
not subject it to the normal rigorous cross-checking and analysis to cor-
roborate its veracity. British intelligence regarded their new source as
the Iraqi equivalent of Oleg Penkovsky, the Soviet spy who provided
U.S. president John F. Kennedy with details of Russia's nuclear weapons
during the Cuban Missile Crisis. "You don't necessarily need to corrobo-
rate a source when you've got a Penkovsky on your books," remarked a
senior British intelligence officer who was closely involved in drawing
up the intelligence dossier.[22]

Blair's Downing Street officials took a direct interest in drawing up
the dossier, which the prime minister wanted ready by September 24,
when he had recalled Parliament for an emergency debate on Iraq. Alastair
Campbell was in constant touch with John Scarlett, the JIC chairman
who was responsible for drafting the dossier. Campbell was anxious that

the dossier be as convincing as possible, and on September 9, he wrote to Scarlett: "The media/political judgment will inevitably focus on 'what's new?' and I was pleased to hear from you and your SIS colleagues that, contrary to media reports today, the intelligence community are taking such a helpful approach to this in going through all the material they have. It goes without saying that there should be nothing published that you and they are not 100 percent happy with." Jonathan Powell, Blair's chief of staff, also took a keen interest. At one point, he e-mailed Scarlett, asking for a key section of the dossier to be redrafted, because it did "nothing to demonstrate a threat, let alone an imminent threat from Saddam." He also wondered, in another e-mail, what headline the dossier would generate in London's *Evening Standard* newspaper on the day of publication. The intense pressure from Downing Street led Britain's spy chiefs to bypass the checks they would normally apply to their intelligence assessments. As Lord Butler was to conclude in his report, "Because of the scarcity of sources and the urgent requirement for intelligence, more credence was given to untried agents than would normally be the case."[23]

Blair was fond of producing briefing documents for the public when he was contemplating military action. The most recent one had been published in October 2001, during the war in Afghanistan, and had dealt with al-Qaeda's responsibility for the 9/11 attacks. But the dossier Blair intended to publish on Iraq broke new ground in several ways. British intelligence had never before been asked to produce a public document, and the authority of British intelligence had never before been called upon to justify government action. But after the Camp David summit, Blair was aware he had to use all the material available to him if he was to be successful in persuading the skeptics that Iraq was a legitimate target for military action. Three days after returning from Camp David, Blair tried to rally support among British trade union members when he said, in a speech to the Trade Union Congress, "I, for one, do not want it on my conscience that we knew of the threat, saw it coming, and did nothing . . . If the will of the UN is ignored, action will follow."[24] Robin Cook saw Blair the following day to discuss the arrangements for the recall of Parliament, and noted that the prime minister "attaches great

importance to the forthcoming dossier." Cook was emerging as a prominent cheerleader of the antiwar campaign in Britain. He found Blair optimistic that he could turn public opinion around both in Britain and in
Europe. He believed that the majority would back intervention if there
were a Security Council resolution in support of it. He also believed that
a number of European countries—he named France, Italy, the Netherlands, and Denmark—would join an international coalition if military
action against Iraq became necessary.[25]

The intelligence dossier was presented with some fanfare to the House
of Commons as planned, on September 24. The fifty-page document bore
the title "Iraq's Weapons of Mass Destruction: The Assessment of the
British Government," and it was billed as presenting definitive proof of
Saddam's continued involvement in WMD. Opening the debate on Iraq,
Blair told a packed House of Commons that, based on the report of the
UN weapons inspectors after they were thrown out of Iraq in December
1998, significant quantities of WMD-related materials were still unaccounted for, including 360 tons of bulk chemical warfare agents, 1.5 tons
of VX nerve agent, 3,000 tons of precursor chemicals, growth media sufficient to produce 26,000 liters of anthrax spores, and more than 30,000
munitions—including ballistic missiles—for the delivery of chemical
and biological agents. Nor was Blair in any doubt that Saddam was still
pursuing his WMD programs. "His WMD program is active, detailed,
and growing. The policy of containment is not working. The WMD program is not shut down. It is up and running."

Despite its star billing, most of the report's contents consisted of little
more than a rehash of the concluding reports of the UN weapons inspectors when they were unceremoniously removed from Iraq in 1998. The
most eye-catching passages related to the new material that SIS's agents
had recently reported, namely that Saddam had chemical and biological
weapons and could deploy them within forty-five minutes of an order to
do so. This particular piece of intelligence was treated with a degree of
derision by the CIA, where George Tenet, the director, took to calling it
the "they-can-attack-in-forty-five-minutes shit." The CIA had strong reservations about the reliability of the new SIS agent who had provided the
intelligence in the first place, and warned London not to rely too heavily

on the new information.[26] Another passage related to intelligence reports that Iraq had made "repeated attempts to acquire a very large quantity (sixty thousand or more) of specialized aluminum tubes. The specialized aluminum in question is subject to international export controls because of its potential application in the construction of gas centrifuges used to enrich uranium." In other words, Saddam was still attempting to develop an atom bomb.

Further evidence of Saddam's attempts to acquire nuclear weapons, which were later to cause controversy in the United States, included the assertion that "there is intelligence that Iraq has sought the supply of significant quantities of uranium from Africa." This related to a visit an Iraqi delegation was reported to have made to the West African state of Niger in 1999. Uranium ore accounts for three quarters of Niger's exports, and the Iraqis were known to have purchased material from Niger for their atomic weapons program in the late 1970s. The presence of an Iraqi delegation in Niger suggested that Saddam was reactivating his interest in Iraq's atomic weapons program, although SIS was not sure whether the Iraqis were merely seeking to acquire uranium from Niger or had successfully concluded a deal.

When SIS checked with the CIA, Langley advised caution about any suggestion that Iraq had succeeded in acquiring uranium from Africa, although it agreed that there was evidence that the Iraqis had sought it. The CIA's advice was heeded, and the dossier went no further than stating that the Iraqis were seeking uranium ore from Africa. President Bush used the same formulation referring to the claim during his speech on January 28, 2003, when he said, "The British government has learned that Saddam Hussein recently sought significant quantities of uranium from Africa." Although it was later claimed by opponents of the war in the United States that this information was incorrect, and should never have been inserted into the State of the Union address, the Butler inquiry into British intelligence on Iraq, which was published in July 2004, concluded that the president's statement had been "well founded."[27]

Blair's primary purpose in publishing the document was to convince the public that Saddam, if left unchallenged, would pose a direct threat to Western security. In his foreword to the document, Blair wrote that he believed Saddam's WMD "to be a current and serious threat to the U.K. national interest."[28] In drawing up the dossier, Britain's spy chiefs had included all the material that they could lay their hands on, even material—such as the intelligence provided by the new Iraqi agent—that could not be subjected to the usual checks. John Scarlett, who personally wrote most of the report, took great care to phrase the dossier's language in the carefully modulated form used by intelligence officers. His careful choice of language, however, was not reflected in the headlines of many British national newspapers the following morning, when they reported on publication of the dossier.

"Brits 45 Minutes From Doom," screamed the banner headline on the front page of the pro-Labour tabloid *Sun* newspaper. At the prompting of Alastair Campbell, Blair's press secretary, the *Sun*, in common with several other leading British newspapers, had mistakenly—it was later claimed that it was deliberate—confused two distinct pieces of material from the dossier to provide stories that were far more alarmist than anything either Blair or the dossier had claimed. "British servicemen and tourists in Cyprus could be annihilated by germ warfare missiles launched by Iraq," read the *Sun* report. "They could thud into the Mediterranean island within 45 minutes of tyrant Saddam Hussein ordering an attack." Even the distinguished defense correspondent of the *Times,* which was widely regarded as Britain's newspaper of record, offered a similar report, writing that Saddam's missiles could hit British military bases in Cyprus in just forty-five minutes.

The dossier itself made no such claims. What it said, in two separate and distinct items, was first, that "some of the WMD" could be ready "within 45 minutes of an order to use them," and second, that Iraq was attempting to build a ballistic missile that had a range capable of hitting Cyprus, as well as a number of key American military bases in the Gulf region. At no point did the dossier say that Iraq had the capability to fit WMD warheads to its missile systems. The forty-five-minute intelligence related solely to battlefield munitions, such as mortars and rockets, although this was not explained in the dossier. When this glaring discrepancy was later made public, Sir Richard Dearlove, the head of SIS, was forced to issue a public apology, in which he expressed his regret over the "misrepresentation" of an intelligence report that was supposed to refer to "battlefield" weapons but was taken to mean "weapons with a longer range." Such distinctions, however, did not seem to unduly concern Downing Street in the autumn of 2002. Blair himself later admitted that he was not aware whether the forty-five-minute claim related to battlefield weapons or ballistic missiles.[29] Certainly Blair's staff showed little interest in the technical details and were more concerned with the media coverage that the dossier's publication had generated. They hoped that it would help to bring British public opinion behind the government's position on Iraq. A measure of the growing opposition Blair faced at home was revealed following the emergency parliamentary debate on Iraq later that day, when fifty-six Labour MPs voted against their leader's policy.

By playing fast and loose with the available intelligence material, Blair and his aides laid themselves open to accusations that they were deliberately exaggerating the case for war to suit their political ends. Campbell's propaganda ploys might have helped to drum up anti-Saddam sentiment in Britain, but Blair's intervention did little to impress his European allies, who were becoming more and more skeptical about the prime minister's seemingly unequivocal support for Bush. Both the French and German intelligence agencies had access to material similar to that of SIS and CIA on Iraq, and government officials in Paris and Berlin were well aware that the more lurid claims being made about Saddam's WMD capability in the British press could not be substantiated by the known evidence. "We were aware that there were concerns within the Western intelligence community about Saddam's WMD," said a senior French diplomat who was involved in the Iraq issue at the time. "We knew that Saddam was always trying to get hold of chemical and biological material, but we were not convinced that Saddam had the means to use them—assuming that he had them. We felt that both the Americans and the British were trying far too hard to make the case against Saddam."[30]

Washington did not feel the need to publish an intelligence dossier—there was still overwhelming American public support for prosecuting the war on terror, irrespective of the target. Instead, in early October 2002, the CIA published a National Intelligence Estimate on Iraq, which reflected the level of cooperation between the CIA and SIS. It reached conclusions similar to those contained in the British dossier, without generating apocalyptic newspaper headlines. The CIA report stated simply that "since the inspections ended in 1998, Iraq has maintained its chemical weapons effort, energized its missile program, and invested more heavily in biological weapons." It also contained the prediction that if Saddam's regime was able to acquire fissile material, Iraq would be capable of developing its own atom bomb within a year.

MUCH OF BLAIR'S ENERGY during the autumn of 2002 was now channeled into the diplomatic effort to secure approval among the permanent members of the UN Security Council for action against Iraq. A drafting process that was initially scheduled to take two weeks ended up lasting nearly two months, mainly on account of the French government's refusal to approve a resolution that sanctioned military action against Baghdad. Apart from the compelling international and domestic arguments for securing a new resolution, Blair believed it would actually make the task of confronting Saddam easier. If Baghdad could be persuaded to allow the inspectors to return—something that Blair had been campaigning for ever since Operation Desert Fox in 1998—he was confident that they would be able to confirm the intelligence reports he had been receiving on a weekly basis, namely, that Iraq still had biological, chemical, and nuclear programs. If that was the case, the inspectors would be able to insist on the Iraqis making a full disclosure of their banned weapons, which could then be destroyed, thereby avoiding the necessity of going to war. "Our primary objective throughout this period was to get rid of Saddam's WMD," explained one of Blair's senior aides. "If Saddam had come clean on his WMD capability, there would have been no reason to go to war."[31]

The French were the most vociferous opponents of military action against Iraq, and made it clear that they would oppose any resolution that authorized it. The initial stage of the drafting process, however, was carried out by the Americans, and the other delegations were kept waiting while the various U.S. departments battled each other over the precise wording. Initially, the Americans wanted a short, blunt resolution to the effect that if Saddam failed to make a full declaration of his WMD, then the United States and its allies were authorized to take military action. Britain was opposed to this, mainly because Downing Street was aware that such a resolution would never win the approval of the Security Council, and if Security Council approval was not forthcoming, then Blair would have difficulty fulfilling his promise to back Washington militarily. Blair understood that the new resolution needed to sanction the return of the weapons inspectors. If Saddam—as expected—impeded their work, then the allies would have a clear-cut case for going to war.

As these sensitive negotiations took place, the more hawkish elements in the Bush administration appeared determined to wreck the whole process, which they regarded as an unnecessary impediment to America's plans to attack Iraq. On one occasion, Lewis "Scooter" Libby, Cheney's chief of staff, revealed his lack of understanding for the delicacy of Blair's position when he asked a British official why it was that the British prime minister was getting so worked up about the UN, since he "is going to be with us anyway."[32] On another occasion, Libby told a British diplomat that the hawks—including Cheney, Libby's boss—were desperate to avoid a new weapons inspection process, as they were all but "locked on" to the spring 2003 window for a military assault against Iraq.[33] Blair was unphased by the efforts of the hawks to derail the process, and kept faith in Bush's pledge that the United States would give the UN one last chance to resolve the Iraq issue. Working on that assumption, Blair threw himself into another frantic round of shuttle diplomacy in Europe to win over the skeptics.

Blair also had his work cut out rallying domestic support, and in early October, he attended the annual conference of his increasingly fretful Labour Party. The strength of opposition to his Iraq policy were spelled out when nearly 40 percent of the delegates voted in favor of an anti-American motion that claimed Bush had reneged on his promise to consult with world leaders and set on launching military action against Iraq. Blair's supporters worked hard to rally support for an alternative motion, to the effect that military action against Iraq should only take place "with the authority of the United Nations."[34] In his keynote speech to the conference, Blair sought to win support for his policy by directly linking

Saddam's noncompliance with the UN with the Middle East peace process. "Some say the issue is Iraq. Some say it is the Middle East peace process. It's both," said Blair. His determination to make Saddam abide by his international obligations was equal to his enthusiasm for reviving the Middle East final status negotiations. "UN resolutions should apply here as much as to Iraq," Blair declared, and received the most prolonged applause of the whole speech.

Blair's willingness to link Saddam's WMD to the stalemate in the Israel-Palestine peace dialogue was unlikely to win him much support in Washington. Nor was his decision to invite former president Bill Clinton to address the conference. Blair had kept in touch with Clinton, and often sought his advice on how to handle delicate issues with the White House. Blair welcomed Clinton to the conference as "a great friend of Britain" and a "friend of the Labour Party." The former president, while supporting the latest attempt by America and Britain to force Saddam to disarm, insisted that the issue must be handled with the consent of the UN. "We must respond in a way that is consistent with the larger obligation we all have to build a more integrated global community," he said. "If the inspections go forward, and I hope they will, perhaps we can avoid a conflict." While Clinton received a standing ovation from the conference delegates, his views were almost diametrically opposed to those of the Bush administration. Clinton also paid tribute to Blair's diplomatic efforts, singling him out as the only world leader who seemed interested in getting an international consensus on Saddam. "I appreciate what the prime minister is trying to do in terms of bringing America and the rest of the world to a common position. If he weren't there to do this, I doubt if anyone else could."[35]

As if to emphasize the differences between the Blair-Clinton approach and the White House, the *New York Times* caused much consternation within the Blair camp when it published a draft of an uncompromising U.S. resolution on Iraq while the Labour conference was still under way. The resolution stipulated that the UN inspection teams could be joined by experts "from any permanent member of the Security Council," and that any breach by Saddam would give member states the authority "to use all necessary means to restore international peace and security in the area." The principle of "automaticity"—whereby a single resolution linked a new round of weapons inspections directly to military action—was anathema to both the French and Russians, who insisted that military action should be authorized by a second resolution only after it had been clearly demonstrated that the inspection process had failed. When Blair learned the details of the resolution, he was obliged to lock himself away with Jack Straw, the foreign secretary, in a secure room to make hasty phone calls to Washington to find out what was going on.

During the UN drafting process, Blair and Bush left the minutiae of the negotiations to their key officials—in Blair's case, Straw—and only got involved when the discussions reached a crucial stage. In America, the negotiations at the UN were accompanied by an intensification of military preparations. In September, Congress gave Bush the green light to use armed force against Iraq as deemed "necessary and appropriate." Later that same month, the U.S. National Security Strategy gave official endorsement to the new Bush doctrine of preemptive action, whereby the United States claimed the right to use its undisputed military prowess to overthrow governments if, in its view, they attempted to acquire weapons of mass destruction or harbored terrorists. Cheney helpfully suggested that this could include no fewer than sixty states worldwide. Meanwhile, the Pentagon was concentrating all its efforts on preparing for military action to overthrow Saddam in the spring of 2003.

The growing mood of militancy in Washington did little to help Blair in his efforts to win international support, particularly in Europe, for action against Iraq. "It was an uphill struggle," said a Downing Street aide. "We were fighting on two fronts—in the White House and Europe. Blair was convinced that Iraq had to be dealt with one way or another, but he needed the White House to engage the UN, and for the Europeans to back the new resolution. It was very much a high-wire act."[36] Given the difficulties involved, Blair showed remarkable fortitude in persevering with the process, especially as he encountered mounting hostility to the very notion of going to war against Iraq both at home and abroad. "For Blair, it was all about having the courage of his convictions," said an aide. "Saddam had to be dealt with, one way or another, and Blair believed that it was in everyone's interest if there was a degree of international consensus on this rather than leaving the Americans to act on their own."[37]

The Russians and French appeared to be determined to rule out a resolution that gave America and Britain the right to attack Iraq if the inspections failed. The emotional solidarity that had shaped Europe's response to 9/11 the previous autumn had all but evaporated. The French minister Hubert Vedrine sarcastically denounced America as a "hyperpuissance" that sought to impose its will on the rest of the world, while Chirac tried to lobby support for a resolution that only authorized a resumption of inspections. Chirac attended a conference of Francophone Arab states in Beirut, which gave their wholehearted support for the French position. President Putin, meanwhile, made his displeasure known when Blair visited him in Moscow in mid-October. The bonhomie that had characterized their previous meetings was noticeably absent as Putin seemed to go out of his way to ridicule Blair's position on Iraq. Putin dismissed the British government's recently published intelligence dossier as "propagandist," adding, "Russia does not have any trustworthy data which would support the existence of nuclear weapons or any other weapons of mass destruction."[38]

Amid this frenzy of diplomatic activity, Osama bin Laden's al-Qaeda terrorists launched a devastating terrorist attack on the idyllic Indonesian resort in town of Kuta, Bali. On the first anniversary of the start of the war in Afghanistan, al-Qaeda launched two carefully simulated bomb attacks—designed to cause maximum casualties—against a nightclub that was packed with Western holidaymakers, many of them from Australia. More than two hundred people were killed in the attacks, including about thirty British tourists. The group held responsible for the attack, an Indonesian Islamic fundamentalist group called Jemaah Islamiyah, was found to have close links to al-Qaeda, and many of its members had received training at bin Laden's camps in Afghanistan. A few days later, bin Laden issued a grainy videotape that was broadcast on the Al-Jazeera Arabic satellite television network. "We warned Australia before not to join in the war in Afghanistan . . . It ignored the warning until it woke up to the sounds of explosions in Bali."[39]

Bin Laden's bloody reemergence served to highlight the juxtaposition of the campaign to eradicate al-Qaeda and the looming war with Iraq. While Bush and Blair were quick to condemn the terrorist outrage in Bali, they found themselves under pressure to explain why they were so intent on concentrating their energies on Saddam Hussein when Osama bin Laden, the perpetrator of the 9/11 attacks, was still at large and continuing with his terror operations. The high casualty toll among British holidaymakers resulted in Blair being questioned as to whether the concentration of British intelligence resources on Iraq meant that warning signals about a possible attack on Bali had been missed. During an emergency debate on the bombings, Blair insisted that dealing with Iraq's WMD was just as important as fighting international terrorism. "Both are new threats facing the post–Cold War world," he said. "Both are threats from people or states who do not care about human life, who have no compunction about killing the innocent."[40] Blair's position was echoed in Washington by President Bush, who pledged to wage the war on terror on two fronts. Responding to criticism that American threats of war against Iraq were undermining the global campaign against terrorism, Bush said America would "fight the war on terror on two fronts if need be. We've got plenty of capacity to do so."

Blair's objective was to ensure that the UN passed a new resolution authorizing the return of the weapons inspectors to Iraq. While Blair continued to lobby for international support of a new resolution, Straw and Powell worked closely on drafting a new resolution. During this period, they were in such constant contact they had secure telephone lines installed in their respective homes so they could keep in touch. "Straw's message to Powell was very simple," said a senior Downing Street advisor. "It was, 'If we are going to be with you, we must have a legal basis for taking action'"—i.e., UN approval.[41] Some of the toughest negotiations Straw had was with the Bush administration, where the hawks were pushing for a hard-line resolution that stood no chance of being acceptable to the other Security Council members. Rumsfeld, for example, at one point demanded that the weapons inspectors be guarded by U.S. troops, a suggestion that was brusquely rejected by Blair.

Toward the end of October, it seemed that the main obstacles to a new resolution were slowly being overcome. Although Putin had caused Blair a degree of public embarrassment during their mid-October meeting, in private, the Russian leader had indicated that he would not oppose a new resolution so long as Moscow's $10 billion Iraqi debt was taken care of. Powell was in close contact with Dominique de Villepin, the French foreign minister, and by the end of October, Washington and London had narrowed their differences with Paris to the extent that all the parties agreed on a new draft resolution by early November. Security Council Resolution 1441 was eventually passed with a resounding 15-0 majority on November 8—a "slam dunk," as one White House official called it.[42] Sir Jeremy Greenstock, the British ambassador to the UN, who worked hard over several weeks to secure the resolution, was surprised that the French agreed to it. "The French were very difficult throughout the negotiations for 1441," he said. "I was very surprised that they voted yes for a resolution that did not contain their bottom line, which was that the UN retained control. In the end, they decided not to fall out with the U.S. over a regime like Iraq, which was, to say the least, unsavory."[43]

Bush and Blair were delighted to secure the resolution and satisfied with its uncompromising wording. It declared that Saddam had failed his responsibilities under a range of UN resolutions going back to the 1990 invasion of Kuwait, and gave him one final opportunity to comply or face "serious consequences." Apart from his intervention with Putin, Blair played a key role in lobbying support among the other members of the fifteen-member Security Council, and in explaining Washington's position to a skeptical international audience. From Blair's point of view, securing 1441 was crucial to the survival of the transatlantic alliance. "Without Blair's intervention, I think it is highly unlikely that the U.S. would have bothered with the UN," said a senior Downing Street official. "And without Resolution 1441, Britain would not have been able to support the U.S. militarily. Without 1441, there would have been no legal basis for military action, and Blair would have had no domestic political support for his close alliance with Washington."[44]

The intense political and diplomatic struggles of the autumn of 2002 tested Blair's resolve to the limit, but at no point did he display any symptoms of self-doubt. "He was a particularly driven man during this period," said one of his Downing Street advisors. "He did not stop to think whether or not dealing with Iraq was necessary. He felt intensely that this was something he had to do. Nor was there any calculation about what was in it for him. Blair is an instinctive politician. He had this very strong vision that this was a turning point for the world and that a broad coalition was required to meet the challenge."[45]

The no-nonsense tone of the resolution helped to allay the reservations of the hawks who now persuaded themselves that going to the UN was actually in their interests. As a White House advisor who was against pursuing the UN explained, "We saw it as a 'twofer'—a two-for-one. If the UN succeeded in getting Saddam to disarm—and it was a remote possibility, I admit—then there was no need to go to war. And if the UN failed, then the institutional weakness of the UN would be exposed and we would do the job ourselves."[46] The hawks were being rather disingenuous about their motives, because their ultimate objective was Saddam's removal, not Iraq's disarmament. Even if the UN succeeded in disarming Saddam, the more hawkish members of the Bush administration were not prepared to allow Saddam to remain in power under any circumstances.

Even the Pentagon, which had expressed strong doubts about the UN process, conceded that it was a "good resolution" because it allowed the military planners to intensify the preparations for war. "Having a resolution suited us, because it allowed us to put other options on the table apart from diplomacy, such as our military plans," said a senior Pentagon official. "And because we could be explicit that there was a military option if Saddam did not comply, it meant that we could have serious discussions with our allies about how they might participate. Before 1441, it was politically difficult for other countries to do this. But because everything was now out in the open, we could discuss with them what kind of a military contribution they could make. We all understood that going to the UN gave us an opportunity to build a coalition. Going to the UN was, therefore, a price worth paying."[47]

Indeed, expectations were high at the Pentagon that Washington would be able to put together the kind of grand coalition that had defeated Saddam's forces in 1991. "The UN route was sold to the Bush administration on grounds other than getting Blair out of a hole at home," said another senior Bush administration official. "One of the reasons that Colin Powell put forward for going to the UN was that it would bring the whole international community behind us, in particular France and Germany. The French were even discussing with us how they were prepared to commit ten thousand troops to military action in Iraq."[48] Apart from Britain, whose participation in a military campaign against Iraq—should it be necessary—was taken for granted, other European countries, such as Italy, Spain, and Poland, had discussions with Washington about their possible participation should the crisis result in war. For a few days after 1441 was passed, it seemed that Blair's desire for international consensus on handling Iraq would be met and that if military action became necessary, it would be undertaken by a coalition of like-minded allies acting on behalf of the UN. But these hopes were soon to be dashed, as the reality of the deep divisions that had already formed between the United States and Europe became even more acute.

Ten

COUNTDOWN

———◆—◆———

THE FAULT LINES THAT would create the greatest fissure in relations between the United States and Europe since the Second World War opened up as the architects of Resolution 1441 came to radically opposing conclusions over how it should be both interpreted and implemented. Many of the countries that voted for it did not regard it as a "trigger" for war if Saddam failed to comply fully with the tough weapons inspection that the resolution authorized. The Americans and British, on the other hand, were confident they had succeeded in getting the principle of "automaticity" enshrined in the resolution—i.e., any failure by Saddam to comply would be an automatic authorization for war. So far as Washington and London were concerned, the onus was on Baghdad to comply fully with the resolution. "If we find anything in what they give us that is not true, that is the trigger," said a Bush administration spokesman shortly after 1441 was passed. "If they delay, obstruct, or lie about anything they disclosed, then this will trigger action." [1]

The French, Russians, and Chinese had a different interpretation. Paris, in particular, was skeptical that Washington would refrain from ousting Saddam, even if he did comply. While the other permanent members of the Security Council were prepared to authorize tough new inspections of Iraq's WMD programs, they insisted on avoiding any automatic triggers for military action, and on leaving final control over any decision to act in the hands of the Security Council. To ensure the resolution's approval, various changes had been made in the wording so that each side believed that the final draft meant what they wanted it to mean. In essence, the dispute came down to what was meant by "serious consequences." For the British and Americans, it meant a trigger for war, while for the others, it meant bringing the issue back to the UN Security Council for further discussions that might lead to a second resolution authorizing war, depending on the scale of Saddam's defiance.

British officials seemed unaware of this potentially divisive difference in interpretation between the five permanent members of the Security Council. "So far as we were concerned, even the Syrians had signed up to it," said a senior Downing Street official. "In fact, our main worry was with Washington. The White House had signed up to this, and it meant that they would have to accept yes for an answer if Saddam complied with all the terms. It was very difficult for the U.S., because they knew there was a fear that Saddam would comply, and that would be it."[2] Another Downing Street official who was closely involved in drafting 1441 said that the British government believed that the argument over a second resolution had been won in London's favor during the intense negotiations over the resolution. "The argument was made during the negotiations for 1441 for a second resolution, and it was lost," the official said. "As far as we were concerned, there was no commitment in 1441 for a second resolution. By the same token, we could not have gone to war if Saddam had shown real cooperation."[3] Sir Jeremy Greenstock, the British ambassador to the UN, who was heavily involved in the negotiations, was more wary. "The French were very difficult throughout the negotiations for 1441 and, frankly, I was surprised that they voted for it, as it did not contain their bottom line, which was that the UN retained control of the whole process. I suppose they calculated that it was not in their interests to cross the U.S. over a state like Iraq that they knew to be unsavory."[4]

The focus now turned toward Baghdad, where Saddam had spent the autumn refusing to be intimidated by the mounting threat to his regime's survival. In one defiant speech, he told the Iraqi people that anyone who attacked Iraq would die in "disgraceful failure," and claimed that the Security Council was unfairly biased against Iraq. On several occasions, he indicated that Baghdad would comply with weapons inspections, but only on his terms—terms which, unsurprisingly, were not acceptable to Washington. In October, Saddam held a referendum on his presidency in which he secured a 100 percent "yes" vote, and he further sought to improve his standing with the Iraqi public by releasing hundreds of common criminals from Baghdad's infamous Abu Ghraib prison. Saddam's initial reaction to 1441 was to get Naji Sabri, the Iraqi foreign minister, to send a letter to the UN in which he harshly criticized the UN mandate for its "bad contents" and accused the resolution's cosponsors—the United States and Britain—of being part of a "gang of evil." In his letter to the UN, Sabri dared the weapons inspectors to find any trace of Iraq's nuclear, biological, or chemical weapons. For all the bluster, ultimately Saddam was well aware of the danger the resolution posed, and he accepted the resolution and the return of UN weapons inspectors to Iraq.

Washington had deep reservations about the effectiveness of UN weapons inspection teams, and was particularly suspicious of Dr. Hans Blix, the former Swedish diplomat who had been appointed the UN's chief weapons inspector. Some American officials believed Blix was more interested in avoiding military conflict with Iraq than investigating Saddam's WMD programs. The Pentagon was so concerned about Blix's approach that they asked the CIA to investigate him. "Cheney and Rumsfeld believed there was a lack of credibility in the inspection process, particularly with the appointment of Blix," said a senior Pentagon official. "Everyone in the White House held their nose over Hans Blix."[5] Downing Street officials, too, had their reservations about Blix's effectiveness, but felt that he should be given the opportunity to demonstrate he was up to the job by recommencing the inspections process.

The two most pressing practical requirements of 1441 were that Saddam allow a return of the weapons inspectors to Iraq, and that Baghdad provide a definitive account of its WMD programs and missile systems. The first requirement was met on November 25, when members of the UN Monitoring, Verification and Inspection Commission (UNMOVIC)

and the International Atomic Energy Agency (IAEA) returned to Baghdad for the first time in four years. At first, the inspections went well, and
the UN teams were allowed to visit sites that had been closed to them
when they last visited Iraq. But the biggest challenge Iraq faced was to
provide, within thirty days of 1441 being passed, a "currently accurate,
full and complete declaration" of its WMD arsenal. This the Iraqis duly
delivered on December 7—a day early—when a 12,807-page dossier was
presented to the UN base in Baghdad. The dossier was immediately
flown to the UN headquarters in New York for a detailed examination.
A week later, Washington declared that most of the information contained in the dossier was old, and that there were many glaring discrep-
ancies between the WMD capability Iraq was known to have had in the
1990s and what it was now claiming. A British diplomat dismissed the
Iraq declaration as "the mother of all gobbledygook," and British and
American officials believed that the omissions in the Iraqi declaration
gave them a prima facie case for finding Saddam to be in material breach
of 1441.

In London, Blair did his best to conceal his disappointment that Saddam had failed to comply with the UN requirements. "He hasn't done it,
has he?" he asked when told of the conclusions American intelligence
experts had reached after their preliminary examination of the Iraqi dossier. "That was Saddam's big moment, and he's blown it."[6] Up to that
point, Blair had still held on to the possibility that Saddam would comply, and there would be no need to take military action. "Our expectation
even after 1441 was that war was not inevitable—far from it," said a senior Blair aide. "If Saddam had cooperated properly, then war would have
been impossible. That was the preferred outcome. But that all changed
with Saddam's declaration, which was complete baloney. The great mys-
tery is why Saddam did not take the opportunity to avert war. It was a
real possibility he did not take. But after December 8, the argument became how long do you leave it—three months or three years? The French
wanted to give it three years; we thought Saddam has already had twelve
years. Enough is enough."[7]

American officials took an even starker view of the Iraqi dossier. "For
us, December 8 was the crucial day," said a senior Pentagon official. "That

was the opportunity for Saddam to demonstrate that he was willing to comply. He did not do it, and from that moment, the countdown to war began in earnest. There was no secret plot to go to war. Everything hinged on what Saddam decided to do. It was clear to us that the president would not flinch, and after Saddam failed to make a proper declaration, that was it." While the UN inspectors continued their work in Iraq, the American military buildup in the Gulf region intensified, although Pentagon officials insisted that the increased buildup was part of the diplomatic process. "If Saddam saw one hundred thousand troops surrounding him from different countries, there was always the possibility that he might see sense and cooperate."[8] Even so, the Pentagon's plans for a military assault on Iraq were well advanced, and in November, the *New York Times* had reported with some accuracy that the attack would involve a total of two hundred thousand troops—four U.S. divisions and one British armored division.[9]

On December 19, Powell informed the UN Security Council that Iraq was in "material breach" of Resolution 1441. The previous day, Bush had a private meeting with José María Aznar, the Spanish prime minister, one of the few European leaders to take an uncompromising view of the Iraq issue. Bush was dismissive of the Iraqi weapons statement. "The declaration is nothing," Bush told Aznar. "It's empty, it's a joke, but we will be measured in our response." The president then shared his private view of what was likely to happen to Saddam. "At some point, we will conclude enough is enough and take him out. He's a liar and he has no intention of disarming," said Bush. "War is my last choice. Saddam Hussein is using his money to train and equip al-Qaeda with chemicals, he's harboring terrorists."[10] Bush determined to intensify the propaganda war against Saddam.

Blair, too, was aware that Saddam's preference for brinkmanship over complete transparency on his WMD programs meant that military action had moved a significant step closer. "It was an absolutely clear sign that he had no intention of shutting this stuff down," said Blair. The declaration marked the start of "an agonizing period when I could see exactly what needed to happen but I couldn't get people to do it."[11] By that Blair meant that he wanted the UN to respond to Saddam's failure to comply with 1441. British officials detected a change of mood in Washington after Powell's declaration to the UN, and reported back to Blair that the White House was moving from diplomacy toward war. Britain was by now increasing its military buildup in the Gulf region, but Blair still saw this as a means of putting pressure on Saddam, not removing him.

Blair spent Christmas with his family at Chequers while the Bushes went to Crawford. For the Blairs, it was a particularly uncomfortable time, as a few weeks previously, a British newspaper had revealed that Cherie Blair had inadvertently used the services of a convicted Australian con man to purchase a couple of apartments in Bristol, which provoked controversy about the couple's private lives. Before retiring to Chequers, Blair made a quick visit to British troops deployed in the Gulf, where he apologized for the "uncertainty" over the possibility of conflict with Iraq. In his New Year's message, Blair painted a bleak picture. "I cannot recall a time when Britain was confronted simultaneously by such a range of difficult problems," he said. High among his list of concerns was "Iraq, and the prospect of committing U.S. troops to act if Saddam Hussein continues to flout international law; the mass of intelligence flowing across my desk that point to a continuing threat of attack by al-Qaeda, the lack of progress in the Middle East peace process and . . . the disturbing developments over North Korea's nuclear program. (The North Koreans had recently announced they were restarting their one, functional nuclear reactor.) Whether we survive and prosper or decline in the face of this insecurity depends crucially on the political decisions Britain now takes." Before leaving to spend the holiday at Crawford, Bush confessed to being stressed. "Yeah, I felt stressed. My jaw muscles got so tight . . . There was a lot of tension during that last holiday season."[12]

By early January 2003, it was clear that the veneer of international unity that had appeared evident when 1441 was passed was rapidly disintegrating, the most serious consequence of which was the damaging rift that was developing in relations between the United States and Europe. While the British and Americans believed Saddam's "material breach" constituted a casus belli, the French and Germans took the contrary view that Saddam's halfhearted compliance showed that 1441 was working and that the inspectors should be given more time to investigate Iraq's WMD programs. Although Bush had still not committed himself to war, that was not how many in Europe saw it.

The main opposition to a military confrontation with Iraq came from the French and the Germans, and their position had as much to do with the internal politics of Europe as their attitude toward the war on terror. Relations between Berlin and Washington had been strained since the previous autumn, when Gerhard Schröder made his antiwar stance a key issue in the German election campaign. Schröder's campaign strategy had infuriated Bush who, before the September election, had promised the German chancellor that military action against Iraq would not take place before the German poll, which Schröder believed would have seriously affected his chances of reelection. Bush was under the impression that he had received a personal commitment from Schröder that he would not exploit the strong antiwar lobby in Germany for personal electoral gain, and when he did so, Bush felt betrayed. "Bush sets great store in people being straight with him," said a Downing Street official. "He did not think that Schröder behaved well during the German election, and that was the end of the relationship so far as the White House was concerned. With Bush you don't get a second chance."[13]

Schröder's ostracism from the White House resulted in the German chancellor seeking to restore Germany's historic alliance with France, which had been strained by Chirac's open courtship of Edmund Stoiber, Schröder's main challenger in the German election. Chirac himself had been empowered by his own election success the previous spring, when he had won reelection for a second presidential term. At the same time, he secured a majority of his right-wing supporters in the National Assembly, thereby ending years of uneasy cohabitation between a Gaullist presidency and a Socialist parliament. Until Schröder's reelection, Chirac had been trying hard to improve the historic entente cordiale between Britain and France, and had sought closer cooperation with Blair on issues such as the creation of a European defense force. But Blair was also close to Schröder, whose Social-Democrat politics, despite his antiwar stance, were more in tune with Blair's. The British prime minister hoped that by maintaining cordial relations with Berlin he would be able to persuade the Germans to resume their more traditional pro-American position.

By the autumn of 2002, the French had become suspicious of the Anglo-German alliance; the Franco-German alliance, after all, had been the driving force behind the European Union for many years. Chirac made a deliberate effort to repair relations with Germany, and by late October, the two countries were working closely together on European reform issues. Blair was made brutally aware of the geopolitical realignment taking place in Europe in late October when he attended a European summit and was ambushed by a Franco-German fait accompli on the controversial subject of agricultural reform. Blair reacted angrily, so angrily, in fact, that Chirac canceled a scheduled Anglo-French summit in December and personally berated the prime minister, telling him, "You are very rude and I have never been spoken to like this before." Thus, by the time Saddam was found in material breach of 1441, the two significant military powers in Western Europe—Britain and France— were barely on speaking terms.

In January, the Germans were given added influence to pursue their antiwar campaign when they took up one of the rotating seats at the UN Security Council, which enabled them to make a direct contribution to the debate about how to handle Iraq. By mid-January 2003, the Franco-German alliance had become an influential rallying point for the antiwar lobby at the UN, although Blair and Bush were still unsure about which way the French would jump, and both Washington and London regarded Paris as the more influential partner in the relationship. In his New Year's message, Chirac had warned that the French military could soon be involved in "new theaters," and the French aircraft carrier *Charles de Gaulle* was made ready for military action. Chirac issued a statement on January 7, in which he warned his armed forces to be "ready for every eventuality" and to be "especially attentive to the way in which Iraq adheres to the UN Security Council Resolution 1441." Chirac even sent a senior French military officer on a secret mission to Washington for discussions about a potential French contribution of some fifteen thousand troops, one hundred airplanes, and the use of significant naval assets, including an aircraft carrier group.[14] At this point, both Britain and the United States thought Chirac would ultimately sign up for a military action against Saddam.

Dr. Hans Blix, the head of the UN weapons inspections team, came to a very different conclusion after he visited Chirac during a stopover at the Élysée Palace in Paris on January 17. According to Blix, Chirac's "thinking seemed to be dominated by the conviction that Iraq did not pose a threat that justified armed intervention."[15] Blix's hunch proved correct, and any hope of achieving an international consensus on Iraq was brutally dashed on January 20, when Dominique de Villepin, the French foreign minister, chose Martin Luther King Day to ambush Colin Powell at the UN with a bitter attack on American preparations for war. "If war is the only way to solve this problem, we are going down a dead end," de Villepin declared. "Nothing today justifies envisaging military action." And asked whether France would use its veto if a second UN resolution were put forward authorizing military force against Iraq, de Villepin replied, "Believe me, in a matter of principles, we will go all the way to the end."

De Villepin's intervention effectively ended any hope of transatlantic cooperation on Iraq. At this juncture, the UN was waiting for an interim report from Dr. Blix on Iraq's compliance on 1441, which had been ordered in response to Iraq's failure to make a satisfactory declaration on its WMD programs in December. If Blix's report, which was due on January 27, confirmed Saddam's noncompliance, Washington would take it as a trigger for war. In fact, Bush had already given up on Blix and the weapons inspectors. From late December onwards, Rice had briefed Bush that the new inspections regime was a sham. The inspectors were inspecting Iraqi warehouses that had already been sanitized, and Blix was not conducting the kind of aggressive, no-holds-barred inspections that Bush desired. The Iraqis were preventing scientists suspected of involvement in the various clandestine weapons programs from being interviewed in private by the weapons inspectors, as 1441 stipulated. On January 13, Bush informed Powell that he had decided to go to war to remove Saddam from power. Powell still had strong reservations about military action, not least because he feared that Iraq would descend into chaos if Saddam were overthrown. But Powell's hopes of trying to make the UN process work disappeared after de Villepin's UN démarche. Powell felt particularly betrayed by the French, because the previous night he had met de Villepin at the Waldorf-Astoria in New York, and the French foreign minister had given him no hint of what he was planning. Powell had lost an important ally in his attempt to prevent the Bush administration from going to war with Iraq.

"It was a complete betrayal by the French," said a senior Downing Street official. "Up until Christmas, Chirac had been very cooperative. And then, suddenly, he completely changed direction. We thought that the Germans and the French were egging each other on to outdo each other in their anti-Americanism, but de Villepin's behavior at the UN was unacceptable. Powell was furious, and concluded that you could not trust the French."[16] The White House was equally incandescent. "The French behavior was appalling," said a senior administration official. "Had there been international consensus on Iraq, then there was always the possibility that Saddam may have fled, and there would have been no need for a war and the loss of thousands of lives. This should weigh heavily on the collective conscience of the French."[17]

The about-turn in the French position ended any hope Blair may still have entertained of holding together the transatlantic alliance. Even though he had anticipated stiff opposition from Chirac, like Bush, he had believed that in the end the French would come around. Chirac's decision to oppose military action meant that Blair was virtually alone in Europe in supporting Washington's declared policy of effecting regime change in Baghdad. Certainly, Britain was the only European country prepared to make a significant military commitment to deal with Saddam. "Blair went through a roller-coaster ride of emotions during that winter," said one of his close Downing Street aides. "He went from great excitement about 1441 to deep despair when he realized that his attempt to hold the transatlantic alliance together was falling apart."[18]

By the time the French and German political establishments gathered together on January 22 in Versailles to celebrate the fortieth anniversary of the Élysée Treaty that cemented the Franco-German alliance, the diplomatic cracks between Europe and America were fast becoming a chasm.

On the evening of the meeting, Schröder told his local party workers, "Don't expect Germany to approve a resolution that would give legitimacy to war," while Chirac reiterated his view to a Franco-German gathering that "War is always an admission of failure. Everything must be done to avoid it." The behavior of the French and the Germans provoked a characteristically caustic response from Donald Rumsfeld, who dismissed them as being part of "old Europe," as compared with the "new" Europeans, such as Poland and the other formerly communist countries of Eastern Europe. Some of the more conservative American media castigated the French as "cheese-eating surrender monkeys," while the Franco-German alliance was dismissed as an "axis of weasel." Blair's response was to sign a letter drafted by a group of European leaders, including Silvio Berlusconi of Italy and José María Aznar of Spain, which was published in the *Wall Street Journal* on January 29, in which the eight signatories stressed the many values Europe shared with America, including "democracy, individual freedom, human rights and the rule of law." The letter went on to state that "the Iraqi regimes and its weapons of mass destruction represent a clear threat to world security . . . We must remain united in insisting his regime is disarmed." [19]

As the transatlantic political tensions increased, Hans Blix and the UN weapons inspectors were preparing their interim report to the Security Council on January 27. Initially, Blix had wanted to report in mid-March, but the White House had objected to the long timeframe, which Bush administration officials believed would encourage the Iraqis to believe that the UN was not serious about forcing them to comply. Blair had raised the issue of what he called an "elongated timeline" when Blix briefly met with him at Chequers on his way back to Baghdad in mid-January. So far as Blair was concerned, the military buildup taking place in the Gulf region was necessary to get Iraq to cooperate, but he warned Blix that the United States could not keep its troops idling in the area for months. If there were to be a continued lack of "honest cooperation" on the part of the Iraqis, then serious decisions would have to be taken around March 1. [20]

When Blix addressed the Security Council on January 27, Bush and Blair were gratified by his criticisms of the Iraqis' conduct. "Iraq," said Blix, "appears not to have come to a genuine acceptance—not even today—of the disarmament which was demanded of it and which it needs to carry out to win the confidence of the world." UN weapons inspectors had found eight empty chemical warheads, there were "strong indications" that Iraq had produced more anthrax than it had declared, and stashes of nuclear documents had been found at the homes of Iraqi scientists. Despite the evidence of Iraqi obfuscation, Blix and Mohamed El-Baradei, the head of the IAEA, asked for "a few months" to complete the inspection process. According to ElBaradei, the extra inspection time would be a valuable "investment in peace, because they could help us to avoid war."

Neither the Bush administration nor the Blair government were convinced. During his State of the Union address the following day, Bush gave notice that his patience with the UN inspection process was starting to wear thin. "Let there be no misunderstanding," said Bush. "If Saddam Hussein does not fully disarm, for the safety of our people and the peace of the world, we will lead a coalition to disarm him. The course of this nation does not depend upon the decision of others." By this point, Bush had already made the decision to remove Saddam, but the growing discord within the transatlantic alliance, and the uncertainty over how the UN should proceed, provided Blair with a dilemma. If America went to war while the UN was still advocating weapons inspections, Blair would find himself in an impossible position, both at home and abroad. In order both to maintain his close alliance with Washington and to win over the skeptics in Britain and Europe, Blair concluded that he would need a new UN resolution that authorized military action.

ON JANUARY 31, BLAIR flew to the United States to see Bush to discuss the next step in disarming Iraq. Before his departure, Blair encountered the full force of the mounting rebellion he was facing from Labour backbench MPs during the weekly session of prime minister's questions. Blair was constantly heckled by MPs shouting "Who's next?" and "When do we stop?" Looking visibly rattled, Blair retorted, "We stop when the threat to our security is properly and fully dealt with."[21] The opposition Conservative Party supported military confrontation with Iraq, but a significant, and voluble, antiwar faction was developing within Blair's own Labour Party. In his last cabinet meeting before leaving for Camp David, Blair was warned by Gordon Brown, the chancellor of the Exchequer and his long-standing rival for the Labour leadership, that he faced a huge battle to win over public opinion. Brown, who maintained close ties with senior Democrats, said the issue was "a lack of identification" with the United States and that the British public did not trust the Bush administration.[22]

On arrival in the United States, Blair found himself even more isolated when he discovered that Colin Powell had joined Washington's prowar camp. As a former soldier, loyalty was ingrained in Powell's DNA. Thus when Powell was summoned to the Oval Office by America's commander-in-chief on January 13, he had no qualms about promising Bush his support. "I'll do the best I can," Powell replied when Bush asked whether he could count on him. "Yes, sir, I will support you. I'm with you, Mr. President."[23] Blair had been due to meet Bush at Camp David, but atrocious weather meant that the meeting was rescheduled at the White House. Blair's message to Bush was simple and to the point: he needed to get a second UN resolution in order to get Labour Party backing for military action.

It had been four months since the two leaders had met at Camp David, and Bush had committed the United States to taking the UN route rather than acting unilaterally. But Bush had never had much faith in the ability of the UN to deliver what he wanted, namely Iraq's disarmament and the removal of Saddam's regime, even if the second requirement contravened the UN charter. Iraq's failure to make a full disclosure on its WMD programs, the Iraqis' grudging cooperation with the weapons inspectors, and Blix's interim report confirmed the Bush administration's view that Saddam had no intention of complying with the numerous UN Security Council resolutions that had been passed since 1990. Consequently, Blair found not only Bush but the entire U.S. war cabinet—including Powell—firmly opposed to returning to the UN Security Council to obtain a second resolution. In fact, this was one of the rare occasions in the first Bush administration when Cheney agreed with Powell. Both Cheney and Powell had, of course, been involved in securing the original UN ceasefire resolution (687) at the end of the Gulf War in 1991, and were well aware of Saddam's history of defiance and noncompliance. After seventeen resolutions, they saw no need for an eighteenth. The last resolution, 1441, had taken seven weeks to negotiate, and a new resolution would take even longer. Pentagon officials were planning for military action to commence before the end of March, and there was a serious risk that a new diplomatic initiative would interfere with the military preparations. "We didn't think there was a need for a second resolution," Powell later explained, "and we were quite sure of very serious problems with the French, but the U.K. needed and very badly wanted a second resolution."[24]

Blair had to deploy all his powers of persuasion and draw upon all his reserves of political capital in Washington to get Bush to change his mind. Blair's pitch to Bush was little more than a direct appeal for help. Blair needed a second resolution because, without it, he would be damaged politically. A second resolution that unequivocally authorized the use of military force against Iraq would enable Blair to overcome the fierce resistance he was encountering in Britain and Europe to his alliance with the United States. Without it, Blair would have serious difficulty in committing Britain to military action. In essence, his message to Bush was, if you want Britain to fight by your side, then I must have this resolution. Reluctantly, Bush agreed. He respected and admired Blair, and what was the point of friendship if you could not help out your buddy? "If that's what you need, we will go flat out to try and help you get it," Bush told Blair. Bush later referred to Blair's visit as "the famous second-resolution meeting," and said that the British prime minister "absolutely" asked for help. "Blair's got to deal with his own Parliament, his own people, but he has to deal with the French-British relationship as well, and its context within Europe," said Bush. "And so he's got a very difficult assignment. Much more difficult, by the way, than the American president, in some ways. This was the period where slowly but surely the French became the issue inside Britain."[25]

Bush's agreement to go to the UN was a significant concession to Blair, and demonstrated that, when it came to the crunch, the British leader did have leverage at the White House. None of the principal members of the Bush administration thought a new resolution was either necessary or helpful. Powell believed that 1441 provided the necessary authorization, view that was also held by a number of British officials. The French, however, had continued to argue that a second resolution was imperative. After the transatlantic split occurred in mid-January, Blair was increasingly vulnerable to claims from his opponents that his actions had no international legitimacy. By going back to the UN, Blair was gambling that he could force the French into a corner, even taking into account de Villepin's threat in New York to veto a second resolution. "We knew that the French did not want to approve a resolution that led to war, but we also knew the Americans would not allow a resolution to be put forward that did not contain a 'trigger' for war," said a senior Downing Street official. "It was a battle of wills."[26] According to the White House, the French were well aware of this, and told the Bush administration not to bother with a second resolution. "The French told us that they would be happy for us not to seek a second resolution, but Blair wanted us to go for a second resolution for his own domestic reasons," said a senior official. "The French attitude was, just do it. But don't ask us for approval."[27] Bush set out the approach the United States would be adopting to a new resolution at a press conference held after meeting with Blair. "Should the UN decide to pass a second resolution, it would be welcomed if it is yet another signal that we're intent upon disarming Saddam Hussein."

The hawks in the Bush administration, particularly Cheney and Rumsfeld, could have done without the inconvenience of a second resolution. Cheney thought that going back to the UN would get the United States entangled in a briar patch and cause unnecessary delays for the military preparations. In fact, the Pentagon was relieved by the diplomatic delay, as it was struggling to get everything in place for February 15, the original date that had been set for an attack against Iraq. Letting the schedule slip back to March suited the Pentagon planners. There was also an understanding within Bush's war cabinet that special allowances should be made for Blair. "The senior members of the administration held him in high regard," said a senior Pentagon official. "Throughout the whole buildup to the war, the president was in constant contact with him. And if someone said we are doing this because it is important to

Blair, then people sat up and took notice. His name topped the list of our allies. No one else came close."[28]

As was usual in his meetings with Bush, Blair raised the perennial issue of the Middle East at the White House. Both Washington and Israel were wary of Blair's attempts to revive the Israel-Palestine peace process, but Blair persisted in the belief that resolving the Arab-Israeli dispute was integral to winning the war on international terrorism. The British government had invited a Palestinian delegation to London in January to discuss political reform, but the conference had to be abandoned after a suicide car-bomb attack in Tel Aviv, and the Israeli government, after consulting with its allies in the Bush administration, banned the delegation from traveling. Undeterred, Blair sent his personal envoy Lord Levy to Ramallah to see Yasser Arafat, to get his agreement to appoint a Palestinian prime minister, a key Washington demand. Arafat gave Levy a letter to pass on to Blair, saying that he was prepared to appoint Mahmoud Abbas as prime minister. Blair's diplomacy had won an important breakthrough with the Palestinians. In Washington, Blair pressed Bush about the Middle East and the road map that had been discussed for creating a two-state solution by 2005. Bush said he would publish the road map once the Iraq issue had been resolved.

A White House official who attended the meeting between Blair and Bush said that the president agreed to help because of his respect for the prime minister. "When Bush saw Blair, he saw a man with iron in his veins who had stood by him at a time of personal crisis," said the official. "There was real warmth between them, and Bush understood perfectly that he needed to do this for Blair. If it caused us problems, so be it."[29] Bush's action was not entirely altruistic, because he did not want America to be fighting alone in Iraq, and Britain was the only country whose armed forces had the training, equipment, and capability to fight effectively alongside the Americans.

At the end of the five-hour meeting, Bush and Blair announced that Saddam had "weeks, not months" to disarm, and that if he failed to do so, he would face the consequences. The consensus was that the coalition was still six weeks away from being ready for military action, and Bush and Blair agreed that the intervening period should be used to bring public opinion around. When Blair got back to London, he called Robin Cook, the most prominent antiwar member of the government, to brief him on the visit. He told Cook that he was encouraged that Bush had been as strong as he had ever heard him on the Middle East, and left with the impression that Bush was willing to push the Israelis into making peace. On the question of a second resolution, Blair said he had found Bush "hard over" on the problems of returning to the UN.[30]

Blair's first move toward rallying public support in Britain was to publish another intelligence dossier detailing human rights abuses in Saddam's Iraq. However, the event became a public relations disaster. The dossier was not made up of intelligence at all but had been plagiarized from the dissertation of an American Ph.D. student. Straw, who was responsible for SIS, had not been informed about Downing Street's latest propaganda ploy, and complained bitterly. Blair and Alastair Campbell then decided to implement what Campbell called the "masochism strategy," whereby Blair toured television studios confronting hostile audiences and made more regular appearances in Parliament. In dealing with the British public, Blair said he would subject himself to "as much beating up by members of the public as you can possibly have," to get across his argument. Blair believed that his strategy worked, because while many of his critics came across as being unreasonable, he was able to argue his case from a point of principle.[31] But he had a far harder task of convincing the politicians. On February 3, while reporting back to the House of Commons on his Washington trip, Blair admitted that he was "risking everything" because of his support for Bush over Iraq. But although his political future was at stake, Blair insisted that he did not want to go down in history as the prime minister who ignored the threats posed by Saddam Hussein and international terrorism. By now, the British press was drawing parallels between Blair and Anthony Eden, who had resigned as prime minister over the 1956 Suez Crisis, and with Lyndon B. Johnson, who decided not to run for a second presidential term because of his unpopularity over the Vietnam War. But Blair said he was determined to resolve the Iraq issue once and for all. "Eight weeks have now passed since Saddam was given his final chance," Blair told the assembled MPs. "Six hundred weeks have passed since he was given his first chance." The following week, there appeared a subtle shift in Blair's argument for war against Iraq when he made his weekly appearance at the Commons. Previously, his main argument had been over Saddam's WMD arsenal; now he argued that war would be preferable to the continuation of the UN sanctions because of the suffering and malnutrition that sanctions caused. Blair was quietly preparing for the day when the UN declined to authorize the use of force to deal with Saddam's WMD.

In Washington, the Bush administration's attempts to rally support were concentrated on the presentation Colin Powell was due to give to the UN Security Council on February 5, which the United States said would contain conclusive proof of Saddam's guilt. Powell spent three days at the CIA's Langley headquarters, searching through the available intelligence, and received a sixty-page dossier from the Pentagon's alternative intelligence-gathering outfit, the Office of Special Plans, run by Abram Shulsky, a leading neocon. Cheney and Libby were still pushing the links between Saddam and al-Qaeda, and even Saddam's involvement in the 9/11 attacks. Powell was skeptical about some of the information he was given, but was aware that the credibility of the United States was on the line when he made his presentation. Caught between his reservations over the quality of the available intelligence and his duty to serve his country, Powell did his best to sound convincing when he arrived at the UN headquarters to make his presentation. He played a transcript of an intercepted conversation between two Iraqi officers, in which they seemed to be talking about concealing Saddam's WMD stockpiles. Using satellite photographs, he argued that the Iraqis had been cleaning up and storing their WMD stockpiles before the arrival of the UN weapons inspectors, and that the Iraqis had mobile laboratories and unmanned aircraft to process and deliver biological weapons. There was evidence that Iraq had imported aluminum tubes that could be used for centrifuges intended for nuclear weapons. Finally, he accused Saddam of providing a safe haven for al-Qaeda in northern Iraq, an area over which Saddam had no control.

Powell hoped that his seventy-six-minute submission would have the same impact as Adlai Stevenson's presentation to the Security Council during the 1962 Cuban Missile Crisis, when the secretary of state produced a compelling set of photographs detailing the Soviet military buildup. Powell's speech certainly helped to win over some of the skeptics in the United States, with even antiwar *Washington Post* columnists writing that they had been impressed by his arguments. But others, particular those familiar with the available intelligence, were less impressed. Hans Blix had actually visited some of the sites Powell had talked about in his presentation, "and at none of the many sites we actually inspected had we found any prohibited activity."[32]

British intelligence officers were surprised to find details of the alleged Saddam–al-Qaeda link in Powell's presentation, because they had told the CIA repeatedly that the evidence was very shaky. "We were in daily contact with our opposite numbers at the CIA, and we told them that there was no institutional link between Saddam and al-Qaeda," said a senior British intelligence official. "There may have been the odd meeting between an Iraqi official and an al-Qaeda operative, but that was all it amounted to. There was nothing to suggest Saddam was working with al-Qaeda, and we did not regard the inclusion of erroneous information in such an important showcase event as helpful."[33] Powell himself insisted that the entire presentation had been cleared personally by Tenet and the other U.S. intelligence chiefs. "Every word in that presentation was screened and approved by the intelligence community," he said.[34]

The next important date on the diplomatic calendar was February 14, when Blix was due to give his latest report to the Security Council on Iraqi cooperation with the weapons inspection teams. Blix was angry that Washington was trying to undermine the inspectors, with Powell's presentation suggesting that the United States was doing a better job at exposing Saddam's noncompliance than the UN. Blix wanted to set the record straight, and in London, Straw learned that Blix was not only going to attack Powell's presentation but praise the Iraqis for their great cooperation. Blix's report was not as negative as Straw feared. There were still, Blix said, 8,500 liters of anthrax, 1.5 tons of VX nerve agent, and thousands of chemical shells that were unaccounted for, and the Iraqis' al-Samoud missile program was in breach of the stipulated 150-kilometer range. However, the Iraqis had allowed some of their scientists to be interviewed, and handed over documents relating to the destruction of chemical agents. So far as Blix was concerned, the weapons inspections were making progress and, given more time, they would be able to make a more definite assessment on the state of Saddam's WMD. Blix concluded his report by criticizing elements of Powell's presentation earlier in the month, suggesting that the interpretation of the satellite pictures he had used could be wrong.

Powell was furious, and said the gestures made by Iraq amounted to nothing more than a cat-and-mouse game. "To this day, we have not seen the level of cooperation that was hoped for," he said. "We cannot allow this process to be endlessly strung out." De Villepin responded by calling for the inspectors to be given more time. "The option of inspections has not been taken to the end. The message comes to you today from an old country," he said, a barbed reference to Rumsfeld's comments on old Europe. This old country, he continued, had "never ceased to stand upright in the face of history and before mankind." In Washington, Blix's appeal for more time did nothing to avert the military juggernaut of the war preparations, while in London, Blair was despondent that the growing transatlantic rift had been so publicly exposed. British officials believed that Blix had been "got at" by the French, who pressured him that he would have blood on his hands unless he found a way to stop the war. "The problem with Blix was that he was a typical diplomat," said a Downing Street official. "He did not want to upset anyone—not even the Iraqis."[35]

The day after Blix's report, millions of Europeans turned out for anti-war demonstrations across the continent. In London, an estimated one million people from all over the country converged on the capital to participate in the largest demonstration in British history. Those taking part in the "stop-the-war rally" came from all walks of life, and reflected a wide variety of political views. Many of them were sturdy, middle-class Britons who had voted Labour for the first time in 1997, and had continued to support New Labour. Blair spent the day in Glasgow, addressing Labour's spring conference. Aware that Blix was winning the argument that 1441 authorized the continuation of the weapons-inspection process, Blair again shifted his grounds for justifying the war. "The moral case for war has a moral answer," he said. "It is not the reason we act. That must be on weapons of mass destruction. But it is the reason, frankly, why, if we do have to act, we should do so with a clear conscience. I do not seek unpopularity as a badge of honor. But sometimes it is the price of leadership and the cost of conviction." As he had done in Chicago in 1999, Blair was falling back on the moral argument to justify war.

But Blair was facing an uphill struggle to convince the doubters of the justice of his cause. Opinion polls showed that a clear majority of the British public did not think the case for war had been made, even though they accepted that Saddam had WMD and had close links with international terror groups, including al-Qaeda.[36] The most significant setback to Blair came on February 26, when 121 Labour MPs voted against the government on the motion that "the case for military action against Iraq is as yet unproven." It was the biggest government rebellion in the Commons since William Gladstone had introduced his Home Rule Bill in 1886 to give Ireland independence from Great Britain. It would have been bigger had the government whips not managed to reassure some of the potential rebels that no action would be taken without a second UN resolution.

Toward the end of February, Blair finally managed to persuade Bush to table a second resolution. Throughout the turbulent days of February, the Bush administration seemed unaware that their key ally was fighting for his political life. Washington's primary focus was to make sure that all the military preparations were in place for the planned attack on Iraq, which was now scheduled for mid-March. It was only after the American Embassy in London dispatched a number of increasingly frantic cables to Washington, highlighting Blair's predicament, that Bush was finally moved to address the issue, and he did so with reluctance. On February 20, Blair had talked to Blix at the UN and told him of Washington's displeasure with his February 14 report. The Americans were, however, attracted to the idea of a second resolution, and in Blair's view, this would help prevent the UN from being marginalized, and the international community split. Blair told Blix that he wanted to give Saddam an ultimatum to force him to truly cooperate. Failure to do so would be deemed a breach of 1441. In Blair's view, the Iraqis could have signaled a change of heart in their December 8 declaration. Their failure to do so indicated that Saddam was not willing to cooperate. At this point, Blix himself was of the opinion that "Iraq still concealed weapons of mass destruction, but I needed evidence."[37]

Cheney and Rumsfeld, as in the past, were against UN involvement, and Bush insisted that a second resolution would have to be dealt with quickly, so as not to interfere with the military preparations. Blair wanted Washington to give the UN until the end of April before a vote was taken, by which time he hoped the weapons inspectors would have found the "smoking gun"—a hidden stash of WMD, or some equivalent breach of 1441—that would justify war. It would also give him time to rally support at the UN and quell the dissident ranks within the Labour Party. But Bush was insistent that the new resolution should be dealt with by mid-March at the latest. Any further delay would mean U.S. troops going into battle in scorching temperatures.

BLAIR NOW EMBARKED ON the most intense political and diplomatic period of activity of his entire career. At stake was not just his own political survival, which would be put in serious jeopardy if he failed to get a second resolution; if Blair could not get the necessary support to commit Britain to war, then the entire fabric of the transatlantic alliance would be torn apart, perhaps irrevocably. "Given the pressure he was under, Blair was remarkably composed throughout this time," said a Downing Street official who worked closely with Blair during this period. "In times of crisis, he never lost his temper. He was under immense pressure and very tired, but he coped very well. It is the antithesis of his nature to take his frustrations out on those around him."[38] Blair and his key officials—Powell, Campbell, and Manning—were starting work at Downing Street at 7 a.m. and not finishing until midnight. The punishing schedule caused some of his officials to fear that he was taking on too much, and that his health might suffer as a consequence. "He was very self-aware throughout this period," said another Downing Street aide. "He did not think he could walk on water. When people were hostile to him, he would say, 'Well, you can decide what to do with me at the election.' He did not get depressed about the political implications but he was anxious about how it was going to turn out. He was determined to do anything possible to avoid war, but if it came, he was determined to do it and live with the consequences."[39]

Even at this late stage, Downing Street believed that war was still not a foregone conclusion. British army units had been deploying in the Gulf region since late January, and it was anticipated that thirty-five thousand troops—more than a quarter of the British army—would be ready to support the American-led campaign to overthrow Saddam by early March. "Blair was very frustrated about the collapse of the international coalition after 1441," said one of his aides. "He believed that if everyone had held together at the Security Council after 1441, there was still a chance that Saddam would be kicked out by his own people, or would cave in to the demands of the UN. But once the split emerged, Saddam was up to his old tricks of playing countries off against each other, with Saddam the main beneficiary."[40]

Like Bush, Blair had received reports from his intelligence chiefs that Saddam's family was putting out feelers about going into exile. In early February, Gamal Mubarak, the son of the Egyptian president, told Bush that a representative of Saddam's family had approached Cairo about the possibility of establishing a safe house in Egypt and depositing $2 billion in cash. Bush was dismissive of the offer, pointing out that the United States took a dim view of countries that harbored known terrorists and, so far as Washington was concerned, that was Saddam's status.[41] Egypt was not the only Arab country to receive an approach from the Hussein clan, and there was muted excitement in Downing Street that the entire crisis could be resolved by Saddam going into exile. "We thought there was a genuine possibility that this could happen," said a senior Downing Street official. "Some Arab governments were very interested in this option. The only problem was that Saddam himself seemed impervious to the idea. He was only interested in his family going into exile, not him."[42]

Washington was torn about helping Blair. The White House did not want to go into battle on its own, but it had lost faith in the UN process. "We would not have gone back to the UN had it not been for Blair," said a senior State Department official. "But we didn't want to do this thing on our own, and Blair's support was crucial."[43] From the White House's point of view, sticking with the UN route meant that the war had to be justified on the basis of WMD, when Bush believed that there were other reasons for taking action. "There were many other justifications for war," said a senior Bush administration official. "Saddam posed a threat to the region, and he had conducted a bloody tyranny against his own people. We believed that the world would be a better and safer place without Saddam Hussein in power." For all the difficulties, the White House admired the way Blair conducted himself through the most critical period of his premiership. "Blair did not do this for political advantage. Far from it. He did it because he believed in it," said a senior White House aide. "He made the case for war very strongly, and he made the moral case for war. He made a crucial contribution to the debate at the time."[44]

There followed an intense diplomatic struggle to rally support at the UN for a second resolution. On February 22, Bush met with José María Aznar, the Spanish prime minister, at his ranch at Crawford, and they had a four-way conversation with Blair and Berlusconi, the Italian prime minister. The four leaders agreed that the second resolution should declare that Saddam had failed to comply with Resolution 1441. A draft resolution put forward by the United States stated that the Security Council had "repeatedly warned Iraq that it would face serious consequences as a result of its continued violations of its obligations," and concluded that "Iraq has failed to take the opportunity afforded to it in Resolution 1441." Aznar's support was crucial to Bush and Blair, as Spain had a seat on the fifteen-man Security Council. Blair knew he could count on the votes of the United States and Bulgaria. But he faced formidable opposition from the antiwar lobby, as represented by France, Germany, Russia, Syria, and China. That left six states—Angola, Cameroon, Chile, Guinea, Mexico, and Pakistan—holding the balance, and both the prowar and antiwar camps indulged in an intensive lobbying campaign of the unsure countries to secure their votes. At the back of Blair's mind was the warning he had received from Labour whips at the House of Commons that without a second resolution, the number of rebel Labour MPs could rise from the 121 who had rebeled on February 26 to more than 200—more than half of the parliamentary Labour Party. If that happened, then Blair would be obliged to resign, having lost the confidence of his own party. If the Conservative opposition, which broadly supported the war, decided to vote with the Labour rebels, then the government would fall.

Britain and France competed with each other in a frantic scramble to get the necessary votes at the Security Council. Of the six remaining countries, Pakistan's general Musharraf had decided he had already taken more than enough gambles in backing the U.S.-led war on terror, and indicated that he would side with the French. Blair thought his best bet was to concentrate his energies on persuading the Chilean president, Richard Lagos, the country's first left-wing leader since the CIA-backed overthrow of Salvador Allende in 1973. But Lagos was in a difficult position, as he faced deep hostility within his own party to an American-led war. Blair also dispatched Baroness Amos, a Foreign Office minister, to Africa to lobby support, where her every movement was shadowed by the irrepressible Dominique de Villepin pushing the French case. Faced with this combined diplomatic onslaught, the middle six decided to stick together for mutual protection; none of them wanted to be the one that gave the UN endorsement for war. It was a very frustrating experience for the British officials working to break the impasse in New York. "The six were just like sheep waiting to be rounded up," said a British diplomat. "They found it a deeply uncomfortable experience, with ministers marching around their capitals demanding their loyalty."[45]

Amid all this frenetic activity, Blair traveled with his family to the Vatican to meet Pope John Paul II. Cherie Blair was a practicing Roman Catholic and Blair, a Protestant, often accompanied her to mass. Blair's strong Christian faith was the foundation of his moral approach to handling international conflict, although he was reticent to talk about his personal beliefs in public. Blair was the first British premier to meet the pope since Winston Churchill, and Blair wanted to discuss his religious beliefs with the pontiff. As the prospect of war loomed ever closer, Blair studied the work of the Catholic medieval saint St. Thomas Aquinas, and in particular his theory of a just war. Pope John Paul II had already made it clear that he condemned military action, and during his fifteen-minute audience with Blair, he emphasized that his views had not changed. After the meeting, the Vatican issued a statement saying that the pope had urged Blair to avoid "the tragedy of war" and to "make every effort to avoid new divisions in the world." But, speaking on Blair's behalf, Alastair Campbell said that the onus was on Saddam, not the prime minister, to avoid war. "We acknowledge the pope's concern and we share the desire to avoid war," Campbell said, "but ultimately the decision will be a decision for Saddam."[46]

An insight into Blair's thinking at this critical juncture was provided in a newspaper interview he gave on February 27 while flying to Madrid to see Aznar. Blair said that history had already proved him right on his decisions to take military action in Kosovo, Sierra Leone, and Afghanistan, and that he would be proved right over Iraq. "I've never claimed to have a monopoly on wisdom," he said, "but one thing I've learned in this job is you should always try to do the right thing, not the easy thing. Let the day-to-day judgments come and go: be prepared to be judged by history." He refuted any suggestion that he was behaving like Bush's poodle, and portrayed himself as a hawk in his own right. "It's worse than you think," he told the left-wing *Guardian* newspaper. "I believe in it. I am truly committed to dealing with this, irrespective of the position of America. If the Americans were not doing this, I would be pressing for them to be doing so." Comparing his position with that of Neville Chamberlain, the prewar British prime minister who signed the Munich Pact with Hitler, Blair said the appeasers of the 1930s had been good people, but they had been wrong. Chamberlain was "a good man who made the wrong decision." He also defended the work of the intelligence services whose information formed the main basis for Britain's justification of the war. While he was not in a position to disclose all the intelligence he saw, "in the end people have just got to make up their minds whether they believe me or not, I'm afraid."[47]

Blair's diplomatic efforts were getting nowhere. "The French were chasing around China and Africa lobbying against us. It rapidly became the most divisive issue in the history of transatlantic relations," said a Blair aide. "The French tactics were not very subtle, and their whole attitude left a very sour taste in the mouth. Villepin behaved in a way that was a complete betrayal."[48] The Russians were more measured, merely advising Blair to distance himself from Bush, and dropping heavy hints that they would not support the proposed second resolution. They fa-

vored giving Blix more time to continue with his inspections. The diplomatic tensions intensified on Friday, March 7, when Blix made his third
presentation to the Security Council, in which he gave the Iraqis a favorable report. According to Blix, the level of Iraqi cooperation had increased,
thirty-four al-Samoud missiles—with a range in excess of the 150 kilo-
meters permitted by the UN—had been destroyed, and no evidence had
been uncovered of Iraq's biological weapons. In Blix's view, the inspections were working and, given several more months, the inspectors would
be able to complete the disarmament of Iraq.

Not surprisingly, the White House, which had amassed nearly two
hundred thousand American troops on the Kuwaiti border, took a different view. The very fact that the Iraqis had been concealing their al-Samoud
missiles proved that they had no intention of complying with the UN, and
that they were only prepared to declare and destroy those aspects of their
WMD programs that were uncovered by the inspectors. The British response was provided by Jack Straw, who was determined to avenge himself
on what he regarded as French duplicity. Responding to de Villepin's pre-
dictable insistence that Blix's report did not justify war, Straw said, "The
choice, Dominique, is not ours as to how this disarmament takes place, it
is Saddam Hussein's." Straw then tabled an amended draft resolution that
called on Iraq immediately to "take the decisions necessary in the interests
of its people and region" to complete the disarmament process. The new
resolution contained the ultimatum that Blair had discussed with Blix on
February 20, giving Saddam until March 17 to demonstrate its "full, un-
conditional, immediate, and active cooperation" in yielding possession of
all its WMD programs. Blix thought that the new resolution might help
to avoid war. All Saddam needed to do was make a speech and hand over
the prohibited items. Blix had one, significant reservation about whether
the March 17 deadline could prevent war. "It occurred to me that the
Iraqis would be in greater difficulty if, as they had been saying, there truly
were no weapons of which they could 'yield possession.'"[49] But Bush was
not in the mood to quibble. The day after Blix's report, he called a press
conference at the White House at which he said the United States would
push ahead with a second resolution no matter what. "The resolution says
Saddam Hussein is in defiance of 1441 . . . And it's hard to believe anybody

is saying he isn't in defiance of 1441, because 1441 said he must disarm . . . No matter what the whip count is, we're calling a vote."

Sir Jeremy Greenstock, the British ambassador to the UN, who drafted the second resolution, believed that the French could still have been persuaded to sign up with the coalition if evidence of WMD was found in Iraq. "The French were waiting for a smoking gun," he said. "If we had found two thousand shells in Iraq, instead of half a dozen, the French would have been there with us. Chirac would have been there and they would have authorized the use of force against Saddam." Greenstock regarded the American "bullying" of Blix as counterproductive. "I had no problems with Hans Blix, and we were combing through the Iraqi declaration to find information that might help him to find something. Blix had the right degree of expertise, and was skeptical about Saddam's motivation." Greenstock nevertheless sensed that Blix was going out of his way to show that he was not being used by the Americans, and as a consequence, Blix "was softer on the Iraqis than he should have been."

The British ambassador thought it important that the prowar lobby should draft the new resolution so that they could keep control of the agenda at the UN. "If one of the other, antiwar member states had put down the resolution, it might not have suited us, and caused us trouble. It was something we needed to end the vacuum created by the inspections process. We felt that the inspectors would eventually find some WMD. Going for a second resolution was the best way to assert Security Council control. Saddam had to understand that the game was up."

Blix's report did nothing to ease the domestic pressure on Blair. During the weekend following Blix's report, five junior Labour ministers indicated that they would resign if Britain went to war without a second resolution, while there were expectations that the two leading left-wing members of Blair's cabinet, Robin Cook and Clare Short, would also resign. On Sunday, March 9, Short went public in a BBC radio interview about her opposition to war, launching a personal attack against Blair himself, describing the prime minister's strategy as "reckless," and threatening her resignation. Downing Street officials warned that such action was likely to precipitate a wider revolt within the party.

That same Sunday, Bush called Blair at Chequers to express his concern at Blair's domestic political predicament. The previous day, Manning had met Rice and explained the complexities of the British parliamentary system, and how a backbench revolt could bring down the prime minister. Rice had passed on Manning's concerns to Bush, who asked her, "Do you think he could lose his government?"

Rice replied, "Yes."

"Would the British really do that?" Bush persisted.

"Remember Churchill." The wartime British prime minister was one of Bush's political heroes, and the president needed no reminding of how Churchill had been ignominiously dumped out of office in 1945 after winning the Second World War.[50]

Bush talked to Blair about the various voting permutations at the Security Council, which would enable them to secure the nine-man majority they needed for the new resolution. Bush was deeply concerned that if Blair went down, he would not only lose a key ally, he would get the blame. And the overthrow of one of Saddam's leading opponents would strengthen the Iraqi dictator's hand.

"If they don't vote with us," said Bush, "what I want to say to you is that my last choice is to have your government go down. We don't want that to happen in any circumstances. I really mean that." By this time, more than thirty-five thousand British troops were assembled across the southern Iraqi border, ready to join an American-led invasion force. If it would help, Bush said, he would let Blair drop out of the coalition and they would find some other way for Britain to participate. But Blair would have none of it.

"I said I'm with you, I mean it," Blair insisted. Bush continued to press the premier, suggesting they could think of another role for the British forces, "a second wave, peacekeepers or something. I would rather go alone than have your government fall." Bush said he really meant it that it would be OK for Blair to opt out. "You can bank on that."

"I know you do," Blair said, "and I appreciate that. I absolutely believe in this, too. Thank you. I appreciate that. It's good of you to say that. But I'm there to the very end."[51]

"We were really taken aback by the strength of Blair's commitment to this," said a close Bush aide. "He did the right thing against tremendous pressure at home."[52] Bush himself was also coming under domestic pressure, but to act, particularly from the powerful neoconservative lobby. Leading neocon intellectuals, such as William Kristol, the editor of the influential *Weekly Standard*, and Charles Krauthammer, a columnist for the *Washington Post*, met regularly with Karl Rove, Bush's chief of staff, and complained that the president was moving too slowly, and the opportunity to overthrow Saddam might be missed. Bush was aware of the criticism, although he thought it better to be "criticized as moving too slowly than moving too fast." As he later told Bob Woodward, "I began to be concerned at the blowback coming out of America: 'Bush won't act. The leader that we thought was strong and straightforward and clear-headed has now got himself in a position where he can't act.' And it wasn't on the left. It was on the right."[53]

At the same time as Bush and Blair were discussing the likely fate of the Security Council resolution, the prime minister was entertaining his old friend and ally Bill Clinton at Chequers for the weekend. Clinton had secretly arrived at Chequers to advise Blair on how to deal with his deepening political crisis. Clinton had already made one telling intervention on Blair's behalf when he addressed the Labour Party the previous autumn on the need to deal with the Iraqi threat. But Labour unrest had intensified, and Blair needed all the help he could get to survive the UN quagmire. While Clinton was at Chequers, Blair was constantly on the phone to the Chilean president asking for his support, and Clinton advised the prime minister about how to deal with both the Chilean leader and Vicente Fox of Mexico. Neither Lagos nor Fox were thrilled to find themselves at the center of this unseemly diplomatic tug of war, and the Mexicans in particular were disinclined to support what they regarded as a Yankee colonial war. Clinton favored giving the weapons inspectors more time, as did Blair; his problem was that Bush would not give him more time. Three days after his return to Washington, Clinton delivered a speech in which he praised Blair's leadership, but also asked that Blix and the weapons inspection teams be given more time to finish their job.

By the time Clinton spoke, the debate had become academic. On Monday, March 10, Jacques Chirac dealt the UN process a fatal blow when he announced on French television that he would veto a second resolution "whatever the circumstances." Chirac's blunt announcement was his riposte to Bush's challenge of the previous Saturday to call a count at the UN. The French president justified his decision by France's desire to "live in a multipolar world"—i.e., one that was not dominated by the Americans. France would block a new ultimatum to Iraq, "because France believes this evening that there is no reason to make war to reach the objective we have given ourselves, the disarmament of Iraq." Prior to Chirac's television appearance, de Villepin had spent March 9 touring Angola, Guinea, and Cameroon, trying to persuade those countries not to support the new resolution. De Villepin told the respective leaders that France "would not let a new resolution pass that would open the way to war on Iraq," and that France would "assume its responsibilities as a permanent member of the security council." The British and Americans denounced de Villepin's trip as the height of treachery.[54] The British, meanwhile, were concentrating their diplomatic activity on the UN, where Sir Jeremy Greenstock was working around the clock trying to lobby support. Blair was in constant contact with Greenstock, asking him how many votes there would be in favor of a second resolution. Greenstock had told him that the best they could hope for was eight votes, one short of the majority needed.

British officials later insisted that they could have got the ninth vote, but after Chirac's broadcast, both London and Washington believed that the prospect of getting a second resolution had been severely damaged. British intelligence had warned Blair that Chirac was determined to ruin him politically in Europe, and they had reported back snippets of the president's private conversation that he would like to see Blair fall.[55] But by showing his hand so early, Chirac unwittingly gave Blair an escape clause. If the second resolution had proceeded to a vote at the Security Council and been defeated, then it would have been impossible for Blair to commit British troops to war. Chirac's declaration, however, enabled Blair to argue that a new vote was now impossible because the French were threatening an "unreasonable" veto.

Some British officials blamed the failure to get the resolution on Washington's disinclination to take the process seriously. And Sir Jeremy

Greenstock detected Washington was moving away from the UN process long before Chirac delivered his coup de grace. "The Americans were gradually drifting away from WMD as the main issue," said Greenstock. "They started talking about things like regime change, democracy in the Arab world, how horrible Saddam's regime was. Anything but WMD."[56]

THE UN PROCESS LIMPED on for a few more days as Blair desperately sought to find a way around the French position. Blair remained under tremendous domestic political pressure with senior cabinet ministers, such as Cook, making it clear that they would resign if a second resolution were not secured. Shortly after Chirac's announcement, a group of hard-left Labour MPs had even floated the idea of calling a special conference to debate Blair's future as party leader. They had been encouraged by Clare Short's outburst against the prime minister the previous weekend. But the notion quietly died after more moderate antiwar Labour MPs realized that the party would disintegrate if the hard left had its way. Even so, the antiwar MPs still hoped to get 206 Labour MPs—more than half the parliamentary party—to vote against war, a result that would force Blair's resignation.

Continually aware of Blair's deepening political crisis at home, Bush reluctantly agreed to allow British diplomats one last chance to circumvent Chirac's veto threat and find a second resolution by other means. Greenstock was persistent on lobbying the six undecided countries to see if a compromise resolution could be found. A proposal was devised whereby Iraq would be given a new ultimatum of thirty days, and that a set of six benchmarks, or tests, should be placed alongside the deadline. The benchmarks stipulated that Saddam must surrender his chemical and biological agents and their production facilities, allow the thirty most important Iraqi scientists to travel to Cyprus to be interviewed by UN inspectors, destroy the remaining al-Samoud missiles, and provide a full account of its undeclared drone aircraft program. When Greenstock put the proposal to Blix, he was surprised to find the Swede enthusiastic about the benchmarks. The same could not be said about the White House, which saw the proposal as yet another delaying tactic. So far as Bush was concerned, Saddam had already been given one ultimatum with Resolution 1441, and he saw no reason to give him another. Rumsfeld was particularly irritated at the suggestion that the military planning could be further delayed by the elusive search for a second resolution. "I am learning to hate the British," he confided to a friend.[57]

Despite the opposition he was encountering from Rumsfeld and Cheney, Blair talked regularly to Bush to see if there was any leverage the Americans could bring into play, particularly with Chile and Mexico. On March 12, at Blair's request, Bush called the two presidents to discuss their position on a second resolution. With public opinion in both countries ambivalent about the prospect of war, the Latin American leaders saw no political gain in sticking their necks out for a resolution that the French were sure to veto. Despite these reservations, the Chileans were finally persuaded to table a proposal on March 14 along the lines Greenstock had outlined, setting Saddam a thirty-day deadline to comply with six inspection benchmarks. But the Americans immediately made it clear that they would not accept it, and the proposal was withdrawn just twenty minutes after it was put forward. The prospects of securing a second resolution were rapidly receding.

Hoon phoned Rumsfeld after Chirac's statement, to warn him that if Blair was unable to secure the necessary political support, British troops would not be able to participate in the forthcoming conflict. Rumsfeld took this as a signal to make one of his unhelpful public comments, when he dismissed Blair's dilemma as a "workaround," prompting Blair to make yet another call to Bush to smooth things over. Rumsfeld thought he was being helpful to the British, but he was wrong to suggest that the U.S. military could cope without British support. British withdrawal would have left a massive hole in American military planning as the British and American armed forces were closely entwined at an operational level. British withdrawal would itself have caused the start of hostilities to be delayed by weeks.

The other storm cloud hovering on Blair's horizon was whether or not military action against Iraq was legally justified. Both the Foreign Office and the Ministry of Defence had expressed concern that Blair was considering military action without proper legal backing, which would leave British troops open to war crimes charges brought by the International Criminal Court. Until early March, Lord Goldsmith, the attorney general, shared the same view as the Foreign Office's legal team, that military action could only be justified by a second UN resolution. He also pressed for definite proof that Iraq was in breach of the UN. But on March 7, Goldsmith changed his mind, setting out a thirteen-page legal opinion for Blair, in which he argued that military action could be justified without a second resolution, although this position might be open to legal challenge. Foreign Office lawyers were deeply unhappy by Goldsmith's change of plans, which they believed had been caused by intense political pressure from Downing Street.

With no prospect of a second resolution, Blair now agreed with Bush that military action should commence the following week unless Saddam complied with an ultimatum to stand down. "This was when it really dawned on Blair that Britain was going to war," said a senior Blair aide. "Up to this point, Bush and Blair were saying to each other, 'There's a way out of this.' It was really up to Saddam. But by the time they got to the Azores, they knew the game was up."[58] They agreed to meet to discuss the final tactics, but Blair was reluctant to fly to Washington for fear of arousing further accusations of being "Bush's poodle." Bush was happy to come to London, but was talked out of it by a nervous Downing Street that thought the American president's presence in London would attract widespread antiwar demonstrations, which would not be helpful to planning for the war effort. They decided to have a war summit at the U.S. military base on the Portuguese Azorean Islands, together with Spanish prime minister Aznar and their Portuguese hosts. Apart from deciding on the timetable for military action, Blair was mindful that on his return he faced a crucial debate at the House of Commons, where MPs would vote on whether to back war. Labour whips were still warning that up to two hundred Labour MPs might rebel, crippling the government and putting an end to any chance of British participation. As Robin Cook observed when he went to see Blair on March 13 to discuss his impending resignation, he found the prime minister "mystified as to quite how he got into such a hole and baffled as to whether there is any way out other than persisting in the strategy that has created his present difficulties."[59]

Before setting off for the Azores, Blair returned to the one other subject where he believed he had influence over Bush: the Israel-Palestine dispute. Bush had been holding off from publishing the long-awaited road map outlining the new peace process until Arafat fulfilled his promise—made to Blair's special envoy in January—to appoint a new prime minister. Arafat finally complied on March 8, when Mahmoud Abbas, who had helped to negotiate the Oslo Accords, was appointed to the post. On March 14, Bush, flanked by Powell and Rumsfeld, stepped onto the White House lawn to announce that he would publish the road map to a full Middle East settlement as soon as Abbas's appointment had been confirmed by the Palestinian Authority. He said that the Israelis and Palestinians had arrived at "a hopeful moment for progress."

Bush's announcement was a much-needed fillip for Blair, who could now attempt to persuade the doubters within the Labour Party that while he was unable to get a second resolution, it was worth sticking with the United States, because he could influence policy in Washington in other ways. Blair and his advisors set off for the Azores on Sunday, March 16. On arrival, Bush, Blair, and Aznar got straight down to business. Although the Spanish were not making any military contribution to the war, Aznar's support was seen by both Bush and Blair as an important counterweight to the entrenched opposition of those "old Europeans," France and Germany. The meeting was dominated by the American president's agenda. Coalition forces were ready and primed for an attack on Iraq, and Bush believed the diplomatic track, which had now lasted for six months, had run its course. He was prepared to put a blunt, new resolution to the Security Council the following morning, authorizing the use of force if Saddam failed to disarm. If there was no agreement, then the attack would commence. Bush showed Blair a copy of the speech he was preparing to give once the UN process ended. "I'm going to have to give Saddam Hussein an ultimatum," Bush said. He would give the Iraqi dictator and his two sons forty-eight hours to get out of Iraq. "That's what I am going to do, OK?"[60] This was not a matter for discussion. Bush had made up his mind to act. As Saddam was unlikely to respond

positively to the ultimatum, the war would start on March 19. As a courtesy, Bush let Blair read a copy of the ultimatum speech. Even at this
stage, American officials insisted that war was not inevitable. "This wasn't
like the First World War, where everything was determined by the tyranny of the train timetables," said a senior Bush administration official.
"If Saddam had complied with the ultimatum and stood down, the war
would not have taken place."[61]

When the three leaders emerged for the press conference, Bush looked
relaxed while Blair looked tense and tired. Bush declared that the "moment of truth" had arrived for the world over disarming Saddam. Asked
whether the diplomatic window was closing, Bush replied, "That's what
I am saying." Blair said he would continue to work hard during the remaining hours to get a majority at the Security Council, or get France to
drop its veto. But he conceded that time was running out. After twelve
years of failing to disarm Saddam, "now was the time to decide." The
American delegation noticed the nervousness in Blair's demeanor, and
Rice was fully aware of the prime minister's precarious position as she
watched the British party depart. "Gee, I hope this isn't the last time we
see them," said Rice.[62] On the plane home, Blair expressed his gratitude
for Bush's understanding of his domestic predicament. "I like George's
directness. I like the way he has understood my political problems. Has
he offered to ring seventy of my MPs, say he's going to end global warming, sign up to the Kyoto Accord, and return America to an agrarian
economy? No. Has he been as helpful as he can? Yes."[63]

Blair was clutching at straws so far as the UN was concerned: the diplomatic process had been all but exhausted the previous week, and in a
telephone call he made to Chirac before leaving for the Azores, the French
president had reaffirmed his intention to veto any resolution that authorized war. The moribund UN process was finally put to an end the following morning on March 17, when Britain's draft second resolution was
formally withdrawn. Soon afterwards, the White House announced that
Bush would make a speech at 8 p.m. Washington time, in which he
would declare that in order to avoid military conflict, Saddam Hussein
must leave the country.

The die was cast, and for Blair, the sole priority now was to gather support within his own Labour Party for the crucial parliamentary debate that was due to take place the following day. Resentment at Chirac's tactics and disdain for Short's self-serving attack on Blair the previous weekend had combined to weaken support for the antiwar lobby in the Commons, and the whips predicted that the number of Labour rebels was more likely to be 150 than the 200 that had been previously touted. But Blair was insistent that he did not want to rely on the Conservative opposition to win the vote. He wanted his own party to give him a mandate for war. At the same time, he was well aware that this could be the end of his political career, and instructed Andrew Turnbull, the cabinet secretary, to make arrangements to handle his resignation if he lost the Commons vote.

Blair's position was not helped by Cook's resignation shortly after the abandonment of the second resolution had been announced. Cook had been preparing to resign for some weeks, but felt he should see the UN process through before making his decision final. That evening, Cook gave the most articulate exposition of the antiwar case when he made his resignation speech at the Commons. The centerpiece of his argument was that, as foreign secretary, he had seen much of the intelligence material upon which the justification for military action was now being based. He had also received an updated briefing from John Scarlett, the head of JIC, on the latest intelligence. And from what he had seen, Cook did not think the intelligence was strong enough to merit war. "Iraq probably has no weapons of mass destruction in the commonly understood sense of the term—namely, a credible device capable of being delivered against a strategic city target," he said. "It probably still has biological toxins and battlefield chemical munitions, but it has had them since the 1980s." Cook, one of the best parliamentary debaters of his generation, pulled no punches as he dissected the government's case. "Why is it now so urgent that we should take action to disarm a military capability that has been there for twenty years and which we helped to create?" he demanded.

After the war, Cook said that Blair's determination to ally himself with America at any cost was the reason Britain had no option other than to fight. "What was propelling the prime minister was a determination that he would be the closest ally to George Bush and they would prove to the United States administration that Britain was their closest ally. His problem was that George Bush's motivation was regime change. It was not disarmament. Tony Blair knew perfectly well what he was doing. His problem was that he could not be honest about that with either the British people or Labour MPs, hence the stress on disarmament."[64] Cook's was the only cabinet-level resignation Blair received, although several junior ministers resigned their posts in protest. But Clare Short, who had been more vociferous than Cook in her criticism of Blair, backed down on her threat to resign, arguing that she felt it was her duty to stay to help with the postwar reconstruction of Iraq.

Blair spent most of March 18 with his senior ministers, trying to persuade dissident Labour MPs not to vote against the government in the debate that was due to take place in the Commons that evening. Constitutionally, the government was not obliged to have a vote, but Straw had argued that the Commons should be consulted: "I just thought in the modern age it is not possible to commit troops without the approval of the Commons."[65] Straw, like Blair, was aware that if the vote did not go their way, they would have to tender their resignations. "I was simply conscious of the fact that if it went wrong—if we did not get the support we needed in the Commons—he (Blair) would almost certainly have to go and I would go with him. I did give it quite a bit of thought."[66] Unlike Blair, Straw still had doubts about signing up to the war. After the Azores summit, Straw wrote Blair a "personal minute," in which he suggested that, without a second resolution, Britain might consider offering full moral and political support to the United States instead of a military commitment. British troops could be deployed at the end of the war for peace enforcement. Blair rejected Straw's suggestion. British troops were deployed and ready for action. It was too late to pull out.

Blair's other cabinet colleagues kept whatever reservations they had about the looming conflict to themselves. Blair had patched up his differences with his archrival Gordon Brown, who had until very recently been excluded from the war planning. Brown commanded enormous respect within the parliamentary Labour Party, and his support for Blair was crucial in the campaign to persuade renegade MPs to vote for the government. Blair's prospects were boosted by the attorney general's decision to publish a summary of the legal advice he had presented to Blair on the legal justification for the war. In Lord Goldsmith's view, military action against Iraq was allowed under three UN Security Council resolutions going back to 1990: 678, by which the UN authorized force against Iraq following its invasion of Kuwait in August 1990; 687, the ceasefire resolution passed after the Gulf War, in which Saddam undertook to disarm; and 1441, which gave Saddam a final opportunity to comply. Lord Goldsmith's brief summary of the thirteen-page opinion he had given the prime minister on March 7 did not contain the caveats included in the original documentation, such as military action without a second resolution could be open to legal challenge. Indeed, Matrix Chambers, the legal practice founded by Cherie Blair, had prepared an opinion for the left-wing pressure group, the Campaign for Nuclear Disarmament, arguing unequivocally that Britain would be in breach of international law if it were to use force against Iraq without a second resolution. Lord Goldsmith's legal opinion was further undermined a few days later, when Elizabeth Wilmhurst, the deputy legal advisor at the Foreign Office, resigned in protest at the conclusions he had reached.

So far as Blair was concerned, Goldsmith's statement helped him to convince wavering Labour MPs that war against Iraq was legitimate, even without a second resolution. Blair and his allies conducted a military-style campaign to win over the doubters. Individual ministers were assigned groups of MPs to lobby, while Cherie Blair even phoned the wives of some MPs. As one minister later commented, "this was no longer about what you say to your local paper, this was about whether you want to keep the government in business." But the main task of winning support fell to Blair himself. At 10 a.m. on the morning of March 18, he made the short trip from Downing Street to the House of Commons to address a meeting of the parliamentary Labour Party, at which he laid down the challenge, "Don't vote for me out of loyalty. Vote because it is the right thing to do." Blair's passion and courage made a deep impression on the meeting, even with those MPs who were opposed to the war conceding that Blair's performance had been impressive.

Later that day, Blair opened the crucial debate at the House of Commons. He told the packed chamber that the decision facing MPs was whether to withdraw British troops from the Gulf and allow Saddam Hussein to emerge strengthened. If that were to happen, future tyrants and terrorist organizations would believe that the international community would never wage war against them, while the United States would develop a powerful impulse to act alone. "This is the time for the House, not just this government or indeed this prime minister, but for this House to give a lead, to stand up and vote for what we know to be right. To show we will confront the tyrannies and dictators and terrorists who put our way of life at risk. To show that at the moment of decision, we have the courage to do the right thing." In a crucial new angle to his argument, Blair said his unflinching support for the United States would steer it to a "larger global agenda" that would involve restarting the Middle East peace process. And rather than be made irrelevant by invasion of Iraq without its permission, the UN would be asked for a new resolution for the "administration and governance of Iraq." This last point was important in winning over some of the waverers. In all Blair, spoke for fifty minutes, and his arguments carried the day. When the vote was finally held nearly nine hours later, 139 Labour MPs voted against war, and 40 abstained. A clear majority of Labour MPs had backed Blair, and he had avoided having to rely on the Conservatives to win the debate. The crisis was over.

The following day, Bush phoned Blair to congratulate him. "Not only did you win, but public opinion has shifted because you are leading," the president said, expressing his conviction that people and nations will follow in the "slipstream" of leaders who take strong stands and define their missions. "That is why the vote happened the way it happened. It's the willingness of someone to lead."[67] To show its approval, the White House's Office of Global Communications posted a section of Blair's speech on its Web site as its "quote of the day." White House officials were impressed both by Blair's determination and the content of his speech. "He made the case for war very strongly in that speech, and he made the argument for war," said a senior White House official.[68]

Blair was under no illusions about how close he had come to ending his political career. "In the end, it is a decision you put the whole of your premiership on the line for," Blair later recalled. "The point is that some people are actually going to go and die as a result of your decision. In the end, if you lose your premiership, well, you lose it. But as least you lose it on the basis of something you believe in." He revealed that the crisis had placed enormous pressure on his family, especially his eldest son, Euan, who was then a nineteen-year-old university student. "He was on the phone virtually every night just, you know, giving me lots of support. And Cherie was tremendously supportive." But despite the strain, once he had decided to go to war, Blair had no second thoughts. "Once I had made what I thought was the right decision, I never lost any sleep over all the hassle and abuse and the disagreement and the wrangling. When you are in my position, what dwarfs any of that is the ultimate responsibility for a life-and-death decision. That is the thing that really weighs on your mind—that the decision that you make is going to result in many people's lives being changed forever and some people's lives being ended."[69]

Eleven

HOW TO LOSE A WAR

THE DAY BEFORE THE war started, Tony Blair relaxed in Downing Street with his family and close aides, catching up on official paperwork. In times of crisis, Blair took refuge within the comforting confines of family life. After the exhausting and punishing schedule of the most critical week in his premiership, Blair badly needed to rest before entering the next phase of the high-stakes Iraq crisis. He felt no great sense of triumph about his Commons victory. If anything, he was exasperated that so many members of the Labour Party, which by tradition campaigned against injustice, could not understand the moral imperative of dealing with a brutal and menacing tyrant such as Saddam Hussein. "He was not given to doubts, but he was well aware that thousands of British soldiers were about to risk their lives for a war that was his personal responsibility," said one of his close aides. "He needed time to collect his thoughts."[1] As the Downing Street staff drifted home for a good night's rest before the conflict began in earnest, Blair retired to his private quarters where, after dinner with his family, he spent the evening watching football on television while finishing work on the remaining official papers. In order to remain in good physical condition, Blair, who was only ever a modest drinker, resolved to give up alcohol for the duration of the conflict and to adopt a healthier lifestyle, watching what he ate and exercising as regularly as his responsibilities would allow.

During the twenty-minute conversation he had with Bush on March 19 after the Commons vote, the American president had dropped a heavy hint that there might be a surprise development in the opening phase of the war. Bush did not want to be too explicit, even though the two leaders were talking on a secure telephone. The top secret intelligence that Bush was unable to tell Blair directly was that CIA teams operating inside Iraq had picked up highly reliable information that Saddam Hussein, his sons, and other key members of the regime were to meet at a complex in the southern outskirts of Baghdad called Dora Farm. The farm was mainly used by Saddam's first wife, Sajida, but Saddam's inner circle, always fearful of assassination attempts, liked to stay on the go, and his estranged wife's home provided perfect cover for the key regime members to meet to discuss their war plans. Throughout the day, Tenet continued to receive intelligence reports from the CIA team stationed in northern Iraq that it was almost certain that Saddam would be at Dora Farm that evening. After consulting with the key members of his war cabinet, at 7.12 p.m. Washington time, Bush gave the order to General Tommy Franks, the U.S. commander of the invasion force, to launch a bombing raid against the complex. Two hours later, two F-117 stealth bombers from the Eighth "Black Sheep" Fighter Squadron dropped four 2,000-pound bunker-buster bombs on the Dora Farm complex.

Blair was fast asleep in London when Bush gave the order for the bombing raid. Hostilities had started a day earlier than planned. At Bush's request, Rice woke up Manning at home. "David," she said, "there's a little change in plans. And I'm sorry to say this, but I think you better wake the prime minister."[2] Manning woke Blair, who watched the news breaking on satellite television. Blair may have been Bush's most important ally, but there was no question who was calling the shots once military operations began in earnest. The initial intelligence reports after the bombing were that the "decapitation" strike had been successful. Satellite reconnaissance photographs showed fleets of ambulances and emergency vehicles rushing to the scene while CIA agents on the ground reported that the complex had been so badly damaged that it was unlikely that anyone inside could have survived. The principal CIA agent who provided the original information was killed in the bombing raid, but as day broke, the intelligence reports suggested that Saddam and his two sons had survived, although one of them had been badly injured. Confirmation that Saddam had survived the attack came a few days later, when the Iraqi dictator appeared in a videotape released on Iraqi television. Looking distinctly disheveled and wearing thick-rimmed reading glasses, Saddam remained defiant. "The criminal little Bush has committed a crime against humanity. We pledge to you in our name and in the name of our leadership and in the name of our heroic army, in the name of Iraq, its civilization and its history, that we will fight the invaders. Draw your sword and be not afraid."

Once he had digested the following morning's intelligence reports, Bush phoned Blair at 4 p.m. London time on March 20. "Thank you for understanding that plans change," said Bush. "My opinion is that if the military comes with an option and highly recommends it, then everybody adjusts to the plan. And that's what happened."

Blair appeared unphased by the sudden change of plan. "I kind of think that the decisions taken in the next few weeks will determine the rest of the world for years to come," said Blair. "As primary players, we have a chance to shape the issues that are discussed. Both of us will have enormous capital, and a lot of people will be with us."[3]

Although the bombing mission against Saddam failed to achieve its objective, it served to demonstrate that the principal war aim was the destruction of Saddam's regime; this was not to be a war against the Iraqi people. Apart from the bombing raid on Dora Farms, the Allies fired forty-four cruise missiles at Saddam's key command and control facilities in and around Baghdad, with the effect that from the first day of the war the Iraqi leader was unable to issue effective orders to the Iraqi armed forces. So far as CentCom commanders were concerned, Saddam ceased to be militarily relevant after the first night of hostilities.[4]

At the time hostilities commenced there were nearly three hundred thousand coalition troops based in the Gulf region—nearly half the size of the force that had participated in Desert Storm in 1991. Americans constituted more than three-quarters of the military personnel, and they were joined by forty-one thousand British troops, two thousand from Australia, and two hundred from Poland. The total fighting force amounted to one hundred and eighty-three thousand, against an estimated Iraqi deployment of four hundred thousand troops, although the allies' overwhelming air superiority meant that the Iraqis could put up little more than token resistance to the advance of coalition troops, which began in earnest at 6 a.m. on Friday, March 21, when the First Marine Division crossed the Kuwait-Iraq border, closely followed by the Army's Third Infantry Division. Within twenty-four hours of Operation Iraqi Freedom being launched Franks reported to Bush that U.S. and British special forces had taken control of the vast western desert area—25 percent of Iraqi territory—while the Third Infantry Division had moved 150 miles into southern Iraq, securing most of the oil fields on the way. By the second day, British Royal Marines had managed to capture the strategically important port of Umm Qasr, at the head of the Shatt al-Arab River, leaving the way open for a direct assault on Basra, Iraq's second largest city.

Britain's First Armored Division comprised one-third of the invasion force, and was given special responsibility for capturing and securing Basra and the Shiite heartlands of southern Iraq while the two American divisions undertook the advance on Baghdad, the Iraqi capital. The decision to give the British army its own defined area of military operations was made during the detailed planning that took place in early 2003. General Franks allotted the British a special and separate task from that of his American formations. He correctly recognized that the American divisions, with their unmatched capacity to cover ground and resupply themselves while doing so, were the best suited to make the long-distance strike up the central valley to Baghdad. He equally recognized that the British, with their long experience of peacekeeping operations and their historic connections with the Gulf region, would be better suited to tackling Basra and the surrounding area.[5] There was also the political dimension to the division of labor—the Pentagon wanted be in control of post-Saddam Iraq, and so it made sense that American troops should be given responsibility for the capture of Baghdad.

"The Americans wanted Baghdad," said General Sir Mike Jackson, who oversaw planning for the British army's contribution to the conflict. "They wanted to head north as fast as possible, and so we agreed that the British would secure the south. In military terms, it was plain common sense."[6] From the Pentagon's perspective, the only country they were interested in as an active military ally was the British. "We saw real value in the British capability," said a senior Pentagon military officer. "We had huge respect for their military professionalism, and we knew what they could do from their performance in the Gulf War. The American and British armies are used to working with each other. They train with each other and have similar equipment, and that enables them to fight alongside each other. A French division would have been useless, because they have different equipment and a different mindset." British and American soldiers enjoyed a deep mutual respect for each other, which derived from joint training exercises and cross-posting of personnel. The Pentagon was resistant to offers of military assistance from other friendly European countries such as the Dutch, who were prepared to offer the use of their air force but wanted to attach conditions about how they could be used. "We did not want to get tied down over operational control," said the officer. "And this was not a problem we encountered with the British."[7]

The decision to start the war with a joint American-British operation had been taken in December 2002, although work on the battle planning was still going on until well into March. Initially, Franks had hoped to open a northern front from Kurdistan at the same time the offensive was launched in the south, but this had to be rethought when on March 1 the Turkish parliament rejected an offer of $6 billion in U.S. aid to allow sixty-two thousand coalition troops to deploy along its border. "We were working on different plans all the time," said General Jackson. "But the actual decision to go to war was not taken until the last minute. At any point, we could have thrown the plans in the wastepaper bin, packed up, and gone home. Our job was to give the politicians options, and one of those options was to invade Iraq. But just because we were working on a plan to invade Iraq did not mean that a decision had been made to do so."[8]

The Pentagon took the same view, even though it was no secret that Rumsfeld had long believed that Washington had no alternative other than to remove Saddam by force. "The decision to go to war was not taken until the president gave the go-ahead, and that did not come until the decapitation strike against Saddam," said a senior Pentagon official. "We had to give the president the option and we were moving forces into theater. Our reading of Saddam was that he was not going to give us satisfaction. But the president had the option to stand down, if he chose, right up until the last minute."[9] The Pentagon's planning for the war was so meticulous that more than three thousand strategic targets had been drawn up for the bombing campaign, of which twenty-four needed White House approval because of their close proximity to sensitive civilian locations such as schools and hospitals. Every building in Baghdad had Global Positioning System coordinates attached to it, so that there would be no repeat of the infamous mistake during the Kosovo war when U.S. warplanes accidentally bombed the Chinese embassy. "We were determined to make it clear that we were waging war against Saddam's regime and his supporters, not ordinary Iraqis," said a senior Pentagon official who was closely involved in the war planning. "For that reason, we did not target the Iraqi civilian infrastructure. Bombing ordinary Iraqis would have been counterproductive to our mission. We wanted to fight a war of liberation."[10]

Saddam's Fedayeen were aware of the coalition's sensitivity about civilian casualties, and from the opening phase of the war they forced Iraqi civilians to occupy obvious bombing targets, such as Baath Party buildings and other locations that were directly related to the regime. Blair, in particular, lived in dread of coalition forces incurring what the military referred to as "collateral damage"—civilian casualties—and was mindful of the controversies that had been generated during the Gulf War, when the allies had been accused of bombing a baby-milk factory in Baghdad, and during the Kosovo war, when the allies bombed Belgrade's television station. Once the conflict had begun in earnest, Blair monitored developments closely from Number 10. He started each day with briefings from his military and intelligence chiefs, and talked regularly to Straw and his other cabinet colleagues about the diplomatic and political implications of the conflict. For all the high political drama that preceded the conflict in Britain, once hostilities began, public opinion swung solidly behind the government and the armed forces: whatever the merits of the war, few in Britain had much sympathy for Saddam Hussein and his tyrannical regime.

Blair was particularly affected by the deaths of British servicemen, the first of which occurred in the early phase of combat operations when twelve British marines were killed after their helicopter was shot down by "friendly fire" near Kuwait. During these difficult moments, Blair, like Bush, was sustained by his deep Christian faith. "I am ready to meet my Maker and answer for those who have died or have been horribly maimed as a result of my decisions," Blair later told a political confidant.[11] Bush, too, believed that he would ultimately answer to God for his actions. "There is a higher father that I appeal to," he confided to Bob Woodward. Blair's concern about the progress of the war led him to become actively involved in every aspect of the military campaign, so much so that he had to be restrained from turning his Downing Street office into a replica of the bunker that Winston Churchill had used to mastermind the Second World War. "We wouldn't let him. It would have looked awful," said Sally Morgan, a close political advisor. "He really would have liked a sandpit with tanks."[12]

The day after the war began, Blair had to fly to Brussels to attend an EU summit, where he would be obliged to see Chirac. Blair did not want to go, but realized that his nonappearance would generate negative publicity. Before leaving, Blair recorded a television address announcing the start of hostilities and appealing to the British public to rally around their troops. In the five-minute address, Blair conceded that his strategy on Iraq had "produced deep divisions of opinion in our country. I also know the British people will now be united in sending our armed forces our thoughts and our prayers. They are the finest in the world, and their families can have great pride in them." For Blair, the objective of the war was "to remove Saddam Hussein from power, and disarm Iraq of its weapons of mass destruction." From the intelligence reports he had seen, Blair was convinced that the post–Cold War world faced the new threat of "disorder and chaos born either of brutal states like Iraq, armed with weapons of mass destruction, or of extreme terrorist groups. Both hate our way of life, our freedom, our democracy." Britain had no alternative other than to go to war to prevent catastrophe affecting both Britain and the wider world. "Britain has never been a nation to hide at the back," he declared.

Having recorded the broadcast, Blair then set off for Brussels for the EU summit. The British and French leaders hardly spoke during the twenty-four-hour meeting, and when Blair and Chirac briefly shook hands, the greeting was described by their aides as a decidedly frosty moment. Their only encounter was toward the end of the meeting, when Chirac took Blair to one side without their respective aides to warn him that when the war was over, the two leaders would need to work closely with each other to rebuild European unity. But this sentiment was not reflected in Chirac's comments at the end of the summit. With European public opinion firmly behind him, the French president refused to commit France to making any contribution to the reconstruction effort to rebuild Iraq once hostilities had ended. He did, however, send a note of condolence to Blair on the deaths of the British servicemen killed in action.

The day after Blair's return from Brussels, on Saturday, March 26, 2003, he and Bush consulted on the progress of the war so far. British marines, with American support, had secured the Fao Peninsula and the all-important oil wells, many of which had been halfheartedly booby-trapped by the Iraqis. Meanwhile, General Franks was able to report to Bush that the Third Infantry Division was 150 miles into Iraq, and continuing to make rapid progress on the 350-mile sweep toward Baghdad. "The body language of Tommy and all the commanders is pretty positive," Bush told Blair. "They are pleased with the progress, pleased that no WMD has been shot at us, and we are looking and we'll find the stuff." Coalition commanders had encountered isolated pockets of stiff resistance from the Iraqis, but the overall picture was that the Iraqis had no stomach for a fight. "Thousands are just taking off their uniforms and going home," said Bush.

"Yes, they are just melting away," said Blair.[13]

The British leader was anxious that the public be made aware that a large number of Iraqi oil wells had been mined by Saddam's regime, which in Downing Street's view constituted a "pernicious threat to the country's future prosperity."[14] In London, a crowd of two hundred thousand took to the streets to protest against the war, but Blair took comfort from the fact that it was only a fraction of the estimated one million who had taken part in the main antiwar rally the previous February.

Even at this early stage in the conflict, both leaders were highly conscious of the fact that its success would be judged as much by the evidence they uncovered of Saddam's WMD as the coalition forces' success on the battlefield. Prewar intelligence reports received both by the CIA and SIS had indicated that Saddam's forces were likely to use WMD battlefield munitions, although only as a last resort.[15] All frontline coalition troops had been equipped with protective clothing, and the risk of an Iraqi WMD attack was high on coalition commanders' list of battlefield priorities. On the first weekend of the war, Franks was so concerned about the possibility of an Iraqi WMD attack that he ordered the coalition's advance formations to disperse, because they presented too easy a target for the enemy. A lone helicopter with a gallon of chemical or biological weapons could have brought the whole coalition advance to an abrupt halt.[16]

While the coalition commanders concentrated their energies on the battlefield WMD threat, Bush and Blair were equally aware that uncovering evidence of Saddam's WMD programs was essential to winning the wider public relations battle. Blair was eager to try to manage expectations, and at a Downing Street press conference on March 25, he cautioned that it might be some time before coalition forces discovered the truth about Saddam's WMD. "The idea that we can suddenly discover this stuff is a lot more difficult in a country the size of Iraq, but of course once the regime is out, then there will be all sorts of people that will be willing to give us the information we seek." For the first time Blair let slip that removing Saddam from power was every bit as important as dealing with the WMD issue. He confessed to being "uncomfortable" with the limitations imposed by the "confines of international law and UN resolutions," because "if Saddam had voluntarily disarmed, he could have remained in place . . . In one sense, I feel more comfortable now, where we are saying quite plainly to people, the only way now to disarm him is to remove his regime." This was not a sentiment Blair could have dared to express a week earlier, when he was fighting for his political life and trying to persuade the Labour Party to back the war. Regime change in Baghdad had never been official British government policy, as it was in Washington. But on a personal level, it was a policy that very much appealed to Blair.

The desire to prove the WMD case led some of the prowar media organizations, particularly in the United States, to be too hasty in reporting that evidence of Saddam's WMD had been uncovered. On the first Sunday of the campaign, for example, an American news channel reported a potential chemical weapons find at a one-hundred-acre site near the Iraqi town of Najaf. The story was widely circulated by other news networks until coalition commanders were forced to concede that no such find had been made. The story was later put down to a "zealous overinterpretation of a briefing." In London, Downing Street was more concerned about what it considered to be the antiwar bias of much of the coverage by the British media, particularly the BBC, which Campbell thought was concentrating too heavily on negative aspects of the military campaign.

The opening thrust of Operation Iraqi Freedom proceeded mainly according to plan, but Washington and London still encountered strong criticism from those countries that opposed the war. Both Russia and France issued statements condemning the "shock and awe" bombing campaign that was being conducted against key strategic targets. In Washington, the State Department had taken preemptive measures against any international condemnation of the war by announcing that it had put together a "coalition of the willing." Countries such as Eritrea, Albania, El Salvador, and Ethiopia, which made no tangible contribution to the military campaign, were added to the list of more than thirty countries that the State Department listed as supporting the conflict.

The early promise of the first days of the conflict started to fade as coalition forces began to sustain significant losses. On Sunday, March 23, ten U.S. marines were killed, fourteen wounded and fourteen more, including two British soldiers, went missing during a fierce gun battle at the strategic town of Nasiriyah. Iraqi television broadcast graphic images of four dead American soldiers and of five captured soldiers, which were then beamed around the world by the Arabic satellite station Al-Jazeera.

The British, meanwhile, encountered stiff resistance around Umm Qasr, which, despite earlier claims that it had fallen to coalition forces, was still being hotly contested by Fedayeen fighters. Downing Street was particularly aghast when Al-Jazeera showed the mutilated bodies of two British soldiers who, in Blair's words, had been "executed." Blair said the deaths were "cruelty beyond comprehension" and breached all the proper conventions of war. The battlefield picture was further complicated by foul weather and sandstorms, so, by midweek, both Bush and Blair were under pressure from a critical media claiming that the coalition advance was getting bogged down, and Iraq was becoming a "quagmire" for coalition troops. This erroneous assessment appeared to be confirmed by American officers on the ground in Iraq, who suggested that the war could take months rather than weeks. At his regular weekly Question Time session on March 26, Blair tried to reassure the faint hearts. "There are bound to be difficult days ahead, but the strategy and its timing are proceeding according to plan," he declared.

Later that day, Blair and his key officials—Manning, Campbell, and Straw—flew to Washington to attend a war summit with Bush. It had only been ten days since Blair and Bush had met for their final prewar summit in the Azores, but during the intervening period, British officials had become concerned about American intentions for postwar Iraq. At the Azores meeting, Bush had given a commitment that the postwar administration would be under UN control. Since then, Whitehall had picked up signals that the White House was going cool on the idea. Lord Goldsmith, the attorney general, had warned Blair that any postwar administration in Iraq that did not have UN approval would be illegal under international law. Blair himself was ambivalent about the role of the UN, and took the pragmatic view that he would support UN involvement only if it appointed the right candidate to run post-Saddam Iraq. "A lot depends on who the UN coordinator for Iraq is going to be," Blair confided to a British journalist at Camp David. "If they choose a good man, someone who doesn't faff about, that's fine. If they choose the wrong man, I won't back them, either." [17]

At the official press conference, both men heaped praise on each other. "America has learned a lot about Tony Blair over the last weeks," said

Bush. "We've learned he is a man of his word. We've learned that he's a man of courage, that he's a man of vision. And we're proud to have him as a friend." "I believe the alliance between the U.S. and Britain has never been in better or stronger shape," said Blair in response. Pressed on how long the military conflict was likely to last, Bush insisted that the campaign would take "however long it takes . . . And that's important for you to know, the American people to know, our allies to know, and the Iraqi people to know." The two leaders then went for a walk in the Camp David woods, where Blair pressed Bush hard on the UN issue and the Middle East peace process. So far as the UN was concerned, Bush was prepared to tolerate a degree of UN involvement, but nothing like the central role that Blair desired and felt was necessary if the international divisions caused by the war were to be repaired. On his way back to London, Blair stopped off in New York to see Kofi Annan, the UN secretary-general, who made clear his displeasure that the Iraq War was being conducted without UN approval.

By early April, the weather had cleared, the coalition's forward units were resupplied, and the military campaign began to regain its momentum. After a particularly fierce encounter, in which the U.S. Third Infantry Division defeated Iraqi forces to take control of the Karbala Gap, the main River Euphrates crossing point south of Baghdad, coalition forces were able to make a rapid advance on Baghdad, reaching the city's outskirts and taking control of the sprawling Baghdad international airport complex, twenty miles to the west of the capital, on April 2. Many military experts had predicted that Saddam would concentrate the defense of his regime on turning Baghdad into another Stalingrad. But the speed of the American advance had left the city's defenses in a state of chaos, and to maintain their advantage, U.S. commanders launched the first in a series of "thunder runs"—heavily armed reconnaissance missions—into the heart of Baghdad to test the strength of Iraqi resistance. By this time, most of the major Republican Guard formations—Iraq's elite military units—had been destroyed by a combination of the coalition's intensive bombing campaign and the mass desertion of Iraqi troops.

The main resistance encountered by U.S. forces as they entered Baghdad came from groups of irregular Fedayeen fighters, hundreds of whom were killed as they launched what amounted to suicide missions against the heavily armed American forces. In Basra, meanwhile, British forces finally succeeded in taking control of the city on April 5 as columns of British troops overwhelmed the last remnants of the Iraqi forces loyal to Saddam. On April 7, acting on new intelligence on Saddam's supposed whereabouts, coalition commanders launched another "decapitation" strike, this time against a restaurant in the al-Mansour district of Baghdad, where Saddam and key members of the regime were supposed to be meeting. Although the U.S. Air Force dropped four 2,000-pound bombs on the restaurant, Saddam and his entourage had left the building half an hour before the bombs hit their target.

By the time Blair and Bush met at Hillsborough Castle in Northern Ireland later that day, Saddam's regime was on the point of collapse, and the two leaders could look forward to a quick military victory. Blair had chosen Hillsborough, the queen's official residence in County Down, because he wanted somewhere that would serve as a British equivalent to Camp David, and the castle's opulent rooms and manicured lawns provided a tranquil backdrop for the two leaders to continue their discussions on how to manage postwar Iraq. Blair succeeded in persuading Bush to agree that the UN should have a "vital role" in rebuilding the country, although the American president was not prepared to hand over complete control of liberated Iraq to the UN. Bush was under pressure from Rumsfeld and Cheney for Washington to have overall responsibility for administering the country post-Saddam, and the Pentagon had already flown a team of two hundred advisors to Kuwait to take control of vital areas, such as government, finance, law, and media, as soon as the fighting was over. This was all done under the command of retired general Jay Garner, who would be appointed the first civilian administrator of liberated Iraq. Blair was unhappy at the prospect of the American military running Iraq, but realized that there was little he could do at this juncture other than to ensure that the UN was involved in some capacity or other. In Paris, Jacques Chirac demonstrated that his opposition to the war had not mellowed, despite the success of the military campaign. He rejected Bush and Blair's halfhearted commitment to the

UN, declaring that rebuilding Iraq "is a matter for the UN and for it alone."

The end of Saddam's regime came two days later on April 9, when American troops finally seized control of central Baghdad, and helped a crowd of Iraqis to topple an imposing statue of Saddam in al-Fardus Square in the city center. Saddam and his two sons, Uday and Qusay, had spent the final days of the war trying to organize some vestige of resistance against the advancing American units, but were limited to sending groups of Fedayeen fighters on the equivalent of suicide missions. As late as April 8, Saddam was still in Baghdad trying to organize the city's defenses, and Arabic television later showed him touring Baghdad's northern suburbs on the same day that his statue was being pulled down in the center of the city. But soon afterwards, the Iraqi dictator and his sons fled north to their tribal heartland around Tikrit in northern Iraq.

Blair watched Saddam's statue being pulled down on television in Downing Street. That morning, his military advisors had told him that the military campaign was not complete, and he was surprised by the media coverage given to the events taking place in al-Fardus Square. "It's just one statue," he remarked to an aide. "I don't know what all the fuss is about."[18] Blair's official spokesman later issued a statement that read: "We are delighted at what we are seeing in the reaction on the ground. We have seen today the scales of fear falling from the people of Iraq." Bush, meanwhile, was attending a meeting with Rumsfeld at the moment the statue actually came down, but his spokesman said that the president had been "moved" by the celebrations of the Iraqis.

Military operations continued for a few more days as coalition forces continued to move north, and by April 14, combat operations were effectively ended with the capture of Tikrit. Blair now allowed himself to talk about the "victory" that had been achieved in Iraq, and expressed the hope that the Iraqis would be able to hold democratic elections in Iraq within a year. "We are nearing the end of the conflict," Blair told MPs in the Commons. "But the challenge of the peace is now beginning. We took the decision that to leave Iraq in its brutalized state under Saddam was wrong. Now there is a heavy responsibility to make the peace worth the war. We shall do so not in any spirit of elation, still less of triumpha-lism, but with a fixed and steady resolve that the cause was just, the vic-tory right, and the future for us to make in a way that will stand the judgment of history." During his statement to the Commons, Blair placed more weight on his belief that regime change was the primary objective of the war as opposed to WMD. On that front, he said progress was "bound to be slow" until all the suspect Iraqi facilities had been thor-oughly examined, and the estimated five thousand Iraqi scientists who were involved in the illicit programs had been fully debriefed.

Bush did not make his victory speech until May 1, when, speaking on the deck of the aircraft carrier *Abraham Lincoln*, he declared that major combat operations were over. Like Blair, Bush vowed to continue the hunt for Saddam's WMD, but his main interest was in celebrating an important "victory in a war on terror that began on September 11, 2001, and still goes on." For Bush, victory in Iraq went some way to avenging the deaths of those who had died in the 9/11 attacks. "We have not for-gotten the victims of September 11, the last phone calls, the cold-blooded murder of children, the searches in the rubble. With those attacks, the terrorists and their supporters declared war on the United States, and war is what they got . . . The liberation of Iraq is a crucial advance in the campaign against terror. We have removed an ally of al-Qaeda, and cut off a source of terrorist funding. And this much is certain: no terrorist network will gain weapons of mass destruction from the Iraqi regime, because that regime is no more."

THE MILITARY CAMPAIGN FOUGHT by the Anglo-American coali-tion to remove Saddam Hussein from power achieved a remarkable vic-tory in only twenty-one days, for the loss of 155 military personnel—122 Americans and 33 British. Before the war, coalition commanders had predicted that the conflict could last as long as three months, depending on the level of resistance that they encountered from the Iraqi armed forces. The Iraqis fielded an army of four hundred thousand to defend the country against an invading force only half its size, but the overwhelming military superiority of the coalition forces, and the marked disinclination of the Iraqi forces to fight, meant that the allies were able to achieve a crushing military victory in a remarkably short period of time. Although the Americans provided the majority of strength on the ground and, overwhelmingly, the majority in the air and at sea, the British military contribution was significant. "The speed of the American advance on Baghdad was greatly assisted by the great work the British did in capturing and securing the south," said a senior Pentagon official. "We would not have been able to get to Baghdad in twenty-one days and achieve such a swift victory without the British." [19]

But if the Iraq War of 2003 was an unqualified military success, the same could not be said for the coalition's administration of a country that had just been liberated from thirty-five years of Baath Party tyranny. Planning for the administration of postwar Iraq had taken several months before the war. So far as Britain was concerned, the main responsibility for postwar planning was in the hands of the Foreign Office, which could draw on its wealth of colonial experience and expertise in running failed states. In Washington, the situation was more complicated, with both the Pentagon and the State Department competing for the privilege of taking charge of post-Saddam Iraq.

The intense rivalry between Powell and Rumsfeld over Washington's Iraq policy in the buildup to the war spilled over into the approach of their respective departments. The State Department had supported Powell's opposition to the war, and subscribed to his view that Iraq was likely to collapse into anarchy if Saddam's regime was overthrown. The Pentagon, particularly the ideologically driven neoconservative civilian contingent working under Rumsfeld and Wolfowitz, rejected what they regarded as Powell's unduly pessimistic assessment. In their view, post-Saddam Iraq provided a wonderful opportunity to export the neocon vision of bringing democracy to the Middle East. Having been freed from Saddam's tyranny, they believed the liberated Iraqis would leap at the opportunity to establish a functioning, Western-style democracy, which would provide a model for the other autocracies of the Middle East.

Both Downing Street and the Foreign Office were concerned at the prospect of the Pentagon taking control of Iraq's postwar administration, particularly as the U.S. military was not set up to handle peacekeeping operations in the same way as the British army, which had many years of experience of handling hostile civilian populations in places such as Northern Ireland and Cyprus. Blair had raised his concerns directly with Bush, and hoped that if the UN was given a key role after the conflict, the activities of the more ideologically minded members of the Bush administration would be curbed. But with much of the energy of both governments taken up with the political and diplomatic battles that preceded Operation Iraqi Freedom, planning for post-Saddam Iraq had not been the priority.

"It was very difficult to do postwar planning, because until the war actually started, we were all trying to avoid a war," said Sir Jeremy Greenstock.[20] Downing Street officials conceded that more work should have been undertaken on postwar planning. "People had just not given enough thought to what might happen," said one of Blair's key aides. "There was talk of a humanitarian crisis, and of civil war. None of these things happened. But other things did, and we were not prepared for them." Downing Street, like the White House, was under the impression that the coalition would receive a warm welcome from the Iraqi people, whereas, in fact, most Iraqi civilians simply withdrew to their homes for the duration of the conflict, and, for the most part, were neither welcoming nor hostile. "We had this somewhat misplaced feeling that we would be welcomed as liberators by the population," said Blair's aide. "This was true to an extent with the Shia, but not the Sunnis, who resented the dispersal of their powers." Blair's team were particularly critical of Clare Short and her overseas development department, which, in their view, failed to make adequate preparations for the military victory. "Clare Short was the most culpable," said a senior Downing Street official. "She ordered her department not to do anything, because she thought the war was illegal. We all thought she was guilty of a gross dereliction of duty."[21]

Pentagon policymakers, who were eventually given control of running Iraq, were aware of the shortcomings of their plans for administering Iraq, but argued that their first priority in early 2003 was to ensure that the military campaign was a resounding success. "Every aspect of what we did in Iraq after the war could have been done better," said Douglas Feith, the Pentagon official responsible for postwar planning in Iraq. "So far as the military campaign was concerned, we wanted to achieve tactical surprise and to avoid a protracted war. We accomplished this by launching the attack with a force of less than two hundred thousand. Saddam had been expecting us to build a force of five hundred thousand, and so, despite the drawn-out process at the UN, we still retained the crucial element of surprise. Saddam was not prepared for what we did. All the bridges were left intact, and he did not have time to blow up the oil wells, as he did in Kuwait in 1991." The price the Pentagon paid for achieving such a quick victory was that it had insufficient troops on the ground to impose order once Saddam's regime had been overthrown.

Even so, the Pentagon rejected charges that it had given insufficient thought to the problems it would encounter after the war. "Before the war, Rumsfeld got us to draw up a memorandum for the president on all the issues we were likely to face," said the official. "Everything was in there, such as what would happen if we did not find any WMD, how to deal with a refugee crisis, potential terror attacks in the U.S., and what happened if we didn't find Saddam. We thought through all the things that could go wrong, to make sure we were prepared for every eventuality. Rumsfeld wanted everyone at the top of the administration to know what we faced."[22]

Bush's decision to give Rumsfeld responsibility for running postwar Iraq caused serious difficulties for the British government. "Basically, we had been dealing with the State Department," said a senior Foreign Office diplomat. "All our postwar planning had been undertaken with American diplomats. Suddenly, we found we had been working with the wrong part of the American machine." The British situation was complicated by the fact that the one area where there was not a close bond between the respective department heads was in defense. While senior British military officers worked well with their American counterparts, the same could not be said of Hoon and Rumsfeld, a state of affairs that had existed since Hoon's awkward first encounter with the newly appointed American defense secretary. Blair could pick up the phone any time he pleased, to talk to Bush, and Manning could do the same with Rice. Straw and Powell were not only close, but shared a similar worldview. Rumsfeld and Hoon, on the other hand, maintained a formal, distant relationship, so the British defense secretary was never privy to what his American counterpart was thinking. This did not matter unduly when it came to military planning, because senior British and American officers were used to working in close proximity. But it did matter when it came to policy issues, such as the postwar administration of Iraq, where Hoon had not been involved in the planning. "Rumsfeld was so secretive not even the White House knew what was going on," said a senior Blair aide. "And not having a line through to the Pentagon made life very awkward indeed."[23]

Having castigated "old Europe" during the diplomatic fallout before the war, Rumsfeld was so determined to exclude "old Europe" from the new Iraq that he insisted on the Pentagon taking control of the whole planning operation. Said a senior Foreign Office official, "When the State Department presented our postwar plan to Rumsfeld, he simply dumped it in the dustbin." The Foreign Office warned Blair that they thought it was a serious mistake to let the Pentagon take control of running Iraq. "The American military was simply not capable of going from high-intensity combat to soft post-conflict peacekeeping," said a senior Foreign Office official. "They had a very heavy-handed military garrison presence, where you shoot first and ask questions later. It was not the best way for an army of liberation to handle the indigenous population."[24]

In fact, trying to keep abreast of the power battles taking place in Washington became an almost full-time occupation for British officials after the war. While Blair could deal directly with Bush, he could never be sure whether the president had been persuaded to change his mind the minute the British prime minister was out of earshot. Manning was on the phone to Rice several times a day, making sure that the policy decisions agreed upon by Bush and Blair were adhered to. Rice was a reliable informant, and was generally sympathetic to Blair's concerns.[25] But compared with Rumsfeld and Cheney, she was a relative novice in the power politics of the American capital. Unlike Bush and Rice, neither the vice president nor the defense secretary had much inclination to maintain a dialogue with their counterparts in London, and both Downing Street and the Foreign Office fretted whether Rumsfeld and Cheney were persuading Bush to adopt policies that were both contrary to British interests and the understandings that had been reached between the president and the prime minister.

While Downing Street's main contact was Rice, the Foreign Office made full use of the close friendship that had developed between Powell and Straw. Downing Street understood that Rice had the ear of the president, but the problem for the Foreign Office was that Powell was regarded as a pariah by the more hawkish members of the Bush administration, particularly after his failure to secure a second resolution at the UN. "By the spring of 2003, it had got to the point where if Powell wanted to know what was going on in Washington, he would phone Straw in London," said a senior Downing Street official.[26] Blair's team believed that the Foreign Office did not help its cause by trying to side with the warring factions. "Our only interest was in knowing what Bush wanted to do and, where we could, to influence his thinking," said a close Blair aide. "We had a dialogue with the president himself, which was straightforward and to the point. The Foreign Office tried to side with those in Bush's camp, such as Powell, that might be able to influence the president in some way. But we did not have time for those games."[27]

An added difficulty for the Foreign Office was dealing with the rival factions at the State Department. While Powell and his deputy, Richard Armitage, were seen as allies, John Bolton, the number-three official who was in charge of international security policy, was regarded as an ally of the neoconservative ideologues running the Pentagon. British diplomats were concerned that Bolton would leak sensitive information to sympathetic newspapers, such as the *Wall Street Journal*. For that reason, the Foreign Office deliberately did not inform him about the crucial diplomatic breakthrough that had been achieved with Libya at the start of the year, when Libyan leader Colonel Muammar Gadhafi indicated that he was prepared to surrender his country's WMD program.[28]

But the real victims of the power battles in Washington were the Iraqi people for whom the war had been fought in the first place. One major consequence of the coalition's rapid military success was the complete collapse of the Iraqi security infrastructure. Most of the Iraqi armed forces units had simply disbanded and gone home, and the sudden disappearance of Saddam and other key members of the regime encouraged the nation's police officers to follow suit. "The simple fact is that the speed of the regime's collapse surprised us," said a senior Pentagon official. "It collapsed much more quickly than we anticipated, and very quickly a power vacuum developed. The army had disappeared, and the police were unusable."[29] With U.S. forces still involved in mopping up operations throughout the country, American commanders had neither the manpower nor the inclination to maintain law and order. Lieutenant-General David McKiernan, the Third Army commander who had control of Baghdad after the war, refused requests from the civilian administrators to undertake peacekeeping duties. "McKiernan simply refused to transfer his division's role from offensive operations to maintaining law and order," said a senior British diplomat involved in Iraq's postwar administration.[30]

Consequently, within days of Saddam's overthrow, thousands of Iraqis had taken to the streets and indulged in looting that went on for several days. Their first targets were the regime's office buildings, and in just a few days, seventeen of the twenty-three ministries were ransacked. One of the few ministries that was not destroyed was the Ministry of Oil, which did little to allay suspicions that the entire conflict had been fought over Iraq's precious natural reserves. The looters, some of whom were common criminals who had been pardoned and relaeased by Saddam before the war, then moved on to nongovernmental institutions, such as schools and hospitals, stealing anything they could carry, with computers and air-conditioning units being particular favorites. The lawlessness that erupted in Baghdad was all the more noticeable because of the relative order the British were able to establish in and around Basra. The Shiite Muslims of southern Iraq, having borne the brunt of Saddam's genocidal repression for so many years, were better disposed to the coalition forces than the Sunnis in Baghdad, as they had been the country's ruling elite for more than eighty years. Nevertheless, the British army's long experience of peacekeeping operations, and the pragmatic approach taken by its commanders, helped to ensure that a semblance of law and order was quickly established in the south, and work undertaken on restoring essential services.

Far from condemning the lawlessness in Baghdad, Rumsfeld gave the impression that he condoned it. Pentagon officials said it was natural that the Iraqis wanted to "let off steam" after being repressed for so many years, and they had no objection to them avenging themselves against institutions that represented Saddam's repressive regime. The looting had gone too far, but the coalition seemed disinclined to do anything to curb it, even after looters put thirty-three out of Baghdad's thirty-five hospitals out of use. And when Iraq's priceless treasures were looted from the National Museum, Rumsfeld seemed to dismiss the catastrophe when he remarked that "It's the same picture of some person walking out of some building with a vase." Some Pentagon officials who arrived in Baghdad to help administer the country said it would be "a good thing" if every building and institution that was associated with Saddam's regime was "razed to the ground." As one official involved in the reconstruction remarked, "We are going to build a new country in Iraq, a country that works. We don't need any of Saddam's stuff. We've got to demonstrate to the Iraqis that this is a new beginning, not more of the same."[31]

Apart from being in contravention of the Geneva Convention, the looting had a disastrous impact on relations between the coalition forces and the local population. During the military campaign, most of the Iraqi population had been ambivalent about the invasion of foreign troops into their country. Few Iraqis had much affection for Saddam's regime, but they were not keen to be occupied by foreign forces, either. The suggestion made before the war that coalition troops would be greeted as liberators by ecstatic crowds of well-wishers in scenes reminiscent of the liberation of Paris in 1944 did not come to pass. There were occasional displays of gratitude, such as when the crowds pulled down Saddam's statue in al-Fardus Square and British troops eventually entered Basra. But on the whole, the Iraqis remained neutral, waiting to see what the future had in store for them.

During Operation Iraqi Freedom, coalition commanders had taken great care to ensure that civilian casualties were kept to a minimum, and that the country's civilian infrastructure remained intact. Consequently, when hostilities ended, most of the key services were functioning. But in the weeks immediately after the war, the looters inflicted more damage on the country's infrastructure than the military campaign. They stripped copper wire out of the telephone networks and electrical power supplies, thereby bringing the country to a standstill. Important documents were destroyed or stolen from key government ministries, which would later make it difficult for war-crimes investigators to prosecute key figures in Saddam's regime for war crimes, and to discover the truth about the regime's WMD programs. Even Iraq's nuclear research facility at Tuwaitha was looted amid suspicions that sensitive materials and equipment had been shipped across the Iraqi border to Iran.

Attempts to restore order on the ground in Iraq were not helped by the continuing power battles taking place in Washington. Rumsfeld was successful in persuading Bush to allow the Pentagon to oversee the democratization of Iraq. A retired general, Jay Garner, who had served in Iraq during the 1991 Gulf War and had close ties to the neocons, was appointed the head of the Office of Reconstruction and Humanitarian Assistance (ORHA), which was given responsibility for the postwar administration of Iraq. ORHA was comprised of hundreds of U.S. civilians who had been specially vetted by the Pentagon and were to oversee the transformation of Iraq's institutions from autocracy to democracy, while ORHA itself reported to General Tommy Franks, the commander of all coalition forces. Tensions quickly developed between the two organizations, particularly over security issues, with American commanders on the ground refusing to divert their forces from military operations to peacekeeping duties.

There were also continued tensions between the State Department and the Pentagon, with the former smarting from the fact that all the hard work that American Middle East specialists had put into postwar planning had been to no avail. The State Department handed Pentagon officials an elaborate collection of policy documents titled the "Future of Iraq Project," which laid out guidelines for reconstruction and transitional government procedures. The Pentagon ignored it. The State Department responded by effectively withdrawing its cooperation. "The State Department would not do even simple things, like helping to train the Iraqi police force," said a senior Pentagon official. "Whenever we asked them for practical help, their response was: 'It's not our job.'"[32] Richard Armitage, Powell's number two, blamed Rice and the NSC for not exercising more control over the Pentagon, and complained bitterly that the NSC was failing in its duty to enforce discipline throughout the various departments of the Bush administration. Bush eventually attempted to redress the balance of power in Rice's favor at the expense of the Pentagon when, in October 2003, he gave her new authority and responsibility for coordinating the task of stabilizing and rebuilding Iraq.[33]

The bitter turf battles that erupted in Washington after the war were viewed with alarm and dismay in Downing Street, where Blair was concerned that the opportunity to capitalize on the gains of the military success would be lost. Blair and his team were particularly alarmed by what they regarded as the inept performance of General Garner, who, they quickly concluded, was not up to the job of running Iraq. "It was clear to us from a very early stage that Garner simply did not know what he was doing," said one of Blair's close aides. "Rumsfeld and the Pentagon thought that they knew better than anyone else how to run Iraq, and so they seized control of everything from the State Department. But they were wrong. They didn't know what they were doing, either."[34] Responding to pressure from Downing Street and the coalition's military commanders, Bush replaced Garner in early May with Paul Bremer, a State Department counterterrorism expert with close ties to the Pentagon. "Bremer was a big improvement on Garner, and had some strong points. But even he made mistakes," said Blair's aide.

Another cause of postwar tensions between Washington and London was the de-Baathification program that was undertaken in Iraq once hostilities had ceased. One of the first acts of the occupying forces had been to decree the disbandment of the Iraqi armed forces. The Pentagon's policy was heavily influenced by Ahmed Chalabi, the INC leader, who argued that the entire country needed to be purged of Baathism before it could be transformed into a functioning democracy. In essence, this was a technical move, as most of Iraq's military personnel had abandoned their positions during the fighting. The coalition followed this by disbanding the police force. In one stroke, the coalition had removed Iraq's entire security apparatus without having anything to put in its place. This not only resulted in the lawlessness that continued throughout the country long after the war was finished, but it meant that there were tens of thousands of disaffected young Iraqis with nothing better to do than cause trouble. Bremer's arrival in May saw an intensification of the de-Baathification program, which was loosely modeled on the denazification program that had been carried out in Germany after the Second World War. Bremer was determined to make a clean sweep of all of Iraq's institutions to ensure no trace of Saddam's Baathist regime remained, and his policy meant that yet more tens of thousands of Iraqis were left without jobs.

While Downing Street approved the principle of de-Baathification, Blair was concerned that it should not be too extensive. As in Nazi Germany under Hitler, not everyone in Iraq who joined the Baath Party did so because they supported Saddam; in many cases, it was the only means of obtaining employment, whether as an army officer or schoolteacher. "We understood the need for de-Baathification, but we did not want it to go too deep," said a senior Downing Street official. "Denazification did not work in Germany. To get the country running again, the allies had to bring back many former Nazis. We felt it was important to keep the main Iraqi institutions functioning, and to do that, it was clear, we would have to work with some members of Saddam's old regime. We thought it was more of a case of sorting out those we could work with and those we couldn't."[35]

Before the war, British intelligence had provided an assessment that strict limits would need to be placed on de-Baathification. "Our advice to Downing Street was very strongly against widespread de-Baathification," said a senior British intelligence officer. "We argued that it was necessary to keep the Iraqi army and security forces in place to maintain order. There was unanimity on this throughout the intelligence community and the Foreign Office. The message was loud and clear. But Washington simply took no notice."[36] The widespread de-Baathification program was firmly resisted by Iraqi political leaders such as Dr. Ayad Allawi, who had returned to Baghdad from exile with the coalition forces. Allawi was forthright in arguing that the wholesale removal of the Baathists would cause immense ill-will toward coalition troops.[37]

The inability of coalition forces to maintain law and order in Baghdad, and the resentment generated by the de-Baathification program, resulted in the anarchy of the looting being replaced by a well-organized and vicious insurgency, mainly directed by former regime members but assisted by scores of foreign fighters who entered Iraq during and after the war to wage jihad, or holy war, against the coalition. So far as the Iraqi people were concerned, the liberators soon came to be perceived as occupiers, and by May, the coalition had already lost the all-important battle for hearts and minds. Fearing that the situation on the ground was spiraling out of control, and concerned that the Pentagon seemed oblivious to outside advice, Blair decided to appoint his own personal envoy to Baghdad.

John Sawers, the British ambassador to Cairo, had worked closely with Blair in Downing Street during the Kosovo crisis, and was asked to be Blair's eyes and ears on the ground and to keep an eye on Bremer. "Sawers was alarmed to find that Bremer had basically come out with orders from Wolfowitz to raze everything associated with Saddam's regime to the ground," said a senior Foreign Office diplomat. "The Americans were drawing comparisons with the Nazis in 1945. We preferred to draw comparisons with the Russians in 1991, when the Communists were overthrown but many Communist Party members continued in their jobs." British diplomats felt strongly that they were at a disadvantage because of the almost nonexistent state of relations between Hoon and Rumsfeld. "The only place that was deciding policy on Iraq was the Pentagon, and the one place where we had no influence was the Pentagon," said the diplomat.[38]

By the time Sawers and Bremer arrived, the insurgency was well established. Apart from conducting classic terrorist attacks against coalition patrols, the insurgents used suicide bombers to ensure the maximum number of casualties. They also proved highly effective at carrying out sabotage operations against key infrastructure targets, such as oil, electrical, and water installations, with the effect that coalition attempts to bring utility supplies to prewar levels were severely hampered. The resilience of the insurgents surprised coalition commanders, who had expected the Iraqis to be largely acquiescent once Saddam had been overthrown. Indeed, the majority of Iraqis were grateful to see the back of Saddam. A poll taken by the University of Baghdad in May showed that 80 percent of Iraqis approved of Saddam's overthrow.

But this made no impact on the insurgency, which was masterminded by Saddam loyalists and Baath Party veterans. Saddam himself had warned that the coalition would face stiff resistance if it occupied Iraq, and set out plans, complete with arms caches, for the fighters. Some Pentagon officials had anticipated that, once Saddam had been removed, the Iraqis would embrace the future, as had happened in the Soviet-dominated Eastern European countries after 1989. "We were surprised that Saddam's regime showed a lot more staying power than the Cold War countries that collapsed in 1989," said a senior Pentagon official involved in the postwar planning for Iraq. "The hard core of the nomenclature was very organized and determined."[39]

Bremer's arrival in Baghdad did, however, have the effect of legitimizing the coalition's presence. In the weeks immediately after the war, the Bush administration gave every impression of wanting to return to its old, unilateralist ways. The White House refused to let teams of UN weapons inspectors return to continue the work they had been doing before the war on the grounds that disarming Iraq was now a task that would be undertaken by the coalition. Not surprisingly, those countries, such as Germany, France, and Russia, that had stridently opposed the war continued to do so. When Washington sought to have UN sanctions lifted to enable humanitarian supplies to be moved into Iraq, the French objected, arguing that this could not be approved until the UN inspectors had completed Iraqi disarmament. Finally, after weeks of wrangling, UN Resolution 1483 was passed on May 22. It lifted the sanctions and authorized Bremer's Coalition Provisional Authority (CPA), which had replaced Garner's ineffectual ORHA, to run the country.

The new resolution did little to legitimize the coalition in the eyes of ordinary Iraqis, particularly after the Pentagon awarded key reconstruction contracts to two U.S. companies with close ties to the White House. Halliburton, the world's largest oilfield services company, which had once been run by Dick Cheney, was given the oil contract, and Bechtel, which was close to the Pentagon, was given the task of rebuilding the infrastructure that had been destroyed by the looters. British companies were not awarded any of the major contracts.

While security remained a key concern, an even bigger one for Blair was the coalition's failure to find stockpiles of Saddam's WMD. The Pentagon dispatched two thousand U.S. weapons experts to Iraq, led by Dr. David Kay, who had run the UN weapons inspection teams in the 1990s. Kay's Iraq Survey Group (ISG) was given a list of 150 sites that the Western intelligence community believed contained elements of Iraq's WMD programs. British officers from SIS, who were responsible for some of the more controversial claims made about Saddam's WMD capability in the buildup to the war, were also involved in the hunt for the elusive Iraqi weaponry. Within two weeks of the end of the war, half the sites had been searched, and nothing found. Critics of the war began to raise the WMD issue, particularly in Britain, where it had been Blair's main justification for military action during the crucial parliamentary debate on March 18. On April 22, Dr. Hans Blix bitterly criticized the way he had been treated before the war, and declared that London and Washington had built the case for war on "very, very shaky" evidence. Labour MPs in London, who had been persuaded to vote for Blair because of his insistence that Saddam's WMD posed a "current and serious threat to the U.K. national interest"—as he had written in the foreword to the government's September intelligence dossier—demanded an inquiry into whether they were misled about the intelligence used to justify the war.

At the White House, Bush was sanguine about the WMD issue, even if no stockpiles of battlefield munitions had been found. For the American president, the fact that Kay's inspection teams had found abundant evidence that Saddam retained the technology to produce chemical and biological weapons, and was actively seeking nuclear technology, was sufficient. "We have found weapons programs that could be reconstituted," he told Bob Woodward. "And so, therefore, given that, even if that's the very minimum you had, how could you not act on Saddam Hussein?"[40] For a nation still traumatized by the events of 9/11, the mere possibility that Saddam might have WMD at some point in the future was sufficient to justify the war, even though Bush, like Blair, had insisted before the war that Saddam had active WMD programs.

But mere intent was not enough for Blair to defend his position. The British public had not forgotten such apocalyptic press headlines as "Brits 45 Minutes From Doom," nor Robin Cook's withering comment during his resignation speech that "Iraq probably has no weapons of mass destruction in the commonly understood sense of the term." This view appeared to be confirmed during the preliminary interrogation of Iraqi generals and scientists who were known to have worked on Saddam's WMD programs. All of them insisted that Iraq had purged itself completely of WMD after the Gulf War in 1991. Blair's discomfort was highlighted by President Putin, when the prime minister flew to Moscow at the end of April on a diplomatic fence-mending exercise. "Where is Saddam Hussein?" he asked a grim-faced Blair. "Where are those weapons of mass destruction, if they ever were in existence? Is Saddam sitting in a bunker, sitting on cases containing weapons of mass destruction, preparing to blow the whole place up?"[41] A few weeks later, Rumsfeld made his own, typically forthright contribution to the debate when he told the Council of Foreign Relations in New York that "the weapons may not exist. We don't know what happened. It is also possible that [Saddam's government] decided they would destroy them prior to the conflict."

There were, nevertheless, a few bright spots for Blair in the aftermath of the war. British opinion polls showed that 73 percent of the public supported the war, and three weeks after the fall of Baghdad, the long-awaited road map on the Israel-Palestine peace process was finally published. The two-thousand-page document set out a bold agenda: "A settlement, negotiated between the parties, will result in the emergence of an independent, democratic and viable Palestinian state living side by side in peace and security with Israel and its other neighbors." Even though officially the document had been drawn up by the "quartet" of the European Union, UN, Russia, and the United States, Blair could take a great deal of the credit for making sure that the proposal reached fruition. He had continued to raise the subject with Bush since he first brought it up during the two leaders' discussions in the immediate aftermath of 9/11. "We always felt that this was a crucial issue within the context of the war on terror, and that we should keep nagging away at the White House, even if at times they did not hear what we had to say," said one of Blair's close Downing Street aides.[42]

The biggest stumbling block to the successful implementation of the road map, however, remained Bush's refusal to deal with Yasser Arafat.

In a wide-ranging interview with the NBC anchorman Tom Brokaw after the war, Bush provided one, simple reason for having nothing to do with the Palestinian leader. "I saw what he did to President Clinton."[43] Bush did, however, welcome the appointment of Mahmoud Abbas as Palestinian prime minister, and promised that he would play host to him at the White House "one of these days." Bush had been reluctant to engage in the Middle East peace process, and it was to Blair's credit that the American president finally agreed to travel to the region in June, when, at the Jordanian resort of Aqaba, he met with both Sharon and Abbas. "All here today now share a goal: the Holy Land must be shared between the state of Palestine and the state of Israel, living at peace with each other and with every other nation of the Middle East," the president said. Bush's publicly stated commitment to a two-state solution was controversial for some members of the administration, particularly those with close links to Sharon's Likud Party, which was ideologically opposed to the concept of a Palestinian state. But it was Arafat who remained the main stumbling block to genuine progress on the peace front, as it soon transpired that he was not prepared to devolve his powers to Abbas.

The faint flicker of hope that was generated by the Aqaba Summit was finally extinguished in September, when Abbas resigned because he found his position untenable due to Arafat's constant interference. So long as Arafat could lay claim to be the sole, legitimate representative of the Palestinians, the prospects of genuine progress in the peace process were limited. "The White House did not support the road map, but went along with it to humor Blair," said a senior Bush administration official. "We regarded Blair as being hopelessly optimistic on the Middle East, and he paid lip service to the Palestinian cause, but it had virtually no impact or influence here." But Arafat's refusal to let Abbas have any power finally led Bush to conclude that it was pointless for him to waste his energy on a process that had no chance of success. "Bush lost it after Arafat appointed Abbas and then refused to let him do anything. That was it for Bush. He would have nothing to do with the Palestinian leadership so long as Arafat was in control."[44]

Blair was disappointed with the failure of the Middle East peace initiative, and the failure to uncover any evidence of WMD. The deteriorating

security situation in Iraq continued to take the gloss off the military victory, and domestic political pressure intensified against Downing Street
over its Iraq policy. In mid-May, Clare Short, the left-wing overseas development minister, resigned because she claimed Blair had not fulfilled his
commitment to let the UN take a leading role in Iraq's postwar administration. While her departure generated controversy, it was not as damaging for Blair as it might have been had she resigned at the same time
as Cook. The impact of Short's resignation was somewhat undermined by
the approval of UN Resolution 1483 the following week, which legiti-
mized the coalition's administration of Iraq. The WMD issue, on the
other hand, refused to go away. Despite the reports Blair was receiving on
an almost daily basis from SIS that the search for Saddam's WMD was
making little headway, he continued to live in hope that evidence would
soon emerge to justify his actions. At his monthly Downing Street press
conference on May 22, Blair said he remained confident that evidence of
Saddam's WMD capability would eventually be produced, but that it
would take some time.

At the end of May, Blair flew to Iraq to pay tribute to the British troops
who had participated in Operation Iraqi Freedom. His visit was part of a
five-nation tour aimed at rebuilding some of the diplomatic rifts caused by
the war. He flew into Basra on a C130 transporter amid tight security, the
first world leader to visit Iraq since the end of the war. After visiting an
Iraqi school that had been rebuilt with British aid, Blair paid tribute to the
"huge, mighty, and momentous" role the British armed forces had played in
winning the war. But any hope Blair had entertained of basking in the
limelight of the military victory was overshadowed by a controversial BBC
radio report that claimed Downing Street had deliberately "sexed up," or
exaggerated, the intelligence on Saddam's WMD in the "45 minutes" intelligence dossier that had been published the previous September.

The report was based on a briefing a BBC reporter had received from
Dr. David Kelly, a British member of the UN weapons inspection teams.
Even though it was later shown that the BBC reporter had himself exaggerated Kelly's views, the report confirmed the growing suspicion among
the British public that it had been misled by the government on the need
to go to war in the first place. The rest of Blair's trip, which took in Po-

land, Russia, and France, was, much to Blair's profound irritation, dogged by constant questions about Downing Street's role in drawing up the dossier and whether Blair had deliberately exaggerated the intelligence available to him. A press conference in Warsaw, which was supposed to concentrate on Anglo-Polish relations, was almost entirely devoted to questions about Downing Street's involvement in drawing up the dossier. Blair insisted that the dossier was the work of British intelligence officers, and not politicians. "The idea that we authorized or made our intelligence agencies invent some piece of evidence is completely absurd," said Blair. "People who have opposed these actions throughout are now trying to find fresh reasons to say this wasn't the right thing to do . . . We have just got to have a little bit of patience. I have absolutely no doubt at all that evidence will be found and I have absolutely no doubt that it exists."

The political row over the British government's WMD intelligence continued into the summer, and two parliamentary committees began investigations into the handling of the intelligence before the conflict. The political row between Downing Street and the BBC became increasingly bitter, with the news corporation refusing to apologize for its erroneous report and Alastair Campbell seemingly intent on pursuing a personal vendetta against a news organization that he believed was institutionally biased against the government. Blair was alarmed by his communications director's behavior, but seemed unable to control him. The prime minister was also becoming increasingly exasperated with Washington, publicly blaming the Americans for the chaotic situation that had developed in Iraq, and the failure of the ISG to make any headway on locating Saddam's WMD. The ISG teams were severely hindered both by the mounting lawlessness in Baghdad and by the disappearance of key documentation that was destroyed either by Saddam's regime during the war or by the looters after it.[45]

SIS, which still held out the hope that WMD evidence would be found, informed Blair in June that the chaos of the occupation was impeding the hunt for WMD, and that the U.S. military and the CIA were mishandling captured members of the regime and Iraqi scientists.[46] Scientists were afraid to cooperate for fear of reprisals by Saddam loyalists, and senior regime members saw no reason to assist without the promise of an amnesty from prosecution, which the Americans were unwilling to offer. Blair raised his concerns with Bush during their weekly video conferences, but Washington showed little interest in the WMD issue, which many senior members of the Bush administration regarded as a red herring, even after Congress decided to hold an inquiry into the quality and use of U.S. intelligence on Iraq before the war. Paul Wolfowitz summed up the view of many in the Bush administration when he remarked, "For bureaucratic reasons, we settled on one issue, weapons of mass destruction, because it was the one reason everyone could agree on."

Bush and Blair did not meet again until mid-July, when the prime minister flew to Washington to take up an invitation to address a joint session of Congress. The invitation was a privilege that was bestowed on few foreign leaders; Margaret Thatcher was the last British prime minister to have been afforded the honor. In addition, the Senate and the House of Representatives had voted to award Blair the Congressional Medal of Honor. By the time he arrived in Washington, Blair's personal popularity in Britain was in freefall, as the political debate over the use of prewar intelligence refused to abate. The Commons's powerful Intelligence and Security Committee had commenced its investigation into Downing Street's use of SIS intelligence. When its conclusions were published the following September, it found no evidence that Blair had deliberately misled the country. But it was critical of the prominence given to the forty-five-minute claim in the September dossier that suggested Saddam had the capability to hit Europe with ballistic missiles fitted with WMD warheads. It concluded that the claims made about Iraq attempting to seek quantities of uranium from Africa should have "been qualified to reflect the uncertainty" about the evidence.[47]

Washington afforded a welcome respite for Blair from his domestic travails and, as he remarked when he received the first of nineteen standing ovations during his address to Congress, "This is more than I deserve and more than I am used to, frankly." Blair had put much thought into his address to the American body politic. For all the difficulties his alliance with the Bush administration had caused him both at home and abroad, Blair was unrepentant about his status as America's first ally. In fact, although he sought to give some friendly advice about the need to "listen as well as lead," the unapologetically pro-American tone of Blair's speech demonstrated his almost unequivocal commitment to the transatlantic alliance, and his respect for America's undisputed position as the world's sole superpower. He said that the United States should not apologize for wanting to spread "the light of liberty" around the world, and that it was America's destiny to do so. "The spread of freedom is the best security for the free. It is our last line of defense and our first line of attack."

Blair repeated his view that he was prepared to be judged by history for his decision to go to war, whether or not WMD were found. "Can we be sure that terrorism and WMD will join together?" he asked. "Let us say one thing. If we are wrong, we will have destroyed a threat that, at its least, is responsible for inhuman carnage and suffering. That is something I am confident history will forgive. But if our critics are wrong, if we are right—as I believe with every fiber of instinct and conviction I have that we are—and we do not act, we will have hesitated in the face of this menace when we should have given leadership. That is something history will not forgive." And he was critical of France and Germany—without naming them—for seeking to cause a rift in the transatlantic alliance. "Any alliance must start with America and Europe," said Blair. "Believe me, if Europe and America are together, the others will work with us. But if we split, all the rest will play around, play us off, and nothing but mischief will be the result of it." He ended his speech with a rousing declaration of American values. "Tell the world why you are proud of America. Tell them when the 'Star-Spangled Banner' starts, Americans get to their feet, not because some state official told them to but because whatever race, color, class, or creed they are, being American means being free."

The standing ovation Blair received at the end of his speech lasted a full four minutes. Even his wife, Cherie, received an ovation when she took her seat with First Lady Laura Bush. With the congressional applause still ringing in his ears, Blair and his party left Washington to fly to the Far East. As Blair slept on the aircraft, his aides received the devastating news that Dr. David Kelly, the British scientist who had briefed the BBC about his concerns over the September dossier, had committed suicide. Kelly had been devastated by the harsh treatment he had received after it was revealed that he was the source of the BBC dossier story. His death meant that, if anything, the political debate in Britain about Blair's role in the war would get worse, not better, irrespective of the rapturous reception he had just received in Washington. Wherever he turned, it seemed that Blair could not shake off the specter of Saddam's WMD.

Twelve

THE RECKONING

———◆———

IT WAS THE MOMENT Tony Blair had been dreading. Ever since 9/11, Blair and his security chiefs had known that al-Qaeda was determined to commit a similarly headline-grabbing atrocity in Britain. Blair's uncompromising support for the Bush administration and its war against Islamic terrorism meant that Britain and British interests had become a prime target for Osama bin Laden's terror organization, and it was only through the diligence and good fortune of Britain's security and intelligence services that Britain had not been attacked. But Blair's worst fears were confirmed on the morning of July 7, 2005, when his security officials informed him that three London Underground trains and a bus had been bombed, all within the space of a few minutes. It appeared that Osama bin Laden had finally fulfilled his threat to bring carnage to the streets of London.

That morning, Blair was at the Scottish hotel resort of Gleneagles where he was hosting a summit of the G8 heads of state. For all the difficulties Blair had experienced in the two years since the Iraq War, the G8 summit promised a rare opportunity for him to move the political agenda away from Iraq and international terrorism and to issues with broader appeal, such as tackling poverty in Africa and trying to make progress on the contentious issue of global warming. Blair had started his day by taking a walk with President Bush around the grounds of one of Britain's finest hotels. Blair was pushing Bush hard to soften Washington's position on debt relief for Africa, but whatever progress he managed to make during their informal discussions was overshadowed when news of the attacks broke.

Blair was due to chair the opening session of G8 at 9.30 a.m., but, within minutes of the meeting commencing, his aides informed him of the bombings in London. He left the meeting immediately and went to a secure room to talk to British security chiefs in London about the extent of the damage. He returned to the conference room half an hour later to brief the other G8 leaders on the events unfolding in London. They immediately agreed that Blair should return to London, but that the summit should continue in his absence. To cancel it would send a signal to the terrorists that the leaders of the industrialized world could be intimidated. Before leaving, Blair made a brief statement on the hotel steps, with President Bush standing at his side, as the hotel flag flew at half-mast out of respect for those who had been killed and maimed in London. His voice trembling with emotion, a clearly shaken Blair said it was "particularly barbaric" that the bombings had taken place "on a day when people are meeting to try to help the problems of poverty in Africa and the long-term problems of climate change and the environment." He had nothing but contempt for the terrorists. "Whatever they do, it is our determination that they will never succeed in destroying what we hold dear in this country and in other civilized nations throughout the world." A few hours later, Blair was in his underground COBRA bunker in Downing Street, taking charge in the never-ending war on terror.

The London bombings of July 7, or 7/7 as they became known, were not the first time that al-Qaeda had attempted to attack Britain. An al-Qaeda plot to spread the deadly biological agent ricin throughout a shopping mall in central England was uncovered in early 2003. Another al-Qaeda plot, to bomb the Heathrow Express train link between London's busiest airport and the capital, was foiled the following year through good intelligence work. Nevertheless, al-Qaeda had demonstrated its ability to attack British overseas interests in November 2003, when Islamic terrorists with links to bin Laden bombed the British consulate in

Istanbul and the nearby HSBC bank headquarters. The British consul general Roger Short was among the twenty-five people killed in the attacks, which were timed to coincide with President Bush's state visit to Britain. The massive security operation undertaken to protect the American president meant that it was out of the question for al-Qaeda to attack him while he was in London, so bin Laden opted to remind the world of his presence by attacking relatively undefended British targets overseas.

Al-Qaeda operatives are renowned for the care that they take with the timing of their operations so that they generate maximum publicity, and the Istanbul bombings succeeded in upstaging Bush's visit to London on the day he was due to dine with the queen. Bin Laden's terror group had carried out a similarly well-timed attack against a number of Madrid commuter trains the following March, killing 191 people and injuring 1,460. The bombings were planned to coincide with the Spanish general election and draw attention to the staunch support José María Aznar's government had provided to Washington, particularly over the Iraq War. The bombings had the desired effect. When Spaniards went to the polls a few days later, Aznar's government was overthrown, and one of the first acts of the new Socialist prime minister, José Luis Rodríguez Zapatero, was to withdraw the 1,300 Spanish troops that his predecessor had sent to serve in Iraq with the U.S.-led coalition.

Al-Qaeda had learned from its long campaign of terror against the West that transportation systems—whether aircraft or trains—enabled it to inflict a high level of casualties. With that in mind, the terrorists launched their attacks on London at the height of morning rush hour. The police investigation later revealed that the attacks were carried out by four Muslim suicide bombers from the north of England. The bombings killed fifty-two people and injured more than seven hundred, and brought the underground network to a standstill for several weeks as rescue teams struggled to remove the wreckage from deep underground tunnels. Given that bin Laden and his associates made no secret of their desire to detonate a "dirty" nuclear bomb in London, the damage caused by the bombers was nowhere near as bad as it would have been had al-Qaeda's operational infrastructure not been severely disrupted by the coalition's military campaign. And any doubt that al-Qaeda was responsible for the

attacks was dispelled in September, when Ayman al-Zawahiri, bin Lad-
en's Egyptian-born deputy and mastermind of the 9/11 attacks, issued a
videotape, in which he explicitly acknowledged that "the London attack
is one of the attacks that al-Qaeda had the honor of carrying out."[1]

While the CIA had been alerted to the 9/11 attacks, British intelligence had no prior warning of the 7/7 attacks. "Security was tight because of the G8 summit, and most of our resources were focused on that,"
said a senior British intelligence officer. "But there was nothing to indi-
cate a specific plot to bomb London."[2] After the bombing, the British
security establishment was alarmed to discover that the 7/7 plotters were
all British-born and had managed to carry out the attacks without outside help or assistance. In the three years since coalition forces had decisively
defeated the Taliban and destroyed al-Qaeda's operational infrastructure in
Afghanistan, the group had quietly regrouped and managed to set up a
new network of operational cells under the noses of Britain's security forces.
The threat posed by radical British Muslims was highlighted two weeks
later, when another cell attempted to carry out a repeat bombing campaign that failed only because the bombers' homemade explosive did not
detonate.

Nor was there much doubt about the bombers' motivation for carrying
out the attacks. In early August, Ayman al-Zawahiri issued a grainy videotape, in which he suggested that Blair's support for Washington in the
war on terror was to blame for the bombings. "Blair has brought you
destruction in central London, and he will bring more of that, God willing," said Zawahiri. The attacks would continue so long as "the nations of
the Crusader alliance" continued to occupy Iraq and Afghanistan, "the
land of Islam." A few weeks later, in early September, a video statement
from the leader of the London bombers, Mohammad Sidique Khan, was
broadcast on the Arabic TV channel Al-Jazeera. Recorded shortly before
he committed his "martyrdom" operation, Khan said he was sacrificing
his life because "your democratically elected governments continuously
perpetrate atrocities against my people all over the world . . . your support
of them makes you directly responsible, just as I am directly responsible
for protecting and avenging my Muslim brothers and sisters. Until we
feel security, you will be our targets. And until you stop the bombing,

gassing, imprisonment, and torture of my people, we will not stop this fight. We are at war, and I am a soldier. Now you, too, will taste the reality of this situation."[3]

Neither Zawahiri nor Khan specifically linked the London bombings to Blair's support for the Iraq War. But it was implied, and the vocal antiwar lobby in Britain and elsewhere in Europe lost no time in blaming the attacks on Blair's unflinching support for Bush in the war on terror. While government ministers stood resolutely behind Blair, left-wing Labour MPs who had opposed the war from the outset now blamed the attacks on Blair's Iraq policy. Ken Livingstone, the mayor of London who had played a leading role in the antiwar movement, claimed that the Iraq War had influenced the bombers to attack London, while George Galloway, who had been expelled from the Labour Party for his extreme antiwar views, said Blair had "paid the price" for the Iraq conflict. Charles Kennedy, the leader of the Liberal Democrat Party, said the invasion of Iraq had "fuelled the conditions" in which terrorism flourished and that terrorists would not shrink from using Iraq to recruit supporters. The prominent Conservative politician Kenneth Clarke claimed that Blair's "disastrous decision" to invade Iraq had made Britain one of the main targets for Islamic extremists. A few days after the bombings, a report by the Royal Institute for International Affairs, the influential foreign policy think tank, accused Blair of being the "pillion passenger" of a policy drive by George Bush, and claimed that the war and its bloody aftermath had damaged Britain's ability to fight terror at home. Even some of the relatives of the victims sought to blame Iraq for the attacks. Mark Reynolds, the stepfather of twenty-six-year-old bomb victim Helen Jones, said she was "a victim of a war that we did not want to be in."[4] An opinion poll taken ten days after the bombings showed that two-thirds believed there was a direct link between the terror attacks in London and Blair's decision to invade Iraq.[5]

Blair himself was adamant that there was no direct connection between the bombings and Iraq. Speaking at a conference of senior Labour Party activists a few days later, he insisted that the bombers had been motivated by an "evil ideology" rather than opposition to his Iraq policy, and warned that it would be a "misunderstanding of a catastrophic order" to think that if Britain adopted a different policy, the terrorists would change theirs. "If it is Iraq that motivates them, why is the same ideology killing Iraqis by terror in defiance of an elected Iraqi government? What was September 11, 2001, the reprisal for? Why, if it is the cause of Muslims that concerns, them, do they kill so many with such callous indifference?" Blair had no intention of following the dubious precedent set by the Spanish government after the Madrid bombings and ordering British troops to pull out of Iraq. Instead he called for a concerted effort, both in Britain and abroad, to tackle Islamic extremism. "We must pull this up by the roots," he said. "Within Britain, we must join up with our Muslim community to take on the extremists. Worldwide, we should confront it everywhere it exists."[6] Blair was insistent that Britain would have been a target for al-Qaeda irrespective of whether he had committed Britain to war in Iraq. Certainly it is true that, while Britain was not directly threatened by al-Qaeda before the 9/11 attacks, it undoubtedly became a target the moment that Blair decided to declare war on the Taliban and al-Qaeda.

The debate as to whether or not the Iraq War caused the London bombings made little impact on Blair's approval ratings. Indeed, Blair's handling of the immediate aftermath of the bombings saw his position as prime minister strengthened rather than weakened. An opinion poll taken two days after the bombings showed that his satisfaction rating had shot up from 32 percent to 49 percent.[7] As one leading political commentator wrote a week later, "all but his bitterest and most sneering critics are relieved that he is Prime Minister now. Just as Margaret Thatcher was able to speak as a national leader across party lines at times of crisis . . . so does Mr. Blair now in expressing the public mood over the terrorist attacks."[8] A Scottish columnist went even further in his praise for Blair. "Britain has had few modern politicians to compare to the great American presidents: only Winston Churchill and Margaret Thatcher could truly boast global stature. But to that list, we must now add Tony Blair. He does not yet compare with their achievements, and perhaps he never will, but in terms of global stature and acclaim he is now among them."[9] Not everyone in Britain, by any means, subscribed to this somewhat rose-tinted view of the British prime minister, although the favorable press he received seemed to highlight the central paradox of the British public's relationship to their prime minister in the summer of 2005. While the majority held him responsible for the Iraq War, they did not blame him for the London bombings.

ON A PERSONAL LEVEL, the bomb attacks on London were a particularly cruel blow for Blair. The night before the bombers struck Blair had enjoyed one of the most exhilarating moments of his political career. For two years, Blair had spearheaded a campaign to bring the 2012 Olympic Games to Britain, and during the crucial weeks leading up to the final vote, he invested a great deal of energy trying to persuade the delegates to choose London ahead of the other main contenders—Paris and New York. The final decision was to be made on July 6, and in a last-ditch attempt to win over the fifty Olympic delegates, Blair flew with his wife, Cherie, to Singapore, where the delegates would announce the winning city. The couple spent two days trying to persuade the Olympic officials of the merits of the British bid over that of the French, who had emerged as the favorites to secure the nomination as the contest drew to a close.

By the time the decision was due to be announced, Blair had returned to Britain and was at Gleneagles preparing for the G8 summit. An indication of the amount of effort Blair and his wife had personally invested in the British bid was reflected in the fact that neither of them could bear to watch the result announced on television. When Downing Street finally informed Blair that the British bid had triumphed, he was so thrilled by the result that he hugged Jonathan Powell, his chief of staff. As Blair remarked later that day, after addressing thousands of jubilant supporters celebrating in Trafalgar Square, "It's not often in this job that you punch the air and do a little jig and embrace the person next to you."

Blair's success in securing the 2012 Olympics for Britain capped a remarkable turnaround in his political fortunes. Only two months before, he had been fighting for his political life as he sought to persuade a deeply skeptical, not to say hostile, British public during the May 2005 general election to be reelected for a third term as prime minister. The election campaign was dominated by a single issue—Iraq. From the outset of the campaign, Blair's political enemies turned the contest into a judgment over whether Blair had made the right decision in leading Britain into war against Iraq, and whether he had deliberately misled the British people about the necessity of war. Blair's personal popularity was at such a low ebb during the election that many Labour Party candidates declined even to feature a picture of Britain's most successful Labour prime minister in their campaign literature. As Blair electioneered around the country, he was frequently jeered by crowds of Labour sympathizers, who taunted him with chants of "liar." Michael Howard, the Conservative opposition leader, repeatedly accused Blair of lying to the British public, and Conservatives displayed anti-Blair campaign posters bearing the caption "If he's prepared to lie to take us to war, he's prepared to lie to win an election." Apart from being heavily criticized for his conduct over Iraq, Blair was castigated for his close alliance with President Bush. Opposition politicians quickly realized that the best way to persuade undecided voters not to vote for Blair was to show them a picture of the prime minister with Bush.

For all the vitriol directed at him during the election campaign, Blair still managed to emerge victorious on election day on May 5, albeit with his parliamentary majority halved to just sixty-seven seats. Blair's victory owed more to the poor quality of the opposition than his own popularity, and within hours of Labour's election victory being announced, there were widespread calls, both from within his own Labour Party and in the media, for him to step down and allow his colleague Gordon Brown, who had maintained a neutral stance over the Iraq War, to take his place. Blair may have won Labour a historic third consecutive term in office, but it appeared as though he was just barely clinging to power.

The extreme discomfort that Blair suffered during the month-long election campaign was the result of the deep sense of betrayal many Britons felt over his handling of Iraq. When British troops had gone into action to assist the U.S.-led coalition to overthrow Saddam Hussein's regime in March 2003, the majority of Britons supported the war. But by the summer of 2003, as suspicions began to develop that Saddam's WMD arsenal was nowhere near as potent as Blair had claimed before the war, support began to fade. And after Dr. David Kelly took his life following the BBC report that the September intelligence dossier had been deliberately "sexed up" by the government to make the case for war, Blair found himself embroiled in a political firestorm that seemed to become more inflamed by the day. Blair reacted to Kelly's suicide by immediately appointing Lord Hutton, the former lord chief justice of Northern Ireland, to investigate the circumstances surrounding his death. This was the third inquiry to be set up to look at the way the Blair government handled prewar intelligence.

Blair and his advisors took the view that Kelly's death was simply a personal tragedy caused by the scientist's naïveté in having unauthorized meetings with a journalist who then sensationalized his remarks. But the British media, egged on by Blair's antiwar opponents, sensed political blood, with some of the more conspiracy-minded British commentators suggesting that the Kelly affair could ultimately become Blair's "Watergate." The mood of hysteria surrounding Kelly's death, and the BBC's allegation that Blair had exaggerated the available intelligence on Iraq to justify the war, meant that even the killing of Saddam's sons Uday and Qusay by U.S. forces in late July did little to reassure the wider British public of the merits of the war.

The hearings for the Hutton inquiry began in mid-August. Blair and his intelligence chiefs provided a plausible account of how the intelligence dossier on prewar intelligence on Iraq was put together. John Scarlett, the head of the Joint Intelligence Committee (JIC) and Sir Richard Dearlove, the head of SIS, took responsibility for the dossier's contents, which had been published with their approval. But the inquiry heard evidence from a number of defense experts who openly questioned the validity of the government's claim that Saddam had the capability to fire WMD within forty-five minutes. Even the intelligence officers were forced to admit that the WMD claim related to battlefield munitions, and not to missile systems targeted at Israel or southern Europe. The inquiry shed unwelcome light on the informal nature of Blair's government, where key decisions were made by a small coterie of close advisors sitting on sofas in his "den," his private study in Downing Street. This meant that senior ministers and officials were rarely consulted. The role of Blair's spin doctors— Alastair Campbell, in particular—was also brought into the open. In his evidence to the inquiry, Campbell claimed that he had "no input, output, or influence" on the contents of the dossier. But when his correspondence with Scarlett was published, it transpired that the language on the forty-five-minute claim had been strengthened at Campbell's request, after he complained that it was "weak."

Lord Hutton's forensic examination of the intelligence dossier and Dr. Kelly's death failed to unearth any evidence that Blair had deliberately misled the country on the intelligence available to him before the Iraq War. But the conduct of his close officials in seeking to manipulate the few facts that were available on Iraq's WMD for their own political ends did nothing to improve Blair's already battered popularity. When the cross-party Intelligence and Security Committee published its conclusions on the use of intelligence in early September, it unanimously exonerated Blair of "sexing up" the intelligence dossier of the previous year, and found no evidence that his officials had interfered with the contents. But the report was dismissed by the antiwar lobby as an establishment stitch-up, and it singularly failed to dismiss the accusations of dishonesty that were still being heaped on Blair. At the end of the month, a leading opinion poll revealed that 64 percent of British voters no longer trusted Blair, while almost half wanted him to quit as prime minister.[10] Private polls of Labour MPs indicated that a significant number believed Blair should step down in favor of Gordon Brown. At the annual Labour Party conference at the end of the month, Blair hit back at his critics, insisting that he had no intention of stepping down. "I want to carry on doing the job until the job is done," he declared. And he remained convinced that the intelligence picture he had presented before the war was accurate. "This wasn't an invention of British intelligence or the CIA. The intelligence that we got was essentially correct. In my experience of intelligence, not every single item is correct, but if there is a pattern as strong as the pattern here, then it is correct.[11]

Blair's attempts to justify the Iraq invasion were undermined by the country's rapidly deteriorating security situation. While the Iraqis were glad to see the dissolution of Saddam's regime, they did not take kindly to having their country occupied and administered by a foreign force. Although Britain and America had gained UN Security Council approval for their occupation of Iraq in May, the insurgency intensified during the summer as disillusioned Iraqis joined the ranks of the insurgents and *Jihadis*, foreign fighters from countries such as Syria, Saudi Arabia, Yemen, and Somalia, who flocked into the country to take advantage of the opportunity to attack the "infidel" coalition forces. The heart of the resistance was concentrated in the "Sunni triangle" of the Sunni-dominated population area between Baghdad, Tikrit, and Fallujah.

In August, the insurgents succeeded in driving a suicide truck bomb into the headquarters of the UN in Baghdad, killing seventeen people, including Sérgio Vieira de Mello, the special representative to Iraq appointed by the UN secretary-general. This resulted in the UN withdrawing most of its operational staff from Iraq. By the fall, the CIA estimated that the number of insurgents participating in the resistance was more than fifty thousand. The deteriorating security situation forced President Bush to seek an extra $87 billion from Congress to pay for the reconstruction of Iraq and Afghanistan—ten times more than the United States has ever spent on any country in a given year. In a televised address, Bush appealed for international support to help the U.S.-led coalition defeat the insurgents, but the appeal fell on deaf ears. Hopes that "friendly" Muslim countries, such as Pakistan and Saudi Arabia, would bail out Washington were dashed in October, when their governments pointedly insisted that they would wait for an invitation from the Iraqi people before committing troops. The Iraqi people had no say in the matter though, so there was really no prospect of such an offer forthcoming.

The failure of David Kay's Iraq Survey Group to find evidence of Saddam's alleged WMD stockpiles also increased the political pressure on Blair. Kay's interim progress report to the CIA in October found no evidence of an "imminent threat." It provoked a fresh barrage of attacks on Blair from the antiwar lobby, even though the small print in Kay's report confirmed that Saddam had been engaged in covert biological programs in breach of UN resolutions, and had mounted an elaborate drive to disperse, hide, and destroy documents and materials even after the war had started. Robin Cook, the former foreign secretary, led the charge, accusing Blair of going to war before UN weapons inspectors had been given sufficient time to complete their work. "If we had given the UN inspectors extra time, we would now know what the Iraq Survey Group is telling us, which is Saddam Hussein simply did not have any weapons of mass destruction and did not pose a threat to ourselves or indeed to our neighbors."[12]

The seemingly endless criticism of Blair took a heavy toll on the prime minister's confidence, and by November, Blair had come to the drastic conclusion that he had irretrievably lost the confidence of the British public and should therefore resign. During a private dinner on November 6, 2003, hosted by John Prescott, the deputy prime minister, Blair informed Gordon Brown, whom most Labour Party members regarded as the prime minister's heir apparent, that he intended to step down in the autumn of 2004. He told Brown that he had reached the painful conclusion that he had lost the trust of the electorate over the way he had led Britain into war in Iraq. "I think in the end I will be vindicated (over Iraq)," said Blair. "But I'm not going to turn this around for a very long time. Therefore, I am going to stand down before the next election."[13] The next general election was expected in the spring of 2005, and he asked for Brown's help to get him through the next year.

It was against this unpromising backdrop that Bush flew to Britain in November for his long-awaited state visit. A poll taken on the eve of the visit revealed that half of Britons thought that Blair's relationship with Bush was bad for the country. Ken Livingstone, the London mayor, even went so far as to describe Bush "as the greatest threat to life on this planet." Blair dismissed the criticism, insisting that it was exactly the right moment for Bush to visit the capital, as Britain and America were involved in a "battle of seminal importance for the early twenty-first century," one that would "define relations between the Muslim world and the West. It will have far-reaching implications for the future conduct of American and Western democracy." Public hostility to the visit was so strong that Bush and his entourage were hardly seen during the three days he spent in Britain. Even a planned visit by the president to lay a wreath at a memorial to the 9/11 victims located in Grovesnor Square outside the American embassy was canceled over fears that it would attract antiwar demonstrators. And while Blair and Bush tried to put a brave face on the value of the visit, it was ultimately overshadowed by the al-Qaeda attacks on the British consulate and HSBC bank in Istanbul, which demonstrated in graphic detail the price Britain was paying for being America's "closest friend in the world," as Bush described the trans-atlantic alliance during his visit.

In their private discussions, Bush informed Blair that the deteriorating security situation in Iraq made it imperative that power be transferred to the Iraqis at the earliest opportunity. Bush had reached this decision during crisis talks with Paul Bremmer, the U.S. administrator in Baghdad, before flying to London. Blair was relieved to hear the news, especially as Downing Street had been pressuring the White House to change course for several months. "We had argued all along that the sooner we handed control over to the Iraqis, the better," said a senior Foreign Office official. "It was crucial that the Iraqis felt that they were running the country, not us. Unfortunately, the neoconservatives in Washington thought they knew better, and the result was chaos."[14] Bush and Blair agreed on a timetable for a full handover of power to the Iraqis in the summer of 2004.

AFTER ALL THE DIFFICULTIES Blair experienced in the aftermath of the Iraq War, he hoped that a corner might have been turned at the end of the year, when a team of U.S. Special Forces announced that they had captured Saddam Hussein hiding in a foxhole in the grounds of a farm on the outskirts of Tikrit. Saddam's capture was a significant propaganda coup: one of the great failings of the Afghan War had been the coalition's failure to capture the leadership of al-Qaeda and the Taliban. Now the dictator who had brought so much misery to his long-suffering people was safely locked up in American custody. Saddam's capture offered the hope that a turning point had been reached in the insurgency. Coalition intelligence chiefs were convinced that Saddam had arranged the insurgency before the war, and had directed it while on the run. With Saddam in custody, coalition commanders were optimistic that the insurgency would gradually subside. There was also quiet optimism in London and Washington that Saddam might be persuaded to reveal the truth about his WMD programs.

Another totally unexpected development occurred in late December, which enabled Blair to claim that the coalition's strategy in the world-wide war on terror was achieving its objectives. The maverick Libyan leader Colonel Muammar Gadhafi announced that he had agreed to give up his WMD arsenal, which included an advanced nuclear bomb program he had managed to conceal from the regular inspections made by UN's nuclear watchdog, the International Atomic Energy Agency. Gadhafi's bombshell was the result of nine months of top-secret negotiations between British and Libyan officials, which started at the same time as coalition forces launched their invasion of Iraq. Unlike Saddam, Gadhafi did not underestimate the determination of the coalition to tackle rogue states, and he instructed his officials to make a deal rather than run the risk of being the next target in the coalition's war on terror. As a senior Pentagon official remarked shortly after the Libyan deal was announced, "This is one for the good cop. Saddam got the stick and Gadhafi accepted the carrot. The way the Bush-Blair relationship works, you either talk with Blair or you risk ending up in a fight with Bush." [15]

Blair was further buoyed at the end of January 2004, when the Hutton inquiry into the death of Dr. Kelly published its findings. Lord Hutton unequivocally cleared Blair and his government of "sexing up" the September intelligence dossier, and directed all his criticism at the BBC, concluding that the central allegations it had made against the government were "unfounded." But, as was so often the case during Blair's roller-coaster ride on the Iraq issue, his relief at Hutton's findings proved short-lived. As Downing Street digested the conclusions of the Hutton report, the White House announced it was setting up an independent commission to investigate the CIA's intelligence failings on Iraq's WMD. Blair had so far managed to avoid setting up an independent inquiry into the issue in Britain: the three inquiries that had taken place had either been conducted by Parliament or, in the case of Hutton, with their terms of reference strictly limited.

But Bush found himself under pressure on Iraq's WMD after David Kay, the head of the Iraq Survey Group, resigned his position on January 24, admitting that Saddam had most likely got rid of all his WMD soon after the Gulf War in 1991. Four days later, Kay told the Senate Armed Services Committee, "It turns out we were all wrong, probably, in my judgment, and that is most disturbing." Bush responded by setting up a bipartisan, independent inquiry along the lines of the Warren Commission that looked into President John F. Kennedy's assassination in 1963. "I want the American people to know that I, too, want to know the facts. I want to be able to compare what the Iraq Survey Group has found with what we thought prior to going into Iraq."

The big problem for Blair was that no one in Washington had thought to inform Downing Street of the president's decision, which put Blair under pressure to set up an independent inquiry of his own, something he and his officials had strenuously sought to avoid. "It would have been nice if Washington had kept us in the loop," said a senior Downing Street official. "Bush's decision [to hold an independent inquiry] put us in a difficult position."[16] A few days later, Blair announced that he was appointing Lord Butler, who had been Downing Street's most senior civil servant when he first became prime minister, to conduct an independent inquiry into Britain's prewar intelligence on Iraq's WMD. Now it was Washington's turn to be upset. Butler would report in July—just as the American presidential election campaigns would be moving into top gear. Unlike the three previous British inquiries into Saddam's WMD, the Butler report was critical of the government. Although Butler cleared Blair of "deliberate distortion or culpable negligence" in the way in which he portrayed the threat posed by Saddam, Lord Butler was highly critical of the intelligence material on which Britain's decision to go to war was based. He found that much of the intelligence was "seriously flawed" and "open to doubt," and the September dossier should have carried warnings on the limitations of the available intelligence. Perhaps the most startling revelation in Butler's report was the fact that most of Britain's key intelligence was based on information from just three Iraqi spies, none of whom had access to the inner sanctum of Saddam's regime.

Blair's sense that he might never escape the effects of the Pentagon's chaotic handling of postwar Iraq further deepened in April, with the devastating revelation that Iraqi detainees held at Abu Ghraib prison on the outskirts of Baghdad had been subjected to horrific and degrading treatment by their American prison guards. CBS broadcast on television pictures that had been taken inside Abu Ghraib the previous November and December. One showed a group of Iraqis naked—except for hoods—stacked in a human pyramid, and another showed naked prisoners being forced to pretend to have sex with one another. The Abu Ghraib scandal completely undermined the coalition claim that Saddam's overthrow would bring an end to the systematic abuse that Iraqis had suffered under his dictatorship. And it raised further questions in Britain about Blair's support for an administration that appeared to have scant regard for human rights. Blair had already suffered much criticism over the treatment of three Britons who had been held at Guantanamo Bay, the U.S. naval base in Cuba used to hold suspected al-Qaeda supporters captured during the Afghan War. The Iraqi prisoner abuse scandal merely served to bolster the view in Britain that Blair was seeking to defend the indefensible.

Indeed, signs of tension in the transatlantic alliance were apparent when Blair visited Bush in April 2004 to discuss the handover arrangements for Iraq. By the spring, the situation on the ground in Iraq was threatening to spiral out of control. Saddam's capture the previous December had made no impact on the insurrection, which was rapidly taking on the appearance of a widespread revolt. One hundred and thirty-six U.S. troops were killed that April, the bloodiest month since the war began. Coalition forces were engaged in a bitter fight with Sunni insurgents at Fallujah and against Shiite Muslim rebels in the south of the country, led by the pro-Iranian cleric Muqtada al-Sadr. Bush and Blair were in agreement that the only hope of curtailing the violence was to ensure that the planned handover of power to the Iraqis took place as planned at the end of June. But while the two leaders agreed to allow the UN to oversee the Iraq handover, Blair was embarrassed to discover that Bush had made a secret deal with Ariel Sharon, the Israeli prime minister, on pulling Israeli troops out of the Gaza Strip in return for keeping a number of Jewish settlements on the West Bank.

Throughout his dealings with Bush, Blair had persistently raised the Israeli-Palestinian issue, often to no avail. But on the one occasion that tangible progress was being made, Washington had not informed Blair. In fact, the Gaza withdrawal plan had been negotiated by Elliott Abrams, a leading neoconservative brought into the White House to work on the "road map." At no point was Blair or his officials allowed to participate in the talks. "We weren't negotiating with the British government, we were negotiating with the Israelis," Abrams responded brusquely when asked why Blair had not been involved in the talks. "We kept European and Arab governments informed, but it was not play-by-play information."[17] Yet again, Blair had been brutally made aware of the limits of his influence at the White House. Still, despite this obvious snub, at the Rose Garden press conference at the end of the summit, Bush continued to refer to Blair as America's "staunchest" friend. "We have no more valuable friend than Prime Minister Tony Blair," said Bush. "As we say in Texas, he's a standup kinda guy. He shows backbone, courage, and strong leadership."

Unbeknown to Bush, some of that "courage" appeared to desert Blair briefly when he returned home to London. For it was the day after he returned from Washington that Blair came closest to offering his resignation. He was deeply depressed by what he regarded as Washington's mismanagement of postwar Iraq, which seemed to be epitomized by the appalling scandal of Abu Ghraib. The fact that a number of British soldiers were about to be charged with war crimes for their own role in torturing Iraqis confirmed Blair's private view that he would never again be able to recover the trust of the British public. Another factor that weighed heavily on him at that time was the impact the continuous public criticism had on his family, particularly his teenage children. According to his close aides, Blair was on the verge of resigning on April 19, 2004. It was only because of the intervention of close cabinet colleagues and his wife, Cherie, that he was eventually persuaded to change his mind and fight for another term in office. Blair's change of heart about stepping down gradually leaked out the following month, when his supporters let it be known that the prime minister was determined to stay in office at least until the situation in Iraq had stabilized. "He said that he cannot go until he has sorted this out," said one of his close colleagues. "He feels that he got us into this and he has got to get some improvement in Iraq before he thinks of standing down."[18]

Following the April "wobble," as it became known among his close acquaintances, Blair seemed to take a more realistic view of what he was likely to achieve in Iraq. He understood completely that it was the defining issue of his premiership, but realized that the crucial question of whether he was right or wrong to go to war would not be resolved while he was in office. Even so, after the carnage of the previous year, by the summer of 2004, he could point to tangible signs that progress was being made in Iraq when power was formally transferred to Iraq's interim government at the end of June 2004. And having been forced to take a back seat as the Pentagon assumed almost absolute control for administering postwar Iraq, British officials were privately delighted when Ayad Allawi was nominated as the head of the new Iraqi government. Allawi had been a protégé of both the Foreign Office and British intelligence, and Downing Street regarded him as a much better bet than his main rival, Ahmed Chalabi, the darling of the Pentagon and Washington's neoconservatives. On the day of the handover, Bush and Blair attended a joint press conference at the NATO summit in Turkey. "The battle for Iraq and its future is in a genuine sense the frontline of the battle against terrorism," said Blair. "We will stay as long as it takes."

With Bush increasingly focusing his energy on winning reelection, Blair thought it prudent to keep his distance from the American president, lest he be accused of bias in the event of a Democratic candidate winning the November contest. Most of the Democratic candidates, moreover, were, at the very least, critical of the Iraq War, if not downright hostile. Howard Dean, the early Democrat frontrunner from Vermont, made his antiwar stance the cornerstone of his campaign, and expressed his confusion over Blair's close relationship with Bush. "We don't know what to make of Tony Blair," he said. "He was a strong friend of Clinton, and now he's an ally with Bush." [19] Blair felt far more comfortable with Senator John Kerry, who secured the Democratic nomination, because his criticism of the war was more tempered than that of some of his rivals, and, in his public statements, he expressed his admiration for the steadfast support Blair had given America since 9/11. While he was critical of Bush's "arrogance," which he said had alienated the international community, he also said America could find much "to inspire us" in Blair's achievements and Britain's approach to the war on terror. But Blair's sensitivity about offending Bush led him to ban Labour ministers and officials from traveling to the Democratic Convention in Boston in July for Kerry's official coronation as the Democratic candidate, although he later admitted to having met Kerry twice in private when the two politicians "had more than an exchange of pleasantries."[20]

Bush secured reelection, and whatever Blair privately thought about having to continue working with Bush, he kept his feelings to himself. Blair had gone to bed the night of the election believing that Kerry had won, and only discovered that Bush had been reelected when he got up the following morning. He phoned Bush a few days later and had an informal discussion with the president on his plans for the second term. "There is a real sense that in the second term the president has space and energy to develop an agenda that I hope can unify Europe and America," Blair said of the conversation. "That means reaching out on both sides." And he appealed to the Europeans in particular to play their part in mending the transatlantic rift that had emerged during the first Bush administration. "President Bush is there for four years. In a way, some people are in a state of denial. The election has happened, America has spoken, the rest of the world should listen. It is important that America listens to the rest of the world, too."[21] But many European leaders, rather than adopting Blair's pragmatic approach, took a very different view. The leaders of France, Germany, and Spain, meeting in Brussels days after the American election, signaled the formation of a new alliance that would act as a counterbalance to the second Bush administration. Jacques Chirac, the French president, said that Bush's reelection had left the world "more multipolar than ever."

Blair flew to Washington to meet with Bush a week after the election, and Blair began the meeting by raising the Palestinian issue. Blair had pressed Bush hard for four years on Israel-Palestine, with little success. But by a quirk of fate, Bush's reelection had coincided with the death of the Palestinian leader Yasser Arafat. Previously, Bush's refusal to deal with Arafat had been the main stumbling block to implementation of the "road map." But with Arafat out of the picture, the American president now had no excuse for not reengaging in the region, and Blair succeeded in getting Bush to make a public commitment to establish a Palestinian state before the end of his second term. Bush also committed himself to undertake a fence-mending trip to Europe, although he was cool to the point of being dismissive when Blair suggested holding a European peace conference on

the Middle East. While the meeting confirmed that there were still significant differences of approach between the American president and the
British prime minister, Bush was nevertheless gracious about working
with Blair. He said he felt a "lucky president" to be in office at the same
time as Blair, who was "the kind of person I like to deal with."

By the end of the year, it was Blair's turn to concentrate his energy on
seeking reelection. Blair's acknowledgment of his own political mortality
was primarily aimed at reassuring skeptical Labour voters that by voting
the party back into office they were not necessarily voting for him. The
mauling he subsequently suffered during the election campaign indicated that his instincts were right, and that while many voters were prepared to vote Labour, few of them wanted to vote for Blair. Thus, when
Labour was reelected to office with a greatly reduced majority, a significant number of Labour MPs—including Robin Cook, the former foreign
secretary—called on Blair to step down immediately, arguing that he
had become an electoral liability. Many of them reported that they had
been shocked at the degree of hostility to Blair they had encountered
from voters during the campaign.

But Blair was insistent that he would serve for a full third term, which
meant that he would remain in power for the duration of the second Bush
administration. At a meeting of the parliamentary Labour Party a week
after the election, Blair faced his critics and appealed to Labour MPs to
give him enough time to prepare for an orderly handover of power. During the meeting, Blair made no mention of his intention to serve for another four years, and to his surprise, he found more MPs speaking out in
his defense than calling for his immediate resignation. Blair responded
by saying it was his "historic responsibility" to ensure that his successor
was in the strongest possible position to win Labour a fourth term of office at the next election, which would most likely be held in 2009.

In fact, if anything, the 2005 election result appeared to signal the
return of Blair's self-confidence. Aware that the worst was behind him,
Blair rediscovered some of the old swagger that had made him such a
formidable political operator for more than a decade. By the eve of the
London bombings in July, and in the space of just two months, Blair had
achieved a remarkable turnaround. Buoyed by the near collapse of the

Conservative Party opposition immediately after the election, Blair was given another political lifeline when French and Dutch voters rejected a new constitution for the European Union. Blair had committed himself to hold a similar vote in Britain, where his own pro-EU sympathies would have been severely tested by Britain's powerful anti-EU lobby. Cabinet colleagues reported that Blair seemed reinvigorated and that the weekly cabinet meetings were far more relaxed than before the election. And his statesmanlike handling of the London bombings and their aftermath appeared to strengthen his position as prime minister, so much so that in July, there were good odds that Blair would end up serving a fourth term.[22]

But after the London bombings, Blair was in no position to enjoy the brief revival in his political fortunes. The attacks on London and the continuing carnage in Iraq meant that the Iraq War and the wider war on international terrorism would remain the defining issues of his premiership. The long and painful transformation of Iraq from dictatorship to democracy continued to take a heavy toll on the prime minister. While the first democratic elections in Iraq's modern history had taken place the previous January, the new Iraqi government was incapable of halting the insurgency, which continued to inflict significant coalition casualties. By September, as Labour activists gathered for their annual conference at Brighton, there were growing calls for Blair to formulate an exit strategy for British troops in Iraq. An opinion poll showed that half the British people wanted British troops out of Iraq within three months. And speculation continued about the timing of Blair's departure from Downing Street. Gordon Brown's hopes of positioning himself as Blair's heir apparent received a sharp rebuff from Blair's wife, Cherie. When asked by the BBC about the couple's plans after Downing Street, Mrs. Blair replied witheringly, "Darling, that is a long way in the future. It is too far ahead for me to even think about it."

As for Blair himself, he made it clear that he intended to see out the full four-year term, irrespective of the criticism he received over Iraq. During the general election the previous spring, Blair had been robust in defending his decision to go to war, telling his inquisitors that it was the "right thing to do." He had insisted that he had nothing to apologize for.

"If you want me to apologize for the war in Iraq, I'm afraid I cannot say that I'm sorry we removed Saddam Hussein," he said.[23] Blair was both defiant and insistent that he was taking the right course of action. And he was equally robust in handling the call for Britain to withdraw its troops from Iraq. "I have absolutely no doubt as to what we should to," he said in an interview during the Labour conference. "We should stick with it. There is absolutely no doubt in my mind that what is happening in Iraq is crucial for our own security. Never mind the security of Iraq or the greater Middle East. It is crucial for the security of the world. If they are defeated—this type of global terrorism and insurgency in Iraq—we will defeat them everywhere."[24]

NOTES

CHAPTER ONE: THE MAKING OF AN ALLY

1. Andrew Rawnsley, *Servants of the People* (London: Hamish Hamilton, 2000), p. 1.
2. John Rentoul, *Tony Blair, Prime Minister* (London: Little, Brown, 2001), p. 39.
3. *Spectator* (London), October 1, 1994.
4. *Vanity Fair,* March 1995.
5. Speech, Manchester, April 21, 1997.
6. *New York Times,* April 13, 1996.
7. Private interview.
8. Hillary Rodham Clinton, *Living History* (New York: Simon & Schuster, 2003), p. 423.
9. Private interview.
10. John Major, *The Autobiography* (London: HarperCollins, 1999), p. 456.
11. Private interview.
12. Quoted in James Naughtie, *The Accidental American* (London: Macmillan, 2004), p. 71.
13. Ibid., p. 72.
14. Interview, William Kristol.
15. Interview, Lord Renwick.
16. Private interview.
17. Margaret Thatcher, *Statecraft* (London: HarperCollins, 2002), p. 301.
18. *Sunday Times*, April 23, 1995; May 28, 1995.
19. *Times,* July 17, 1995.
20. Interview, Lord Powell.
21. Anthony Seldon, *Blair* (London: The Free Press, 2004), p. 448.

22. Interview, Lord Powell.
23. *Blair*, p. 317.
24. Ibid., p. 319.

CHAPTER TWO: ENEMY TARGET
 1. Anthony Seldon, *Blair* (London: The Free Press, 2004), p. 386.
 2. Lord Butler of Brockwell, *Review of Intelligence on Weapons of Mass Destruction* (London: The Stationery Office, July 14, 2004), p. 31.
 3. Private source.
 4. *Review of Intelligence on Weapons of Mass Destruction*, p. 47.
 5. Con Coughlin, *Saddam: King of Terror* (New York: Ecco, 2002), p. 295.
 6. Ibid., p. 304.
 7. Private interview.
 8. Private source.
 9. *The 9/11 Commission Report* (New York: W. W. Norton and Company, 2004), p. 60.
10. Ibid.
11. Ibid., p. 61.
12. Paddy Ashdown, *The Ashdown Diaries, Volume 2: 1997–1999* (London: Allen Lane, 2000), p. 127.
13. Interview, Lord Guthrie.
14. Speech, Foreign Office, London, May 12, 2004.
15. Private source.
16. Private source.
17. BBC TV, *Endgame in Ireland,* December 2, 2003.
18. *Blair*, p. 353.
19. Ed Maloney, *A Secret History of the IRA* (London: Penguin, 2002), p. 380.
20. Private interview.
21. *Blair*, p. 350.
22. Private interview.
23. Private interview.
24. *Blair*, p. 353.
25. Private interview.
26. Speech, Belfast, May 16, 1997.
27. Ibid.
28. Philip Stephens, *The Price of Leadership* (New York: Penguin, 2004), p. 199.
29. Private interview.
30. Andrew Rawnsley, *Servants of the People* (London: Hamish Hamilton, 2002), p. 123. (Rawnsley provides one of the most definitive accounts of the travails Blair suffered in negotiating the Good Friday Agreement.)
31. Ibid., p. 136.
32. Ibid., p. 140.
33. Bill Clinton, *My Life* (New York: Knopf, 2004), p. 784.

34. Private interview.
35. *Blair*, p. 361

CHAPTER THREE: TAKE AIM

1. *Comprehensive Report of the Special Advisor on Iraq's WMD*, September 30, 2004, (Regime Finance and Procurement Summary), p. 1.
2. *Times*, October 8, 2004.
3. *Forbes,* July 1997.
4. *New York Times,* June 22, 1997.
5. Iraq Television, June 22, 1997.
6. CNN, June 28, 1997.
7. Peter Riddell, *Hug Them Close* (London: Politicos, 2003), p. 91.
8. Quoted in *Hug Them Close*, p. 91.
9. Private interview.
10. Private interview.
11. Speech, Georgetown University, Washington, D.C., March 26, 1997.
12. Madeleine Albright, *Madam Secretary: A Memoir* (New York: Talk Miramax Books, 2003), p. 275.
13. Paddy Ashdown, *The Ashdown Diaries, Volume 2: 1997–1999* (London: Allen Lane, 2000), p. 127.
14. Con Coughlin, *Saddam: King of Terror* (New York: Ecco, 2002), p. 307.
15. Seymour Hersh, "Saddam's Best Friend," *New Yorker,* April 5, 1999.
16. Bill Clinton, *My Life* (New York: Knopf, 2004), p. 769.
17. *Madam Secretary*, p. 277.
18. House of Commons *Hansard* Debates, November 25, 1997.
19. Speech, Mansion House, London, November 10, 1997.
20. *Madam Secretary*, p. 277.
21. Ibid., p. 275.
22. *Hansard,* November 19, 1997.
23. Private interview.
24. Private interview.
25. *Weekly Standard,* December 1, 1997.
26. *Letter to President Clinton on Iraq,* Project for the New American Century, January 26, 1998.
27. Sidney Blumenthal, *The Clinton Wars* (New York: Farrar, Straus and Giroux, 2003), p. 308.
28. Hillary Rodham Clinton, *Living History* (New York: Simon & Schuster, 2003), p. 425.
29. Ibid., p. 308.
30. *Guardian*, May 14, 1998.
31. *New Yorker,* April 21, 1997.
32. *New York Times,* April 23, 1997.
33. *Hug Them Close*, p. 80.

34. Downing Street Press Briefing, January 27, 1998.
35. *Daily Mail*, February 5, 1998.
36. *BBC Newsnight,* February 4, 1998.
37. Lord Butler of Brockwell, *Review of Intelligence on Weapons of Mass Destruction* (London: The Stationery Office, July 14, 2004), p. 45.
38. *Observer*, February 8, 1998.
39. John Rentoul, *Tony Blair, Prime Minister* (London: Little, Brown, 2001), p. 432.
40. *Hug Them Close*, p. 85.
41. Anthony Seldon, *Blair* (London: The Free Press, 2004), p. 388.
42. *Comprehensive Report of the Special Advisor on Iraq's WMD* (Regime Strategic Intent Key Findings), p. 1.
43. *Review of Intelligence on Weapons of Mass Destruction*, p. 45.
44. Ibid., p. 52.
45. Private interview.
46. *Independent*, February 25, 1998.
47. *The 9/11 Commission Report* (New York: W. W. Norton and Company, 2004), p. 67.
48. Ibid., p. 66.
49. *Al-Quds Al-Arabi*, February 23, 1998.
50. *PBS Frontline,* May 1998.
51. Private source.
52. Private interview.
53. *Review of Intelligence on Weapons of Mass Destruction*, pp. 31–32.
54. *The 9/11 Commission Report*, p. 109.
55. Ibid., p. 114.
56. Downing Street statement, August 20, 1998.
57. *My Life*, p. 803.
58. Private interview.
59. *Hansard,* March 10, 1999.
60. Quoted in *Blair*, p. 377.
61. Private interview.
62. *Independent*, November 16, 1998.
63. BBC, *Breakfast With Frost,* December 20, 1998.
64. *Hansard,* December 1998.
65. Private interview.

CHAPTER FOUR: MISSION ACCOMPLISHED
1. Douglas Hurd, *Memoirs* (London: Little, Brown, 2003), pp. 459–60.
2. Private interview.
3. Ivo Daadler and Michael E. O'Hanlon, *Winning Ugly: NATO's War to Save Kosovo* (Washington, D.C.: Brookings Institution, 2000), p. 35.
4. Anthony Seldon, *Blair* (London: The Free Press, 2004), p. 393.
5. Interview, General Sir Mike Jackson.

Notes 361

6. Adam LeBor, *Milosevic* (London: Bloomsbury, 2002), p. 286.
7. Madeleine Albright, *Madam Secretary: A Memoir* (New York: Talk Miramax Books, 2003), p. 405.
8. Ibid., p. 397.
9. Andrew Rawnsley, *Servants of the People* (London: Hamish Hamilton, 2000), p. 258.
10. Ibid.
11. *Madam Secretary*, p. 406.
12. Ibid.
13. Private interview.
14. Private interview.
15. *Hansard,* March 23, 1999.
16. Private interview.
17. Private interview.
18. Ibid.
19. Prime Ministerial Broadcast, March 26, 1999.
20. *Blair*, p. 395.
21. Interview Lord Robertson.
22. *Servants of the People*, p. 262.
23. Sidney Blumenthal, *The Clinton Wars* (New York: Farrar, Straus and Giroux, 2003), p. 641.
24. John Rentoul, *Tony Blair, Prime Minister* (London: Little, Brown, 2001), p. 395.
25. *Sunday Telegraph*, April 4, 1999.
26. *Sky News,* April 3, 1999.
27. Wesley K. Clark, *Waging Modern War* (New York: Public Affairs, 2001), p. 244.
28. *Blair*, p. 396.
29. *Observer*, July 18, 1999.
30. Private interview.
31. Margaret Thatcher, Speech to the International Free Enterprise dinner, London, April 20, 1999.
32. *The Clinton Wars,* p. 640.
33. *Waging Modern War*, p. xxxiv.
34. *Madam Secretary*, p. 415.
35. Ibid.
36. *Servants of the People*, p. 271.
37. *Washington Post*, April 23, 1999.
38. Prime minister's speech, *Doctrine of the International Community,* Chicago, April 22, 1999.
39. *Financial Times*, April 23, 1999.
40. *Blair*, p. 399.
41. *Weekly Standard,* April 19, 1999.
42. Ibid., April 26, 1999.

43. *Associated Press,* May 6, 1999.
44. *Sunday Telegraph* (London), April 25, 1999.
45. *Servants of the People,* p. 274.
46. Ibid., p. 276.
47. Peter Riddell, *Hug Them Close* (London: Politicos, 2003), p. 113.
48. *Hansard,* May 10, 1999.
49. *Servants of the People,* p. 281.
50. *Financial Times,* May 17, 1999.
51. Private interview.
52. *Servants of the People,* p. 285.
53. Private interview.
54. Lance Price Diary, May 7, 1999, quoted in *Blair,* p. 402.
55. *Blair,* p. 407.
56. Downing Street comments, June 10, 1999.
57. Private interview.
58. Bill Clinton, *My Life* (New York: Knopf, 2004), p. 855.
59. Ibid., p. 858.
60. Ibid., p. 859.
61. *Sunday Telegraph,* March 18, 2001.

CHAPTER FIVE: CHANGING THE GUARD
1. Peter Riddell, *Hug Them Close* (London: Politicos, 2003), p. 135.
2. Private interview.
3. Private interview.
4. *Evening Standard* (London), June 29, 2005.
5. Anthony Seldon, *Blair* (London: The Free Press, 2004), p. 607.
6. Private interview.
7. Private interview.
8. Private interview.
9. Robert Kagan and William Kristol, *Present Dangers: Crisis and Opportunity in American Foreign and Defense Policy* (New York: Encounter Books, 2000), pp. viii–ix.
10. Interview, Bill Kristol.
11. James Mann, *Rise of the Vulcans: The History of Bush's War Cabinet* (New York: Viking Penguin, 2004), p. xvi.
12. *Blair,* p. 611.
13. Bob Woodward, *Bush at War* (New York: Simon & Schuster, 2002), p. 34.
14. *Sunday Telegraph,* July 25, 1999.
15. Philip H. Gordon and Jeremy Shapiro, *Allies at War: America, Europe and the Crisis over Iraq* (New York: McGraw-Hill, 2004), p. 49.
16. Interview, Gary Schmidt, Project for the New American Century.
17. Condoleezza Rice, "Promoting the National Interest," *Foreign Affairs,* v. 79, no. 1, January/February 2000.

18. Interview, Lord Robertson.
19. *Hug Them Close*, p. 136.
20. Ibid.
21. Private interview.
22. Private interview.
23. *Sunday Telegraph,* March 18, 2001.
24. Private interview.
25. Private interview.
26. Private interview.
27. Private interview.
28. *Sunday Telegraph,* March 18, 2001.
29. Private source.
30. Private interview.
31. Testimony of Samuel L. Berger to the National Commission on Terrorist Attacks upon the United States, March 24, 2004.
32. Bill Clinton, *My Life* (New York: Knopf, 2004), p. 935.
33. *Bush at War*, p. 39.
34. Private interview.
35. *Bush at War*, pp. 38–39.
36. Berger testimony.
37. Private interview.
38. *The 9/11 Commission Report* (New York: W. W. Norton and Company, 2004), p. 120.
39. Ibid., p. 132.
40. Ibid., p. 193.
41. Ibid., p. 199.
42. Ibid., p. 119.
43. CNN, "Ahead of the Curve," October 13, 2000.
44. *The 9/11 Commission Report,* p. 202.
45. Private source.
46. Private interview.
47. Lord Butler of Brockwell, *Review of Intelligence on Weapons of Mass Destruction* (London: The Stationery Office, July 14, 2004), p. 34.
48. Private interview.
49. *Review of Intelligence on Weapons of Mass Destruction*, p. 56.
50. Ibid., pp. 58–61.
51. Philip Stephens, *The Price of Leadership* (New York: Penguin, 2004), p. 269.

CHAPTER SIX: APOCALYPSE
1. Bob Woodward, *Bush at War* (New York: Simon & Schuster, 2002), p. 15.
2. Ibid., p. 17.
3. Private interview.
4. Tony Blair, "Campaign Against Terror," *Frontline* (WGBH Boston), 2002.

5. Ibid.
6. Private interview.
7. Private source.
8. *The 9/11 Commission Report* (New York: W. W. Norton and Company, 2004), p. 259.
9. Intelligence and Security Committee, *Annual Report 2001–2002* (London: The Stationery Office, 2002), p. 22.
10. Private source.
11. Private interview.
12. Intelligence and Security Committee, p. 22.
13. BBC interview with David Blunkett, the Home Secretary, *On the Record*, September 24, 2001.
14. Peter Riddell, *Hug Them Close* (London: Politicos, 2003), p. 149.
15. Private interview.
16. "Campaign Against Terror."
17. *Bush at War*, p. 42.
18. Ibid., p. 43.
19. Ibid.
20. Bob Woodward, *Plan of Attack* (New York: Simon & Schuster, 2004), p. 25.
21. *Bush at War,* p. 49.
22. Private interview.
23. *Washington Post,* January 28, 2002.
24. Private interview.
25. Private interview.
26. Private interview.
27. *Washington Post,* January 30, 2002.
28. *Bush at War*, p. 45.
29. Interview, Lord Robertson.
30. Private interview.
31. *Bush at War*, p. 81.
32. *Financial Times,* September 27, 2001.
33. *Washington Post,* September 26, 2001.
34. *National Journal,* April 6, 2002.
35. Private interview.
36. Private interview.
37. Private interview.
38. Private interview.
39. Private interview.
40. Private interview.
41. Private interview.
42. Private interview.
43. Richard B. Cheney, Remarks by the Vice President to the Heritage Foundation, October 10, 2003.

44. Private interview.
45. Anthony Seldon, *Blair* (London: The Free Press, 2004), p. 615.
46. *Hansard,* September 14, 2001.
47. *Bush at War*, p. 38.
48. Private interview.
49. Private interview.
50. *Bush at War*, p. 63.
51. *Washington Post,* January 30, 2002.
52. *Bush at War,* p. 74.
53. *Washington Post,* January 30, 2002.
54. *Washington Post,* January 31, 2002.
55. Ibid.
56. *Blair*, p. 496.
57. *Washington Post,* September 21, 2001.
58. "Blair's War," *Frontline* (WGBH Boston), 2003.
59. "Campaign Against Terror."

CHAPTER SEVEN: DECLARATION OF WAR
1. Prime minister's statement, October 7, 2001.
2. Private interview.
3. Private interview.
4. Responsibility for the Terrorist Atrocities in the United States, 11 September 2001—An Updated Account (Downing Street, October 4, 2001).
5. Private interview.
6. *Sunday Telegraph,* October 7, 2001.
7. Private interview.
8. Private interview.
9. Private interview.
10. Private interview.
11. Private interview.
12. Private interview.
13. Private interview.
14. Private interview.
15. Interview, General Sir Mike Jackson.
16. Ibid.
17. Interview, Lord Robertson.
18. Private interview.
19. Private interview.
20. Her Majesty's Government's Campaign Directives, October 21, 2001.
21. Al-Jazeera, October 7, 2001.
22. Tony Blair, "Campaign Against Terror," *Frontline* (WGBH Boston), 2002.
23. *Daily Telegraph*, October 11, 2001.
24. *Daily Mail*, November 1,2001.

25. *Times*, November 3, 2001.
26. Interview, Lord Powell.
27. Private interview.
28. Private source.
29. David Frum, *The Right Man* (New York: Random House, 2003), p. 256.
30. Private interview.
31. Private interview.
32. Private interview.
33. *Daily Mail,* November 2, 2001.
34. *Times,* November 2, 2001.
35. *New York Times,* November 8, 2001.
36. John Kampfner, *Blair's Wars* (London: The Free Press, 2003), p. 138.
37. White House Press Conference, November 7, 2001.
38. *Sun*, November 10, 2001.
39. *Times,* November 10, 2001.
40. Private interview.
41. "Campaign Against Terror."
42. Jane Corbin, *The Base* (London: Simon & Schuster, 2003), p. 267.
43. Ibid., p. 270.
44. *Atlantic,* October 2004.
45. Private interview.
46. Interview, General Sir Mike Jackson.

CHAPTER EIGHT: PREPARE FOR BATTLE

1. State of the Union Address, January 29, 2001.
2. David Frum, *The Right Man* (New York: Random House, 2003), p. 224.
3. Bob Woodward, *Plan of Attack* (New York: Simon & Schuster, 2004), p. 95.
4. Bob Woodward, *Bush at War* (New York: Simon & Schuster, 2002), p. 99.
5. Richard A. Clarke, *Against All Enemies* (London: Simon & Schuster, 2004), p. 32.
6. *Wall Street Journal*, June 14, 2002.
7. Private interview.
8. *Plan of Attack*, pp. 96–100.
9. Private interview.
10. *Daily Telegraph,* September 18, 2004.
11. Interview, Sir Jeremy Greenstock.
12. Private interview.
13. Lord Butler of Brockwell, *Review of Intelligence on Weapons of Mass Destruction* (London: The Stationery Office, July 14, 2004), p. 63.
14. Ibid.
15. Private interview.
16. Private interview.
17. Private interview.

18. Philip Stephens, *The Price of Leadership* (New York: Penguin, 2004), p. 287.
19. Private interview.
20. Anthony Seldon, *Blair* (London: The Free Press, 2004), p. 573.
21. Robin Cook, *Point of Departure* (London: Simon & Schuster, 2003), p. 115.
22. Ibid., p. 116.
23. Private interview.
24. "Blair's War," *Frontline* (WGBH Boston), 2003.
25. *Plan of Attack*, pp. 108–9.
26. Private interview.
27. Private interview.
28. *Review of Intelligence on Weapons of Mass Destruction*, p. 67.
29. Ibid., pp. 68–69.
30. Private interview.
31. ABC Television (Australia), February 28, 2002.
32. *Times* (London), March 1, 2002.
33. ABC Television (Australia), March 3, 2002.
34. Private source.
35. *Daily Mail*, March 12, 2002.
36. Private interview.
37. ITN News, April 5, 2002.
38. *Plan of Attack,* p. 119.
39. Private interview.
40. Private interview.
41. Private interview.
42. Private interview.
43. Private interview.
44. Interview, General Sir Mike Jackson.
45. Private interview.
46. "Blair's War."
47. Private interview.
48. *Point of Departure*, p. 135.
49. *London Evening Standard,* March 21, 2005.
50. *Vanity Fair,* June 2003.
51. Peter Stothart, *30 Days* (London: HarperCollins, 2003), p. 70.
52. Ibid., p. 161.
53. Private interview.
54. Private interview.
55. Private interview.
56. *Blair*, p. 576.
57. Private interview.
58. Private interview.
59. Private interview.
60. Private interview.

CHAPTER NINE: A QUESTION OF RESOLVE

1. *Daily Telegraph*, February 26, 2005.
2. Speech to Veterans of Foreign Wars, Nashville, Tennessee, August 26, 2002.
3. *BBC Panorama,* March 21, 2005.
4. Private interview.
5. Private interview.
6. *Sunday Telegraph,* September 8, 2002.
7. Private interview.
8. Private interview.
9. Bob Woodward, *Plan of Attack* (New York: Simon & Schuster, 2004), p. 178.
10. Private interview.
11. *Sunday Telegraph,* September 8, 2002.
12. Private interview.
13. Private interview.
14. Private interview.
15. *Guardian,* April 26, 2003.
16. Interview, Sir Jeremy Greenstock.
17. Lord Butler of Brockwell, *Review of Intelligence on Weapons of Mass Destruction* (London: The Stationery Office, July 14, 2004), p. 72.
18. Ibid., p. 74.
19. Ibid., p. 100.
20. *Review of Intelligence on Weapons of Mass Destruction*, p. 73.
21. Ibid., p. 74.
22. Private interview.
23. *Review of Intelligence on Weapons of Mass Destruction*, p. 152.
24. Speech to Trade Union Congress, September 10, 2002.
25. Robin Cook, *Point of Departure* (London: Simon & Schuster, 2003), p. 203.
26. Bob Woodward, *Plan of Attack* (New York: Simon & Schuster, 2004), p. 190.
27. *Review of Intelligence on Weapons of Mass Destruction*, p. 123.
28. *Iraq's Weapons of Mass Destruction The Assessment of the British Government* (London: The Stationery Office, 2002), p. 3.
29. *Sunday Telegraph*, February 6, 2004.
30. Private interview.
31. Private interview.
32. Peter Riddell, *Hug Them Close* (London: Politicos, 2003), p. 218.
33. Anthony Seldon, *Blair* (London: The Free Press, 2004), p. 585.
34. *Daily Telegraph,* October 1, 2002.
35. *Daily Telegraph,* October 3, 2002.
36. Private interview.
37. Private interview.
38. *Times,* October 12, 2002.
39. *Al-Jazeera,* November 12, 2002.

40. *Hansard,* October 15, 2002.
41. Private interview.
42. Private interview.
43. Interview, Sir Jeremy Greenstock.
44. Private interview.
45. Private interview.
46. Private interview.
47. Private interview.
48. Private interview.

CHAPTER TEN: COUNTDOWN
1. *New York Times,* September 28, 2002.
2. Private interview.
3. Private interview.
4. Interview, Sir Jeremy Greenstock.
5. Private interview.
6. Con Coughlin, *Saddam: The Secret Life* (London: Macmillan, 2005, rev. ed.), p. 332.
7. Private interview.
8. Private interview.
9. *New York Times,* November 10, 2002.
10. Bob Woodward, *Plan of Attack* (New York: Simon & Schuster, 2004), p. 240.
11. *The Price of Leadership*, p. 310.
12. *Plan of Attack,* p. 251.
13. Private interview.
14. Gordon and Shapiro, p. 142.
15. Dr. Hans Blix, *Disarming Iraq* (London: Bloomsbury, 2004), p. 127.
16. Private interview.
17. Private interview.
18. Private interview.
19. *Wall Street Journal,* January 29, 2003.
20. *Disarming Iraq*, p. 130.
21. *Hansard,* January 29, 2003.
22. *Sunday Times,* January 26, 2003.
23. *Plan of Attack,* p. 271.
24. *Daily Telegraph,* February 26, 2005.
25. *Plan of Attack,* p. 297.
26. Private interview.
27. Private interview.
28. Private interview.
29. Private interview.
30. Robin Cook, *Point of Departure* (London: Simon & Schuster, 2003), p. 277.
31. *Guardian,* April 26, 2003.

32. *Disarming Iraq*, p. 156.
33. Private interview.
34. *Daily Telegraph,* February 26, 2005.
35. Private interview.
36. *Times,* February 11, 2003.
37. *Disarming Iraq*, pp. 192–94.
38. Private interview.
39. Private interview.
40. Private interview.
41. *Plan of Attack,* p. 314.
42. Private interview.
43. Private interview.
44. Private interview.
45. *Guardian,* April 26, 2003.
46. *Sunday Telegraph,* February 23, 2003.
47. *Guardian,* March 1, 2003.
48. Private interview.
49. *Disarming Iraq*, p. 213.
50. *Plan of Attack*, p. 338.
51. Ibid.
52. Private interview.
53. *Plan of Attack*, pp. 333–34.
54. Gordon and Shapiro, p. 151.
55. Philip Stephens, *The Price of Leadership* (New York: Penguin, 2004), p. 320.
56. Interview, Sir Jeremy Greenstock.
57. *Sunday Telegraph,* March 16, 2003.
58. Private interview.
59. *Point of Departure*, p. 320.
60. *Plan of Attack*, p. 358.
61. Private interview.
62. *Plan of Attack*, p. 361.
63. *30 Days*, p. 70.
64. *Sunday Times,* March 20, 2005.
65. *Guardian,* April 26, 2003.
66. *Times,* April 26, 2003.
67. *Plan of Attack*, p. 377.
68. Private interview.
69. *Sun,* April 18, 2003.

CHAPTER ELEVEN: HOW TO LOSE A WAR
1. Private interview.
2. Bob Woodward, *Plan of Attack* (New York: Simon & Schuster, 2004), p. 393.
3. Ibid., p. 399.

4. Williamson Murray and Major General Robert H. Scales Jr., *The Iraq War* (Cambridge, Mass.: Harvard University Press, 2003), pp. 154–55.

5. Sir John Keegan, *The Iraq War* (London: Hutchinson, 2004), pp. 168–69.

6. Interview, General Sir Mike Jackson.

7. Private interview.

8. Interview, General Sir Mike Jackson.

9. Private interview.

10. Private interview.

11. *Times,* May 3, 2003.

12. Anthony Seldon, *Blair* (London: The Free Press, 2004), p. 597.

13. *Plan of Attack*, p. 403.

14. Peter Stothart, *30 Days* (London: HarperCollins, 2003), p. 117.

15. Private source.

16. *Plan of Attack*, p. 404.

17. *30 Days*, p. 162.

18. Ibid., p. 233.

19. Private interview.

20. Interview, Sir Jeremy Greenstock.

21. Private interview.

22. Interview, Douglas Feith.

23. Private interview.

24. Private interview.

25. Private interview.

26. Private interview.

27. Private interview.

28. Private interview.

29. Private interview.

30. Private interview.

31. Private interview.

32. Private interview.

33. *Plan of Attack*, p. 414.

34. Private interview.

35. Private interview.

36. Private interview.

37. Interview, Dr. Ayad Allawi.

38. Private interview.

39. Private interview.

40. *Plan of Attack*, p. 422.

41. *Times*, April 30, 2003.

42. Private interview.

43. NBC News, April 26, 2003.

44. Private interview.

45. Interview, Dr. David Kay.

46. Private source.

47. Intelligence and Security Committee, *Iraqi Weapons of Mass Destruction—Intelligence and Assessments* (London: The Stationery Office, 2003), p. 52.

CHAPTER TWELVE: THE RECKONING

1. *Al-Jazeera,* September 19, 2005.

2. Private interview.

3. *Al-Jazeera,* September 2, 2005.

4. *Daily Express,* August 8, 2005.

5. *Guardian/ICM* poll, July 19, 2005.

6. Speech, Labour National Policy Forum, July 16, 2005.

7. *Daily Telegraph* (London), July 9, 2005.

8. *Times,* July 14, 2005.

9. *Scotland on Sunday* (Edinburgh), July 10, 2005.

10. *ICM/News of the World,* September 28, 2003.

11. *Observer,* September 28, 2003.

12. *Times,* October 3, 2003.

13. *Sunday Telegraph,* January 9, 2005.

14. Private interview.

15. Private interview.

16. Private interview.

17. *Sunday Telegraph,* April 18, 2004.

18. *Sunday Telegraph,* May 16, 2004.

19. *Daily Mirror,* August 19, 2004.

20. *Times,* October 27, 2004.

21. *Times,* November 5, 2004.

22. *Daily Telegraph,* July 16, 2005.

23. *BBC Newsnight,* April 20, 2005.

24. *BBC AM,* September 25, 2005.

INDEX